MW00615708

JAMES HILLMAN UNIFORM EDITION

3

Uniform Edition of the Writings of James Hillman
Volume 3

Copyright © 2005 by James Hillman

Published by Spring Publications, Inc.
28 Front Street, Suite 3, Putnam, CT 06260
www.springpublications.com

Distributed by The Continuum International Publishing Group
www.continuumbooks.com

First edition 2005

Printed in Canada

Designed by white.room productions, New York

Cover illustration:
James Lee Byars, *Untitled*, ca. 1960. Black ink on Japanese paper.
Estate of James Lee Byars, courtesy Michael Werner Gallery, New York

Library of Congress Cataloging-in-Publication Data

Hillman, James.
    Senex & puer / edited and introduced by Glen Slater. — 1st ed.
       p. cm. — (Uniform edition of the writings of James Hillman ; v. 3)
    Includes bibliographical references.
    ISBN-13: 978-0-88214-581-5 (hardcover : alk. paper)
    ISBN-10: 0-88214-581-9 (hardcover : alk. paper)
       1. Archetype (Psychology) 2. Psychoanalysis.   I. Slater, Glen.
    II. Title. III. Title: Senex and puer. IV. Series: Hillman, James. Works.
    2004 ; v. 3.
    BF175.5.A72H56 2005
    155.2′64—dc22
                                                        2005025796

∞The paper used in this publication meets the minimum requirements of the
American National Standard for Information Sciences — Permanence of Paper
for Printed Library Materials, ANSI Z39.48-1992.

JAMES HILLMAN

SENEX

&

PUER

Edited and Introduced by
Glen Slater

SPRING PUBLICATIONS, INC.
PUTNAM, CONNECTICUT

THE UNIFORM EDITION OF THE WRITINGS OF JAMES HILLMAN

1

ARCHETYPAL PSYCHOLOGY

2

CITY AND SOUL

3

SENEX AND PUER

4

FROM TYPES TO IMAGES

5

ALCHEMICAL PSYCHOLOGY

6.1

MYTHICAL FIGURES

6.2

MYTHICAL REFERENCES

7

INHUMAN RELATIONS

8

PHILOSOPHICAL INCLINATIONS

9

ANIMAL PRESENCES

10

CONVERSATIONS AND COLLABORATIONS

The Uniform Edition of the Writings of James Hillman
is published in conjunction with

Dallas Institute Publications, Joanne H. Stroud, Director

**The Dallas Institute of Humanities and Culture
Dallas, Texas**

as integral part of its publications program concerned with
the imaginative, mythic, and symbolic sources of culture.

Additional support for this publication has been provided by

The Fertel Foundation, New Orleans, Louisiana

Pacifica Graduate Institute, and
Joseph Campbell Archives and Library,
Carpinteria, California

Contents

Introduction by Glen Slater   IX

Part One

Openings

1   Senex and Puer: An Aspect of the Historical
        and Psychological Present   30
2   Peaks and Vales: The Soul/Spirit Distinction
        as Basis for the Differences between
        Psychotherapy and Spiritual Discipline   71
3   Notes on Opportunism   96

Part Two

Movements and Pathologies

4   The Great Mother, Her Son, Her Hero,
        and the Puer   115
5   Notes on Verticality: Creation, Transcendence,
        Ambition, Erection, Inflation   158
6   Pothos: The Nostalgia of the Puer Eternus   179
7   Betrayal   193
8   Puer Wounds and Odysseus' Scar   214

Part Three

Senex

9   On Senex Consciousness   251
10   Negative Senex and a Renaissance Solution   271

Part Four

Old and New

11   Coda: A Note on Methodology   311
12   Old and New: Senex and Puer   317
13   Of Milk . . . and Monkeys   327

Appendix A   345
Appendix B   346

Index   349

Introduction

James Hillman undoes. You enter his writing and a conversation or an argument will occur, either with him, with yourself, or with some well-worn belief system. Favorite theories will either be turned on their head or you'll be guarding them all the closer. Passive readers beware: this work engages. Though his approach is not systematic — he doesn't build models of the mind — his reflections are pointed and precise, sharply illuminating whatever terrain he traverses — pathology to politics, nature to nurture, antiquity to Armageddon. Yet his concern is always more vertical than horizontal. Hillman lifts rocks and reveals the strange creatures beneath. He locates fissures of narrow-mindedness and drops into their blind spaces. Unraveling conventional wisdom and codified understanding, he makes room for new ways to be psychological. The undoing always becomes an opening. The result is a different perspective, one that deepens before it explains. The consistent goal: To put psyche (soul) back into psychology.

Today psychology rarely inspires. Materialism and numbers have eclipsed interiority. Cognitive-behaviorism and neuroscience dominate the landscape — flatlands where subjects are quantified, therapies are determined economically, and pills are given before anyone asks, "what's wrong?" Functionality reigns. There is no room for the dream, less for meaning and little for the imagination. Most theorists have abandoned the depth perspectives of Freud and Jung, thinkers whose works constantly ignite discourse in the humanities and remain mainstays of popular soul-searching. Psychology has placed itself inside a Skinner box — a place with an empty interior where psychologists map the brain and observe activity.[1] It is this boxed-in psychology that is grist for Hillman's mill.

When efficiency and functionality become psychology's primary goal, the programmable machine becomes its primary metaphor. Medicine already convinces us that psychopathology is a "chemical imbalance." These trends force complex, multi-faceted soul-realities outside the field. To find "psyche" one must get into Buddhism, read pop psychology books and take New-Age workshops. Whereas these alternate paths may sustain for a time, they are notoriously evasive of the soul's disturbances and they often lack a nose for cultural shadows; they may have *psyche*, but little critical *logos*. Between scientism and self-help, psychology proper, the logos of psyche, finds itself homeless.

Hillman's work reverses this kind of alienation of the psyche. His writings recover an authenticity and vitality within the field. Staying close to emotion, fantasy and metaphor, to the more poetic and imaginative basis of mind, his ideas stir the heart while waking the intellect. Religion and myth are predominant themes, providing expressions that have always been the psyche's mirror. Courting rather than denying mystery, Hillman follows psychological life through its innate forms. He lingers in dark places and rarely settles on easy, unambiguous understandings. The driving concern is for apt *perspective* — insight that satisfies through its very way of seeing, so that the process of *being* psychological, referred to by him as *soul-making*,[2] becomes the focus. Curiosities, confusions and deformities are given their due. They too are part of psychological understanding. As the title of his previous key work suggests, Hillman's archetypal psychology is a psychology *re-visioned*.[3]

Senex and Puer

This volume, for the first time, collects James Hillman's running encounters with a primary psychological pattern, an archetype that arises alongside the very attempt to fashion psychological perspective. *Senex* and *puer* are Latin terms for "old man" and "young man," and personify the poles of tradition, stasis, structure, and authority on one side, and immediacy, wandering, invention and idealism on the other. The senex consolidates, grounds and disciplines; the puer flashes with insight and thrives on fantasy and creativity. These diverging, conflicting tendencies are ultimately interdependent, forming two faces of the one configuration, each face never far from the other. "Old" and "new" maybe the most direct terms for the pair. They represent two very different ways of entering the world, but are oddly dependent on one another.

Senex and puer are not hidden. They do battle on the world-political and social stage, underpinning profound rifts between rigid conservatism and freewheeling expression evident everywhere we turn. Late night television and talk shows face them off as a formula for a capturing an audience, reconfirming the polarity every day. The embers from these collisions fly into living rooms and fire up entire world views. The senex-puer split can start wars and determine the course of history. It may be seen in the political divisions of the Vietnam era (Hillman's writings on this topic began in 1967). It is in the suicide bomber's flight to immortality in the face of monolithic powers. It is in the confrontations between disenfranchised youth and the World Trade Organization. It lives in the psychological and cultural divide between reign of Reagan and the collapse of Clinton, in the tenacity of one and the vulnerability of the other. The puer surfaced in the idealism of flower power. Today he infuses the mercurial minds of Silicon Valley, who show senex faces when their companies move to Wall Street. The puer is in the twinkle-in-the-eye creatives who can never realize their vision; the senex enters at midlife, when the soul turns dry, vision has dimmed and unlived life begins to plague us. This pair is all around, roaming unrecognized and in need of our attention.

As fundamental patterns of psychological life, Hillman sees the senex and puer at work in interior processes. He suggests that "this specific archetype will be involved with the process character of any (psychological) complex."[4] More precisely,

> the puer personifies that *moist spark* within any complex or attitude that is the original dynamic seed of spirit. It is the call of a thing to the perfection of itself, the call of a person to the Self, to be true to itself, to maintain the connection with its own divinely created *eidos*.[5]

Elsewhere he indicates the accompanying role of the senex:

> Therapy . . . becomes a working on Saturn, a *depressive grinding* of the most recalcitrant encrustations of the complex, its oldest habits, which are neither childhood remnants nor parental introjections, but are senex phenomena, that is, *the structure and principles by which the complex endures*.[6]

Puer and senex reside within psychological complexes — those black holes of inner life that bind history and emotion, wound and aspiration, past, present, and future. Jung claimed the complex to be the *via regia* of the unconscious.[7] According to Hillman, work with any complex becomes an encounter with the senex-puer duality. Puer and senex appear along with our attitudes and feelings toward each complex. Psychotherapy is therefore called to recognize *both* the "moist spark" and the "depressive grinding" and find adequate vessels to hold these colliding energies. For instance, an inferiority complex may be draining, debilitating, pulling us back into the past, yet work on the complex may also release sparks of new potential and become fertile ground for future pursuits and callings; the *old* inferiority fuels the *new* determination. New meets old when the imagination searches for openings in constrictions and habits. This approach reunites the pair and maintains the too often broken bonds of symptom and soul.

We could say that sparks and grinding need each other. The deeper the psychic exploration the more apparent this understanding. Yet many psychotherapies tend to identify with one side or the other of this pattern. Transpersonal and humanistic approaches can have too many sparks, always striving for potentials and expansions, transcending rather than facing the more constricting aspects of reality. Cognitive-behavioral therapies have too few sparks, treating emotions as hangovers of poor thinking. Muses and demons are whipped into shape through willful affirmation or banished through denial. Post-modern deconstruction and feminist critiques can evade the weight and determining force of psychic reality, enlightening for a moment then leaving us with idealized value systems or airy nothings. Academic psychology monotonously grinds out the same windowless basement laboratory research, filling journals with micro-scrutinies of phenomena that never hit the street. The rarefied puer can hijack any mind-trip, just as the recalcitrant senex can clog intellectual plumbing and prevent the flow of fresh thought.

An *adequate* psychology will offer some relationship to both sides of the archetype, both dimensions of the complex, recognizing the presence of peak experiences *and* underworld sufferings. But a psychology that claims its basis in imagination and soul — whose forms continually join the highest and lowest, the profound and profane — must hold the *mutual dependence* of both aspects. This conviction lies at the very basis of the work in this volume.

As primary modes of apprehending lived experience, *puer and senex may be the archetypal basis of psychology itself.* Senex style systems, structures and appeals to authority have tended to dominate our ways of seeing, so Hillman enters the problem from the side of the puer. He is the spark within the grinding. Referring to this as the "union of sames"[8] in the form *puer-et-senex*, these writings approach the theme of unification in a body of work focused on the multiplicity and polytheism of the psyche. Yet this unification is not so much a marriage of opposites as a confluence of consciousness — a dance of attitudes and sensibilities: The novel and fresh is seen through the timeless and universal, and the timeless and universal is rediscovered in the everyday world.

Background

Psychology often fails to see its ideas in cultural-historical context. It can become unconsciously bound to trends and fashions, forgetting to consider the spirit of the times, which always infuses views of reality. In Hillman's view, "current events, that which is taking place outside in the historical field, is a reflection of an eternal mythological experience."[9] Today senex destruction is present in American authoritarianism as well as in Islamic fundamentalism, just as puer destruction stems from idealistic, naïve, overly optimistic political and social views blind to their shadows. The present is defined by the past but also by the future — by a *teleological process* that engenders purposefulness, even when a specific goal is not defined. Soul withers without awareness of these influences, and a soul-based psychology is impossible in their absence. Hillman insists that individual problems cannot be divorced from wider cultural problems and must be understood as reflections of each other. The much discussed emptiness, loss of meaning and materialism of our time are the offspring of lost contact with traditions and ancestors, the outcome of an unquestioned falling in with "progress." Psychology needs to connect with the times. So these essays begin with the call to recognize "the *kairos*, this unique moment of transition in world

history . . . [the] transition within the microcosm, within us each individually, as we struggle with psychological connections between past
and future, old and new."[10] No thinker has taken Jung's admonition
to keep our finger on the pulse of the collective psyche as seriously as
Hillman has. This volume also presents a psychological response to
the spirit of the times.

These writings on senex and puer began in 1967, although the
closely related paper "Betrayal" (Chapter Seven) came some years earlier.
A previous volume, Puer Papers [11] combined several of Hillman's essays on
the topic with papers by Henry A. Murray, Randolph Severson, Thomas
Moore, James Baird, and Thomas Cowan. Between then and now, major
essays have been written, most notably "The Great Mother's Son, Her
Hero, and the Puer," which describes at length why puer psychology
cannot be understood within the bounds of the mother-son relationship (Chapter Four). The present collection also includes previously
unpublished material. "Notes on Verticality" (Chapter Five) appears here
for the first time. The endurance of this topical engagement extends to
Hillman's best-selling, The Soul's Code, [12] where he reflects on his puer-
based approach to the question of character and calling. Relevant sections of its "Coda: A Note on Methodology" are extracted here (Chapter
Eleven). The long presence and careful working of these themes exists
alongside the puer's resistance to the completion of projects. In Puer
Papers, Hillman wrote:

> Perhaps this scattered incompletion, together with promises
> of a grander vision, belongs to our divine boy himself who is
> characterized by an unfulfilled failing combined with a longing
> for the wider shores of further comprehension. He does so want
> perfection. This insight that the puer itself is withholding the
> book from completion, even as he publicizes himself in fits and
> starts, allows his laughter to infect the whole project, a project
> that will continue to trick us both, reader and writer, but letting
> us make hay while the sun shines. Better these straws now than
> what tomorrow may never bring. [13]

Whereas these essays may focus mostly on the puer, their *collection*
underscores the senex, who prefers boundaries, continuity, and evidence

of discipline. The persistent return to this topic brings to the fore Hillman's extensive scholarly engagement with one archetypal pattern. The gathering shows the other side of "these straws" (Hillman) — a well-cooked authority. The stage at which we are collecting the author's work must also be taken into account. Although the quick wit and fresh eye are still present, James Hillman is now himself the "old man," recently acknowledging this in *The Force of Character*, a contribution on longevity and growing old. [14] Yet his engagement with the perplexities and burdens of age are held with optimism and a light heart, a befitting way to avoid merely succumbing to senex gravity, in other words, a union of sames. In all, it may be a time for a gathering. But we should also hold this idea lightly; for the puer there is no final word . . .

Archetypal Psychology

There are no introductory texts to archetypal psychology. One plunges into the writings and sinks or swims — or sinks then swims! This absence of an organizing statement has partly to do with the field's adherents, who are drawn from within Jungian thought but also from a number of other disciplines, such as religious studies, literature, communications and the arts. The absence also pertains to the iconoclasm of its founder who, consistent with his psychology, withdraws at the first sign of codification. Mostly it belongs to this psychology's own polytheistic bearing, which resists efforts to centralize and organize. *Revisioning Psychology* provides basic points of orientation — "fenceposts," as Hillman calls them. [15] *Archetypal Psychology: A Brief Account* [16] is a historical and bibliographic overview, oriented around key themes. The former remains archetypal psychology's key text; the latter is a useful but highly condensed overview, which also attempts to describe the salient contributions of other authors. Absent from the literature has been a more thorough look at the essential background of Hillman's thought.

The present volume addresses this deficit. It may be regarded as an arterial expression of archetypal psychology and arguably its most foundational text. The blood that sustains the whole project is coursing through these essays — one is better off listening to the rhythms of the animal than attempting an anatomical mapping. A structural approach will fail here. Still, students and scholars *will* search for a kind of logic in the evolution of the author's views, the critic will find opportunity for reductive personal analysis. Hillman has himself referred to these writings as "a prolonged and still incomplete defense of my traits and behaviors."[17]

The personal factor only underscores the archetypal perspective, which does not attempt to isolate individual traits from the more mysterious impetus that drives a person. An archetypal eye discerns an impersonal guiding force and the idea of calling and embraces the purposeful spark within the neurotic complex, which comes into the world with one's character. Here the deeply personal — worked over, inspired, ground out — *is* the universal and finds universal relevance. Here a passion for a particular idea is indivisible from the instinct for its significance and the faculty for its articulation. Here "personal work" means being caught in a conversation between the ancestors and the zeitgeist. Hillman tackles such notions at length in his book, *The Soul's Code.*

The roots of archetypal psychology may be discovered in the puer-senex problem. Whereas Hillman's writings defy organization into any one *theory*, the chapters of this book may be taken as grounds for his *theoretical orientation*. Equally, these chapters contain the early sparks of later writings. At a minimum, this gathering must be considered a companion piece to *Revisioning Psychology* and essential background to its more honed concepts. In *Revisioning Psychology*, Hillman moves *via negativa* — attacking everything from transcendental philosophy to humanistic psychology. The energy is fierce, the style is combative, the rhetoric passionate. Understanding the puer-senex problem helps us see what Hillman is doing in *Revisioning Psychology*, namely, *working on psychology's own complexes* — loosening rigidities, undoing literalisms, responding to its plight, attempting to release psychology's own archetypal potentials, to release its sparks. He brings puer promise to psychology caught in senex stasis.

Hillman's work proceeds through a fidelity to the *mythic imagination*. Myth provides the irreducible root metaphors of psychological life. Imagination is psyche's most innate activity, apprehending and comprehending all phenomena, satisfying the highest and lowest aspects of being. Myth, like dream, arises from and returns to mystery. Imagination moves the spirit and the instincts. It defies mind-body dualism because it encompasses both abstract principles and gut reactions. Myth and image move psychological perspective beyond the merely personal and displace rationalistic attempts to grasp the psyche. Mythic imagination brings shade and nuance to those fluorescent certainties that dominate life but fail to move us. It pushes psychology from scientific pursuit to poetic vision, preserving psychology's long but fast fraying ties to the humanities. For Hillman the *logos* of *psyche* begins and ends with divine drama, which places meaning, purpose and a sense of fate in the lap of the gods.

When psyche is met on these terms, "the poet," who preserves the forms and essences of experience, will speak prior to "the analyst," who may shrink experiences into concepts and stock interpretations. Indeed, Hillman has suggested that "analytical" is a misnomer for psychology, for it contradicts the rich symbolic emphasis in Freud's and particularly in Jung's approach.[18] We therefore find in Hillman's writings continual reference to the arts and history as records of the imagination and reflections of psychological life. No psychodynamic or structural models appear, though there is concern for the mythologies that animate these notions. Static explanations, notions of cure, and even processes of development are avoided so that the exploration remains focused on fitting modes of perception for the raw and painful events of life. These fitting modes of perception nurse events and turn them into psychological experiences,[19] occasioning the quality we call "soul," a term Hillman has largely resuscitated. Soul arises when the universal meets the unique, when depth is sounded, and open wounds begin to scar over with the skin of reflective engagement. In Hillman's view, soul is present whenever the mythic imagination cradles the sufferings, longings and visions of everyday life. Here the goal of psychotherapy is to invoke this process.

The Jungian Context

Archetypal psychology gives radical emphasis to C. G. Jung's notion of "universals" — archetypal determinants that shape psychological life. However, Hillman is less concerned with the collective unconscious as a structure or "layer" of the psyche and is more taken with Jung's idea that archetypal forms shape thoughts, attitudes and ideas [20] as *modes of apprehension.* [21] Hillman follows closely the phenomenal aspect of Jung's perspective, which underscores images [22] and metaphors [23] as primary archetypal expressions. "Our ideas about the psyche affect the psyche," [24] expresses the essence of this leaning. Hillman's writings are most resonant with Jung's alchemical works, where the overlap of psyche and image is more apparent than in earlier psychodynamic treatments, and where Jung stays closer to the *anima* (soul) than in earlier preoccupations with the journey of the hero.

The archetypal approach examines the thoughts, attitudes and ideas of psychology itself, looking for universals within concepts and models, holding that imagination exists prior to theorizing. Theories themselves are seen as having underlying (usually unconscious) fantasies and are governed by archetypal forms. Along these lines, archetypal psychology first uncovered then avoided *monotheistic* notions of unity that are strong in classical Jungian thought, claiming such ideas invite a single mindedness that is anathema to meeting each psychological event on its own terms. Taking his cue from myth, which is found in fragments, versions, and contradictory details, Hillman's work consistently defies the systematic mindset and underscores the *polytheistic* nature of psychic life. Many Jungians have found this critique untenable; others manage to view the psyche through both monotheistic and polytheistic lenses.

The polytheistic, unsystematic stance of archetypal psychology has meant that keeping its threads together has never been easy, perhaps not even desirable; "loose ends" [25] are preferred. Nevertheless, in his writings on puer-senex we do locate something of a woven thread, at least a place where loose ends might gather. Early on in this work, after presenting the senex and puer separately, Hillman then describes their "secret identity," and it is in this context that he uses the term "union of sames" — a theme that reappears throughout the volume in different guises. When these essays are held as a complement to *Revisioning Psychology,* archetypal psychologists must also contend with the presence of this unifying image lingering somewhere near its concerns with multiplicity. The union of puer and senex is a point of continual return, echoing notions surrounding the *coniunctio* and opposites, which run through Jung's writings — themes that Hillman has otherwise held with wariness. This "union of sames" is not unrelated to Jung's description of the *transcendent function*, which cites the psyche's innate capacity to generate transforming symbolic forms. In this context Jung spoke of the necessity for both "creative formulation" and "understanding,"[26] — the one aspect more spontaneous spirit, the other more objective discipline. Split from each other these qualities can become either ethereal "aestheticization" or deadening "intellectualization."[27] The presence of puer and senex are in these descriptions; in "Puer Wounds and Odysseus' Scar" (Chapter Eight) Hillman even attributes the transcendent function to the "puer archetype."[28] But such comparisons should not obscure the differences between the Classical Jungian and Archetypal orientations. To do so puts us back into the mouth of the negative senex who, split from the puer, loves to swallow provocative ideas and break them down into manure for well-guarded plots. Still, the comparison points to a confluence of perspectives in the cultivation of soul and speaks again to the critical importance of these figures for depth psychology.

There is a more specific issue pertaining to the Jungian context. The lengthy engagement with this topic was initially ignited by Hillman's response to the way Jungians treated puer themes, especially the puer personality, which has strong spiritual strivings while being whimsical and resistant to ordinary life and erotic entanglement. Jungians have linked the puer to the mother complex, suggesting that his movement, flight and escape from commitment are symptoms of an unconscious mother-bound problem. In moving an understanding of the puer into puer-senex phenomena, Hillman challenges this prior emphasis and shifts the gravity of the problem from the mother to the father. Marie-Louise von Franz's book, *Puer Aeternus*,[29] centered on an interpretation of *The Little Prince* by Antoine de Saint-Exupéry, remains the classic expression of this mother emphasis. Taking on the psychopathology of the puer-character occasions two major aspects of Hillman's psychology: the challenge to the dominance of mother-bound theories *in general* and the importance of the prospective, intentional aspect of the symptom. (Something already emphasized by Jung who suggested symptoms need to be fulfilled, not just "resolved"). Whereas the classical Jungian reading of the puer indicates the need for "grounding" — a return to ordinary, everyday reality — Hillman sees the redemption of the puer in the marriage to psyche — in reflection, depth, and complication. This is a return to *psychic* reality, to psychic ground, not necessarily to the literal ground of everyday life. It is the puer's enduring dedication to his vision that leads to a healing of his wounds — a union of sames.

Part Two of this volume is dedicated to this revised approach to the puer personality, its psychology and psychopathology. Psychotherapists will find essential reading in these chapters. The previously unpublished essay in Chapter Five explores the sexuality of the puer and his relation to "ascent" and inflation. Vivid differentiations — a characteristic of Hillman's writing — are sprinkled throughout; the conflation of creativity and fertility is but one issue that receives treatment in this new chapter.

Method

"Coda: A Note on Method" (Chapter Eleven) is Hillman's clearest statement of the puer basis of his perspective and joins with "Notes on Opportunism" (Chapter Three) to reflect on fitting means for approaching archetypal realities. Detailing the archetypal basis of the archetypal method, these essays are primers on how a *psychology of perspective* differs from a psychology of structure. Considering the mythic background of his own approach, Hillman invokes Hermes, the messenger of the gods. Hermes is the only god who moves between all realms — heaven, earth, and underworld. His ability as a messenger comes largely from charming his way through the pantheon, speaking the language of each god, negotiating each situation. Of all the gods, Hermes is the best communicator. The god of opportunity, luck, thresholds, and crossroads, we remember it is also Hermes who inhabits hermeneutics — the philosophy of meaning and interpretation. Hermes himself shows many puer traits and it is this confluence that lives in Hillman's method: a constantly moving, sharply insightful, mercurial crafting that follows the gods wherever they go. For a psychology with polytheistic aims, Hermes is the apt god of method.

Just as Hermes takes a different approach to each divinity, Hillman writes to the specific archetypal situation. He is thus concerned with fitting styles and rhetoric, which are also important in recognizing the gods. So in writing on Hermes himself, Hillman follows this god's style: "Notes on Opportunism," brings the dexterity of Hermes to the fore. The paragraphs are short and concise, the discussion shifts quickly from point to point, grabbing insights from here and there; Hermes is revealed through a series of Hermes leaps. This dexterity, though most evident in this particular essay, is required in all archetypal work. When a theme needs an aesthetic eye, Aphrodite's sense of beauty might prevail; when precision and order are required, Apollo may be called. Like Hermes himself, Hillman moves constantly, sometimes writing through several sensibilities in one essay. He likewise watches for divinities in the writings of others, sensitive to viewpoints that remain stuck in any one style. His critiques may also begin by sniffing out a dismissed god. Thus the concern is with tone and texture as well as content. This is the archetypal "method."

One characteristic of the Hermes-puer style is contradiction. Hillman is criticized for being inconsistent, saying one thing in one context and seemingly its opposite in another. Early in his essay on the Great Mother we find him critiquing Joseph Henderson for speaking of the puer in positive and negative terms, attributing to him a misplaced moral standpoint in psychic terrain,[30] yet having no difficulty discussing the positive and negative senex in another context. Contradictions like this one are not uncommon and not well understood until each discussion is read in terms of its different archetypal situation. The discussion of positive and negative aspects of the senex belongs to the polarizing proclivity of the senex himself: "When he appears, so does the problem of opposites; when opposites appear as a *problem*, so does the senex."[31] For each point a different context, for each context a different point. Once this is understood, one also understands that the same phenomenon can appear quite differently depending on the psychology of the stance. It is this shifting ground that can also make these writings dilettantish and enraging to the usual rational mind.

One prevailing stance in Hillman, his emphasis on soul, is described in his critique of spirituality in Chapter Two — "how the peaks look from the vale"[32] — a *psyche*-logical view of the spirit. Spirit and soul are presented as two distinct modes of discourse, reminding us of soul's downward movement, its life in the "vales," quite a distance from the ascending "peaks" of the spiritual quest. This chapter sensitizes us to spiritual rhetoric in psychology, showing how spiritual perspectives and their proclivity for abstraction can lead away from the ground of the psyche. Hillman describes the spirit-soul dialectic in terms of the puer-psyche marriage, writing,

> reflection in the mirror of the soul lets one see the madness of one's spiritual drive, and the importance of this madness. . . . The spirit needs witness to this madness. Or to put it another way, the puer takes its drive and goal literally unless there is reflection, which makes possible a metaphorical understanding of its drive and goal. [33]

The soul's meandering directions and outright messes vividly contrast with the spirit's need for clarity and consistency. The latter becomes allied with the fantasy of objectivity, which, like a removed third eye, seeks one neutral standpoint from which to survey the whole terrain. But for Hillman, as perhaps for any view faithful to psyche, there is no neutral standpoint, only looking from one psychological place to another. "Neutral" is also a fantasy, full of values and biases, which may be discovered when examined from other angles. Turning to Hermes, the god Jung referred to as "the archetype of the unconscious,"[34] and to soul before spirit, also turns us toward psychic reality.

These reflections give background to Hillman's comments on the puer in Chapter 11:

> Any theory that is affected by the puer will show dashing execution, an appeal to the extraordinary, and a show-off aestheticism. It will claim timelessness and universal validity but forgo the labors of proof. It will have that puer dance in it, will imagine ambitiously and rebel against convention. [35]

Whereas this "puer dance" is a lively one and may not be concerned with "proof," behind the scenes there *is* a concern with substance, rigor and weight. Hillman's work is not short on philosophical underpinnings or literary and historical references. It contains a slew of social, political and cultural amplifications, as well as an unerring devotion to here and now relevancy. The dance is far from erratic, it builds from ponderance and poise, characteristics that may fall into the background but show just as much evidence of the senex concern for scholarship, thus exhibiting the union of sames.

Endings

Archetypal psychology has never shied away from incomplete thought. Psyche rarely ties things up neatly anyway. Myth is itself a world of gaps and unfinished business. Soul so often relies on what's missing to keep the imagination alive, and the final part of this book reflects these values. Whereas each chapter is a fragment, each fragment provides an uncanny glimpse of the project as a whole, illuminating the discussion anew from different angles.

I have already mentioned "Coda: A Note on Method," lifted from a more complete statement in *The Soul's Code*. From *Inter Views*, Hillman's conversation with Laura Pozzo on puer and senex phenomena in culture brings immediacy to the topic. The conversational tone also reveals some of the emotional fuel behind Hillman's concerns. To end, we return to "Of Milk . . . And Monkeys" — elemental themes and reflections on primal being. These are the extracted two final subsections of the original senex and puer lecture, which opens this volume. We thus conclude with writings that are bookends and fragments, returning to the beginning, appreciating these nascent insights all the more having tracked the extended exploration. Employing the perspective won through the rejection of psychology's developmental mono-myth, "Of Milk" returns to questions of *relationship as an archetypal reality*, deliteralizing both mother and breast. Hillman writes, "Milk finally 'represents' the original connection to and continual thirst for the world we long to 'remember'."[36] Here we *do* return to mother, though on an altogether different plane. Last, in "Of Monkeys," Hillman takes up the question with which depth psychology begins: *What happened to the animal within us?* His remarks are striking, even more pertinent today than thirty years ago. I suggest they be read carefully and reread, for we live in a time that is alienating to our animal being. He writes,

> To remain human would require remaining in psychic connec-
> tion with the sub-human at the center, remaining true to one's
> shadow-angel, true to one's own central madness, which is as
> well the wisdom of nature that is unconscious of itself and cannot
> speak in words. [37]

The return to instinct has been, since Freud, the meandering path we have trodden in depth psychology, the base note of the whole thing. And so this volume ends with monkeys, apes, baboons, and with that paradox that the highest is also the lowest, a paradox known only to the wise-fool.

In editing this collection I have endeavored to maintain the original structure and content of the papers as much as possible given the goal of compiling a fresh text with thematic shape. Most edits were aimed at reducing repetition and content overlap. Two longer sections of text — the original opening of "Senex and Puer" (Chapter One) and an excursion on Leonardo da Vinci and his vision of a kite from "The Great Mother" (Chapter Four) — have been placed in appendices. As the project progressed, the author reviewed each chapter thoroughly, correcting, revising and updating as he went. His concern was always for the immediate relevance of the material. At several points, while I argued for preservation and historical record, he pushed for further cuts and lively flow. So senex and puer were with us to the end. Hopefully, something of a union of sames prevailed. Readers new to Hillman will discover in these pages that psychology can be at once daring, elegant, and inspiring. Jungians will find one of the most sustained encounters with a particular archetypal configuration in print. Archetypal psychologists will be glad for this collection of James Hillman's papers in one volume and will be drawn to the previously unpublished material. Psychotherapists will appreciate the insight and challenge of puer psychology. Historians of psychology will draw on this collection for dialogue about the role and significance of archetypal perspectives. Critics will enjoy the full exposure to Hillman's clear preoccupation. Poets, comforted by this meditation on shadows and celebration of eccentricity, will dream on.

Glen Slater
Pacifica Graduate Institute

Notes

C. G. Jung's *Collected Works* are quoted throughout from Bollingen Series XX, ed. and trans. Gerhard Adler and R. F. C. Hull, and published by Princeton University Press.

1. B. F. Skinner was recently named the twentieth-century's most eminent psychologist. In the American Psychological Association's *Monitor on Psychology* 33:7. From a study in *The Review of General Psychology* 6:2. Among factors considered was whether the individual had been a past president of the American Psychological Association. Noteworthy: C. G. Jung came in at number 23.

2. Hillman takes this term from Keats, "Call the world if you please, 'The vale of Soul-making.' Then you will find out the use of the world . . ." See Chapter 2 for a discussion of soul-making.

3. See J. Hillman, *Revisioning Psychology* (New York: Harper and Row, 1975). [Reprinted: Harper Perennial, 1992].

4. Chapter 1, p. 8.

5. Ibid, p. 26. Italics added to "moist spark."

6. Chapter 10, p. 246. Italics added to "depressive grinding."

7. C. G. Jung, *Collected Works*, vol. 8: *Structure & Dynamics of the Psyche*, par. 210.

8. Chapter 1, p. 31.

9. Chapter 1, p. 5.

10. Chapter 1, p. 3.

11. J. Hillman ed., *Puer Papers*, (Dallas: Spring Publications, 1979).

12. J. Hillman, *The Soul's Code*, (New York: Random House, 1996).

13. From "Note to the Reader," in J. Hillman, *Puer Papers*, op. cit., p. 100. The note also states: "It seems that each time I touch the theme of the *Puer Eternus* I tend to begin with a complicated apology for the incompleteness of the work, promising more later. Once again I start out by saying these are only

selected chapters of a larger book, that still not all has been collected in one place, that it is uneven in style and thought because some goes back to 1967 and some has been re-written as late as this Note. Other main pieces that are not included in this volume are listed at the beginning of the notes, together with two articles on the senex which must always be considered background to what we say about the puer." Two years prior to this, in an introductory note to "The Negative Senex and a Renaissance Solution" *Spring* 1975, here reprinted as Chapter 10, he wrote: "Because it is coming home to me that I may never finish and publish the psychological study, begun in 1966, on senex and puer phenomenology, I have taken to slipping into print hunks of the incomplete typescript as the occasions arose. The following therefore belongs within the context of four other pieces: "Senex and Puer: An Aspect of the Historical and Psychological Present"; "On Senex Consciousness"; "The Great Mother, Her Son, Her Hero, and the Puer"; and "Pothos: The Nostalgia of the Puer Eternus." All four papers are included here — Chapters 1, 9, 4 and 6 respectively.

14. J. Hillman, *The Force of Character,* (New York: Random House, 1999).

15. J. Hillman, *Revisioning Psychology,* op. cit., p. xvi.

16. J. Hillman, *Archetypal Psychology: A Brief Account* (Dallas: Spring Publications, 1983). Reprinted in an enlarged and revised edition as J. Hillman, *Archetypal Psychology.* Uniform Edition, vol. 1 (Putnam, CT: Spring Publications, 2004).

17. Preface to the 1992 edition of *Revisioning Psychology* (New York: Harper Perennial, 1992), p. xiii.

18. J. Hillman, *The Myth of Analysis* (Evanston: Northwestern University Press, 1972) pp. 183–90.

19. See J. Hillman, *Revisioning Psychology,* op. cit. p. xvi.

20. C. G. Jung, *Collected Works,* vol. 9.1: *Archetypes and the Collective Unconscious,* par. 45, 69.

21. C. G. Jung, *Collected Works,* vol. 8: *Structure & Dynamics of the Psyche,* par. 277.

22. C. G. Jung, *Collected Works,* vol. 9.1: *Archetypes and the Collective Unconscious,* par. 152.

23. Ibid. par. 267.

24. Chapter 4, p. 107.

25. This term is the title of an earlier collection of papers by Hillman, *Loose Ends: Primary Papers in Archetypal Psychology* (New York/Zurich: Spring Publications, 1975). Note the juxtaposition of "loose" and "primary."

26. "The Transcendent Function," in *Collected Works,* vol. 8: *Structure & Dynamics of the Psyche,* par. 172.

27. Ibid. par. 183

28. Chapter 5.

29. Toronto: Inner City Books, 2000.
30. Chapter 4, p. 8.
31. Chapter 10, p. 243.
32. Chapter 2, p. 47
33. Chapter 2, p. 58
34. C. G. Jung, *Collected Works*, vol. 13: *Alchemical Studies*, par. 299.
35. Chapter 11, p. 285.
36. Chapter 13, p. 304.
37. Chapter 13, p. 310.

Part One

Openings

1

Senex and Puer:
An Aspect of the Historical and Psychological Present [1]

"But it is rather time," saith she, "to apply remedies, than to make complaintes."

— Boethius, *The Consolation of Philosophy*

We are living in what the Greeks called the kairos — the right moment — for a "metamorphosis of the gods," of the fundamental principles and symbols. This peculiarity of our time, which is certainly not of our conscious choosing, is the expression of the unconscious man within us who is changing. Coming generations will have to take account of this momentous transformation if humanity is not to destroy itself through the might of its own technology and science.

— C. G. Jung, *The Undiscovered Self*

Our special problem today is just this: we are essentially primitive creatures struggling desperately to adjust ourselves to a way of life that is alien to almost the whole past history of our species . . . the transition from primitive to sophisticated technology must be made swiftly — the resource problem demands that this be so. Today we are living at a unique moment, neither in the long primitive era nor in the better adjusted prosperous future. It is our century, our millennium, that must perforce take the maximum strain, for it is our fate to live during the transitional phase. And because we live in this special phase we find social difficulties, pressures, situations that defy even the simplest logical processes. We find ourselves in no real contact with the forces that are shaping the future.

— Fred Hoyle, *Of Men and Galaxies*

To have "no real contact with the forces that are shaping the future" (Hoyle)[2] would be to fail the *kairos* of transition.[3] To come to terms with this *kairos* would mean discovering a connection between past and future. For us, individuals, makeweights[4] that may tip the scales of history, our task is to discover the psychic connection between past and future, otherwise the unconscious figures within us who are as well the archaic past will shape the historical future perhaps disastrously. Thus the *kairos*, this unique moment of transition in world history, becomes a transition within the microcosm, within us each individually, as we struggle with the psychological connections between past and future, old and new, expressed archetypally as the polarity of senex and puer.

PSYCHOLOGY AND HISTORY. A polar division between senex and puer is all about us outside in the historical field. We find good example of this in demography which has reached back to an archaic system: peoples are again divided along lines of age and youth. The principle categories of social structure — race, region, religion, class, occupation, economics, sex — are insufficient. Modern urban society emphasizes again the division according to age-levels. There are communities in the United States — new communities, not just the derelict hamlets from which youth has always fled where only "oldsters" live, entire cities of the retired, the "home for the aged" now extended over square miles. There are new suburbs in France where the average age of population is less than twenty-one. In Sweden, in Britain, in the United States, there are communities the size of towns where only young married couples live; and settlements, apartment houses, resorts for only the young or only the old. Two new fields of psychotherapy have been invented — geriatrics and juvenile delinquency — and we have specialists for the psyche of the old and of the adolescent. In this crowded world of our future, the division is between age and youth: on one side the established nations with slower, controlled birth-rates and aging population; on the other, the so-called newer, younger, and needy nations with high birth-rates and the proliferation of children reflected in a low median age.

The division is in the family as the conflict of generations, sometimes no longer a conflict of misunderstandings, but a silence. There
is a division of communication systems between age and youth: the
latter learns today not through traditional forms and printed words
but from altogether other media in our urban collective. Youth forms a
social class, self-enclosed and uninitiated by its elders, and thus largely
without communication outside of itself.

The division is in the political world with its aging leaders and
systems attempting to maintain "law and order," and the rebellions of
youth in the name of "rights and freedom." As one legal philosopher
has put it: never in the history of the United States have we had so
many laws, so much science of law and its enforcement, and never
have we had so much disorder and violence.

> The falcon cannot hear the falconer;
> Things fall apart; the centre cannot hold;
> Mere anarchy is loosed upon the world,
> The blood-dimmed tide is loosed . . .
> The best lack all conviction, while the worst
> Are full of passionate intensity.
> Surely some revelation is at hand;
> Surely the Second Coming is at hand, [5]

said William Butler Yeats in his poem, "The Second Coming."

And theology, also riven by the senex-puer problem, having found
God dead, both Father and Son, awaits some revelation. For when it is
announced: "The King is dead, " immediately follows: "Long live the
King. " At the same moment, the King dies and the Prince becomes
King. If God is dead, what princely power is succeeding? Why the
silence, and where the succession?

The polar division between senex and puer, falcon split from falconer, that is all about us is of course our historical concern. But it is
not only historical and for the historian only. The psyche is not isolat-
ed from history, and psychology takes place not only in a small room
between two people in two chairs walled off from the historical scene.
History is in the room. And just as the psyche is situated in an histori-

cal present that trails behind it the roots of a thousand ancestral trees, so too does history have psychological existence. Mircea Eliade has shown that historical events, those accumulations of irreversible time, are not the primary facts of existence.[6] Historical facts are secondary; they are incomplete and imperfect actions calling for a before and after, historical consequences built on historical antecedents, and are, as such, only accumulations of sins and sufferings that are senseless unless they point inward to central meanings. The historical "facts" may be but fantasies attached to and sprouting from central archetypal cores. Below the tangled pattern of events are experiences, psychological realities of passionate importance, a mythological substrate that gives the soul a feeling of destiny, an eschatological sense that *what happens matters*. And it matters to someone, to a person. Without the person, without the individual's sense of personal soul (that makeweight in the scales) we are simply pre-historic revenants with only collective destiny. Without the sense of soul, we have no sense of history. We never enter it. This core of soul that weaves events together into the meaningful patterns of tales and stories recounted by reminiscing creates history. History is story first and fact later.

The fantasy we call "current events," that which is taking place outside in the historical field, is a reflection of an eternal mythological experience. An historical analysis of these events — old Mao and the Red Guard, the hippie flower youth, the sociology of ageing — will not lead to their meaning. We can no more grasp the soul of the times through the TV news than we can understand the soul of a person only through the events of his case history. (Twenty-two volumes of a Warren Report can never settle or explain the living ferment of a myth.) Nothing can be revealed by a newspaper, by the world's *chronique scandaleuse*, unless the essence is grasped from within through an archetypal pattern. The archetype provides the basis for uniting those incommensurables, fact and meaning. Outer historical facts are archetypally colored, so as to disclose essential psychological meanings. Historical facts disclose the eternally recurring mythemes of history and of our individual souls. History is but the stage on which we enact the mythemes of the soul.

The experiencing that makes history possible and is its *a priori* has been called Clio. And Clio, as first daughter, has a special relation to the mother of muses, Remembering. Clio's name signifies *gloria*, honor, celebration, and she remembers best the actions of heroes. Her interest is hardly in the daily news of the world's case history, or what Mircea Eliade calls "profane time." Rather her interest lies in those unique nuclear moments, the heroic moments through which the archetype at the soul's core is revealed, redeeming events from the blindness of mere fact. As we individuals are fastened to the facts of our personal case histories by what we remember of our personal lives, so is our culture addicted to the history of profane time. An addiction demands more and more, faster and faster. Much of our inventiveness serves merely making, gathering, and reproducing events. As the time of the millennium runs out, events speed up. We need more "information," we have less time to wait. We have even achieved "instant history," which Arthur Schlesinger defends by calling, "Contemporary History," where everything that happens to everyone on the public scene must be recorded and what is recorded must be published — and fast.[7] The profane *chroniques scandaleuse* — the profanities — of the heroes replace the *gloria* of Clio.

In analytical practice we have learned that an archetypal understanding of events can cure the compulsive fascination with one's case history. *The facts do not change, but their order is given another dimension through another myth.* They are experienced differently; they gain another meaning because they are told through another tale. So redemption from the addiction to profane history might come in the same way. This way would show another archetypal organization of the events from which we suffer. But this reorganization first requires a change in memory itself, so that one asks each day not "what happened?" but "what happened to the soul?" For this way of remembering events, memory needs to return again to its reminiscence of primordial ideas, to its original association with the root metaphors of human experience. Memory thus transformed would register first the experiences of the soul and only secondarily the accidents of events. Or rather, it could take up the events psychologically, ritually, no longer only their victim.[8]

This archetypal understanding could regenerate history in the sense of reversing it or cleansing it. Such work is immensely difficult, demanding that heroic intensity that Clio celebrates. For this reason analytical work on the collective levels of the soul is so "heroic." Psychological changes — changes of attitude, changes of personality, those fundamental lustrations of the soul — are also regenerations of history. Transforming my family's attitudes by uncovering patterns in the entwined ancestral roots is not merely a personal analytical problem. It is an historical step towards freeing a generation from a collective pattern. By changing that collective, there is a change in history itself. And each one, anyone, who makes a clearing in his bit of the forest of the past is the hero who redeems time and is the scapegoat who by taking on the sins undoes time. Thus are we makeweights in the historical transition and what we do with our psychological life is of historical import, not merely on the inner plane of salvation of the individual soul from history. More, it is the way in which history, as that which goes on collectively outside us, itself may be washed and healed.

Our polarities — senex and puer — provide the archetype for the psychological foundation of the problem of history. First, in the conventional sense, puer and senex are history as sequence and transition, as a process through time from beginning to end. And second, history as a problem in which I am caught, for which I suffer and from which I long to be redeemed, is given by the same pair as Father Time and Eternal Youth, temporality and eternity, and the puzzling paradoxes of their connection. To be involved with these figures is to be drawn into history. To be identified with either is to be dominated by an archetypal attitude towards history: the puer who transcends history and leaps out of time, and is as such a-historical, or anti-historical in protest and revolt; or the senex who is an image of history itself and of the permanent truth revealed through history.

Our concern with the archetype of senex-puer is determined by the transition of millennia and it indicates the late stage of our culture. Curtius has amassed evidence enough from classical Latin literature to support his statements that the term *"puer senilis* or *puer senex* is a coinage of late pagan antiquity" and that where early cultures may extol youth and honor age, "late periods develop a human ideal in which the polarity youth-age works towards a balance."[9] Thus our concern is itself a reflection of the archetype now manifested symbolically in the culture around us and in the complexes of our inner world. And the constellation of this polarity *as a split* demonstrates the gravity of our historical crisis. Therefore our engagement with this archetype may restore a balance and have an effect on the historical lysis.

We are not concerned with the case history of our times and its anarchy, with the psychology of aging, of revolt and tradition, of youth, of fathers and sons, of stages of life, and such "timely topics." These are diversions. The soul is neither young nor old — or it is both. Our contemporary obsession with age and youth reflects the fall of the soul into the time and measurement system of historical materialism. Behind it all is an archetypal split. Therefore our concern must be with archetypal therapy or therapy of an archetype. And our approach must be radical if we would put history back into the psyche. Thus we take historical problems as psychological symptoms in order to contain the speeding and spreading of these events. We shall try to hold them as psychological problems, regarding the splits in which we are caught as manifestations of an archetypal split within our individual souls.

Furthermore, because of its special relation with time as process, *this specific archetype will be involved with the process character of any complex,* with the youth and age, the temporality and eternity conundrums of any psychological attitude or part of personality. Senex and puer are bound up with the very nature of development. Any attitude as it comes into being can take on the wings of the puer and streak skyward; any attitude as it passes its ripeness can lose touch with revelation, cling to its power, and be out of Tao. Lao Tzu says: "After things reach their prime, they begin to grow old, which means being contrary to Tao . . ."[10] Our puer attitudes are not bound to youth, nor are our senex qualities reserved for age. The complete coincidence of psychological development and the biological course of life is yet to be established. The psyche seems to have its own course, its own timing. The senex as well as the puer may appear at many phases and may influence any complex. So we cannot fit psychological life into the historical conditions or the narrowly biological frames of a "first-half/second-half." To do so would be an early indication that we have ourselves too easily succumbed to the faulted thinking of the split archetype.

If we look about us we see too well that the first-half/second-half scheme simply does not fit. Can the generation that is now to make the transition of the millennium put off until "some time later" the issues of meaning, of religion, of selfhood, meanwhile adapting to sociological and biological norms that have been handed them by another age and have lost their inherent value? A young person today is pressed to take up the problems of the second-half in the first-half. He has been born into a second-half, into the end of an age (as those of us who are older are forced to live a first-half of the wholly new spirit of the next age which is now beginning). We have not only our own problems; we have by historical necessity the collective problem of individuation loaded onto us. We carry a pack of history on our backs and are expected to meet the requirements of an old culture. Thus we start out as a *puer senilis*, both older than our age and struggling heroically against our oldness.

The "puer problem" of today is not only a collective neurosis; it is a psychic expression of an historical claim, and as such is a call. If psychic energy is not able to flow through the usual external channels of tradition, it falls inward and activates the unconscious. The unconscious as "mother" makes it then appear as if all a young person's questioning and mal-adaptation were his own personal mother-complex. But it is a reflection of the transition and, as Jung says, "not of our conscious choosing." It reflects "the unconscious man within us who is changing." Can this unconscious man be put off until the second-half?

The second-half is with us from the beginning, as is Saturn in our birth charts, just as the little boy and his question "why," the child Eros, and the winged angel are with us to the last. The puer inspires the blossoming of things; the senex presides over the harvest. But flowering and harvest go on intermittently throughout life. And do we know finally who takes charge at death — greybeard with his scythe or the young angel?

II POLARITIES IN ANALYTICAL PSYCHOLOGY. Since it will be in the form of a polar split that we shall encounter the archetype puer-senex, we need first to regard polarities, in general, in analytical psychology. Analytical psychology as a structured field depends for this structure upon polar descriptions. Jung's life and thought makes more use of polarities than does any other major psychological vision.[11] The polar model is basic in all his major psychological ideas.[12]

In all of this, the primary poles are conscious and unconscious, whether conceived as topological areas, as modalities of being, or as adjectival descriptions of mental contents and behavior. For psychology, all polarities are subjected to this primary division. This primary polarity, however, is given only as a potential within the archetype, which theoretically is not divided into poles. The archetype per se is ambivalent and paradoxical, embracing both spirit and nature, psyche and matter, consciousness and unconsciousness; in it the yea and nay are one. There is neither day nor night, but rather a continual dawning. The inherent opposition within the archetype splits into poles when it enters ego-consciousness. Day breaks with the ego; night is left behind. Our usual daily consciousness grasps only one part and makes it into a pole. *For psychology, the ontological basis of polarity is ego-consciousness.*

For every bit of light that we grasp out of archetypal ambivalence, illumining with the candle of our ego a bright circle of awareness, we also darken the remainder of the room. At the same moment that we light the candle we create "outer darkness," as if the light were a theft from the penumbra of dawn and twilight, of paradoxical archetypal light. Consciousness and the unconscious are created into a polarity at the same moment out of original twilight states; and they are continually being created at the same moment. The process of making conscious thereby also makes unconscious, or as Jung put this awkward truth: "So we come to the paradoxical conclusion that there is no conscious content which is not in some other respect unconscious. Maybe, too, there is no unconscious psychism which is not at the same time conscious."[13] We may not speak therefore of an evolutionary process of light emerging from darkness, an extension of light at the expense of darkness. The light is not stolen from the dark where there is privation of light; rather the ego concentrates into one pole the divine primordial half-light, thereby also darkening the divine. Snuff the candle and the twilight dawns again at the outer edges of the room which just before were impenetrable recesses of shadow. In other words, for psychology the phenomenon of polarity is not archetypally primary, but is a consequent of the ego's affinity for light, just as the term *polarity* entered Western language with the Cartesian ego and the Enlightenment.[14]

As long as we remain within metaphors of light and vision, it does not matter which comes first or which is best. The metaphors of vision, of intuition, require neither logic nor value. Clarity is enough. Both poles of the archetype are necessary and equal. On this plane of vision, of intuition, one is beyond the opposites, beyond good and evil. But consciousness and unconsciousness require other metaphors, especially those of value. So we find that the basic yea and nay as positive and negative values in all their modes interfere and complicate a simple co-existing polarity. The Bible's God, in the first value judgment of the universe, declares light to be good, and by calling it Day and by separating it from the darkness of Night implies that the latter is not good. Thus are plus and minus signs attached to the primary poles of conscious and unconscious. Thus does the human world begin when feeling values add complexity to perception, and we *feel* the polarities and recognize moral choice.

So when we speak of consciousness we still tend to say good or bad consciousness, attributing at the same time the opposite sign to the unconscious. This tendency works for every pair of opposites. The view and value we have of one pair of a polarity is taken from within the standpoint of the other. Owing to the nature of consciousness as a polarity with the unconscious, we can never be wholly outside our own unconsciousness. Thus, too, the so-called objective standpoint of the conscious observer is actually from within the same archetype but from the opposite pole of it. Does not the most penetrating revelation of the negative senex come from his own son? Is not the most objective critic of the negative puer his own father?

Puer and senex are therefore each both positive and negative. Because these figures are in special relation forming, if you will, a two-headed archetype, or a *Janus-Gestalt*, we shall find it impossible to say good of one without saying bad of the other as long as the two remain in polar opposition, as long as the ego wears only one face.

Nevertheless, though polarities may split into contradictories and even strive against each other as in all the classic puer-senex struggles, they may also be re-approximated. This rapprochement in order to heal a fundamental split is the main work of psychoanalysis. *Our attempt at rapprochement shall go by way of returning to the original condition of the archetype before it has been broken apart and turned against itself.*

May I insist here that we cannot over-estimate the importance of this rapprochement. It is worth every attempt, not for the success or cure that it might bring, but because each attempt makes us aware of the split and thereby begins healing. The division into mutually indifferent or repugnant polarities is tearing the soul apart. The soul itself stands amidst all sorts of opposites as the "third factor." It has always existed half-way between Heaven and Hell, spirit and flesh, inner and outer, individual and collective — or, these opposites have been held together within its unfathomed reaches. From the lyre of Heraclitus to the spectrum of Jung, the soul holds polarities in harmony. It is the psychic connection. But now the ego, having replaced the soul as the center of the conscious personality, cannot hold the tension. With its disjunctive rationalism it makes divisions where the soul gives feeling connections and mythic unities. So the soul has come unstrung; its suffering and illness reflect the torn condition of the split archetype.

As an early sign of this re-union we may expect a new experience of ambivalence. Psychology usually gives to ambivalence a major pejorative judgment. It is associated with schizophrenia. Like the term "twilight state," "ambivalence" tends to be reserved only for a faulty ego. But *ambivalence is natural*, as the necessary concomitant to the ambiguity of psychic wholeness whose light is in a twilight state. Neither ambivalence nor twilight consciousness is per se a pathological condition even though, as with anything psychological, they may present pathological forms. Living in ambivalence is living where yea and nay, light and darkness, right action and wrong, are held closely together and are difficult to distinguish. Psychology usually attempts to meet this condition through reaffirming consciousness by decision and differentiation: solidify and strengthen the ego; turn against the mixture of feelings and the indistinct soft light of the first-half or of old age. But ambivalence, rather than being overcome in this manner, may be developed within its own principle. It is a way in itself.

As there is a way of decision, there is also a way of ambivalence; and this way can comprehend the archetype in its wholeness, leading one down even to the psychoid[15] level. Ambivalence rather than corrected may be encouraged towards encompassing ever more profound paradoxes and symbols, which always release ambivalent feelings that hinder clarity and decisiveness. Paradox and symbol express the co-existence of polarity, the fundamental two-headed duality that is both logically absurd and symbolically true. *Ambivalence is the adequate reaction of the whole psyche* to these whole truths. To cure away ambivalence removes the eye with which we can perceive the paradox, whereas bearing ambivalence places us within symbolic reality where we perceive both faces at once, even exist as two realities at once. That which is not split does not have to be rejoined; thus going by way of ambivalence circumvents *coniunctio* efforts of the ego, because by bearing ambivalence one is in the *coniunctio* itself as the tension of opposites. This way works at wholeness not in halves but through wholeness from the start. The way is slower, action is hindered, and one fumbles foolishly in the half-light and the symbolic. The way finds echo in many familiar phrases from Lao Tzu, but especially: "Soften the light, become one with the dusty world."[16]

III THE SENEX. Let us begin with a prayer to Saturn, an Arabic one from the *Picatrix* of the tenth century, which circulated widely in the late Middle Ages of Western Europe:

> O Master of sublime name and great power, supreme Master; O Master Saturn: Thou, the Cold, the Sterile, the Mournful, the Pernicious; Thou, whose life is sincere and whose word sure; Thou, the Sage and Solitary, the Impenetrable; Thou, whose promises are kept; Thou who art weak and weary; Thou who hast cares greater than any other, who knowest neither pleasure nor joy; Thou, the old and cunning, master of all artifice, deceitful, wise, and judicious; Thou who bringest prosperity or ruin and makest men to be happy or unhappy! I conjure Thee, O Supreme Father, by Thy great benevolence and Thy generous bounty, to do for me what I ask . . .[17]

Appropriately, our starting point is duplex. Kronos-Saturn is on one hand:

> . . . a benevolent God of agriculture . . . the ruler of the Golden Age when men had abundance of all things . . . the lord of the

Islands of the Blessed . . . and the building of cities . . . On the
other hand he was the gloomy, dethroned, and solitary god conceived as "dwelling at the uttermost end of land and sea," "exiled
. . .ruler of the nether gods" . . . prisoner or bondsman in . . .
Tartarus . . . the god of death and the dead. On the one hand he
was the father of gods and men, on the other hand the devourer
of children, eater of raw flesh, the consumer of all, who "swallowed up all the gods" . . . [18]

According to the Warburg Institute's authoritative study of Saturn, in no Greek god-figure is the dual aspect so real, so fundamental,
as in the figure of Kronos, so that even with the later additions of
the Roman Saturn who "was originally not ambivalent but definitely
good," the compounded image remains at core bi-polar. Saturn is at
once archetypal image for wise old man, solitary sage, the *lapis* as rock
of ages with all its positive moral and intellectual virtues, *and* for the
Old King, [19] that castrating castrated ogre. He is the world as builder
of cities *and* the not-world of exile. At the same time that he is father
of all he consumes all; by living on and from his fatherhood he feeds
himself insatiably from the bounty of his own paternalism. *Saturn is image for both positive and negative senex.*

We turned to the *Picatrix,* [20] a popular astro-magical text for a first
description of the senex because astrology provides the best descriptions of character qualities. More than any other field, astrology gives
background for the psychology of personality when personality is
conceived as a collection of stable traits. This fixed characterological
view, personality conceived through heredity, disposition, virtues and
vices, is less to be found in personality theory and psychopathology
today. Personality theory and psychopathology tend to favor psycho-dynamics, learning theory, conditioning and behaviorism, and at
times so extremely that even endogenic and structural disorders have
been considered not as inherent traits but as reaction formations. [21]
The astrological view of personality is saturnine, and Saturn is the
"ruler" of astrology. The psycho-dynamic view is mercurial: nothing is
given and everything can be transformed; all limits may be overcome
and conditions may be altered through re-learning, behavior therapy,

drive reinforcement, and psycho-dynamics. The impetus behind therapy itself owes more to mercurial optimism and less to the saturnine
attitude of fateful limits set by character traits where psychic disposition is congenital. Congenital means synchronous with birth, that is,
astrological.

But the pessimism of Saturn has deeper implications. Although the
virtues and vices of character may be modified, they do not disappear
through cure because they belong to one's nature as the original gift of
sin. Congenital structure is karma; character is fate. Thus personality
descriptions of the senex given by astrology will be statements of the
senex by the senex. It is a description from the inside, a self-descrip-
tion of the bound and fettered condition of human nature set within
the privation of its characterological limits and whose wisdom comes
through suffering these limits.

From astrology, then, from the medicine of the humors, from lore
and iconography, from the collections of the mythographers, we can
piece together the major characteristics of Kronos-Saturn as archetypal image of the senex.[22] His duality we have already mentioned.
In astrology this duality was traditionally handled by the examination of Saturn's place in the birth-chart. In this way, the good and bad
poles inherent to his nature could be kept distinct. His temperament is
cold. Coldness can be expressed also as *distance*; the lonely wanderer set
apart, out-cast. Coldness is also cold reality, things just as they are; and
yet Saturn is at the far-out edge of reality. As lord of the nethermost,
he views the world from the outside, from such depths of distance that
he sees it, so to speak, all upside down, yet structurally and abstractly.
The concern with structure and abstraction makes him the principle of
order, whether through time, or hierarchy, or exact science and system,
or limits and borders, or power, or inwardness and reflection, or earth
and the forms it gives. The cold is also *slow*, heavy, leaden, and dry or
rheumy moist, but always the *coagulator* through denseness, slowness,
and weight expressed by the mood of sadness, depression, or melancholia. Thus he is black, winter, and the night, yet heralds through
his day, Saturday, the return of the holy Sunday light. His relation to
sexuality is again dual: on the one hand he is patron of eunuchs and
celibates, being dry and impotent; on the other hand he is represented

by the dog and the lecherous goat, and is a fertility god as inventor of agriculture, a god of earth and peasant, the harvest and Saturnalia, a ruler of fruit and seed. But the harvest is a *hoard;* the ripened end-product and in-gathering again can be dual. Under the aegis of Saturn it can show qualities of greed and tyranny, where in-gathering means holding and the purse of miserliness, making things last through all time. (Saturn governs coins, minting, and wealth.) Here we find the characteristics of avarice, gluttony, and such rapaciousness that Saturn is *bhoga* (Hindu), "eating the world," and identified with Moloch[23] — which again on its positive side demands the extreme *sacrifice* and can be understood as Abraham and Moses, the patriarchal mentor who demands the extreme.

His relationship to the *feminine* has been put in a few words: those born under Saturn "do not like to walk with women and pass the time." "They are never in favor with woman or wife." So Saturn is in association with widowhood, childlessness, orphanhood, child-exposure, and he attends childbirth so as to be able to eat the newborn, as everything new coming to life can become food to the senex. Old attitudes and habits assimilate each new content; everlastingly changeless, it eats its own possibilities of change.

His *moral aspects* are two-sided. He presides over honesty in speech — and deceit; over secrets, silence — and loquaciousness and slander; over loyalty and friendship — and selfishness, cruelty, cunning, thievery and murder. He makes both honest reckoning and fraud. He is god of manure, privies, dirty linen, bad wind, and is also cleanser of souls. His *intellectual qualities* include the inspired genius of the brooding melancholic, creativity through contemplation, deliberation in the exact sciences and mathematics, as well as the highest occult secrets such as angelology, theology, and prophetic furor. He is the aged Indian on the elephant,[24] the wise old man and "creator of wise men," as Augustine ironically called him in his anti-pagan polemic, which used Saturn for whipping-boy.[25]

This amplification may give a phenomenological description of an archetype, but it is not psychology. Psychology may be based on archetypal themata, but psychology proper begins only when these dominants, experienced as emotional realities through and within our complexes, are felt to pull and shape our lives. The senex is at the core of *any complex* or governs *any attitude* when these psychological processes pass to end-phase. We expect it to correspond to biological senescence, just as many of its images: dryness, night, coldness, winter, harvest, are taken from the processes of time and of nature. To speak accurately, however, the senex archetype transcends mere biological senescence and is given from the beginning as a potential of order, meaning, and teleological fulfillment — and death — within all the psyche and all its parts. So the death that the senex brings is not only bio-physical. It is the death that comes through perfection and order. It is the death of accomplishment and fulfillment, a death which grows in power within any complex or attitude as that psychological process matures through consciousness into order, becoming habitual and dominant — and therefore unconscious again. Paradoxically, we are least conscious where we are most conscious. Where we are in our ego-efficiency, habitual, feeling most certain, ruling from within that which we know best, we are the least reflectively aware. Close to the light our sight is shortest. Our destructivity is felt in the closest neighborhood and is the result of the shadow that issues from the very ego-center of our light. Out of its own light, the ego makes shadow; the ego is its own shadow; perhaps the ego is shadow. So the senex represents just this force of death that is carried by the glittering hardness of our own ego-certainty, the ego-concentricity that can say "I know" — for it does know, and this knowledge is power. It is also dry and cold, and its boundaries are set as if by its own precision instruments.

The hardening process of consciousness has been represented by the symbol of the Old King.[26] The Old King with his sickness is an alchemical image for the negative *lapis*, the *lapis* as petrifaction. This end-phase has also been formulated mainly as a consequent of the absent feminine, resulting in dryness and coldness. Consciousness is out of touch with life. The elixir does not flow and the negative tincture stains the surrounding with blight. The main blame for this condition of the senex has been laid upon the ego, which often gets a moralistic-pedagogical rap over the knuckles for "wrong attitudes." It is the ego's fault that consciousness is ingathered to itself. It is the power-greed of the ego that makes its point of view tyrannical and its consciousness deaf. It is the one-sidedness or the over-rationality of the ego that cuts it off from the living.

Let us reconsider the relation between the ego and the senex. We have just seen from our amplification that it is the senex that in-gathers and hoards. It is the senex that *a priori* is the archetypal principle of coldness, hardness, and exile from life. As principle of coagulation and of geometrical order, it dries and orders, "builds cities" and "mints money," makes solid and square and profitable, overcoming the dissolving wetness of soulful emotionality. It is the senex as certainty principle that directs the ego away from the uncertainty principle, the doubts and provisional confusions of dawn and twilight. No, it is not the ego that gives the senex its authority and ultimate tyranny, but the brief authority in which the ego is dressed depends upon its relation with the senex archetype. Even the ego's notion of itself as authoritative dominant of consciousness results from the archetypal senex. The Old Wise Man and the Old King are there from the beginning, before the ego is born, governing the mysterious ordering aspect of ego-formation by meaningfully structuring contents into knowledge and extending the area of the will's control. As Jung pointed out in discussing the "Stages of Life," knowledge is the hallmark of consciousness and is at the beginning of ego-formation in the child.[27] This knowing precedes the ego that says "I know." The cognitive capacity precedes cognition, which, in turn, precedes ego-subjectivity. The ego does not come *ex nihilo* onto the scene, cognizing the world into existence by turning its attention like a spotlight upon its surround. Rather, the ego is gradually formed "like a chain of islands or an archipelago," from pre-existent fragments of cognitive consciousness.[28] Something prior to the ego cognizes, gives meaning, and patterns into order this fragmentary twilight consciousness. This "something" has been called the Self, which is another name for the archetype of meaning,[29] or the Old Wise Man.

Thus we conclude *that the senex is there at the beginning as an archetypal root of ego-formation.* It makes consolidation of the ego possible, giving its rule as an identity within fixed borders, its tendency to omnivorous rapacious aggrandizement ("swallowing all the gods" and their ambivalent natural light) through the principle of association with consciousness, and its perpetuation through habit, memory, repetition, and time. These qualities — identity of borders, association with consciousness, continuity — we use to describe the ego, and these qualities are each properties of Kronos-Saturn, the senex. The senex as *spiritus rector* bestows the certainty of the spirit, so that one is led to state that ego-development is a phenomenon of the senex spirit that works at ordering and hardening within the ego with such compulsion that it must be — as well as the Promethean thrust of the Hero — an instinctual source of ego energy. Here we approach Freud's notion of Thanatos.

Because the negative senex is not an ego fault it cannot be altered by the ego. The negative senex problem is not merely a matter of moral attitude (as if the ego should do better, be more modest or humble or "conscious"). Nor is it a problem of outdated ideas (as if the ego should keep up with the times), nor of biological vitality (as if the ego should keep fit and active), nor even of the absent feminine. *These ego problems are consequents rather than causes; they reflect a prior disorder in the archetypal ground of the ego.* This ground is *senex-et-puer,* briefly conceived as its order on the one hand, its impetus on the other. Together they give the ego what has been called its *Gestaltungskraft* or intentionality, or meaningfulness of the spirit. When the duality of this ground is split into polarity, then we have not only the alternating plus and minus valences given to one half or the other, but we have a more fundamental negativity, that of the split archetype, and its corollary: ego-consciousness split from archetypal reality, the Gods.

We must further conclude that the negative senex is the senex split from its own puer aspect. He has lost his "child." The archetypal core of the complex, now split, loses its inherent tension, it's ambivalence, and is just dead in the midst of its brightness, which is its own eclipse, as a negative *Sol Niger.* Without the enthusiasm and eros of the son, authority loses its idealism. It aspires to nothing but its own perpetuation, leading but to tyranny and cynicism; *for meaning cannot be sustained by structure and order alone.* Such spirit is one-sided, and one-sidedness is crippling. Being is static, a pleroma that cannot become. Time — called euphemistically "experience" but more often just the crusted accretions of profane history — becomes a moral virtue and even witness of truth, "*veritas filia temporis* (truth is the daughter of time)." The old is always preferred to the new. Sexuality without young eros becomes goaty; weakness becomes complaints; creative isolation, only paranoid loneliness. Because the complex is unable to catch on and sow seed, it feeds on the growth of other complexes or of other people, as for instance the growth of one's own children, or the developmental process going on in one's analysands. Cut off from its own child and fool, the complex no longer has anything to tell us. [30] Folly and immaturity are projected onto others. Without folly it has no wisdom, only knowledge — serious, depressing, hoarded in an academic vault or used as power. The feminine may be kept imprisoned in secret, or may be Dame Melancholy, a moody consort, as an atmosphere emanating from the moribund complex, giving it the stench of Saturn. The integration of personality becomes the subjugation of personality, a unification through dominance, and integrity only a selfsame repetition of firm principle. Or, to reawaken the puer side again there may be a complex-compelled falling-in-love. (Venus is born from imaginal froth — i.e. the repressed fantasies — of dissociated sexuality cut off through Saturn.)

To sum up then with the senex: It is there from the beginning as are all archetypal dominants and is found in the small child who knows and says "I know" and "mine" with the full intensity of its being, the small child who is the last to pity and first to tyrannize, destroys what it has built, and in its weakness lives in oral omnipotence fantasies, defending its borders and testing the limits set by others. But although the senex is there in the child, the senex spirit nevertheless appears most evidently when any function we use, attitude we have, or complex of the psyche begins to coagulate past its prime. It is the Saturn within the complex that makes it hard to shed, dense and slow and maddeningly depressing — the madness of lead-poison — that feeling of the everlasting indestructibility of the complex. It cuts off the complex from life and the feminine, inhibiting it and introverting it into an isolation. Thus it stands behind the fastness of our habits and the ability we have of making a virtue of any vice by merely keeping it in order or attributing it to fate.

The senex as complex appears in dreams long before a person has himself put on his *toga senilis* (*aet.* 60 in Rome). It manifests as the dream father, mentor, old wise man, to which the dreamer's consciousness is pupil. When accentuated it seems to have drawn all power to itself, paralyzing elsewhere, and a person is unable to make a decision without first taking counsel with the unconscious to await an advising voice from an oracle or vision. Though this counsel may come from a dream or revelation, it may be as collective as that which comes from the standard canons of the culture. For statements of sagacity and meaning, even spiritual truths, can be bad advice. These representations — father, elders, mentors, and old wise men — provide an authority and wisdom that is beyond the experience of the dreamer. Therefore it tends to have him rather than he it, so that he is driven by an unconscious certainty, making him wise beyond his years, ambitious for recognition by his seniors and intolerant of his own youthfulness.

The senex spirit also affects any attitude or complex when the creative contemplation of its ultimate meaning, its relation to fate, its deepest "why," become constellated. Then the husk of any habitual attitude deprived of all outward power shrinks to a grain, but imprisoned in the little limits of this seed is all the *vis* of the original complex. Turned thus in on itself almost to the point of disappearing altogether, leaving only a melancholy mood of *mortificatio* or *putrefactio*, in the black cold night of deprivation it holds a sort of lonely communion in itself with the future; and then with the prophetic genius of the senex spirit reveals that which is beyond the edge of its own destructive harvesting scythe, that which will sprout green from the grain it has itself slain.

This duality within the senex itself that is imaged by the positive-negative Kronos-Saturn figure gives each of us those intensely difficult problems in our lives. How does the Old King in my attitudes change? How can my knowledge become wisdom? How do I admit uncertainty, disorder, and nonsense within my borders? How we work out these issues affects the historical transition since we are each a makeweight in the scales.

We might easily believe that the difference between the negative and positive senex is mainly a matter of the difference between the Old King of power and extraversion as a profane end-stage of the Puer-Hero, and the Old Wise One of knowledge and introversion as the sacred end-stage of the Puer-Messiah. But this simplification will

not hold because we are involved with an archetypal structure that
is not only dual as is the image of Kronos-Saturn, reflected by the
universal duality of the senex dominants Chief and Medicine Man.
(These figures stand for the inner polarity of the senex, the two ways
of order and meaning, neither of which is positive or negative *per se*.)
The simplification will not hold because *the duality of the senex rests upon
an even more basic archetypal polarity: the senex-puer archetype.*

Thus the crucial psychological problem expressed by the terms
"negative senex" and "positive senex," ogre and wisdom, which concerns our individual lives and "how to be," and which is determining
the symptoms of the ageing millennium, arises from a fundamental
split between senex and puer within the same archetype. Negative
senex attitudes and behavior result from this split archetype, while
positive senex attitudes and behavior reflect its unity; so that the term
"positive senex" or "old wise man" refers merely to a transformed con-
tinuation of the puer. Here the first part of our thesis reaches its issue:
*the difference between the negative and positive senex qualities reflects the split or con-
nection within the senex-puer archetype.*

IV THE PUER. Unlike the term senex, analytical psychology uses the
concept of *puer eternus* widely and freely. It appears early in Jung's
work (1912)[31] and has been elaborated in various aspects by him and
by many since then.[32] We are especially indebted to Marie-Louise von
Franz for her work on this figure and the problem.[33] The single archetype tends to merge in one: the Hero, the Divine Child, the figures of
Eros, the King's Son, the Son of the Great Mother, the Psychopompos,
Mercurius-Hermes,[34] Trickster, and the Messiah. In him we see a mercurial range of these "personalities": narcissistic, inspired, effeminate,
phallic, inquisitive, inventive, pensive, passive, fiery, and capricious.
Furthermore, a description of the puer will be complicated because archetypal background and neurotic foreground, positive and negative,
are not clearly distinguished. Let us nevertheless sketch some main
lines of a psychological phenomenology.

The concept *puer eternus* refers to that archetypal dominant, which
personifies or is in special relation with transcendent spiritual powers. Puer figures can be regarded as avatars of the psyche's spiritual

aspect, and puer impulses as messages from the spirit or as calls to the spirit. When the collective unconscious in an individual life is represented mainly by parental figures, then puer attitudes and impulses will show personal taints of the mother's boy or *fils du papa*, the perennial adolescence of the provisional life. Then the neurotic foreground obscures the archetypal background. One assumes that the negative and irksome adolescence, the lack of progress and reality, is all a puer problem, whereas it is the personal and parental in the neurotic foreground that is distorting the necessary connection to the spirit. Then the transcendent call is lived within the family complex, distorted into a transcendent function of the family problem, as an attempt to redeem the parents or be their Messiah. The true call does not come through, or is possible only through technical breakthroughs: drugs or death-defying adventure.

The parental complex, however, is not solely responsible for the crippling, laming, or castration of the archetypal puer figures. This laming refers to the especial weakness and helplessness at the beginning of any enterprise. Inherent in the one-sided vertical direction is the Ikaros-Ganymede propensity of flying and falling.[35] It must be weak on earth, because it is not at home on earth. The beginnings of things are *Einfälle*; they fall in on one from above as gifts of the puer, or sprout up out of the ground as daktyls, as flowers. But there is difficulty at the beginning; the child is in danger, easily gives up. The horizontal world, the space-time continuum, which we call "reality," is not its world. So the new dies easily because it is not born in the *Diesseits*, and this death confirms it in eternity. Death does not matter because the puer gives the feeling that it can come again another time, make another start. Mortality points to immortality; danger only heightens the unreality of "reality" and intensifies the vertical connection.

Because of this vertical *direct* access to the spirit, this immediacy where vision of goal and goal itself are one, winged speed, haste — even the short cut — are imperative. The puer cannot do with indirection, with timing and patience. It knows little of the seasons and of waiting. And when it must rest or withdraw from the scene, then it seems to be stuck in a timeless state, innocent of the passing years, out of tune with time. Its wandering is as the spirit wanders, without at-

tachment and not as an odyssey of experience. It wanders to spend or
to capture, and to ignite, to try its luck, but not with the aim of going
home. No wife waits; it has no son in Ithaca. Like the senex, it cannot
hear, does not learn. The puer therefore understands little of what is
gained by repetition and consistency, that is, by work, or of the moving back and forth, left and right, in and out, which makes for subtlety
in proceeding step by step through the labyrinthine complexity of the
horizontal world. These teachings but cripple its winged heels, for
there, from below and behind, it is particularly vulnerable. It is anyway
not meant to walk, but to fly.

The direct connection to the spirit can be misdirected through or
by the Great Mother.[36] Puer figures often have a special relationship
with the Great Mother, who is in love with them as carriers of the spirit; incest with them inspires her — and them — to ecstatic excess and
destruction. She feeds their fire with animal desire and fans their flame
with promise of scope and conquest over the horizontal world, her
world of matter. Whether as her hero-lover or hero-slayer, the puer
impulse is re-inforced by this entanglement with the Great Mother
archetype, leading to those spiritual exaggerations we call neurotic.
Primary among these exaggerations is the labile mood and the dependency of the spirit upon moods. Again, they are described in vertical
language (heights and depths, glory and despair) and we hear echoes
of the festivals for Attis called *tristia* and *hilaria*.[37]

The eternal spirit is sufficient unto itself and contains all possibilities.
As the senex is perfected through time, the puer is primordially perfect.
Therefore there is no development; development means devolution, a
loss and fall and restriction of possibilities. So for all its changeability
the puer, like the senex, at core resists development. This self-perfec-
tion, this aura of knowing all and needing nothing, is the true background of the self-containment and isolation of any complex, reflected
for instance in the ego's narcissistic attitudes, that angelic hermaphroditic quality where masculine and feminine are so perfectly joined that
nothing else is needed. There is therefore no need for relationship or
woman, unless it be some magical puella or some mother-figure who
can admiringly reflect and not disturb this exclusive hermaphroditic
unity of oneself with one's archetypal essence. The feeling of distance

and coldness, of impermanence, of Don Juan's ithyphallic sexuality, of homosexuality, can all be seen as derivatives of this privileged archetypal connection with the spirit, which may burn with a blue and ideal fire, but in a human relationship it may show the icy penis and chilling seed of a satanic incubus.

Because eternity is changeless, that which is governed only by the puer does not age. So, too, it has no maturing organic face that shows the bite of time. Its face is universal, given by the archetype, and so it cannot be faced, confronted in personal confrontation. It has a pose — phallic cavalier, pensive poet, messenger — but not a persona of adaptation. The revelations of the spirit have no personal locus in personality; they are eternally valid statements, good forever.

Yet in this faceless form it captures psyche.[38] It is to the puer that psyche succumbs, and just because it is psyche's opposite; the puer spirit is the least psychological, has the least soul. Its "sensitive soulfulness" is rather pseudopsychological, and a derivative of the hermaphroditic effeminacy. It can search and risk; it has insight, aesthetic intuition, spiritual ambition — all but not psychology, for psychology requires time, femininity of soul, and the entanglement of relationships. Instead of psychology, the puer attitude displays an aesthetic point of view: the world as beautiful images or as vast scenario. Life becomes literature, an adventure of intellect or science, or of religion or action, but always unreflected and unrelated and therefore unpsychological. It is the puer in a complex that "unrelates" it, that volatilizes it out of the vessel — that would act it out, call it off and away from the psychological — and thus is the principle that uncoagulates and disintegrates. What is unreflected tends to become compulsive, or greedy. The puer in any complex gives it drive and drivenness, makes it move too fast, want too much, go too far, not only because of the oral hunger and omnipotence fantasies of the childish, but archetypally because the world can never satisfy the demands of the spirit or match its ideal beauty. Hungering for eternal experience makes one a consumer of profane events. When the puer spirit falls into the public arena, it hurries history along.

And finally, as Henry Corbin has often pointed out, the puer eternus figure is the vision of our own first nature, our primordial golden shadow, our affinity to beauty, our angelic essence as messenger of the divine, as divine message.[39] From the puer we are given our sense of destiny and mission, of having a message and being meant as eternal cup-bearer to the divine, that our sap and overflow, our enthusiastic wetness of soul, is in service to the Gods, bringing eternal refreshment to the archetypal background of the universe.

So the puer personifies that moist spark within any complex or attitude that is the original dynamic seed of spirit. It is the call of a thing to the perfection of itself, the call of a person to his or her daimon, to be true to itself. The puer offers direct connection with spirit. Break this vertical connection and it falls with broken wings. When it falls we lose the urgent burning purpose and instead commence the long processional march through the halls of power towards the heart-hardened sick old king who is often cloaked and indistinguishable from the sick wise old man or woman.

The spark extinguished by this "heroic overcoming" leaves behind sad regrets, bitterness and cynicism, the very emotions of the negative senex. By conquering the parental complexes in the neurotic foreground, we smother the archetypal background. The puer suffers an enantiodromia into senex; he switches Janus faces. Thus are we led to realize *that there is no basic difference between the negative puer and negative senex*, except for their difference in biological age. The critical time in this process that is represented by the midpoint of biological life is as well the midpoint of any attitude or psychological function that ages but does not change. The eros and idealism of the beginning succumb to success and power, to be re-found, as we have seen from our examination of the senex, only at the end when power and success fail, when Saturn is in exile from the world — then eros as loyalty and friendship, and idealism as prophetic insight and contemplation of truth return.

In all this, the greatest damage is done to meaning, distorted from idealism into cynicism. As the spirit becomes meaning through senex order, so the puer is meaning's other face. As archetypal structure, the puer is the inspiration of meaning and brings meaning as vision wherever he appears. A beginning is always meaningful and filled with the excitement of eros. Meaning expresses the invisible coincidence of the positive puer with the positive senex. The puer aspect of meaning is in the *search*, as the dynamus of the child's eternal "why?"; the quest, or questioning, seeking, adventuring, which grips personality from behind and compels it forward. All things are uncertain, provisional, subject to question, thereby opening the way and leading the soul toward further questioning.

However, if persuaded into the temporal world by the negative senex, the puer loses connection with its own aspect of meaning and becomes the negative puer. Then it goes dead, and there is passivity, withdrawal, even physical death. These pueri are only flower-people like Hyacinthus, Narcissus, Crocus, whose tears are but wind-flowers, anemones of the Goddess, and whose blood gives only Adonis-roses and Attis-violets of regret. They are flower-people who are unable to carry their own meaning through to the end, and as flowers they must fade before fruit and seed. Eternal Becoming never realized in Being; possibility and promise only. Or the negative puer may become hyperactive and we find all the traits accentuated and materialized, but without inherent meaning. When the falcon cannot hear the falconer, wingedness becomes mere haste and fanaticism, an unguided missile. A person is caught in the puer activities of social rebellion, intellectual technology, or physical adventure with redoubled energy and loss of goal. Everything new is worshipped because it gives promise of the original, while the historical is discarded because it is of the senex who is now enemy. Personal revelation is preferred to objective knowledge so that minor epiphanies weigh more than the classics of culture. Eventually meaning declines into a philosophy of the absurd, action into the *acte gratuite* or violence, or intoxication, or flight into the future; and the chaos returns, which the puer as archetype is itself called to oppose. By refusing history, by pushing it all down into the unconscious in order to fly above it, one is forced to repeat history unconsciously. In the unconscious the senex position builds up with a compulsive vengeance until with all the force of historical necessity it takes over in its turn, reducing new truths to old cliches again, switching the only-puer into an only-senex, split from the next generation.

The puer gives us connection to the spirit and is always concerned with the eternal aspect of ourselves and the world. However, *when this concern becomes only puer, exclusive and negative, the world is itself in danger of dissolution into the otherworldly*. This danger is especially present in the psyche and history of this fraction of our era.[40] Therefore it is of immense importance that the puer be recognized and valued, for it carries our future — positive or negative — not necessarily as the next step in time, but as the futurity within every complex, its prospective meaning, its way out and way forward, as a possibility of renewal through eros and as a call to meaning built on the eternities of spirit. Therefore it is of immense importance that we attempt the healing of the archetypal split, which divides puer from senex, turning them into a negative antithesis, hardening the heart against one's own puer imagination, thereby demonizing one's angel so that the new, which comes into being through the puer, is demonic. When the archetype is split, the dynamus works independently of the patterns of order. Then we have a too-familiar pattern: action that does not know and knowledge that does not act, fanatic versus cynic, commonly formulated as youth and age. This negative turn happens not only in young people or in the first half of life or in new movements.

We must therefore deny again the usual separation into first and second halves of life, as presented for example by Jacobi, Fordham, and Dunn.[41] It dangerously divides puer and senex. Always the puer is described from within the senex-puer duality and therefore comes out negatively, which also implies a positive senex view of itself.

Let us look at the usual recommendations for the "first-half" of life, or "how to cure a puer": analyze the unconscious, reduce the fantasies, dry the hysterics, confront the intuitions, bring down to earth and reality, turn the poetry into prose. The will is to direct sexuality into relationship; the crippling is to be overcome through the exercise of work; practicality, sacrifice, limits, hardening. The face is to be set, positions defended, the provisional overcome through the panacea of commitment. Concentration, responsibility, roots, historical continuity and identity: in a word, ego-strengthening. Note well: all these images are Saturnian.

Commitment as duty clips the wings and binds the feet, as Saturn is chained through his commitments. Ego-strengthening fosters a revolutionary unattached shadow that would smash all fetters, for the strong ego has the strong shadow, the brilliance makes its own blackness. This path of worldly commitment aims to sever the puer from its own vertical axis; it reflects a senex personality, which has not itself separated the parental from the archetypal and is thus threatened by its own child, its own phallus, and its own poetry.

However we conceive the tasks of youth, or of the beginning of things, they cannot be accomplished without the meaning given by the spiritual connection. Initiation into reality is not to take away the initiant's relation with the primordial origins but only to separate these origins from the confusions of the personal and parental. Initiation is not a demythologizing into "hard" reality, but an affirmation of the mythical meaning within all reality. Initiation "softens" reality by filling in its background with layers of mythological perspective, providing the fantasy, which makes the "hardness" of reality meaningful and tolerable, and at the same time truly indestructible. The puer figure — Baldur, Tammuz, Jesus, Krishna — brings myth into reality, presents in himself the reality of myth that transcends history. His message is mythical, stating that he, the myth — so easily wounded, easily slain, yet always re-born — is the seminal sub-structure of all enterprise. Traditional initiation of the puer by the positive senex confirms this relation to the archetype. Some substitutes for initiation — and analysis can be one — may instead sever this relation.

Relation with any archetype involves the danger of possession, usually marked by inflation. This is particularly true of the puer because of its high-flights and mythical behavior. Of course, possession through the senex brings an equally dangerous set of moods and actions: depression, pessimism, and hardness of heart. Even a minimum of psychological awareness — that I am just what I am as I am — can spare complete archetypal possession. This awareness is made possible through the reflective, echoing function of the psyche. This function is the human psyche's contribution to spirit and to meaning, which noble as they may be can also be, without psyche, runaway destructive possessions. So the main puer problem is not lack of worldly reality but *lack of psychic reality*. Rather than commitment to the order of the world the puer needs to be wedded to psyche, to which the puer is anyway naturally drawn. Rather than historical continuity and roots in the horizontal, he needs devotion to the anima. First psyche, then world; or through the psyche to the world. The anima has the thread and knows the step-by-step dance that can lead through the labyrinth, and can teach the puer the subtleties of left-hand/right-hand, opening and closing, accustoming and refining vision to the half-light of ambivalence.

Let us not mistakenly take this as *Lebensphilosophie* or a psychological prescription for "cure" — i.e., only involvement with a real woman leads a man out of his mother-bound adolescent compulsions. We are discussing rather an archetypal structure, not "how to be." Each "hot idea," at whatever time of life in whomever, wherever, requires psychization. It needs first to be contained within the relationship to psyche, given the soul connection. Each complex needs realization and connection within the psyche, taming the puer's hot compulsions with the common salt of the soul. This salt makes things last and brings out their true flavor. The young and burning sulphur needs union with the elusive quicksilver of psychic reality before it becomes fixed and weighty.

This turning to the soul means *taking in our complexes out of the world,* out of the realm of senex power and system. Only this can slow the speed of history and technology and the acceleration of particle-men into bits of information without souls. It means that the search and questing be a psychological search and questing, a psychological adventure. It means that the messianic and revolutionary impulse connect first with the soul and be concerned first with its redemption. This alone makes human the puer's message, at the same time reddening the soul into life. [42] It is in this realm of the soul that the gifts of the puer are first needed.

V THE UNION OF SAMES. With the phenomenology of the senex and the puer behind us, we now see that we have actually been describing a secret identity of two halves — two halves not of life, but of a single archetype. This secret identity should not astonish us, since a corresponding feminine union of sames (the Mother-Daughter mysteries) has been placed at the center of feminine personality. Archetypal representations of this single figure with double aspects are: Tages, the Etruscan God who was a grey-haired boy appearing out of the furrows of a plowed field; the Islamic Chidr, a beauteous youth with a white beard; and Lao Tzu, whose name means senex-puer, *i.e.*, "Lao" = "old" and "Tzu" = both "master" and "child." (Other literary and hagiographic descriptions of the puer-senex polarity in the same figure are given in detail by Curtius.[43]) Through Jung's work we also know of this union of sames: a) first, on a dangerous and primitive level in the figure of Wotan, both youthful and Kronos,[44] b) in the figures of Mercurius,[45] Dionysus,[46] and Christ, each as *senex-et-puer,* c) in Asklepios, *senex-et-puer* who heals, and d) in the alchemical King and King's Son as two faces of the same dominant. These mythological figures, representing the union of sames which energize (Wotan), which transform (Mercurius, Dionysus), which heal (Asklepios), which renew (King-*cum*-King's Son), and which redeem (Christ), each state the psychological axiom that the archetype is timeless. It seems utterly unconcerned with aging, with historical accumulations; there is no conflict of generations since it is all generations at any moment. Ego-consciousness as the self-divisive instrument of the Self, its "father" or its "son" and thus its "enemy," instigates the factions and the differences. Thus does the ego act as the shadow of the Self.

We are also used to finding a secret identity in those we call in our offhand psychological jargon "typically puer" or "typically senex": the same self-willed petulance and resistance to change, the same egocentricity and coldness of feeling, the same destructive effect on the middleground values of life, regarding them with scurrility, bitterness, and contempt. "Typically puer" or "typically senex" therefore means a possession through one face only. Again, because of the secret identity, it does not matter by which face one is possessed since they are the same. "Typical" therefore means "only," and the typical puer is identical with the typical senex; each is only puer or senex, not *puer-et-senex.* They are the same in a negative identification because they have lost the ambivalent consciousness of the union of sames. That tragedy of changelessness, of being "stuck," of being "unmoved" (expressed symbolically in "deafness," "heart disease," and "feet troubles"), is also accounted for by this negative identification. If the senex will not change and the puer cannot change (change requires listening, feeling, and going step-by-step), it is because the alpha-omega polarity has been negatively identified and thus obliterated. Without this polarity, which is at the essence of the archetype and holds its meaning together, there is perfection but no process, no movement from here to there, from past to future. A tension of ambivalent opposites is the structural precondition for change.

The critical age of change in an individual life is, as Jung noted, around its midpoint in the fourth decade. Then the archetype of the process of life — and life for the psyche is a symbol — can break into two halves, sometimes killing the physical life of the individual who is broken by this symbolic crisis. That critical midpoint, when the puer impulse so often "dies" or becomes converted to senex values, is less a biological fact than a psychic symbol. As such it is governed less by the physiology of life processes than by the archetype of the process of life. This archetype of puer and senex is therefore particularly constellated at the midpoint, when the two faces are so close to each other and yet seem to look in opposite directions. It can be of utmost therapeutic value for the individual to realize (not that one is "getting old" but) that one is in the midst of a symbolic situation characterized by ambivalence of feeling and attitude, and that fears and confusions are appropriate. This realization that one's psyche is now being governed mainly by a union of sames may save one from an only ego view of necessary oppositions and choices. The therapeutic key to the midpoint would lie in the secret identity of the two faces of the same archetype. By continuing true to one's past puer spirit and consciously affirming it, one has already assumed the senex virtue of responsibility and order.

We are able to establish this identity of the two faces not only through psychological observations. It can be confirmed as well through mythographical amplification. A review of the main characteristics of each half shows parallels in symbolic forms with the other:

The Holy Old Man as Attik[47] is concealed and as Saturn has his head covered or cloaked; Harpocrates, the boy, is hooded, faceless or covered; so, too, are Attis[48] and Telesphoros. Saturn has a sparse beard; Mercurius wears his first downy beard or a small beard. Saturn is taciturn and guards secrets; Harpocrates has his fingers to his lips. As Mercurius is winged, so can Kronos-Saturn, as Aion, or on tombstones, be winged. Both are related to the dead, to time and eternity, and to the Golden Age. On a tomb in the Vatican "Saturn appears sadly reflecting, like Attis on other tombs." Both are concerned with truth — and with deceit, craftiness, and thieving. Their animals are the same breed: Goat and Kid, and sometimes Dog. Both show abnormality of the feet: Saturn is lamed and crippled; the feet of Attis are bound, and Mercurius has winged foot-gear and Achilles the vulnerable heel of heroic illusion. One cannot walk, the other can only fly. The deformity points to their each being only half of a whole reality. As Jung says, "they are separated by deformity." Both Attis and Saturn show the castration motif and cold, cut-off satanic sexuality. For some, Mercurius is the principle of reason, governing astrology, mathematics, geometry, writing, knowledge, wisdom; for others, all these areas belong to Saturn. Both can be cold and dry. Saturn is lord of melancholy, yet Mercurius gives depression and worry. Harpocrates wears a wolf-skin, and Mercurius, patron of merchants, shows the greed for gain; yet Saturn is the greedy one, miserly at home and rapacious abroad. Both are wanderers, both outcasts, and Saturn, who governs "magic and revels" (which could as well be said of the puer), is also against the bourgeois canons of society. As the puer is suicidal, Saturn presides over self-destruction. Both show an absence of the feminine, and both may have the ithyphallic attribute. The remoteness of Saturn at the *imum coeli* is matched at the other pole by the ascending puer Ikaros-Ganymede. Yet Ganymede the cup-bearer is also Saturn as Aquarian Water-Carrier, the sign of our new age; and in reverse, the alchemical mercurial spirit is buried deep in the bowels of the earth, in exile and stench, in the lowest of low. The vertical axis, which connects them, gives them the spiritual point of view: both see the world *sub specie aeternitatis*. The one sees through it from below, as criminal or peasant, having suffered it with the privative vision given of melancholy. The other looks down upon it from above and from within as the divine seed-spark that knows the true *eidos* of all things.[49]

We seek this merger in our own lives. We seek a transformation of the conflict of extremes into a union of sames. Our time and its longing to be healed asks that the two ends be held together, that our other half so near to us, so like us as the shadow we cast, enter the circle of our light. Our other half is not only of another sex. The union of opposites — male with female — is not the only union for which we long and is not the only union that redeems. There is also the union of sames, the re-union of the vertical axis, which would heal the split spirit. Adam must re-unite with Eve, but there still remains his re-union with God. Still remains the union of the first Adam at the beginning with the second Adam at the end of history. This division, experienced as the chasm between consciousness and the unconscious, is in us each at the unhealed heart of the process of individuation. No wonder that our theme is so charged, that we cannot take hold of the senex-puer problem anywhere without getting burnt; no wonder that it cannot be fully circumscribed and contained. It cannot become clarified, for we stand in the midst of its smoke. Its split is our pain.

This split of spirit is reflected in the senescence and renewal of God and of civilization. It is behind the fascination with *Lebensphiloso- phie* and the comforting aphorisms of stages of life, which by taking the polarity as its starting point can offer no healing.[50] This split gives us the aches of the father-son problem and the silent distance between generations, the search of the son for his father and the longing of the father for his son, which is the search and longing for one's own meaning; and the theological riddles of the Father and the Son. It tells us that we are split from our own likeness and have turned our same- ness with this likeness into difference. And the same split is in the feminine as the spirit is represented in her by the animus, its poles that divide her and cause her to divide others, leading her into the either/or clarifications of the animus that but further new divisions such as love versus loyalty, principle versus abandon, or find her mothering the inspired puer or being the inspired daughter of the senex. The same split gives the frustrations of homosexual eros, the search for angelic beauty, the fear of ageing, the longing for the union of sames. We find it too in the insoluble difficulties of the master-pupil transference, the senex-teacher who must have a disciple and the puer-pupil who must have his image of the old wise man carried for him.[51] This is the tra- ditional way the spirit is transferred. Yet just this outer constellation reflects the inner division within each. Owing to the split archetype, a negative polarity is inevitably constellated.[52] This leads to the curse between generations, the betrayals, to kings and powers not sages and wisdom, and the inability of the master to recognize his pupil and give him blessing. The pupil then "slays the Old King" in order to come into his own kingdom, only to become an Old King himself in the course of time.

What might this union of sames feel like? How would it be were the polarity healed? We have only hints: some in concepts, some in images.

A primary image of the union of sames is given in that "most widely cherished Renaissance maxim" *festina lente* (make haste slowly). Holding the opposites together in a balanced tension was represented in countless emblematic variations summarized by Wind. The puer-senex or *paedogeron* was one major example of *festina lente*. Maturity in this ideal was not a negation of the puer aspect since the puer was an essential face of "two-fold truth."[53]

Festina lente, in other words, presents an ego-ideal based on the two-faced archetype. It is an ideal that may be achieved, however, only by remaining consequently true to the puer aspect. To be true to one's puer nature means to admit one's puer past — all its gambols and gestures and sun-struck aspirations. From this history we draw consequences. By standing for these consequences, we let history catch up with us and thus is our haste slowed. History is the senex shadow of the puer, giving him substance. Through our individual histories, puer merges with senex, the eternal comes back into time, the falcon returns to the falconer's arm.

The dynamus of one combines with the order of the other. The bipolar spirit becomes ambivalent, logically incoherent but symbolically cohesive, as we see in the paradoxes of mysticism. There will be a curious intermingling of time and eternity, as in nature. Temporal continuity, that causal chain of history, the basis of order and the basis of ego, is broken up or broken through by the eternal. The world of Saturn is pierced through with Mercurius; the silver-quick flow coagulated into solid moments: quantum jumps, spontaneous events, forgetting and foolishness, uselessness in the world of power yet full knowledge, unpredictable — "discontinuity," as Erich Neumann called it.[54] Yet this is not chaos nor random destruction. Rather these ordered happenings within limits are vividly meaningful, happenings having their own meaning, a sense or non-sense that is not dependent upon before or after from which it may be discrete, discontinuous, or only in the same "topological space." So the sense is given wholly by the experience itself as a gift of soul. And one feels through such experiences that there is meaning, that one is in meaning, that one is personally, individually meant. Let us call it meaningful discontinuity or the order of chance governed by fate, or call it living from the principle which Jung circumscribed as synchronicity.

Another hint comes from the paradoxes of knowing and not-knowing, the archetypal mystery, which is behind the phenomenon of dialogue. For dialogue does not rest only on the people who are involved, nor does their involvement rest on some existential para-concept. Dialogue, the union-forming effect of dialectic, the press within us to enter into dialectic to find knowledge and to discover meaning, is already embedded within the archetype of senex-puer relationship — that question "why" and that answer "I know." For meaning is as much in the questioning as in the knowing, or as Jung put it in his autobiography:

> The meaning of my existence is that life has addressed a question to me. Or, conversely, I myself am a question which is addressed to the world, and I must communicate my answer . . . I also think of the possibility that through the achievement of an individual a question enters the world, to which he must provide some kind of answer.[55]

In answering one's own question one is *puer-et-senex*. In questioning one's own answer one is *senex-et-puer*. The two faces turned towards each other in dialogue. This unending dialogue with oneself and between oneself and the world is that which holds one in meaning.

Alchemy gives a further hint in one of the paradoxes of the *lapis*. The stone is not only hard as the senex face might view it, not only a jade of longevity, a diamond body of immortality. The *lapis*, as Erwin Rousselle[56] and Henry Corbin[57] have carefully elaborated, is the *puer eternus*. The end of the *via longissima* is the child. But the child begins in the realm of Saturn, in lead or rock, ashes or blackness, and it is there the child is realized. It is warmed to life in a bath of cinders, for only when a problem is finally worn to nothing, wasted and dry, can it reveal a wholly unexpected essence. Out of the darkest, coldest, most remote burnt-out state of the complex the phoenix arises. *Petra genetrix;* out of the stone a child is born, laughing, tender, unable. The stone, says Sir George Ripley, is "of so tender and oily a substance that it is apt to dissolve in every moist place."[58] So it must be kept as sugar in a dry place. The *ceratio* makes it soft to the touch; lead, Mercurius, and gold have a kindred softness. Because it is wax-like and malleable, it takes the "type" easily, impressions can be struck and then wiped out, forgotten, history leaving no marks. At the human touch, at body temperature, the stone relaxes its form. Oily and fat, it anoints that which it touches, spreads blessing: *Christos, Messias,* anointed; the oily nature which "walks on water" and heals wounds. This stone of changeless substance nevertheless has discontinuity of form and face, of defensive borders. It is easily persuaded into positions and dissuaded out of them again. Though receptive to any imprint, it is not committed to any *eidos* but its own substance. So, of *purus actus,* it is also purely acted upon and is thus a spirit indistinguishable from matter. Highly impressionable yet leaving no trace, it may take on any shape for a little while yet through warmth be ready to dissolve again. The coagulation is always subject to renewed dissolution, the senex certainty always provisionally puer.

These are hints of our healing. To get there where the spirit is whole, where meaning holds together, we have begun on a way of mythical images. There is an advantage in going this way towards archetypal healing, for myth is the language of ambivalence; nothing is only this or that; the Gods and dancers will not stand still. They allow no sharp pictures of themselves, only visions. Besides, as Kluckhohn has paraphrased Lévi-Strauss: ". . . mythical thought always works from awareness of binary oppositions toward their progressive mediation. That is, the contribution of mythology is that of providing a logical model capable of over-coming contradictions."[59]

Do we truly have a choice of ways? The binary oppositions, the polar coordinates, cannot be healed through an effort of mind and will, since the willful mind is the splitting instrument. We are incapable, as Hoyle said,[60] of solving the problems of the day with even the simplest logical processes. Any solution originating from the usual mind would be one-sided; it would be a solution imposed by either the senex or puer components of the ego. Thus the ego must first undergo an archetypal therapy of its split root.

The ego today is a "mind at the end of its tether." All it can do is leave itself open to the possibility of grace and to a renewal which might then take place in its absence. In the *absence of ego* and into its emptiness an imaginal stream can flow, providing mythical solutions for the psychic connection or "progressive mediation" between the senex/ puer contradictions. These mythical solutions will be unclear, ambivalent, foolish. Ego-absence will feel first like ego-weakness; the solutions will seem to regress rather than to advance the problem into new terrain. But at this moment of transition we cannot advance until we have first retreated enough inward and backward so that the unconscious figures within can catch up with us. We cannot bring healing to the split without their cooperation since it is from them that we are split. To elicit their cooperation we must go part of the way, into the penumbral world.[61]

Notes

1. [First presented at Eranos and published in *Eranos-Yearbook* 35 (1967). The paper was republished in *Art International* 15/1 (1971) and in J. Hillman ed., *Puer Papers* (Dallas: Spring Publications, 1979). For this volume the first three paragraphs of the original paper may be found in the appendix.] — Ed.

2. F. Hoyle, *Of Men and Galaxies* (London: Heinemann, 1965), p. 65.

3. [See Chapter 3 for a further exploration of *kairos*, especially in terms of opportunity and opening.] — Ed.

4. ["Makeweight" refers to Jung's question: "Does the individual know that *he* is the makeweight that tips the scales?" Cf. C. G. Jung, *Collected Works*, vol. 10: *Civilization in Transition*, par. 586.] — Ed.

5. W. B. Yeats, "The Second Coming," *Collected Poems* (London: Macmillan, 1952).

6. M. Eliade, *The Myth of the Eternal Return* (New York: Bollingen, 1954); *Images and Symbols* (London: Harvill, 1961); *Myth and Reality* (London: Allen and Unwin, 1964); *The Two and the One* (London: Harvill, 1965).

7. A. Schlesinger, "On the Writing of Contemporary History," *Atlantic Monthly* 219 (1967), sec. 3.

8. [For further discussion of this perspective see James Hillman's *Healing Fiction* (Putnam, CT, Spring Publications, 2004).] — Ed.

9. E. R. Curtius, *European Literature and the Latin Middle Ages* (New York: Pantheon, 1953), pp. 98–101.

10. Wing-tsit Chan, *The Way of Lao Tzu* (*Tao-te ching*) (Indianapolis: Bobbs-Merrill, 1963), sec. 55.

11. Jung does, of course, use other explanatory models for psychic structure, such as: 1) *Schichtentheorie* and a hierarchical schema when describing levels of the psyche or when describing the process of individuation. 2) He uses a situational conditionalism — a major model of thought for the existentialists — when discussing therapeutics and interpretation. 3) He uses as well an organismic functional model when he accounts for the evolutionary, developmental, or transformative aspects of the psyche as a whole. 4) And, further, we find in Jung an atomist-molecular model when describing the associations and constellations of the psyche. These are each but one metaphor for seizing the ungraspable nature of psychic realities. The one which he favored most is that of polar opposites.

12. The main features of Jung's polar model are as follows: 1) The psyche is primarily divided into conscious and unconscious, the relation between which is compensatory. 2) The energy of the psyche flows between two poles which can be variously qualified by opposites. 3) The attitudes of the psyche (introversion and extraversion) and the four psychological functions are described in polar pairs. 4) Instinctual pattern of behavior and archetypal image

are polar ends of a spectrum-continuum. 5) There are recurrent themes of polarities such as: logos and eros, power and love, ego and shadow, spirit and nature, sexuality and religion, rational and irrational, individual and collective, container and contained, as well as the notions of two kinds of thinking, first-half and second-half, *les extrêmes se touchent*, etc. 6) Polarity is fundamental to Jung's writings on practice as a dialectic and his writings about himself, e.g., personality number one and personality number two. 7) Finally, the major theme of his later years: the male-female polarity and union in its various alchemical forms. (*Eranos-Yearbooks* 2: 379–81; 3: 248–53; 4: 298–329; 20: 408–10).

13. C.G. Jung, "The Spirit of Psychology," in Joseph Campbell, ed., *Spirit and Nature: Papers from the Eranos-Yearbooks* (Princeton University Press, 1982), p. 399.

14. O. Barfield, *History in English Words* (London: Faber, 1962).

15. Jung introduced the term "psychoid" in 1946 (*Collected Works*, vol. 8: *Structure and Dynamics of the Psyche*). It refers to that aspect of archetypal reality that suggests an overlap of psyche and matter.

16. *Tao-te ching*, pp. 20, 55.

17. J. Seznec, *The Survival of the Pagan Gods* (New York: Harper Torchbooks, 1961), p. 53.

18. R. Klibansky, E. Panofsky, and F. Saxl, *Saturn and Melancholy* (London: Warburg Institute/Nelson, 1964), p. 134.

19. P. Wolff-Windegg, *Die Gekrönten* (Stuttgart: Klett, 1958).

20. See *Picatrix*, translated into German from the Arabic by H. Ritter and M. Plessner (London: Warburg Institute, 1962).

21. Recent bio-genetic determinism is returning to Saturnian physiological fatalism: e.g., we are our inheritance.

22. My condensation of traditional traits derives from: *Saturn and Melancholy*, especially pp. 127–214; E. Panofsky, "Father Time," in *Studies in Iconography* (New York: Harper Torchbooks, 1965); *Picatrix*, pp. 117, 209, 213ff., 333–35, 360.

23. *Saturn and Melancholy*, pp. 135 n. and 208.

24. Ibid., p. 204

25. Ibid., pp. 161–64.

26. *Collected Works*, vol. 14: *Mysterium Coniunctionis*, sec. IV (Rex et Regina).

27. *Collected Works*, vol. 8: *Structure and Dynamics of the Psyche*, par. 754–55.

28. Ibid., par. 387.

29. *Collected Works*, vol. 9.1: *Archetypes and the Collective Unconsciousness*, par. 66ff.

30. Cf. A. Guggenbühl-Craig, *The Old Fool and the Corruption of Myth* (Dallas: Spring Publications, 1991).

31. C.G. Jung, *Wandlungen und Symbole der Libido* (Leipzig/Vienna: Deuticke, 1912); *Collected Works*, vol. 5: *Symbols of Transformation*, par. 194, 392, 526; Col-

lected Works, vol. 9.2: Aion ("Psychological Aspects of the Mother Archetype," "The Psychology of the Child Archetype," "On the Psychology of the Trickster Figure"); Collected Works, vol. 16: Practice of Psychotherapy, par. 336; Collected Works, vol. 13: Alchemical Studies ("The Spirit Mercurius"); Collected Works, vol. 11: Psychology and Religion, par. 742.

32. H. Baynes, "The Provisional Life," in Analytical Psychology and the English Mind (London: Kegan Paul, 1950); M. van Leight Frank, "Adoration of the Complex," in A. Guggenbühl-Craig, ed., The Archetype (Basel: Karger, 1964); H. Binswanger, Vol de Nuit von A. de St.-Exupéry: Versuch einer Interpretation, Diss., C.G. Jung Institut, n.d.; H.A. Murray "American Icarus," in A. Burton, ed., Clinical Studies of Personality (New York: Harper, 1955).

33. M.-L. von Franz, The Problem of the Puer Aeternus (New York: Spring Publications, 1970); Commentary to Das Reich ohne Raum by B. Goetz (Zurich: Origo, 1962); "Über religiose Hintergründe des Puer-Aeternus Problems," in A. Guggenbühl-Craig, ed., The Archetype (Basel: Karger, 1964).

34. K. Kerényi, Hermes der Seelenführer (Zurich: Rhein, 1944).

35. [For further discussion of this theme see chapter 5.] — Ed.

36. [For more on this issue, see Chapter 4, "The Great Mother, Her Son, Her Hero, and the Puer."] — Ed.

37. M. J. Vermaseren, The Legend of Attis in Greek and Roman Art (Leiden: Brill, 1966).

38. E. Neumann, Amor and Psyche (New York: Bollingen, 1956).

39. Cf. H. Corbin in Eranos-Yearbooks 17, 19, 25, 27.

40. [This paper (1967) was written in the midst of the 1960s social revolution in Western societies.] — Ed.

41. J. Jacobi, Der Weg zur Individuation (Zurich: Rascher, 1965); M. Fordham, "Individuation and Ego Development," Journal of Analytical Psychology 3.2 (1958); I.J. Dunn, "Analysis of Patients Who Meet the Problems of the First Half of Life in the Second," Journal of Analytical Psychology 6.1 (1961); also M.E. Harding, The Parental Image (New York: Putnam, 1965).

42. For a fuller treatment of this important motif see Chapter 2, "Peaks and Vales." [— Ed.]

43. Curtius, European Literature and the Latin Middle Ages, loc. cit.

44. Collected Works, vol. 10, par. 375, 393ff.

45. Collected Works, vol. 13 ("The Spirit Mercurius")

46. Collected Works, vol. 5, par. 184; K. Kerényi, Dionysos: Archetypal Image of Indestructible Life, trans. R. Manheim (Princeton University Press, 1976); W.F. Otto, Dionysos: Myth and Cult, trans. R. Palmer (Bloomington: Indiana University Press, 1965).

47. G. Scholem, "Die mystische Gestalt der Gottheit in der Kabbala," Eranos-Yearbook 29 (1960), p. 175.

48. The Legend of Attis in Greek and Roman Art, p. 54 n.

49. *Saturn and Melancholy*, pp. 196–7; 213; 131–34; 157, 177–79; 203; 266 n.; *The Survival of the Pagan Gods*, pp. 294ff.

50. M. Eliade, "Dimensions réligieuses du renouvellement cosmique," *Eranos-Yearbook* 28 (1959), p. 251.

51. Panofsky, "Father Time," in *Studies in Iconography*, pp. 75, 78.

52. *Collected Works*, vol. 5, par. 184.

53. E. Wind, *Pagan Mysteries in the Renaissance* (Harmondsworth: Peregrine, 1967), pp. 98ff.

54. E. Neumann, "Das Bild des Menschen in Krise und Erneuerung," *Eranos-Yearbook* 28 (1959), pp. 42ff.

55. *Memories, Dreams, Reflections*, p. 318.

56. E. Rousselle, "Seelische Führung im lebenden Taoismus," *Eranos-Yearbook* 1 (1933).

57. H. Corbin, *Temple and Contemplation* (London and New York: KPI and Islamic Publications, 1986), p. 169.

58. G. Ripley, "The Bosom Book" in *Collectanea Chemica* (London: Stuart, 1963), p. 141.

59. C. Kluckhohn, "Recurrent Themes in Myths and Mythmaking" in H. A. Murray, ed., *Myth and Mythmaking* (New York: Braziller, 1960), p. 58.

60. F. Hoyle, *Of Men and Galaxies*, p. 65.

61. [The concluding sections of the 1967 Eranos lecture ("Of Milk . . . and Monkeys") can be found as the last chapter of Part Four of this volume.] — Ed.

2

Peaks and Vales:
The Soul/Spirit Distinction as Basis for the Differences
between Psychotherapy and Spiritual Discipline[1]

> The way through the world
> Is more difficult to find than the way beyond it.
>
> — Wallace Stevens, "Reply to Papini"

IN SEARCH OF SOUL. Long ago and far away from California and its action, its concern, its engagement, there took place in Byzantium, in the city of Constantinople, in the year 869, a Council of the Principals of the Holy Catholic Church,[2] and because of their session then and another one of their sessions a hundred years prior (Nicaea, 787), we are all in this room tonight.

Because at that Council in Constantinople the soul lost its dominion. Our anthropology, our idea of human nature, devolved from a tripartite cosmos of spirit, soul, and body (or matter), to a dualism of spirit (or mind) and body (or matter). And this because at that other Council, the one in Nicaea in 787, images were deprived of their inherent authenticity.

We are in this room this evening because we are moderns in search of a soul, as Jung once put it. We are still in search of reconstituting that third place, that intermediate realm of psyche — which is also the realm of images and the power of imagination — from which we were exiled by theological, spiritual men more than a thousand years ago: long before Descartes and the dichotomies attributed to him, long before the Enlightenment and modern positivism and scientism. These ancient historical events are responsible for the malnourished root of our Western psychological culture and of the culture of each of our souls.

What the Constantinople Council did to soul only culminated a long process beginning with Paul (the saint) of substituting and disguising and forever after confusing, soul with spirit. Paul uses *psyche* only four times in his Epistles. *Psyche* appears in the entire New Testament only fifty-seven times compared with two hundred seventy-four occurrences of *pneuma*.[3] Quite a score! Of these fifty-seven occurrences of the word *psyche*, more than half are in the Gospels and Acts. The Epistles, the presentation of doctrine, the teachings of the school, could expose its theology and psychology without too much need for the word *soul*. For Paul four times was enough.

Much the same is true in regard to dreams and myths.[4] The word *to dream* does not appear in the New Testament; *dream* (*onar*) occurs only in three chapters of Matthew (1, 2, and 27). *Mythos* occurs only five times, pejoratively. Instead, there is stress on spirit phenomena: miracles, speaking in tongues, visions, revelations, ecstasy, prophecy, truth, faith.

Because our tradition has systematically turned against soul, we are each unaware of the distinctions between soul and spirit — therefore confusing psychotherapy with spiritual disciplines, obfuscating where they conflate and where they differ. This traditional denial of soul continues within the attitudes of each of us whether Christian or not, for we are each unconsciously affected by our culture's tradition, the unconscious aspect of our collective life. Ever since Tertullian declared that the soul (anima) is naturally Christian, there has been a latent Christianity, an antisoul spirituality, in our Western soul. This has led eventually to a psychological disorientation, and we have had to turn to the Orient. We place, displace, or project into the Orient our Occidental disorientation. And my task in this lecture is to do what I can for soul. Part of this task, because it is ritualistically appropriate, is to point out C. G. Jung's part in prying loose the dead fingers of those dignitaries in old Turkey, both by restoring the soul as a primary experience and field of work and by showing us ways — particularly through images — of realizing that soul.

‖ PSYCHE AND IMAGE. The three hundred bishops assembled at Nicaea in 787 upheld the importance of images against the enemies of images, mainly the Imperial Byzantine army. Images were venerated and adored all through the antique world — statues, icons, paintings, and clay figures formed part of the local cults and were the focus of the conflict between Christianity and the old polytheistic religions. At the time of the Nicaean Council there had been another of those long battles between spirit and soul, between abstractions and images, between iconoclasts and idolaters, such as occur in the Bible and in the life of Mohammed, and such as those which took place in the Renaissance and in the Reformation when Cromwell's men broke the statues of Christ and Mary in the churches in England because they were the Devil's work and not Christian.

The hatred of the image, the fear of its power, and of the imagination is very old and very deep in our culture.

At Nicaea a subtle and devastating differentiation was made. Neither the imagists nor the iconoclasts got their way entirely. A distinction was drawn between the *adoration* of images and the free formulation of them on the one hand, and the *veneration* of images and the authorized control over them on the other.[5] Church Councils split hairs, but the roots of these hairs are in our heads, and the split goes deep indeed. At Nicaea a distinction was made between the image as such, its power, its full divine or archetypal reality, and what the image represents, points to, means. Thus, images became allegories.

When images become allegories the iconoclasts have won. The image itself has become subtly depotentiated. Yes, images are allowed, but only if they are officially approved images illustrative of theological doctrine.[6] One's spontaneous imagery is spurious, demonic, devilish, pagan, heathen. Yes, the image is allowed, but only to be venerated for what it represents: the abstract ideas, configurations, transcendencies behind the image. Images became ways of perceiving doctrine, helps in focusing fantasy. They become representations, no longer presentations, no longer presences of divine power.

The year 787 marks another victory in our tradition of spirit over soul. Jung's resuscitation of images was a return to soul and what he calls its spontaneous symbol formation, its life of fantasy (which, as he notes, is inherently tied with polytheism).[7] By turning to the image, Jung returned to the soul, reversing the historical process that in 787 had depotentiated images and in 869 had reduced soul to the rational intellectual spirit.

This is history, yet not only history. For each time you or I treat images as representations of something else — Penis, or Great Mother, or Power Drive, or Instinct, or whatever general, abstract concept we prefer — we have smashed the image in favor of the idea behind it. To give to imagination interpretative meanings is to think allegorically and to depotentiate the power of the imagination.

Here I want to remind you of Jung's position, from which I have developed mine. Jung's psychology is based on soul. It is a tripartite psychology. It is based neither on matter and the brain nor on the mind, intellect, spirit, mathematics, logic, metaphysics. He uses neither the methods of natural science and the psychology of perception nor the methods of metaphysical science and the logic of mentation. He says his base is in a third place between: *esse in anima*, "being in soul."[8] And he found this position by turning directly to the images in his insane patients and in himself during his breakdown years.

The soul and its images, having been alienated so long from our conscious culture, could be recognized only by the alienist. (Or by the artist, for whom imagination and madness have long been kissing cousins in our culture's anthropology.) So, Jung said, if you are in search of soul, go first to your fantasy images, for that is how the psyche presents itself directly.[9] All consciousness depends upon fantasy images. All we know about the world, about the mind, the body, about anything whatsoever, *including the spirit* and the nature of the divine, comes through images and is organized by fantasies into one pattern or another. This holds true also for such spiritual states as pure light, or the void, or absence, or merging bliss, each of which is captured or structured in soul according to one or another archetypal fantasy pattern.[10] Because these patterns are archetypal, we are always in one or another archetypal configuration, one or another fantasy, including the fantasy of soul and the fantasy of spirit. The "collective unconscious," which embraces the archetypes, means our unconsciousness of the collective fantasy that is dominating by means of the archetypes our viewpoints, ideas, behaviors

Let me continue for just a moment with Jung — though we are almost through the abstract, thinky part of this lecture — who says, "Every psychic process is an image and an imagining."[11] The only knowledge we have that is immediate and direct is knowledge of these psychic images. And further, when Jung uses the word image, he does not mean the reflection of an object or a perception; that is, he does not mean a memory or after-image. Instead he says his term is derived "from poetic usage, namely, a figure of fancy or fantasy image."[12]

I have spelled all this out because I want you to know what I am doing. I am showing how soul looks at spirit, how peaks look from the vale, from within the fantasy world that is the shifting structure of our consciousness and its formulations, which are always shaped by archetypal images. We are always in one or another root-metaphor, archetypal fantasy, mythic perspective. From the soul's point of view we can never get out of the *vale* of our psychic reality.

III SOUL AND SPIRIT. I have called this talk "Peaks and Vales," and I have been aiming to draw apart these images in order to contrast them as vividly as I can. Part of separating and drawing apart is the emotion of hatred. So I shall be speaking with hatred and urging strife, or *eris*, or *polemos*, which Heraclitus, the first ancestor of psychology, has said is the father of all.

The contemporary meaning of "peak" was developed by Abraham Maslow, who in turn was resonating an archetypal image, for peaks have belonged to the spirit ever since Mount Sinai and Mount Olympus, Mount Patmos and the Mount of Olives, and Mount Moriah of the first patriarchal Abraham. And you will easily name a dozen other mountains of the spirit. It does not require much explication to realize that the peak experience is a way of describing pneumatic experience, and that the clamber up the peaks in search of spirit is the drive of the spirit in search of itself. The language Maslow uses about the peak experience — "self-validating, self-justifying and carries its own intrinsic value with it" — the God-likeness and God-nearness, the absolutism and intensity, is a traditional way of describing spiritual experiences. Maslow deserves our gratitude for having reintroduced *pneuma* into psychology, even if his move has been compounded by the old confusion of *pneuma* with psyche. But what about the *psyche* of psychology?

Vales do indeed need more exposition, just as everything to do with soul needs to be carefully imagined as accurately as we can. "Vale" comes from the Romantics: Keats uses the term in a letter, and I have taken this passage from Keats as a psychological motto: "Call the world, if you please, 'The vale of Soul-making.' Then you will find out the use of the world."

Vale in the usual religious language of our culture is a depressed emotional place — the vale of tears; Jesus walked this lonesome valley, the valley of the shadow of death. The very first definition of "valley" in the Oxford English Dictionary is a "long depression or hollow." The meanings of vale and valley include entire subcategories referring to such sad things as the decline of years and old age, the world regarded as a place of troubles, sorrow and weeping, and the world regarded as the scene of the mortal, the earthly, the lowly.

There is also a feminine association with vales. We find this in the *Tao Te Ching;* in Freudian morphological metaphors, where the wooded river valley teeming with animal life is an equivalent for the vagina; and also we find a feminine connotation of the valley in mythology. For valleys are the places of the nymphs. One of the etymological explanations of the word *nymph* takes these figures to be personifications of the wisps and clouds of mist clinging to valleys, mountainsides, and water sources. [13] Nymphs veil our vision, keep us shortsighted, myopic, caught — no long-range distancing, no projections or prophecies as from the peak.

This peak/vale pairing is also used by the fourteenth Dalai Lama of Tibet. In a letter (to Peter Goullart) he writes:

> The relation of height to spirituality is not merely metaphorical. It is physical reality. The most spiritual people on this planet live in the highest places. So do the most spiritual flowers . . . I call the high and light aspects of my being spirit and the dark and heavy aspect soul.
>
> Soul is at home in the deep, shaded valleys. Heavy torpid flowers saturated with black grow there. The rivers flow like warm syrup. They empty into huge oceans of soul.
>
> Spirit is a land of high, white peaks and glittering jewel-like lakes and flowers. Life is sparse and sounds travel great distances.

There is soul music, soul food, soul dancing, and soul love . . .

When the soul triumphed, the herdsmen came to the lamaser-
ies, for soul is communal and loves humming in unison. But the
creative soul craves spirit. Out of the jungles of the lamasery,
the most beautiful monks one day bid farewell to their comrades
and go to make their solitary journey toward the peaks, there to
mate with the cosmos . . .

No spirit broods over lofty desolation; for desolation is of the
depths, as is brooding. At these heights, spirit leaves soul far
behind . . .

People need to climb the mountain not simply because it is
there but because the soulful divinity needs to be mated with the
spirit . . . [abbreviated]

May I point out one or two little curiosities in this letter. They
may help us to see further the contrast between soul and spirit. First,
did you notice how important it is to be *literal* and not "merely metaphorical" when one takes the spiritual viewpoint? Also, this viewpoint
requires the physical sensation of height, of "highs." Then, did you see
that it is the most *beautiful* monks who leave their brothers, and that
their mating is with the *cosmos*, a mating that is compared with snow?
(Once in our witch-hunting Western tradition, a time obsessively concerned with protecting soul from wrong spirits — and vice versa — the
devil was identified by his icy penis and cold sperm.) And finally, have
you noticed the two sorts of anima symbolism: the dark, heavy, torpid
flowers by the rivers of warm syrup and the virginal petaled flowers of
the glaciers?

I am trying to let the *images* of language draw our distinction. This is
the soul's way of proceeding, for it is the way of dreams, reflections, fantasies, reveries, poems, and paintings. We can recognize what is spiritual
by its style of imagery and language; so with soul. To give *definitions* of
spirit and soul — the one abstract, unified, concentrated; the other concrete, multiple, immanent — puts the distinction and the problem into
the language of spirit. We would already have left the valley. We would
be making differences like a surveyor, laying out what belongs to whom
according to logic and law rather than according to imagination.

Let us turn to another culture a little closer to home even if far away in time: the early desert saints in Egypt, whom we might call the founders of our Western ascetic tradition, our discipline of the spirit.

We must first recall that these men were Egyptians, and as Violet MacDermott has shown, [14] their spiritual moves need to be understood against their Egyptian religious background. As the inheritor of an enduring polytheistic religion, the desert saint attempted to "reverse the psychological effects of the ancient religion." His discipline aimed to separate the monk from his human community and also from nature, both of which were of vital importance to the polytheistic religion in which divine and human interpenetrated everywhere (that is, in the valley, not only at the peak or the desert). By living in a cave — the burial place of the old religion — the desert saint performed a mimesis of death: the rigors of his spiritual discipline, its peculiar postures, fasting, insomnia, darkness, etc. These rigors helped him withstand the assault of the demons or ancestral influences of the dead, as well as his personal and cultural history:

> The world of the Gods was, in Egypt, also the world of the dead. Through dreams, the dead communicated with the living . . . therefore sleep represented a time when his soul was subject to his body and to those influences which derived from his old religion . . . his ideal was to sleep as little as possible. [15]

Again you will have noticed the turn away from sleep and dreams, away from nature and community, away from personal and ancestral history and polytheistic complexity. These factors from which the spiritual discipline works to be free give specific indications about the nature of the soul.

We find another contrast between soul and spirit, couched in different terms from the spiritual ones we have been examining. E. M. Forster's little volume *Aspects of the Novel* lays out the basic components of the art of the novel. He makes a distinction between fantasy and prophecy. He says that both involve mythology, Gods. Then he calls up fantasy with these words:

> . . . let us now invoke all beings who inhabit the lower air, the shallow water, and the smaller hills, all Fauns and Dryads and

slips of the memory, all verbal coincidences, Pans and puns, all that is medieval this side of the grave [by which I guess him to mean the coarse, common, and humorous, the daily, the grotesque and freakish, even bestial, but also festive].[16]

When Forster comes to prophecy we gain yet more images of spirit, for prophecy in the novel pertains to:

. . . whatever transcends our abilities, even when it is human passion that transcends them, to the deities of India, Greece, Scandinavia, and Judea, to all that is medieval beyond the grave and to Lucifer son of the morning [by which last I take him to mean the "problem of good and evil"]. By their mythologies we shall distinguish these two sorts of novels.[17]

By their mythologies we shall also distinguish our therapies.

Forster goes on with the comparison, but we shall break off, taking only a few scattered observations. Spirit (or the prophetic style) is humble but humorless. "It may imply any of the faiths that have haunted humanity — Christianity, Buddhism, dualism, Satanism, or the mere raising of human love and hatred to such a power that their normal receptacles no longer contain them."[18] (You recall the lama mating with the cosmos, the desert saint alone.) Prophecy (or spirit) is mainly a tone of voice, an accent, such as we find in the novels of D. H. Lawrence and Dostoevsky. Fantasy (or soul, in my terms) is a wondrous quality in daily life. "The power of fantasy penetrates into every corner of the universe, but not into the forces that govern it — the stars that are the brain of heaven, the army of unalterable law, remain untouched — and novels of this type have an improvised air . . ."[19] Here I think of the free associations of Freud as a *method* in psychology, or of Jung's mode of writing where a paragraph may not logically follow the one preceding, or of Lévi-Strauss's figure, the *"bricoleur,"* the handyman and his ragtag putting together of collages, and how different this psychological style is from that of intensely focused transcendental meditation, the turning away, the emptying out.[20]

And finally for our purposes Forster says about fantasy novels, or soul-writing, "If one god must be invoked specially, let us call upon Hermes — messenger, thief, and conductor of Souls. . ."[21]

Forster points to something else about soul (by means of his notion of fantasy), and this something else is history. The soul involves us in history — our individual case history, the history of our therapy, our culture as history. (We have seen the Coptic ascetics attempting to overcome ancestral history through spiritual practices.) Here, I too am speaking soul language in going back all the time to historical examples, such as old E. M. Forster, little fussy man in his room in Cambridge, now dead, and dead Freud and Jung, back to old myths and their scholarship, to etymologies and the history in words, and down to specific geographical localities, the actual vales of the world. For this is the way the soul proceeds. This is psychological method, and psychological method remains within this valley world, through which history passes and leaves its traces, our "ancestors."

The peaks wipe out history. History is to be overcome. History is bunk, said Henry Ford, prophetic manufacturer of obsolescence, and the past is a bucket of ashes, said Carl Sandburg, prophetic singer. So the spirit workers and spirit seekers first of all must climb over the debris of history, or prophesy its end or its unreality, time as illusion, as well as the history of their individual and particular localities, their particular ethnic and religious roots (C. G. Jung's ill-favored earlier term "racial unconscious"). Thus, from the spirit point of view, it can make no difference if our teacher be a Zaddik from a Polish *shtetl*, an Indian from under a Mexican cactus, or a Japanese master in a garden of stones, these differences are but conditionings of history, personalistic hangups. The spirit is impersonal, rooted not in local soul, but timeless.

I shall ride this horse of history until it drops, for I submit that history has become the Great Repressed. If in Freud's time sexuality was the Great Repressed and the creator of the internal ferment of the psychoneuroses, today the one thing we will not tolerate is history. No; we are each Promethean with a bag of possibilities, Pandoran hopes, open, unencumbered, the future before us, so various, so beautiful, so new — new and liberated men and women living forward into a science fiction. So history rumbles below, continuing to work in our psychic complexes.

Our complexes are history at work in the soul: father's socialism, his father's fundamentalism, and my reaction against them like Hefner to Methodism, Kinsey to Boy-Scoutism, Nixon to Quakerism. It is so much easier to transcend history by climbing the mountain and let come what may than it is to work on history within us, our reactions, habits, moralities, opinions, symptoms that prevent true psychic change. Change in the valley requires recognition of history, an archaeology of the soul, a digging in the ruins, a re-collecting. And — a planting in specific geographical and historical soil with its own smell and savor, in connection with the spirits of the dead, the *po*-soul sunk in the ground below.

From the viewpoint of soul and life in the vale, going up the mountain feels like a desertion. The lamas and saints "bid farewell to their comrades." As I'm here as an advocate of soul, I have to present its viewpoint. Its viewpoint appears in the long hollow depression of the valley, the inner and closed dejection that accompanies the exaltation of ascension. The soul feels left behind, and we see this soul reacting with anima resentments. Spiritual teachings warn the initiate so often about introspective broodings, about jealousy, spite, and pettiness, about attachments to sensations and memories. These cautions present an accurate phenomenology of how the soul feels when the spirit bids farewell.

If a person is concurrently in therapy and in a spiritual discipline — Vedanta, breathing exercises, transcendental meditation, etc. — the spiritual teacher may well regard the analysis as a waste of time with trivia and illusions. The analyst may regard the spiritual exercises as a leak in the psychic vessel, or an escape into either physicality (somatizing, a sort of sophisticated hysterical conversion) or into metaphysicality. These are conditions that grow in the same hedgerow: both physicalize, substantiate, hypostasize, taking their concepts as things. They both lose the "as if," the metaphorical Hermes approach, forgetting that metaphysics too is a fantasy system, even if one that must unfortunately take itself as literally real.

Besides these mutual accusations of triviality, there is a more essential question that we in our analytical armchairs ask: *Who* is making the trip? Here it is not a discussion about the relative value of doctrines or goals; nor is it an analysis of the visions seen and experiences felt. The essential issue is not the analysis of content of spiritual experiences, for we have seen similar experiences in the county hospital, in dreams, in drug trips. Having visions is easy. The mind never stops oozing and spurting the sap and juice of fantasy, and then congealing this play into paranoid monuments of eternal truth. And then are not these seemingly mind-blowing events of light, of synchronicity, of spiritual sight in an LSD trip often trivial — seeing the universe revealed in a buttonhole stitch or linoleum pattern — at least as trivial as what takes place in a usual therapy session that picks apart the tangles of the daily domestic scene?

The question of what is trivial and what is meaningful depends on the archetype that gives meaning, and this, says Jung, is the self. Once the self is constellated, *meaning* comes with it. But as with any archetypal event, it has its undifferentiated foolish side. So one can be overwhelmed by displaced, inferior, paranoid meaningfulness, just as one can be overwhelmed by eros and one's soul (anima) put through the throes of desperate, ridiculous love. The disproportion between the trivial content of a synchronistic event on the one hand, and on the other, the giant sense of meaning that comes with it, shows what I mean. Like a person who has fallen into love, so a person who has fallen into meaning begins that process of self-validation and self-justification of trivia which belong to the experience of the archetype within any complex and form part of its defense. It therefore makes little difference, psychodynamically, whether we fall into the shadow and justify our disorders of morality, or the anima and our disorders of beauty, or the self and our disorders of meaning. Paranoia has been defined as a disorder of meaning — that is, it can be referred to the influence of an undifferentiated self-archetype. Part of this disorder is the very systematization that would, by defensive means of the doctrine of synchronicity, give profound meaningful order to a trivial coincidence.

Here we return to Mr. Forster, who reminded us that the spirit's voice is humble and the soul's humorful.[22] Humility is awed and wowed by meaning; the soul takes the same events more as the puns and pranks of Pan.[23] Humility and humor are two ways of coming down to *humus*, to the human condition. Humility would have us bow down to the world and pay our due to its reality. Render unto Caesar. Humor brings us down with a pratfall. Heavy meaningful reality becomes suspect, seen through, the world laughable — paranoia dissolved, as synchronicity becomes spontaneity.

Thus the relation of the soul analyst to the spiritual event is not in terms of the doctrines or of the contents. Our concern is with the person, the Who, going up the mountain. Also we ask, Who is already up there, calling?

This question is not so different from one put in spiritual disciplines, and it is crucial. For it is not the trip and its stations and path, not the rate of ascent and the rung of the ladder, or the peak and its experience, nor even the return — it is the person in the person prompting the whole endeavor. And here we fall back into history, the historical ego, our Western-Northern willpower, the very willpower that brought the missionaries and trappers, the cattlemen and ranchers and planters, the Okies and Arkies, the orange-growers, wine-growers, and sectarians, and the gold-rushers arid railroaders to California to begin with. Can this be left at the door like a dusty pair of outworn shoes when one goes into the sweet-smelling pad of the meditation room? Can one close the door on the person who brought one to the threshold in the first place?

The movement from one side of the brain to the other, from tedious daily life in the supermarket to supra-consciousness, from trash to transcendence, the "altered state of consciousness" approach — to put it all it in a nutshell — denies this historical ego. It is an approach going back to Saul who became Paul, conversion into the opposite, knocked off one's ass in a flash.

So you see the archetypal question is neither *how* does the soul/spirit conflict happen, nor *why*, but *who* among the variety of figures of which we are each composed, which archetypal figure or person is in this happening? What God is at work in calling us up the mountain or in holding us to the vales? For archetypal psychology, there is a God in every perspective, in every position. All things are determined by psychic images, including our formulations of the spirit. All things present themselves to consciousness in the shapings of one or another divine perspective. Our vision is mimetic to one or another of the Gods.

Who is going up the mountain: is it the unconscious do-gooder Christian in us, he who has lost his historical Christianity and is an unconscious crusader, knight, missionary, savior? (I tend to see the latent "Christian Soldier" of our unconscious Christianity as more of a social danger than so-called latent psychosis, latent homosexuality, or masked, latent depression.)

Who is going up the mountain: is it the Climber, a man who would become the mountain himself, I on Mount Rushmore — humble now, but just you wait and see . . .

Is it the heroic ego? Is it Hercules, still at the same labors: cleaning up the stables of pollution, killing the swamp creatures, clubbing his animals, refusing the call of women, progressing through twelve stages (all in the end to go mad and marry Hebe, who is Hera, Mom, in her younger, sweeter, smilingly hebephrenic form)?

Or is the one ascending the spiritual impetus of the *puer aeternus*, the winged godlike imago in us each, the beautiful boy of the spirit — Icarus on the way to the sun, then plummeting with waxen wings; Phaethon driving the sun's chariot out of control, burning up the world; Bellerophon, ascending on his white winged horse, then falling onto the plains of wandering, limping ever after? These are the puer high climbers, the heaven stormers, whose eros reflects the torch and ladder of Eros and his searching arrow, a longing for higher and further and more and purer and better. Without this archetypal component affecting our lives, there would be no spiritual drive, no new sparks, no going beyond the given, no grandeur and sense of personal destiny.

So, psychologically, and perhaps spiritually as well, the issue is one of finding connections between the puer's drive upward and the soul's clouded, encumbering embrace. My notion of this connection would avoid two side tracks. The first would take the soul up too, "liberate it" from its vale — the transcendentalist's demand. The second would reduce the spirit to a complex and would thus deny the puer's legitimate ambition and art of flying — the psychoanalyst's demand. Let's remember here that he who cannot fly cannot imagine, as Gaston Bachelard said, and also Mohammed Ali. To imagine in a true high-flying, free-falling way, to walk on air and put on airs, to experience pneumatic reality and its concomitant inflation, one must imagine out of the valley, above the grainfields and the daily bread. Sometimes this is too much for professional analysts, and by not recognizing the archetypal claims of the puer, they thwart imagination.

Let us now turn to the puer-psyche connection without forcing the claims of either figure upon the other.

IV THE PUER-PSYCHE MARRIAGE. The accommodation between the high-driving spirit on the one hand and the nymph, the valley, or the soul on the other can be imagined as the puer-psyche marriage. It has been recounted in many ways — for instance, in C. G. Jung's *Mysterium Coniunctionis* as an alchemical conjunction of personified substances, or in Apuleius's tale of Eros and Psyche.[24] In the same manner as these models, let us imagine in a personified style. Then we can feel the different needs within us as volitions of distinct persons, where puer is the Who in our spirit flight, and anima (or psyche) is the Who in our soul.

Now the main thing about the anima[25] is just what has always been said about the psyche: it is unfathomable, ungraspable. For the anima, "the archetype of life," as Jung has called her, is that function of the psyche which is its actual life, the present mess it is in, its discontent, dishonesties, and thrilling illusions, together with the whitewashing hopes for a better outcome. The issues she presents are as endless as the soul is deep, and perhaps these very endless labyrinthine "problems" *are* its depth. The anima embroils and twists and screws us to the breaking point, performing the "function of relationship," another of Jung's definitions, a definition that becomes convincing only when we realize that relationship means perplexity.

This mess of psyche is what puer consciousness needs to marry so as to undertake "the battle of the sexes." The opponents of the spirit are first of all the hassles under its own skin: the morning moods, the symptoms, the prevarications in which it gets entangled, and the vanity. The puer needs to battle the irritability of this inner "woman," her passive laziness, her fancies for sweets and flatteries — all that which analysis calls "autoeroticism." This fighting is a fighting *with*, rather than a fighting off or fighting against, the anima, a close, tense, devoted embracing in many positions of intercourse. Where puer madness is met with psychic confusion and deviation, and where this madness is reflected in that distorted mirror. It is not straight and not clear. We do not even know what weapons to use or where the enemy is, since the enemy seems to be my own soul and heart and most dear passions. The puer is left only with his craziness, which, through the battle, he has resort to so often that he learns to care for it as precious, as the one thing that he truly is, his uniqueness and limitation. Reflection in the mirror of the soul lets one see the madness of one's spiritual drive, and the importance of this madness.

Precisely this is what the struggle with the anima, and what psychotherapy as the place of this struggle, is all about: to discover one's madness, one's unique spirit, and to see the relationship between one's spirit and one's madness, that there is madness in one's spirit, and there is spirit in one's madness.

The spirit needs witness to this madness. Or to put it another way, the puer takes its drive and goal literally unless there is reflection, which makes possible a metaphorical understanding of its drive and goal. By bearing witness as the receptive experiencer and imager of the spirit's actions, the soul can contain, nourish, and elaborate in fantasy the puer impulse, bring it sensuousness and depth, involve it in life's delusions, care for it for better or for worse. Then the individual in whom these two components are marrying begins to carry with him his own reflective mirror and echo. He becomes aware of what his spiritual actions mean in terms of psyche. The spirit turned toward psyche, rather than deserting it for high places and cosmic love, finds ever further possibilities of seeing through the opacities and obfuscations in the valley. Sunlight enters the vale. The Word participates in gossip and chatter.

The spirit asks that the psyche help it, not break it or yoke it or put it away as a peculiarity or insanity. And it asks the analysts who act in psyche's name not to turn the soul against the puer adventure but rather to prepare the desire of both for each other.

Unfortunately a good deal of the psychotherapeutic cosmos is dominated by the perspective of Hera's social adaptation (and her favorite minion, the strong ego of coping Hercules). Hera is out to get the renegade puer spirit and "do" something sensible with it. The puer spirit is not seen for its authentic archetypal value. Hera's priests and priestesses of psychological counseling attempt to make problems clearer, give therapeutic support, by trying to understand what upsets a person. Psychological counseling then literalizes problems and, by killing the possibility of seeing through to their madness, kills the spirit.

Psychologists who do not attend enough to spirit forget that it is one of the essential components of the conjunction and cannot be dismissed as a head trip, as intellect, as just theology or metaphysics or a puer flight. Spirit neglected comes into psychology through the back door, disguised as synchronicity, magic, oracles, science fiction, self-symbolism, mandalas, tarot, astrology, and other indiscriminations, equally prophetic, ahistorical, and humorless. For it requires spirit to discern among the spirits.

Diakrisis (discernment) itself is a gift of the spirit, and psychologists who refuse the puer chug along empowered by doctrinal mechanisms of dead masters, their own imaginative sails decayed or never even hoisted, circling in the doldrums of low-profile, low-horizon humility: the practice of psychotherapy.

Once the spirit has turned toward the soul, the soul can regard its own needs in a new way. Then these needs are no longer attempts to adapt to Hera's civilizational requirements, or to Venus's insistence that love is God, or to Apollo's medical cures, or even Psyche's work of soul-making. Not for the sake of learning love only, or for community, or for better marriages and better families, or for independence does the psyche present its symptoms and neurotic claims. Rather these demands are asking also for inspiration, for long-distance vision, for ascending eros, for vivification and intensification (*not* relaxation), for radicality, transcendence, and meaning — in short, the psyche has spiritual needs, which the puer part of us can fulfill. Soul asks that its preoccupations be not dismissed as trivia but seen through in terms of higher and deeper perspectives, the verticalities of the spirit. When we realize that our psychic malaise points to a spiritual hunger beyond what psychology offers and that our spiritual dryness points to a need for psychic waters beyond what spiritual discipline offers, then we are beginning to move both therapy and discipline.

The puer-psyche marriage results first of all in increased interiority. It constructs a walled space, the thalamus or bridal chamber, neither peak nor vale, but rather a place where both can be looked at through glass windows or be closed off with doors. This increased interiority means that each new puer inspiration, each hot idea at whatever time of life in whomever, be given psychization. It will first be drawn through the labyrinthine ways of the soul, which wind it and slow it and nourish it from many sides (the "many" nurses and "many" maenads), developing the spirit from a oneway mania for "ups" to *polytropos*, the many-sidedness of the Hermetic old hero, Odysseus.[26] The soul performs the service of indirection to the puer arrow, bringing to the sulphuric compulsions of the spirit the lasting salt of soul.

Likewise, for soul: the bridal chamber intensifies the brooding, gives it heat and pressure, building soul from amorphous clouds into driving needs. And these, by benefit of puer, become formulated into language. There is a sense of process, direction, continuity within one's interior life of dreams and wishes. Suffering begins to make sense. Instead of the repetitious and usual youth-nymph pairings of virginal innocence coupled with seed spilled everywhere foolishly, psychic conception takes place and the opus of one's life begins to form.

The puer-psyche marriage finally implies taking our complexes both out of the world and out of the realm of spiritual systems. It means that the search and questing go through a psychological search and questing, an exploration of soul by spirit for psychic fecundation. The messianic, liberating, transcending movement connects first with soul and is concerned first with its movement: not "what does this mean?" — the question asked of spirit by spirit — but "what does this move in my soul?" — the interiorization of the question. This alone puts psychic body into the puer message and trip, adding to it psychic values, so that the puer message can touch soul and redden it into life. For it is especially in this realm of soul — so lost, emptied, and ignorant — that the gifts of the puer spirit are first needed. It is soul, psyche, and psychology that need the spirit's attention. Come down from the mountain, monks, and like beautiful John Keats, come into the vale of soul-making.

V FOUR POINTS OF DIFFERENCE. At this point I am leaving the puer's enthusiastic perspective to return again to soul. I want to suggest now three fundamental qualities of soul-making in distinction to spirit disciplines. These three are: 1) *Pathologizing*[27]— an interest in the psychopathologies of our lives — that is, an attentive concern to the logos of the pathos of the psyche. By keeping an ear tuned to the soul's pathologizings, we maintain the close link of soul with mortality, limitation, and death. 2) *Anima* — a loyalty to the clouded moods of the water sources, to the seductive twists and turns of the interior feminine figures who personify the labyrinthine path of psychic life, those nymphs, dark witches, lost Cinderellas and Persephones of destruction, and the elusive, illusional fantasies that anima creates, the images of soul in the soul. 3) *Polytheism* — single-minded commitment to discord and cacophony, to variety and not getting it all together, to falling apart, the multiplicity of the ten thousand things, to the peripheries and their tangents (rather than centers), to the episodic, occasional, wandering movement of the soul (like this lecture) and its compulsion to repeat in the valleys of its errors, and the necessity of errancy and error for discovering the many ways of many Gods.

I am aware that these lectures have been organized in order to relate East and West, religious disciplines and psychotherapy, and so I must make a contribution to an issue that I believe is not the main one (the East-West pair). For I believe the true passion is between North and South, between the upper and lower regions, whether they be the repressive Northern Protestantism of Europe and America on the one hand, and on the other, Southland, the oppressed Mediterranean, the Latin darkness below the borders, across the rivers, under the Alps; whether this division be the manic industrial North and the depressive ritualistic South, or between San Francisco and Los Angeles.

But Professor Needleman says the line is blurred between the therapist and the spiritual guide, and he would draw that line spiritually — that is, vertically — creating East and West across the mountain-tops, perhaps like the Continental Divide, whereas I would draw the line horizontally, as rivers flow, downward. The three qualifications I have just made — pathologizing, anima, polytheism — are my way of drawing the line more heavily and bluntly, thick with shadow.

Anyone who is engaged with these three factors, regarding them as important, as religious even, seems to me to be engaged in therapy and psychology. Anyone who tends to dismiss pathologizing for growth, or anima confusions for ego strength or spiritual illumination, or who neglects the differentiation of multiplicity and variety for the sake of unity is engaged in spiritual discipline.

The lines between the two labors I would draw in this way. But I would also suggest that they are drawn not by what a person preaches but according to the weight of importance he lays upon trivia, the little things in daily practice. There are, for instance, many who are called "psychotherapists" and pretend its practice, but who, according to these criteria, are actually daily engaged in spirit. In the emphasis they give and in the values they select, their main concern is with ascension (growing *up*), strengthening, unity, and wholeness. Whereas I believe, though I am less familiar with the spiritual side of things (coming from Switzerland, where our main words are complex, schizophrenia, introvert-extrovert, Rorschach and Bleuler, and the spectrum of drugs from Ciba-Geigy, Sandoz, and Hoffmann-La Roche; that is, our fantasy is more psychiatric, more psychopathological than yours, which is more spiritually determined by your history and geography, this Golden State, its founding missions, its holy spiritual names — Eureka, Sacramento, Berkeley (the Bishop), Los Angeles, San Diego, Santa Cruz, Santa Monica, Carmel, Santa Barbara) I believe that the spiritual masters may, despite their doctrine, very often be engaged in psychotherapy when they follow the female inner figure as guide, the *paredros* or angel, when they allow vision and fantasy to flourish, when they let the multiple voices in the symptoms speak and turn the pathologizings into inner teachers, when they move from all generalities and abstractions to concrete immediacy and the multivalence of events.

In other words, the lines between therapy and discipline, between soul and spirit, do not depend on the kind of patient or the kind of teacher, or whether the patient or teacher was born in the Cascades

or the Himalayas, but rather depend upon which archetypal dominant is working through one's viewpoint. The issue always returns to
"Who" in an individual's subjectivity is asking the questions and giving
the answers.

Pathologizing, anima, and polytheism are, moreover, intimately
connected with one another. It would take us too far in this talk to
attempt to show the internal logic of this connection, and I am not
up to doing it swiftly and succinctly. Besides, this interconnection has
been a main theme of many of my writings, because one soon dis-
covers in work with oneself and others that each of these criteria of
soul-making tends to imply the other. The varied anima figures, elfin
inspirations, and moods that move a person, men and women alike
(for it is nonsense to hold that women can have only animuses, no
souls, as if an archetype or a goddess could be limited to the personal
psychology of sexual gender), give a peculiar double feeling. There is
a sense of me-ness, personal importance, soul sense, that is not an ego
inflation, and at the same time there is an awareness of one's subjectivity being fluid, airy, fiery, earthy, made of many components, shifting,
ungraspable, now close and intimate and helpful as Athene giving wise
counsel, then wily and disappearing, naively pulling one into hopeless
holes like Persephone, and at the next moment fantasizing Aphro-
ditic whisperings in the inner ear, sea foam, pink vulvar bivalves, and
then proud and tall Artemis, keeping everything at bay, oneself at a
distance, at one only with nature, a virgin soul among brothers and
sisters, only.

Anima makes us feel many parts.

Anima, as C. G. Jung said, is an equivalent of and a personification of the polytheistic aspect of the psyche.[28] "Polytheism" is a
theological or anthropological concept for the experience of a many-
souled world.

This same experience of multiplicity can reach us as well through
symptoms. They too make us aware that the soul has other voices and
intentions than the one of the ego. Pathologizing bears witness to both
the soul's inherent composite nature and to the many Gods reflected
in this composition. Here I take my cue from two passing remarks of
Jung's: "The divine thing in us functions as neuroses of the stomach,

or the colon, or the bladder, simply disturbances of the underworld. Our Gods have gone to sleep, and they only stir in the bowels of the earth."[29] And again: "The gods have become diseases; Zeus no longer rules Olympus but rather the solar plexus, and produces curious specimens for the doctor's consulting room . . ."[30]

Sometimes going up the mountain one seeks escape from this underworld, and so the Gods appear from below bringing all sorts of physiological disorders. They will be heard, if only through intestinal rumblings and their fire burning in the bladder.

Similar to going up the mountain, but in the disguise of psychology, are the behavior therapies and release-relax therapies. Cure the symptom and lose the God. Had Jacob not grappled with the Daemon he would indeed have not been hurt, and he would not have been Jacob either. Lose the symptom and return the world back to the ego.

Here my point is that soul-making does not deny Gods and the search for them. But it looks closer to hand, finding them more in the manner of the Greeks and Egyptians, for whom the Gods take part in all things. All existence is filled with them, and human beings are always involved with them. This involvement is what myths are all about — the traditional stories of human and divine interactions. There is no place one can be, no act one can do, no thought one can think without it being mimetic to a God. Thus we study mythology to understand personality structure, psychodynamics, pathologizing. The Gods are within, as Heinrich Zimmer used to say, and they are within our acts, thoughts, and feelings. We do not have to trek across the starry spaces, the brain of heaven, or blast them loose from concealment with mind-blowing chemicals. They are there in the very ways you feel and think and experience your moods and symptoms. Here is Apollo, right here, making us distant and wanting to form artful, clear, and distinct ideas; here is old Saturn, imprisoned in paranoid systems of judgment, defensive maneuvers, melancholic conclusions; here is Mars, having to turn red in the face and kill in order to make a point; and here too is the wood nymph Daphne-Diana, retreating into foliage, the camouflage of innocence, suicide through naturalness.

Finally, I would point to one more, a fourth, difference between peaks and vales, the difference that has to do with death.

If spirit would transcend death in any of several ways — unification so that one is not subject to dissolution; union with Self, where self is God; building the immortal body, or the jade-body; the moves toward timelessness and spacelessness and imagelessness and mindlessness; dying to the world as place of attachments — soul-making would instead hew and bevel the ship of death, the vessel of death, a container for holding the dying that goes on in the soul. It imagines that psychic life refers most fundamentally to the life of the *po*-soul, that which slips into the ground — not just at the moment of physical death but is always slipping into the ground, always descending, always going deeper into concrete realities and animating them.

So I cannot conclude with ultimates, positions, final words, wise statements from masters. There is no end to a wandering discourse, no summation, summit, for to make an end is to come to a stop. I'd rather leave unconcluded and cloudy, no abstracted spiritual message — not even a particular image. You have your own. The soul generates them ceaselessly.

Notes

1. [Revised from a lecture delivered at the University of California Medical Center, San Francisco, in 1975 and first published in J. Needleman and D. Lewis, eds., *On the Way to Self-Knowledge* (New York: Knopf, 1976). Reprinted in J. Hillman, ed., *Puer Papers* (Dallas: Spring Publications, 1979) and in Benjamin Sells, ed., *Working with Images* (Woodstock, CT: Spring Publications, 2000).] — Ed.

2. C. J. Hefele, *Conciliengeschichte* (Freiburg: Herder, 1860), IV: pp. 320, 404 (Canon 11).

3. D. L. Miller, "Achelous and the Butterfly," *Spring* 1973, p. 14.

4. Cf. M. T. Kelsey, *God, Dreams, and Revelation* (Minneapolis: Augsburg Publishing House, 1974), pp. 80–84; A. N. Wilder, "Myth and Dream in Christian Scripture," in J. Campbell, ed., *Myths, Dreams and Religion* (New York: Dutton, 1970). [Reprinted by Spring Publications in 1988], pp. 68–75; H. Schär, "Bemerkungen zu Träumen in der Bibel," in *Traum und Symbol* (Zurich: Rascher, 1963), pp. 171–79.

5. C. G. Hefele, *A History of the Councils of the Church*, trans. W. R. Clark (Edinburgh: Clark, 1896): V, pp. 260–400, esp. pp. 377–85.

6. Hefele, op. cit., p. 402 (Canon 3).

7. C. G. Jung, *Collected Works*, vol. 8: *Structure & Dynamics of the Psyche*, par. 92.

8. C. G. Jung, *Collected Works*, vol. 6: *Psychological Types*, par. 66.

9. C. G. Jung, *Collected Works*, vol. 8: *Structure & Dynamics of the Psyche*, par. 618, 623; vol. 11: *Psychology and Religion*, par. 769.

10. C. G. Jung, *Collected Works*, vol. 8, par. 746.

11. C. G. Jung, *Collected Works*, vol. 11, par. 889.

12. C. G. Jung, *Collected Works*, vol. 6, par. 743.

13. W. H. Roscher, *Ausführliches Lexikon der griechischen und römischen Mythologie* (Leipzig/Stuttgart: Teubner; Hildesheim, 1965) III, 1, "Pan," pp. 1392ff.

14. V. MacDermott, *The Cult of the Seer in the Ancient Middle East* (Berkeley/Los Angeles: University of California Press, 1971). See H. Frankfort, *Ancient Egyptian Religion* (New York: Harper Torchbook, 1961), chapter 1, for an excellent summary of Egyptian polytheistic psychology.

15. Ibid., p. 46.

16. E. M. Forster, *Aspects of the Novel* (Harmondsworth: Pelican, 1971, originally published 1927), p. 115.

17. Ibid.

18. Ibid., p. 129.

19. Ibid., p. 116.

20. [See Chapter 8 for more discussion of the *bricoleur*.] — Ed.

21. Ibid., p. 116.

22. On the relation of humor and psyche, see Miller, "Achelous and the Butterfly," (op. cit.).

23. On synchronicity and Pan, see my "An Essay on Pan" in *Pan and the Nightmare* (with W.H. Roscher) (New York/Zurich: Spring Publications, 1972), pp. lvi–lix.

24. There are many Jungian interpretative attempts on this tale. Cf. M.-L. von Franz, *A Psychological Interpretation of the Golden Ass of Apuleius* (New York/Zurich, 1970); E. Neumann, *Amor and Psyche* (New York: Pantheon, 1956); and my *The Myth of Analysis* (Evanston: Northwestern University Press, 1972), pp. 55ff.

25. For a full exploration of anima, relevant literature, and citations from Jung, see my two papers "Anima" in *Spring* 1973, pp. 97–132, and *Spring* 1974, pp. 113–46. Later published as *Anima: An Anatomy of a Personified Notion* (Dallas: Spring Publications, 1985 [Reprinted in 1996]).

26. [See Chapter 8, "Puer Wounds and Odysseus' Scar."] — Ed.

27. Pathologizing points to the psyche's autonomous ability to create illness, morbidity, disorder, abnormality, and suffering in any aspect of its behavior and to experience and imagine life through this deformed and afflicted perspective; see "Pathologizing," Part 2 of my *Re-Visioning Psychology* (New York: Harper & Row, 1975).

28. C.G. Jung, *Collected Works*, vol. 9.2: *Aion*, par. 427, and my discussion of this theme in "Psychology: Monotheistic or Polytheistic?" *Spring* 1971, pp. 193–208. [Reprinted in B. Sells, ed., *Working with Images* (Woodstock, CT: Spring Publications, 2000)] — Ed.

29. C.G. Jung, "Psychological Commentary on Kundalini Yoga" (from the Notes of Mary Foote, 1932), *Spring* 1975, p. 22.

30. C.G. Jung, *Collected Works*, vol. 13, par. 54.

3

Notes on Opportunism [1]

"Chance" and "system" are other words for puer and senex. Senex consciousness lives from the plotted curve of expectations. Establishment requires predictabilities: we must plan for eventualities, provide for the future, run no risks. Within a senex cosmos chance will be either reduced to meaninglessness by calling it "random events" or fit into order as "statistical probabilities." Otherwise, chance becomes chancey and those who follow it chancers; opportunity becomes opportunism and those who follow it opportunists — major charges against the puer. Puer existence, however, is based on opportunities and therefore an archetypal aspect of existence is reflected through this style. What we may learn about opportunism may tell us as well something about the puer aspect of existence itself.

Let us begin with the word "opportunity." The word derives, according to Onians, most probably from *porta, portus (angiportus)* "entrance," "passage through." Portunus was associated with doors. "*Opportunus* would thus describe what offers an opening, or what is in front of an opening and ready to go through." [2] Onians associates this meaning of opportunity with the Roman *porta fenestella*, a special opening through which Fortune passed, and the word window (*fenestra*) "was used symbolically in the sense of 'opening,' 'opportunity' . . ." [3] Cognate with *porta* and *portus* (meaning "passage," "way," "means") is the Greek *poros*, [4] who, according to Plato's *Symposium* (203b–d), is the father of Eros. Curiously, *poroi* are passages and connections in the body for its flowings (veins, ducts, etc.). [5] "Pores" are openings in our skins.

A similar set of meanings appears in English in connection with the word "nick," [6] another of those words, like chancer and opportunist, that can be applied to the shadowy traits of puer consciousness. "To nick" means "To win at dice, to hit the mark just in the nick of time, or at the critical moment."[7] A nick in time is a hole in it, that slot in the system of law and order through which an opportunity may be seized. The "nick" is slang for prison; to be "nicked" is to be cheated; and a "nickel" is false-copper. "Old Nick," of course, is the Devil, and St. Nicklaus (Santa Claus) who can never be caught, always disguised, slipping down chimneys in the night, was originally a goblin, a kind of *Augenblicksgott* (epiphanic daimon). The close association, even identification, between Old Nick and the Christchild, bringer of miraculous gifts, gives a wholly hermetic, mercurial aspect to the Christmas moment of the Christian year.[8]

The main Greek term for opportunity is *kairos*, which referred in Homeric Greek to a "penetrable opening." Let us listen to this sentence from Onians in terms of the puer-senex opposition: "To get past fortifications, armor, bones, the early Greek archer practised by aiming at an opening or a series of openings . . . *kairos*, as appears from Pindar, Aeschylus, etc., described that at which he aimed."[9]

The same idea of "opening" can be evolved not only from *kairós*, but also from *kaīros*, a term from the art of weaving. Weaving, time, and fate are often connected ideas. An opening in the web of fate can mean an opening in time, an eternal moment when the pattern is drawn tighter or broken through. The weaver shot the spool or shuttle through the opening in the warp-threads at a critical time, the right moment (*kairos*), for "the opening in the warp lasts only a limited time, and the 'shot' must be made while it is open."[10]

The image of Kairos presents another of those astoundingly vivid personifications exemplifying an experience as a puer figure, like Pothos who presents the nostalgias of longing, and Eros who images the burning and moody complexities of love.[11] These puer figures bespeak archetypal experiences. They therefore tell of a consciousness that affects young and old, male and female, and are not limited only to young and special men.

The earliest large-scale visual image of Kairos that has been recorded was fashioned by Lysippos (of Sikyon), the principal sculptor in the Peloponnesos during the fourth century BC. Reconstructions of this statue show Kairos as a wingfooted runner, a naked young man on tiptoes with head shorn except for forelocks. He carries a razor (in his right hand) and a balance-scale, and often stands upon a wheel or sphere.[12] Later he added other attributes, becoming more emblematic, e.g., winged time (wings on his back), hurrying time (carrying a whip).[13] Another trait could not easily be shown: deafness.

The poetic personification of Kairos appears in a fifth-century hymn where he is called the youngest son of Zeus, and he had his cult in association with Zeus of Olympia.[14] (A somewhat comparable figure is Tages of the Etruscans who was a little boy spirit, yet had grey hair. He, too, was an *Augenblicks-Gott*, an epiphanic appearance at a certain moment, who had something to do with insight into time through magic and foretelling).[15]

|| By considering opportunity as a nick in time (senex) through which Kairos (puer) may pass into the established order, we may better understand puer openness and suggestibility. This is a consciousness that must leave its door ajar; nothing closed down; *"toujours ouverte, toujours disponible,"* as maxim for the young man in André Gide's *The Counterfeiters*. We may also better understand the necessity of puer wounds and the supposed weak ego with its omissions and holes. These too are doors, ways for the spirit to come in. The gaps in learning, the absences in remembering, the spottiness in systematic work especially in regard to time (appointments, schedules, deadlines) may be necessary for keeping open and available and superior to the senex style of order. Puer integrity would mean never covering these holes, and so personality integration, when imagined by puer consciousness, always retains gaps and absences, unshielded.

Kairos is vulnerable to the senex who says: "Prove it. How do you know?" Or, more simply, "Say that again." This puer consciousness can never do. It cannot repeat because it is deaf and has never heard what slipped out of its own mouth. And it has no hair on the back of its head. Nothing of the brainstorm can be pulled back after it has skated by. Puer truth may be public but it is not repeatable.

As puer is vulnerable to senex charges, so in turn it threatens senex systems by espying their holes. Often a penetrating shaft simply mobilizes massive defenses and the puer is surprised at what he set off by just a "chance remark." When puer spear is countered with senex shield, a paranoid reaction is the consequent of an opportune insight.

The holes in puer consciousness allow for a two-way traffic. A new idea is never only a wind-fall, an apple to be eaten. It takes hold of us as much as we take hold of it. The hunch that breaks in pulls one into an identification with it. We feel gifted, inspired, upset, because the message is also a messenger that makes demands, calling us to quit a present position and fly out. The puer person is susceptible to the archetypal call of the message, becoming the very angel that has come to him.

What comes through the hole has its source beyond the wall and cannot easily be detached from the gap (chaos) of its entry. Opportunities are not plain, clean gifts; they trail dark and chaotic attachments to their unknown backgrounds, luring us further. One insight leads to another; one invention suggests another variation — more and more seems to press through the hole, and more and more we find ourselves drawn out into a chaos of possibilities.

This chaos that an opportunity initiates also constellates a Zeusian fantasy of cosmic generativity. We feel called to create new schemes, new forms, new visions. At first the puer comes only as a little hole, a brush of wings, as a naked runner on tiptoes; quick now, here, now. And, before we have taken thought, we have been seduced into enterprises beyond our resources. The Zeusian vision of mastery from Olympus takes Ganymede[16] right straight up on eagle's wings way beyond his light-weight body, and a fantasy of lucky power can be the effect of a visitation by Hermes, son of Zeus, messenger of Zeus.

III Although it has been said that kairos "has nothing in the least to do with luck and the fall of the dice, but has much more to do with the propitious moment that must be seized through one's own power and insight,"[17] we do find later associations between kairos and Hermes, Tyche (Fortune) and Nemesis,[18] just as there are similarities between opportunity and luck. "It was good luck to meet him (Hermes), and a piece of good luck was called a gift from Hermes."[19] The older idea of kairos as something to be seized, as a target to hit with one's arrow, emphasizes the heroic puer. Kairos as luck, on the other hand and to make the distinction sharp, stresses the role of the Gods, the hand of Tyche or Fortune in the fall of the dice. Emphasis upon *what one does* with an opportunity (by means of power and insight) helps to bring it into the existing order; emphasis upon the *fall of chance* brings the element of uncontrollable disorder (and thus bad luck, too) to the foreground. Walter F. Otto notes these two divergent aspects of opportunity in connection with Hermes:

> From him comes (both styles of) gain, cleverly calculated, or wholly unexpected, but mostly the latter. That is his true characterization. If a man finds valuables on the road, if a man has a sudden stroke of luck, he thanks Hermes. The regular word for any windfall is *hermaion* . . . It is Hermes in whom the merchant trusts; from him comes the art of sly calculation, but also the lucky chance without which his shrewdness is futile. [20]

When Kerényi differentiates Hermes-Mercurius from the Trickster figure of the American Indians [21] and when Otto differentiates Hermes-Mercurius from Pushan (of the Vedic Hindus), [22] their point is relevant for the order-disorder problems raised by Hermes. For all the similarities of Trickster, Loki, and Pushan with Hermes, the God of classical antiquity did not govern a special section of the world, nor did he represent a separate principle of disorder, or of evil. [23] Hermes' realm and Hermes' order are not distinct from and opposed to our world.

Hermes is the world itself. "Hermes" refers to a way of living in the world, a *Daseinsform* or specific kind of consciousness that creates a "cosmos" (lawful order, intelligible arrangement, beautification) in likeness to itself. [24] Each style of consciousness, such as Hermes, regards the world in a self-consistent way, thereby creating world and mankind according to its image. There are not a multiplicity of worlds and mankinds, yet there are many Gods. Thus for the Gods to create after their likenesses, they must be able to use the same world in many manners, creating styles of being and perception so that our one and only world may participate in a shifting realm of many perspectives, at one moment mimetic to Zeus, and the next to Aphrodite or Ares. Or, they all may be present at the same moment, and we see but one. As the same world can be a likeness of different Gods, consciousness can be qualified by many forms. This very variety of divine forms is the first message of Hermes-Mercurius, who, Jung said, "consists of all conceivable opposites."[25] Hermetic awareness guides souls by bringing consciousness to experience the ego-strictures of opposites as messages of divine multiplicity. Then all things provide divine opportunities for the Gods.

IV The mercurial opportunist, having no fixed position, no sense of being at the center, keeps his eye on the door, the thresholds where transiencies pass over from statement to implication, from fact to supposition, from report to fantasy. Mercurius is messenger of the Gods, so he must be able to hear their messages in whatever is said. This is the hermeneutic ear that listens-through, a consciousness of the borders, as Hermes was worshipped at borders.[26] And borders spring up anywhere as soon as we enter that duplicity of mind that hears two modes at once.

For the opportunistic eye, every wall and every weave presents its opening. Everything is porous. As the surrealists say: "There exists another world. But it is assuredly in this one."[27] The bricks and mortar are firmly real, and surreal at the same moment. These sudden openings that shift perspective with a shaft of insight are hermetic opportunities. The cosmos of one God, via Hermes, suddenly swings open into that of another. We see one viewpoint from that of another. This is Hermes operating in our vision — the God of betweens, keeping us to the world and guiding us out of it at the same instant. "A swing-door is in us leading to the memoryless spaces of a metahuman condition."[28]

Opportunities are also *voiced*. They are seized not only by heroic action or the gambler's hand, but also by hermeneutic formulation. Hermes' gift to Pandora was "voice," and we may hear opportunities as hallucinatory hunches, as dreams speaking direct meanings. A puer waits for these voices, or when he is one, carried by it, he tells you how and what and where, himself an electronic bit of information, a fiery *logos spermatikos*, fervent fugleman of a goldrush.

Because the usual senex ego that we each embody cannot easily grasp these opportunities, they seem slippery and shadowy. We do not trust our hunches and are suspicious of what comes through luck. Puer messages are not familiar; they are so new and young. An opportunity after all is mere *status nascendi*. Sometimes it originates as a schizoid neologism, a fused poetic nugget; or it sounds no better than a pop-slogan or commercial. Yet this almost surrealist absurdity contains a revelation for which puer consciousness will chase to the ends of the earth. The puer word is not composed into solid verbal forms by the elephant of *visuddha*,[29] not established into a commanding voice of authority based on knowledge. Puer consciousness has no footnotes and you can't get a handle on its idea. Its word breezes through the window, freshening but ungraspable. Then to make it concrete, puer consciousness becomes schizoid or surrealist, as André Breton makes a huge literal Manifesto of a little phrase that seems to "tap at the window pane"[30] without warning or premeditation. The Word becomes Flesh in a flash without ever passing through the soul. In the window, out the door: opportunity literalized into a venture.

Puer consciousness neither possesses what it knows nor knows what it intuits. Knowledge, anyway, belongs to the senex, and puer knowing is at the threshold, dawning, where pure meaning is fullness before knowing. It shrugs off knowing its own ideas so that they may remain messages: "I had a thought," "This idea came to me," "Let me tell you this." Mind unsullied by the bowels of digestion.

Opportune ideas come like Hermes, stealthily, or even as actual thefts from others, cryptomnesias, blocked recollections. Kairos is deaf — perhaps in order to hear only his own autochthonous processes. The puer idea flowers in the air of the moment without roots in senex authority. Its hallmark is newness, so that new truths come with puer accoutrements. It is announced as a "discovery" and wholly self-authored (authorized by the Self). Hence those vicious disputes in science about priority in connection with new ideas and inventions, leading into the paranoid senex machines of patent lawyers and copyright offices. When truth is newness and newness truth, then priority is a sign of truth. Opportunism and duplicity are inherent in originality.

Even duplicity does not adequately characterize this conscious-ness, since doubleness implies a fixed position — one foot in and one foot out, fence-sitting, talking out of both sides of your mouth. This is not really a puer place because it literalizes the border into a Janus-Sat-urn stance of the wise-guy who can argue either side. A more precise conception of hermetic opportunism is *eccentricity*, being at the edge, on the windowsill. Then our senses must be acute in order to survive; then we need even a sixth sense. We *have to* listen through, else we lose our luck, and fall. So we find in puer dominated lives an affecta-tion of the crazy, that odd-ball quality in clothes and gait, that signal disconcern for normalcy — a funny hat, a torn sleeve, a car unlike all others, talismans to keep the wall and weave of regular life off center, surrealistically open for chance.

The puer perceives the *discontinuity* of spirit.[31] It comes and goes as do his inspirations and his moods. We are best in touch with it by being discontinuous ourselves, living by chance and loving synchron-icities that prove a secret order is guiding our destiny, beyond senex categories such as time, space, and causality. So puer consciousness worships Kairos at the altar of chance: *I Ching*, a dream, even someone else's dream, spot words on a page will send one off to California. The Dadaist movement elevated chance to a law. Hans Arp was led "to conclude that the laws of chance are 'the highest and deepest of laws, the law that rises from the fundament'"[32]— how much like the new Puer Religion (formulated in senex *Weisheiten*) of Synchronicity. These two Zurich schools, Dadaism and Synchronicity, use similar meth-ods: "When Surrealism interrogates chance, it is to obtain oracular replies."[33] Analysts as usual blame a mother complex for this magical indecisive provisionality. The force at work, however, is not Mama, but Dada.

V In puer consciousness the tendency to lie, to do the devious, to cut out and around the system, would seem a moral problem. Analysts consider the opportunism to belong to the shadow and to result from a weak ego that cannot take a stand and face consequences (as a hero should). But if opportunism has archetypal substrate, having *archetypal necessity* within the puer structure, then we must re-assess the

psychological function of puer deviousness and opportunistic duplicity independently of our preconceptions of right and wrong.

Our usual notion of ego is Emersonian, Faustian, and Apollonic.
The German old man of Weimar, whom Faust spent so many years
creating, died supposedly calling for "more light." If we elevate this
archetypal aspect of our natures by knighting it Sir Ego, we promote
solar consciousness to rulership. But what then of Brother Mephis-
topheles who lives in the twilight?

The thief, the lie, the deception of magic, the surreptitious borderline areas fall into shadow and can but return (opportunistically) to
attention through tricks and theft.

In the sunlight world, the artful dodger is an opportunist. Psychology calls him shadow. But Hermes is not shadow cast off by light, not
Lucifer. He is dark to begin with. He belongs to the night. [34] From the
hermetic perspective and the serpentine eye, it is rather the hero, sun-
fixed and immovably centered who is the benighted one. His is the
consciousness that sees in terms of black and white, and points to evil
to justify the enormous destruction which we always find in his myths.
From the viewpoint of a genuine shadow psychology, a hermetic psychology, the sun-ego is *a sol niger*, in darkness because of its light, like
the untrustworthy blackbirds which appear so often with the sun. [35]

Where there is hero, there is shadow. Depth psychology has too
long insisted that the hero integrate the shadow, whereas maybe the
heroic is actually a product of the shadow. When Hercules was born,
a weasel attendant at his birth was the first to recognize and proclaim
Hercules to the world. [36] The sneaky moment calls up the heroic from
the beginning; something tricky is going on whenever a heroic impulse comes into being. Does the weasel want the hero? And if so, are
our heroisms and egoisms emboldened weaselings? At this point the
terms "ego" and "shadow" begin to dissolve into each other. We have
begun to be guided by Hermes towards the serpentine roots of consciousness, the imagistic impulses that cannot be contained by concepts such as ego and shadow.

When we stand in the image and view hermetically, the problem
of black and white becomes irrelevant: one could as well be the other,
and Hermes' son Autolykos [37] (who is also Odysseus' ancestor) changes

them back and forth, opportunistically in accordance with the situation. Besides, there are so many colors in the spectrum of messages which Hermes carries that black and white need no longer be paired.

Yet, for all the independence of the hermetic viewpoint, Hermes the thief is indeed Apollo's smaller brother.[38] He comes into the world in relation with Apollo, as his shadow, and carries his deception, his cleverness, his weakness. This myth reminds us that the mercurial aspect of the puer is in some shadow league with the Apollonian. When we are Apollonic in ideals, Hermes in his darkest (i.e., most literal) aspect is not far. Together they make a fine pair: the golden gleam of noble ends achieved by sly means. The brothers go together as well in the mercurial ego personality who has a perfectionist computerized shadow.

Rather than following the psychologist's maxim of integrating the shadow, an integration which tends to mean by the hero into the light, we might take the Hermes-Apollo filiation as a model, not of substance, but for its structure. Hermes appears in a "shadow" relation with various Gods, especially these: Hades, Zeus, Athene, Aphrodite, Dionysus. It is within these tandems that shadow can be integrated, not by us, but into them. This is a hermetic mode of shadow perception: noticing how Hermes moves *together with* various structures of consciousness, and this hermetic awareness of archetypal shadow is itself a message of each God through Hermes.

But there is something about Apollo that cannot bear his little brother. Zeus, Dionysus, Aphrodite, even Athene can work well with his wiles. So, what makes it so difficult for Apollonic consciousness to keep this hermetic awareness? Or should we turn the matter on its head? That is, perhaps Apollo is Hermes' shadow, simply cast-off older light, a rationalized and distant awareness that may illumine but no longer has a cutting edge or door into crazyland.

Although the Apollonic temperament loses its Hermes, it is the task of hermetic consciousness to learn to travel with Apollo and with all that light. Hermes can carry messages from any God, Apollo too. Puer consciousness in the Hermetic pattern may follow Auden who says of the Apollo/Hermes strife: "if thou must choose Between the chances, choose the odd."[39] But we must go beyond Auden and the notion of brother strife and opposites, by finding opportunities also for

the even, the clear, and the calm, rather than merely literalizing opportunity into chance and oddity. Hermes literalized is not Hermes, but a
Hermes caught by his Apollonic side, a puer secretly senexed.

VI Now we can return to opportunism from another vantage point.
It manifests not merely the chancy provisionality of puer existence. Opportunism is a way of living the world, creating a Mercurial
cosmos.

We might borrow from the language of existentialism for another
entry into this puer mercurial cosmos. A *kairos* appears as a situation,
where *situs* refers to the invisible structure or lay of things. The puer
spirit is the voice of the moment and the puer spirit seizes the situation
in an instant. The ethics are situationalist.

A situationalist ethic permits one to move in accordance with a
constellation as it is (not as it should be), so that for puer consciousness no situation ever becomes "wrong" or "impossible." There is always
a way, or way out. Every human complexity and every psychological
complex, perceived from the puer perspective, is a situation serving its
own purposes. There is intentionality in all psychic life, when perceived
in terms of the puer. Every situation is always headed somewhere.

Here, mythology shows Hermes knowing the ruse and deception
that opens the way until the constellation shifts. Hermes here is like
Eros, whose father was Poros, "resourcefulness," "way-finder;" love,
too, finds a way, and Hermes had a special function in finding the
way at night for lovers. His ethic was situational, but it favored eros.
Here Hermes is like his descendent Odysseus who too finds his way
through tight spots. Opportunities excite puer consciousness because
they evoke these archetypal spirits of resourcefulness.

Since situations require this opportunistic knowing about where
the openings are and when the time needs voice, *the master of a situation is
the master of the complex.* In an encounter (let us imagine a Mafia negotia-
tion, a master's chess class), the lacuna, the weak place of the other's
psyche gives the opportunity. Perception of opportunities requires a
sensitivity given through one's own wounds. Here, puer weakness provides the kind of hermetic, secret perception critical for adaptation to
situations. We are mimetic to this model when we adapt not as a hero

who coerces situations towards a result but as a thief who pockets what can be made from it. The weak place serves to open us to what is in the air. We feel through our pores which way the wind blows. We turn with the wind; trimmers.

An opportunity requires a cold-snake sense that we call intuition and which reveals the daimon of a situation. The daimon of a place in antiquity supposedly revealed what the place was good for, its special quality and dangers. The daimon was thought to be a serpent, a *familiaris* of the place. To know a situation one needs to sense what lurks in it.

These deeper aspects of awareness give to opportunism a different value. By connecting opportunity with the snake of Hermes, the local snake of the hero cult, and the snake *familiaris* who lives in our neuro-vegetative reactions of fear and greed (below the mind and the will), we see that puer opportunism is also an *instinctual adaptation to psychic realities.* The shiftiness and suddenness is a correspondence between inner genius (complex) and outer daimon (situation), snake speaking with snake through the holes in normalcy. This is the opportunism which the genius of Spanish literature has captured in the genre of the picaresque.

VII Again we are approaching shadow psychology. What is "shad-ow" when we stand in it rather than against it? How do the twilight regions of the serpent look when the threshold is imagined as a doorway and not as a censor — where consciousness itself slithers, slips its skin, and speaks with a forked tongue?

First of all, loss dreams would look different from this shadow psy-chology. The motifs of cheating, robbing, and stealing would indicate a gain for the underworld at the expense of Old Ego up top. It is no longer able to hold its own. It's losing its bag. Its senex accumula-tions are being taken by the little people. Robbery redistributes the wealth, transferring values to the unknown *daimones,* the oppressed and repressed forces in the forest. As Old Ego feels impoverished, deeper, darker values begin to be felt, so that even in our outrage we sense new things uprising. For the Hood is a Robin, harbinger of a new season in our red breast.

Second, "cases" and "symptoms," the very stuff of psychotherapy, betray in their etymologies (a word-game which too belongs to
Hermes) an occasional, opportunistic sense. *Casus, caere, Fall* (in German) refer to the accidental way things fall, how they lie, their situation. "Casualties" and "accidents" also go back to the same Latin root,
caere, to fall. Where the senex systematizes these fallings with accident
and casuality insurance, puer consciousness may move into each fall
as a moment of meaning. Symptoms, too, from the Greek *symptoma*,
refer to anything that has befallen one, a happenstance, a chance. Puer
consciousness can hear case histories and symptoms from this accidental, casual perspective. A symptom can be read as a moment, as one
kens the fall of the *I Ching* sticks, the thrown together dice. There is a
meaningful pattern in the precision of a symptom itself, its picture, its
timing, its immediate effects. Then a case is not only an abnormality,
nor is a symptom merely a disorder. They are opportunities.

Hermetic puer as psychopompos! Puer psychotherapy — not psychotherapy of the puer, but *by* the puer! We seem a long way now
from opportunism, yet we have had to go to the end of an affliction
in order to recover the spirit moving in it. And so, we have found that
opportunism is itself an opportunity when it is imagined from within
the same puer consciousness that is afflicted by it. As healing emerges
from disease, or is the disease when imagined hermetically, so the psychopompos is the psychopathology itself when, as the alchemists say,
it has been "touched by quicksilver."

The shadowy *doppelgänger* brings a sense of ourselves as opportunists, cheats, weasels. At the same time, this duplicity in our consciousness — between what is promised and what is done, what is felt
and what is shown, what is seen and what is said to have been seen
— brings awareness that at least two lives are being led at the same
time. We are here and yet also not here at all, hidden. To focus on the
opposites is to miss the opportunities, the Hermes whose presence is
precisely in the *between*. Perhaps this has been the Hermes function of
the puer all along: to double our awareness by returning a portion of
it to the serpent who can move only by wriggling left and right at the
same moment. Let us imagine Hermetic awareness less as a transcendent function that holds the opposites together, or overcomes them,

and more as a consciousness that requires and even creates a between-ness in which to operate. This sort of awareness must wriggle out of moral oppositions. There is no space for the serpent when the world is set up as either black or white.

For Hermes, whose territory is in the borderlands where many currents live side by side, there is no compartment mentality. He can commit "perjury with the most guileless face;" the baby-faced little brother is also a bare-faced liar. Borders always have two sides and Hermes thrives in this between-world. When psychologists degrade the between into a schizoid gap or a psychopathic lacuna, they eliminate Hermes altogether from their considerations. Then analysts become therapeutic bridge-builders above the gorge, working at "the problem of opposites," rather than workers in the bottom land. If we stay closer to the serpent, by means of duplicity, a kind of in-between consciousness emerges, an awareness — not of opposites — but of relations, the filiation or brotherhood of differences. Consciousness sees parallels, analogies, likenings, family resemblances. Nothing is except *as* it is, in its relations, and these are presented as situations (rather than as opposites). This succession of situations, whether in life, in symptoms or in dreams, requires that each darkness be interpreted in its own light and by the standards it brings with it. Individuation not as tree, spiral, child or union; these paths gone. Instead, individuation as situational hermeneutics, opportunities for kairotic soul-making. It is the moments that are momentous, the pearls not their string.

Once we are able to revalue the soul's divisions in terms of the between, then, like Jung, we are recognizing Mercurius as center of the opus.[40] Then too we can understand the necessity of seeing in terms of opposites: they are made for the sake of the between. They pull apart so as to give opportunity for mercurial space; they give *kairos* a chance. And usually, this space is no bigger than a tiny chink in the armor, a hole in the wall where grand visions do not fit. By seeing with the beady snake-eyes of Mercurius, we make possible the appearance of Mercurius and of a hermetic significance in any situation. Puer consciousness may indeed act as psychopompos.

Notes

1. [Originally published in J. Hillman, ed., *Puer Papers* (Dallas: Spring Publications, 1979).] — Ed.

2. R. B. Onians, *The Origins of European Thought* (Cambridge: Cambridge University Press, 1953), p. 348.

3. Ibid. The window in dreams (coming in through a window, seen through a window, the "woman in the window") can be elucidated in terms of this opening that allows a glimpse "beyond" or permits passage of "wind" into one's "room." For a marvelous constellation of puer imagery interconnecting wind, wings, Eros, windows and doors, see Robert Duncan's "Chords: Passages 14," in *Bending the Bow* (New York: New Directions, 1968), pp. 46–47.

4. Ibid.

5. Ibid., p. 29; Liddell and Scott, *A Greek-English Lexicon* (Oxford: Clarendon Press, 1968): "poros."

6. *The Origins of European Thought*, p. 29.

7. Captain Grose, *A Dictionary of Buckish Slang, University Wit, and Pickpocket Eloquence* (London: C. Chappel, 1811).

8. Clement A. Miles, *Christmas in Ritual and Tradition* (London: Fisher Unwin, 1913), pp. 229–38.

9. *The Origins of European Thought*, p. 345. See T. Thass-Thienemann, *The Interpretation of Language* (New York: Aronson, 1973), vol. 1, p. 371.

10. Ibid., p. 346.

11. These figures are discussed, with references, in Chapter 6, "Pothos: The Nostalgia of the Puer Eternus," and in my *The Myth of Analysis* (New York: Harper & Row, 1978), Part 1.

12. Pauly-Wissowa, *Real-Encyclopädie*, "kairos," p. 1518; also A. B. Cook, *Zeus: A Study in Ancient Religion* (Cambridge: The University Press, 1914–40), II: 2, 859ff., and R. Hinks, *Myth and Allegory in Ancient Art* (London: The Warburg Institute, 1939), pp. 117ff.

13. Ibid. See E. Panofsky, "Father Time," *Studies in Iconology* (New York: Harper Torchbooks, 1962), plate xxi. These later versions bring kairos into visible relation with time, that is, they attempt allegorical connections between puer and senex. This same connection is made by the etymological fantasy which derives Kronos and Kairos "from the same root" (*Zeus: A Study in Ancient Religion*, loc. cit.).

14. Pausanias V, 14, p. 9.

15. "Tages" in W. H. Roscher, *Ausführliches Lexikon der griechischen und römischen Mythologie* (Leipzig/Stuttgart: Teubner; Hildesheim, 1965).

16. Besides the homoerotic, religious, and aesthetic interpretations of the Ganymede image, there is also a Christian reading that carries a useful insight: a gloss on the image refers to Christ's "Suffer little children to come

unto me." The uprush on eagle's wings catches us when we are most childlike, or childish. (See Jean Seznec, *The Survival of the Pagan Gods* [Princeton: Princeton University Press, 1972], p. 103).

17. Pauly-Wissowa, op. cit., p. 1510. (*Der kleine Pauly*, III, Stuttgart, 1969).

18. Ibid.

19. W. K. C. Guthrie, *The Greeks and Their Gods* (London: Methuen, 1968), p. 91.

20. W. F. Otto, *The Homeric Gods* (New York: Pantheon, 1954), p. 108.

21. Karl Kerényi (with C. G. Jung and Paul Radin), *The Trickster* (New York: Greenwood Press, 1956).

22. W. F. Otto, *The Homeric Gods*, p. 121.

23. See K. Kerényi, "The Problem of Evil in Mythology," in *Evil* (Evanston: Northwestern Univ. Press, 1967), pp. 8ff., with reference to W. Grönbech, *Kultur und Religionen der Germanen* (Hamburg: Hanseatische Verlagsanstalt, 1942), on Loki. A correction of Grönbech and Kerényi in regard to Loki has been presented by M. Burri, "Repression, Falsification, and Bedeviling of Germanic Mythology," *Spring* 1978, pp. 91–92. See also, Norman O. Brown, *Hermes the Thief* (New York: Vintage, 1967), pp. 24–25, on similarities and differences between Hermes and Prometheus, Loki, and Trickster.

24. K. Kerényi, *Hermes, Guide of Souls*, trans. M. Stein (Zurich: Spring Publications, 1976), pp. 14 et passim.

25. C. G. Jung, "The Spirit Mercurius," *Collected Works*, vol. 13: *Alchemical Studies*, par. 269, 284; on the Hermes-Mercurius relation, see par. 278–83. For a complete catalogue of the epithets of Hermes — all his traits, powers and associations — see William G. Doty, "Hermes Heteronymous Appellations," *Arche* 2 (1978), pp. 17–35.

26. The border-consciousness of Hermes is brilliantly presented by Rafael Lopéz-Pedraza, *Hermes and His Children* (Einsiedeln: Daimon, 2003). His work extends beyond Hermes manifestations in the puer.

27. Attributed to Paul Eluard by J. H. Matthews in a chapter entitled "A Swing Door," *An Introduction to Surrealism* (University Park, PA: Pennsylvania State University Press, 1967), p. 67.

28. Attributed to Simon Hantai and Jean Schuster in J. H. Matthews, op. cit., p. 62.

29. See C. G. Jung, "Commentary on Kundalini Yoga," *Spring* 1976, pp. 14–17. See J. Hillman "The Elephant in *The Garden of Eden*," *Spring* 50 (1990), pp. 93–115.

30. J. H. Matthews, op. cit., p. 63.

31. "Discontinuity" is a characteristic concept of our times, discussed by physicists, and by thinkers as divergent as Erich Neumann and Gaston Bachelard. It informs our contemporary consciousness also in literary forms (poetry) and in Orient-derived disciplines of "suddenness." (see K. H. Bohrer,

Suddenness: On the Moment of Aesthetic Appearance [New York: Columbia University Press, 1994].) Discontinuity is today invoked as an explanatory principle even in classical scholarship much like "fertility" once was: cf. R. F. Willetts, *Cretan Cults and Festivals* (London: Routledge, 1962), p. 199, on the Minoan Mother Goddess as "continuity" and the "youthful god" as "the element of discontinuity."

32. J. H. Matthews, op. cit., p. 24.

33. Ibid., p. 99; see also p. 110.

34. W. F. Otto, *The Homeric Gods*, pp. 115ff.

35. On the blackbird-sun motif, see *Picatrix*, trans. H. Ritter and M. Plessner (London: Warburg Institute, 1962), pp. 115, 119; it appears in Mithraism, and in late paintings of van Gogh. Apollo was "represented" by a black bird, supposedly meaning his prophetic gift. Why does prophecy that sees so clearly, see doom, and what is the secret desire of Apollo for Cassandra? The inherent relation between the spirit of clarifications and the spirit of destruction remains an enigma, and a tension of the psyche.

36. K. Kerényi, *The Heroes of the Greeks* (London: Thames and Hudson, 1959), pp. 132–33.

37. The tale of Autolykos is told succinctly by both Graves (*Myths* 1:67) and by Kerényi in *The Heroes of the Greeks*, p. 77.

38. See López-Pedraza, *Hermes and His Children*, for insights into the Apollo-Hermes relation.

39. W. H. Auden, "Under Which Lyre," a long humorous poem on the Apollo/Hermes contrast in academia.

40. See C. G. Jung, *Collected Works*, vol. 13, par. 284; *Collected Works*, vol. 14: *Mysterium Coniunctionis*, par. 707–19.

Part Two
Movements and Pathologies

4

The Great Mother, Her Son, Her Hero, and the Puer[1]

Perhaps it would not be too much to say that the most crucial problems of the individual and of society turn upon the way the psyche functions in regard to spirit and matter.

— C. G. Jung

Great Mother Nature has proved most potent . . . down to the present day. It is "she" who does nothing by leaps, abhors a vacuum, is *die gute Mutter*, is red in tooth and claw, "never did betray the heart that loved her," eliminates the unfit, surges to ever higher and higher forms of life, decrees, purposes, warns, punishes and consoles . . . Of all the pantheon Great Mother Nature has . . . been the hardest to kill.

— C. S. Lewis

We are trying to present the puer within a structure that recognizes it primarily as a spiritual phenomenon. We would differentiate puer, hero, and son, and, contrary to the classical analytical view, we would suggest that the son who succumbs and the hero who overcomes both take their definition through the relationship with the magna mater, whereas the puer takes its definition from the senex-puer polarity. The young dominant of rising consciousness that rules the style of the ego personality can be determined by the puer (and senex) or by the son and hero (and Goddess). Nonetheless, analytical psychology has for the most part taken for granted that puer and great mother belong together: the puer-man has, or is, a mother-complex. The puer succumbs to the mother; the hero fights and overcomes her.[2]

Henderson makes one distinction worth noting — and refuting. He associates only the negative puer aeternus with the mother-complex and rightly points to the faulty anima relationship, a main psychological lacuna of the puer-man. But, because he derives this anima peculiarity from the mother-complex, his view too begins and ends with early Jung: puer consciousness is a function of a mother-bound psychology. Henderson's distinction between a "positive" and a "negative" puer aeternus is anyway suspect, since it divides in the morality of mind what is not divided in the reality of psyche. Positive and negative signs affixed to psychic events offer the illusion that there are positive and negative aspects of an archetype per se and that the plus or minus signs we attribute are valid descriptions. But the signs are relative, placed there by the fantasy of the ego, its decisions in terms of its values and realities. Jung never let us forget that the psyche's opposites contain each other, so that every virtue can be a vice, or vice a virtue. To declare a complex negative is to freeze it in hell. What can it do; where can it go? Not only does the idea of positive and negative puer need rethinking, but also the crucial question of the puer in relation with the mother needs fresh examination.

In classical mythology this special entanglement of spirit and maternal world is depicted by the Great Goddess and her young male consort — her son, her lover, her priest. Attis, Adonis, Hippolytus, Phaethon, Tammuz, Endymion, Oedipus are examples of this erotic bind.[3] Each figure in each tale shows its own variation; the Oedipus complex is but one pattern of son and mother that produces those fateful entanglements of spirit with matter which in the twentieth century we have learned to call neurotic. The very desperation of neurosis shows how strong are their mutual needs and that the attempts to untie this primary knot are truly in the ancient sense agonizing and tragic. The primary knot of spirit and matter is personified in the clinging embrace of mother and son.

Alchemy — the fullest and most precise background yet worked out for the processes of analytical work — presents a seemingly similar motif: the extraction of spirit from matter and then their reunion. But the tradition of alchemy pairs the puer figures mainly with the senex (as the young and old Mercurius, as Christ *puer-et-senex*, as King and King's Son), *not* with the mother!

There are many alchemists and many alchemies. There are dragons, devourings, and dissolutions. The material at the beginning is often female and the child at the end often male. Nevertheless, the Great Goddess (as *materia prima*) is not the primary constellating factor of the puer aeternus of renewal. The divine child who is called *renovatus in novum infantum, puellus regius, filius philosophorum* is a new spirit born of an old spirit. The process is rather male to male to hermaphrodite and only takes place within the female as material and vessel. There seems a subtle and yet crucial difference between the alchemical conception of the movement of the spirit (puer) and this same movement in hero myths and heroic fairytales. There the hero is unthinkable without his opposition to a Great Goddess or Dragon Witch in one form or another.

Spirit seems differently imagined in alchemy, implying a different theory of neurosis and of psychic movement. In the hero myths, the psyche moves mainly by means of the will into an enlargement of rational order. In alchemy, it seems to be an enlargement of imagination, a freeing of fantasy from various imprisoning literalizations. When Jung shifted the main analogy for the individuation process from the hero myth in *Symbols of Transformation* (in German, 1911) to *Psychology and Alchemy* (in German, Eranos lectures 1936 and 1937), one result was also a shift from the rational and voluntary faculties of the soul to its third faculty, the imagination or *memoria*.[4]

There may be many historical and philosophical reasons for alchemy's presentation of the puer without the great mother as main counterpart, not the least of them being the Christian doctrine of a God who is both Father and Son. Besides these influences upon alchemy's formulations of the puer, more significant are the spontaneous fantasies of the psyche as expressed in alchemical formulations about redemption. In alchemy too, the embrace of spirit and matter is a suffering and an evil, or what we now call neurotic. However, the way out of this embrace is different. It is not only in terms of a heroic mother-son battle for which St. George and the Dragon has become the major Western paradigm. In alchemy the dragon is also the creative Mercu-

rius and a figuration (or prefiguration) of the puer. The alchemical hero
is devoured by the dragon, or, we would say, imagination takes over.
Then comes the activity of discrimination from within the belly where
nous separates and makes distinctions within the literalizations of *physis*,
the physically concrete fantasies. This process of discrimination is imaged in alchemy as cutting through the belly of the beast from within.

Moreover, the myth of the hero is but one motif of alchemy's hun-
dreds, but one way of proceeding, one operation useful at a specific
moment or within one constellation; whereas the myth of the hero
in modern psychology has become *the* dominant interpretative background for puer psychology.

In yet another way there is a difference between our usual heroic-
ego way of thinking about spirit and matter (puer and mother) and the
images of alchemy. There, spirit is not mainly presented within a Dar-
winian fantasy. The pattern is not usually one of generation, spirit born
out of maternal matter. The alchemical techné aims at another kind of
relationship between *materia* and *spiritus* where polarities become com-
plementaries, different but equal and joined, as king and queen — and
where the close union is *an incest that is a virtue.* Oedipus is altogether
irrelevant here, because the entire process is not heroic, not literalized,
and not viewed from ego-consciousness. The alchemical representation
of development seems never to depart from the unity of the archetype;
development of puer consciousness is not *away* from or *against* matter
(mother) but always a mercurial business involved with her; *puer-et-senex*
needs matter for its foil, for its stuff, for its physicality that gives to its
imagination literal materials upon which to fantasy.

We might consider alchemy, then, to be a discipline that is not
conceived within the mother-complex, because its view of spirit is
not conceived as a derivative of matter. Its psychology differs from
the psychology of science, and so alchemy and science offer different
backgrounds to psychology. Because the science-fantasy implies mas-
tering matter, science works within the archetype of the great mother. And when we look at the psyche scientifically, our consciousness
tends to become appropriated by the archetypal great mother. The
alchemist-fantasy is less bound by the "laws" of matter and by quantitative considerations. Qualitative change and precision of it are more

important. The alchemical way through the material of the mother is the discipline of fantasy, and alchemical psychology is dominated by the puer-senex pair, its tensions and problems, and its relation with anima.

III In our lives the mother/son-complex is the personalized formulation (within that family language so fondly constellated by the very same mother/son archetype) of the matter-spirit relation. "Mother-complex" is another way of stating that spirit cannot present itself, has no effect or reality, except in regard to matter. It only knows itself in contradistinction to matter. If the spirit is heroic, the contradistinction is presented as opposition; if it is materialistic and worldly, it is in that complex's service. Either way its first fascination is with the transformation of matter, earth-shakers, world-movers, city-planners; spiritual acts are materialized in some aspect of concrete reality. The "mother-complex" is such a widespread neurosis, spirit is so immersed in the body of matter, delighting there or squirming to shake free, that we can hardly discover other interpretations of spirit — such as the alchemical — except within a polarity to matter. Whenever we think of spirit in these terms, we are "in the mother-complex."

Is there not another spirit — or other spirits — of nature, or of the seas, the woods and mountains, of fiery volcanoes or of the underworld that comes from the lower Gods (Poseidon, Dionysus, Hades, Hephaistos, Pan) which are male — or hermaphroditic? And is there not a Hermes and a Zeus Chthonios? Must everything below, of nature and of darkness, be mother? The spirit can discover itself by means of another spirit, male with male as parallels, or friends and enemies; so too, the spirit can have as opposite and partner the soul or the body, neither of which must be the Great Goddess. We may question even whether the spirit can know itself, become conscious, within the mother-son polarity. The blindness of Oedipus would indicate the contrary.[5] If psychology is to free itself for other fantasies for comprehending the psyche's immense range of events, it must first free the puer from the mother, else the spirit of psychology can do nothing better than repeat and confirm what mother has told it to do.

Neurosis cannot be separated from *Weltanschauung*, which always is an expression of one or another variety of the spirit-matter issue and is thus loaded with the archetypal problematics of the great mother/puer relation. Hence the therapists of neurosis, as Jung pointed out, are and must be also doctors of philosophy.[6] The puer/great mother relation is also a philosophical problem that can be expressed in philosophical language. The puer cannot be a functioning psychological organ without having its ideational effects. If therapists of neurosis are doctors of philosophy, they should be able to see not only the neurotic in all philosophy but also the philosophical in all neurosis. Metaphysical ideas are hardly independent of their complex roots; so ideas can be foci of sickness, part of an archetypal syndrome. For example, is not the materialism of some natural science a philosophy of matriarchy in which the scientist willy-nilly becomes a priestly or a heroic son? Does not Vedanta and its transcendence of matter reflect a spirit so entangled in the great world mother that it must resort to disciplined exercises to find liberation? In our metaphysics we state our fantasies about the physical and transcendence of it. A metaphysical statement can be taken as a psychological fantasy about the matter-spirit relation. These statements are fantasies whose author is the "archetypal neurosis" of puer and mother, reflected in philosophy by the terms spirit and matter. The archetypal neurosis is collective, affecting everyone with a metaphysical affliction. Working out this affliction is individual, which makes therapy a metaphysical engagement in which ideas and not only feelings and complexes undergo process and change. The appearance of puer figures, particularly in the dreams of women, brings new impetus and new struggles also in the realm of ideas, indicating transformations of *Weltanschauung* in regard to all that is included by the term *physis*.

IV Now we must inquire more precisely into this archetypal contamination of mother and puer. What occurs when the puer as a fundamental structure of the psyche loses its self-identity, its position within the senex-puer whole, and is subtly replaced by the figure of the mother's son?

When the father is absent, we fall more readily into the arms of the mother. And indeed the father is missing; God is dead. We cannot go backward by propping up senex religion. The missing father is not your or my personal father. He is the absent father of our culture, the viable senex who provides not daily bread but spirit through meaning and order.[7] The missing father is the dead God who offered a focus for spiritual things.

Unable to go backward to revive the dead father of tradition, we go downward into the mothers of the collective unconscious, seeking an all-embracing comprehension. We ask for help in getting through the narrow straits without harm; the son wants invulnerability. Grant us protection, foreknowledge; cherish us. Our prayer is to the night for a dream, to a love for understanding, to a little rite or exercise for a moment of wisdom. Above all we want assurance through a vision beforehand that it will all come out all right. Here is the motif of protection again and a protection of a specific sort: invulnerability, foresight, guarantee that all shall be well, no matter what.

Just here we catch one glimpse of a difference between puer and son. Existential guarantees are given by mothers. Loyalty to her gives her loyalty in return. She won't let you down if you remain loyal to her. Mother assures safety and gives life, but mother does not give true spirit that comes from uncertainty, risk, failure — aspects of the puer. The son does not need the father, whereas the puer seeks recognition from the father, a recognition of spirit by spirit that leads to eventual fatherhood in the puer itself. As we cannot get to the father through the mother, so we cannot get to the hot sperm seed of logos through its imitations in moon-magic.

Psychology is not dissolution into psychic magic; psychology is a *logos* of the psyche; it requires spirit. Psychology advances not only through philosophies of the mother: evolution in growth and development, naturalism, materialism, the social adaptation of a feeling-loaded humanism, comparisons with the animal realm, reductions to emotional simplicities like love, sexuality, and aggression. Psychology requires other patterns for advancing its thought and other archetypal carriers, such as the puer which might liberate psychology's speculative fantasy and insist upon psychology's spiritual significance.

Without the father we lose also that capacity which the Church recognized as "discrimination of the spirits:" the ability to know a call when we hear one and to discriminate between the voices, an activity so necessary for a precise psychology of the unconscious. But the spirit that has no father has no guide for such niceties. The senex-puer division puts an end to spiritual discrimination; instead we have promiscuity of spirits (astrology, yoga, spiritual philosophies, cybernetics, atomic physics, Jungianism, etc. — all enjoyed currently) and the indiscrimination among them of an all understanding mother. The mother encourages her son: go ahead, embrace it all. For her, all equals everything. The father's instruction, on the contrary, is: all equals nothing — unless the all be precisely discriminated.

The realm of the Great Goddess is characterized by the passive inertia and compulsive dynamus of nature; the protective, nourishing, generative cycle in animal and plant from seed to death; an affinity for beauty, timelessness, and emotionality; a preference for opacity, obscurity, coagulation, and darkness; a mystique of the blood per se or in kinship ties.[8] All these areas under the domination of the Great Goddess, with but a slight shift of emphasis toward the spiritual, could as well be reflected by the puer. Thus, the puer impulse is *exaggerated* by the mother-complex. A contamination of any two archetypes may reinforce them both, or it may depotentiate one in favor of the other.[9] In the special case of the mother-puer confluence, the mother seems to win out, not only by depotentiating spirit but by exaggerating it. Mother, as giver and nourisher, as natural life itself, supplies the puer with an overdose of energetic supplies, and by reinforcing certain of the puer's basic traits she claims him as her dependent son.

When the mother gets hold of these traits, she draws them in extreme. The puer pensiveness becomes an ineffectual daydream; death becomes no longer a terror but a welcomed and natural comfort; laming, instead of an opening into human vulnerability, is turned exaggeratedly by mother into a castration, a paralysis, a suicide. The vertical flights so authentic to the root of the puer become instead a contemptuous soaring over a corrupt and shoddy world; the family problem takes on a religious mystique: all the family members, personages in a matriarchal epic. Then, too, eternity, instead of being an aspect of events and the way in which puer consciousness perceives through to archetypal significance, is distorted into a disregard for time, even a denial of all temporal things. Or a materialistic opportunism appears instead of the genuine puer sense of opportunity, its way of proceeding by hunch and luck, its ambition carried by play and Mercurius. There is materialism too in a peculiar concretism of metaphysical ideas (they must be put in force, acted out in body and clothes and community), in ethics, in sexuality, money, diet, as the mother's matter, repressed, returns in the literalizations of puer abstractions. The cycle of nature (which in puer consciousness is a field out of which to draw metaphors to make jokes upon, play and experiment with) in son-consciousness becomes a pious nature "out-there," a shack in the woods, soiled clothes, Hatha Yoga; and beauty, which for the puer reflects Platonic ideals and is a revelation of the essence of value, narrows instead into the vanities of my own image, my own aesthetic productions and sensitivities.

The close association of mother and son in the psyche is imaged as incest and experienced as ecstasy and guilt. The ecstasy goes in both vertical directions, divine and hellward, but the guilt is not assuaged. The great mother changes the puer's debt to the transcendent — what he owes the Gods for his gifts — into a debt of feeling, a guilt toward her symbols in the round of material life. He overpays society in family, job, civic duties and avoids his destiny. Through her, his relation with material life oscillates between ecstatic springing of its binds or guilty submission to them. In the sexual sphere, psychoanalysts have called this "oscillation," the continual back and forth between lust and guilt, guilt and lust.

The ecstatic aspect in a man carried by the conjoined archetype of mother-son takes him yet further from the father's inhibitions of order and limit. Ecstasy is one of the Goddess's ways of seducing the puer from its senex connection. By overcoming limit, puer consciousness feels itself overcoming fate which sets and is limit.[10] Rather than loving fate or being driven by it, the puer escapes from fate in magical, ecstatic flight. Puer aspirations are fed with new fuel: the potent combustible of sexual and power drives whose source is in the instinctual domain of the Great Goddess.[11] These exaggerations of the puer impulse set him afire. He is the torch, the arrow, and the wing, Aphrodite's son Eros. He seems able to realize in his sexual life and his career every wish of his childhood's omnipotence fantasies. It's all coming true. His being is a magic phallus, glowing and strong, every act inspired, every word pregnant with deep, natural wisdom. The Great Goddess behind the scenes has handed him this ecstatic wand. She governs both the animal desire and the horizontal world of matter over which she offers promise of conquest.

Due to the emotionality of the great mother, the dynamus of the son is unusually labile, unusually dependent upon emotion. Inspiration can no longer be differentiated from enthusiasm, the correct and necessary ascension from ecstasy. The fire flares up and then all but goes out, damp and smoky, clouding vision and afflicting others with the noxious air of bad moods. The dependence of spirit upon mood described in vertical language (heights and depths, glory and despair) has its archetypal counterpart in the festivals for Attis, Cybele's son, which were called *hilaria* and *tristia*. [12]

When the vertical direction toward transcendence is misdirected through the great mother, the puer is no longer authentic. He takes his role now from the relationship with the feminine. Ecstasy and guilt are two parts of the pattern of sonship. Even more important is heroism. Whether as hero-lover, or hero-hermit denying matter but with an ear to nature's breast, or hero-conquerer who slays some slimy dragon of public evil, or as Baldur, so perfect and so unable to stanch the bleeding from his beautiful wounds, puer has lost its freedom. Direct access to the spirit is no longer there; it requires drama, tragedy, heroics. Life becomes a performance acted out through a role in the relationship with the eternal feminine who stands behind every such son: martyr, messiah, devotee, hero, lover. By playing these roles, we are part of the cult of the Great Goddess. [13] Our identities are given by the enactment of these roles and thus we become her sons, since our life depends on the roles she gives. She thus can affect even the way that the puer seeks the senex: exaggerating the discipleship of the student to his master, the swagger of the battler with the old order, the exclusivity of the messiah whose new truth refuses everything that has gone before. The mother-complex dulls *the precision of the spirit;* issues become quickly

either/or, since the Great Goddess does not have much comprehension of the spirit. She only grasps it in relationship to her; that is, the
mother-complex must make of spirit something *related*. It must have
effects in the realm of matter: life, world, people. This sounds "only
human" and full of "common sense," again terms too often expressing
the sentimentalism of the mother-complex. Even should a man recognize the mother in his actions and take flight from her relatedness into
lofty abstraction and vast, impersonal fantasy, he is still the son filled
with the animus of the Goddess, her pneuma, her breath and wind. And
he serves her best by making such divisions between his light and her
darkness, his spirit and her matter, between his world and hers.

   This is the animus thinking of sonship, found as much in men
as women. It is a thinking of coagulations and oppositions between
them, rather than a thinking in distinctions between perspectives. For
it is not that the mother is this or that and the puer this or that, as
describable objects, things, but rather that mother and puer are ways
of perceiving. More or less the same "facts" can be found in puer and
in the mother's son, so the real difference between them lies in the
way in which we perceive these facts. But the mother does not want
to be seen through. She throws up her veils of darkness, her opacity
and emotionality, and presents crude, materialized divisions between
God and Caesar, this world and the next, time and eternity, sacred and
profane, introvert and extravert, and so on, *ad infinitum*, keeping her
animus-son eternally occupied, preventing his need for an eternality
of another sort. This eternality of the puer would see through all such
opposites in terms of their fundamental likeness as a way of thought.
The movement from son to puer, that is, the movement of restoration
of the original puer vision, occurs when one sees through the challenge of opposites that the Great Goddess embroils us in so that one
can refuse to do battle with her in the field of her entangling dilem-
mas. By this I do not mean that the puer vision is that of a Nietzschean
superman, beyond good and evil. Rather I mean that the puer vision,
because of its inherent connection with the senex, can live within this
field, as the field of necessity, simply by seeing through to that ambiguity which is the identity of opposites. There is no need either to
force choices as does the hero-son or to make a theology of conflict

in the fashion of the priest-son. The puer vision is transcendent and beyond in the sense that it is not caught in her literal animus-game; therefore, puer consciousness does not have to be literally transcendent, leave the scene, cut out, blow.

V   There is also the anti-hero or hero-in-reverse, who is another puer substitute, another form of the great mother's son. He lives in her lap and off the lap of the land. Rather than all phallus, he is all castration — weak, gentle, yielding to life and its blows. He chooses to lose and his is the soft answer to wrath, which spirit he is unable to meet without the father. His way follows nature, the path of least resistance, eventually into the primeval swamp, bogged. Like water he flows downward, slips out of sight, and has effects underground, so like water that he evokes the divine child in the water-rushes. But this son is not separated from the water by cradle, basket, boat; he is the water. He gives the illusion of being on the right way, wending around obstacles, as the Tao is called "water" and "child." But unlike Icarus he does not plunge into the water vertically, nor does he serve Olympian archetypal principles with wet enthusiasm as does Ganymede the cupbearer. He just goes along with what is going, a stream slipping through the great body of mother nature, ending ultimately in the amniotic estuary streaming into oceanic bliss. Whether hyperactive with theatrics or ecstatics, or passive, the flow of energy results from the mother archetype. The anti-hero attempts to resolve the puer-complex through the degradation of energy. The individual follows along, letting things happen, dropping out from the demands put upon the heroic ego. He makes few demands even on himself, wanting little and needing less and less. As tensions equalize he believes himself in rare balance, becoming cooler and less personal. His images and ideas become more archetypal, reflecting universal levels of the collective unconscious.

Because there appears to be a spiritual advance in visual, poetic, and metaphysical ideas, the term "regression" is refused as a misnomer. Regression means return to more childish or historically earlier behavior patterns, but the passive son seems so obviously to be making spiritual advancement toward ever-widening values and general symbols, progressing through the perennial philosophy into truths of all religions — even if requiring sometimes financial support or hallucinogenic reinforcement. One can hardly be "regressing" while quoting Hesse, Don Juan, Gurdjieff, Tagore, Eckhart, Merton, and Socrates! The philosophy, however, has a defensive note providing a wraparound shield against heroics, will, and effort. For example, the anti-heroics of Ramakrishna, "The nearer you get to God, the less he gives you to do": These traits and the predictable pattern of the anti-hero — what he will do, read, say next — disclose that in his spiritual progress he is actually following the degradation of energy in its entropic direction, which is, in another language as Freud pointed out, Nirvana — or death. The entropy in a system is characterized by cooling and running down, by increase of statistical probability, equalization of tension, generalization (randomness), degradation from higher to lower descriptions of energy, and increasing disorder. All of this appears in individual behavior as well as in the behavior of any complex when it "gives up."

Although the theme of "giving up" belongs in another chapter,[14] we may note a difference between the puer and the hero or antihero in this respect. The puer gives up because of an inadequate survival sense. Separated from the senex, it does not know how to defend itself or keep itself in order. The hero/anti-hero gives up owing to the mother. It would free psychic energy by getting rid of complexes altogether. But, as Jung points out, complexes are the mother of psychic energy, so to conquer them, overcome them, or cure oneself of them, is another way of trying to rid oneself of the mother.

Puer and hero also differ in their self-destructiveness. The puer is self-destructive because it lacks psyche — containment, reflection, involvement. And it lacks, when separated from the senex, the ability to father itself, to put a roof over its head and a wall around its property. The self-destructiveness of the puer in any complex arises because the complex does not understand itself: it sees, it knows, it makes — but it does not see or know or make itself. There is an absence of psychic reflection of the spirit and an absence of spiritual realization within the psyche.

The hero is self-destructive because it would have done with the complex, and this may occur in various ways. It may appear as eros idealism, the inspiration of transforming the complexes into wholeness. It may appear as anti-heroic cooling of the complexes, depotentiating everything of tension (or its reverse, burning everything up in enthusiasm). It may appear as the cure of loving acceptance — which is also a death-wish, revealing how close eros and thanatos are to each other. For to be healed and made whole by love or to give up the tension by death are close indeed. Both refuse the complex as the fundamental necessity of psychic life, the only cure for which is death. Death alone puts an end to the complexes which are "normal phenomena of life"[15] and like the mother are the fundament of each individual's existence. We are complexed beings, and human nature is a composition of complexities. Without complexes there is no living reality, only a transcendent Nirvana of the Buddha whose last supposed words point to the complexity of the psyche as life's primary given: "Decay is inherent in all composite things — work your salvation with diligence."

Getting rid of and giving up this complexity through any formula for overcoming opposites, or dropping out, or curing misses psychic reality. Psychological therapy is less an overcoming and a getting rid than it is a decay, a decomposing of the way in which we are composed. This the alchemists called the *putrefactio*, the slow time-process of transformation through affliction, wastage, and moral horror. Both heroic getting-rid and passive giving-up attempt to speed decay and have done with it; they would avoid the work of psychic reality by escape into spiritual salvation. *But the cure is the decay.*

When the puer lives authentically to its structure, there is this smell of decadence, a fond attachment to one's mess, which is part of its resistance to analysis. In this sense the puer — seemingly so quick and flame-like — is slow to change, shows no development, seems forever stuck in the same old dirty habits. His putrefaction is in his intractable symptoms of colon and digestion, of eczema and acne, of piles, in his long, slow colds and sinuses, his chronic genital complaints, his money peculiarities, or in his low-life fascinations. These things analysis has wrongly attributed to the shadow repression owing to the mother-complex: he is bound to the mother in a compensatory materialistic way and cannot fight free. But against the background of decay, the slowness and the dirt in the puer can be seen as a way of following the path of putrefaction toward finding the outcast senex. As such it is a digestive, fermentative process that should not be heroically hurried. Nor should rot be forcefully "rubbed in" as a treatment to integrate the shadow. The puer is not a dog; puer consciousness needs not house-breaking and heeling but a new attunement of his sensitivity to the odors of his own decay. His individuation is in the pathologizing process itself and not in his heroic efforts to overcome.

We can anyway not rid ourselves of complexes until they have given us up. Their decaying time is longer than the life of the individual personality, since they continue in a kind of autonomous existence long after we have left the scene; they are part of the psychic inheritance of our children and their children, both natural and spiritual. The complexes are our dosage of sin, our karma, which if given up is really only passed on elsewhere. In the analysis of those men called "puer," one needs a nose for decay, for waste, for moldering ruin. By nursing the mess along we keep the puer alive and in touch with the *prima materia;* by whitewashing with bland acceptance (giving-up) or hurrying the process to get going (getting-rid), we put the authentic spirit into the old bottle marked "Mother."

VI   In our consideration of puer and mother we should look, if only briefly, at Dionysus.[16] He has, of course, been perceived as a typical mother's son. The nurses, the milk, the emotionality, the dance, his unheroic behavior and weaponlessness, his softness and effeminacy, the women's favorite — all this has meant to our simple, so-called psychological minds nothing but one more striking archetypal example of the mother-complex.[17]

But Dionysus may also be seen within the puer-senex structure. His name means Zeus-Son; his mythologems are in many aspects almost interchangeable with those of the Cretan Zeus, and in one of his birth performances he is delivered from the thigh of his father, male born of male. It is questionable whether we may call Dionysus puer in our modern psychological sense, even though *puer* was one of his Latin epithets. But since Dionysus was one of the young Gods and since his cult presented him, especially in later antiquity, in child form,[18] he shows some traits relevant for our thoughts here, even if the quality of his masculinity differs from what our historical consciousness under its Greco-Roman and Judeo-Christian heroic dominants has decided is masculine. So we have written off "the Dionysian" to the mother; therewith we have missed the spiritual significance implied by Dionysus *puer,* and we have misappreciated the wine, the theatrical and its tragedy, the style of madness and phallicism, and other aspects of his nature and cult that bear on puer consciousness. Puer may find in Dionysus a background to traits and experiences that are not to be taken literally and acted out in dancing troops with tambourines but which offer another and softer means for the puer-senex, father-son, reunion. Dionysus presents the spiritual renewal in nature or the natural renewal of the spirit, encompassing in himself the cyclical and generative traits of mother nature with the culture, inspiration, and irrational excitement of puer consciousness.

Dionysus, they say, has several mothers. Demeter, Io, Dione, Persephone, Lethe, and Semele have been variously named. And the relationship between his mothers is *discontinuous.* Semele is killed by Zeus while still pregnant; Zeus is his second mother; he is mothered by nymphs in a cave, by Persephone, by his grandmother Rhea, who puts back together his dismembered pieces.

This discontinuity in the mother is not exclusive to Dionysus. Other Gods and heroes are "motherless," i.e., abandoned, suckled by animals, raised by foster mothers or nurses, the natural mother having disappeared or died. Psychoanalysis has made much of this theme of "the two mothers." It has become the good and bad breast; and Jung, too, devoted a large piece of his *Symbols of Transformation* to "The Dual Mother," by which is meant two sides of the same figure, a positive life-cherishing and a negative life-endangering aspect.

But I would look at the two (or more) mothers from another angle, not as different kinds or faces of one figure, but as an interruption in the relation between mother and child. I suggest that the rupture in natural continuity (Semele's not carrying the child to term) offers another way of regarding the relation between *mater* and *puer.* Owing to the intervention of Zeus's thunderbolt — or whatever other spiritual

inroad into the natural continuity between mother and son, whether from Pharaoh in the Moses tale or from the oracle in the case of
Oedipus — the son does not have to force a break with the mother. It
has happened. It is given with his condition. He is no longer only her
child. The only-natural has been broken because the spiritual has inter-
vened, and so a separation of puer consciousness from mother occurs
without the necessity of cutting or killing. Evidently, another archetype
is activated to which the son also belongs, and this other archetype is as
signal to his fate as is the mother from whom he is separated.[19]

VII When we stand within the consciousness influenced mainly by
the great mother, all puer phenomena seem derivative of the
mother complex, and even our consciousness itself becomes "her son,"
a resultant of the primordial matrix of the unconscious. Yet, there is
no such thing as "the mother-complex." If we are strict and are not
just led along by easy language, complexes do not belong to any specific archetype. The complexes — power, money, illness, sex, fear,
ambition, jealousy, self-destruction, knowledge, etc. — which form
the energetic cores and provide the fantasy stuff of our afflictions and
transformations do not belong to any single God.

First, there are no single Gods. In polytheism each God implies
and involves others. *Theos* and *deus* (as well as the Celtic and Nordic
roots of our God consciousness) arise in a polytheistic context where
reference to God always meant a field of many Gods. A single God
without others is unthinkable. Even our Judeo-Christian second commandment makes this statement, albeit in a negative fashion ("Thou
shalt have no other Gods before me"). Second, the Gods interpen-
etrate, as the archetypes interfuse. The archetypes do not so much rule
realms of being as they, like the Gods, rule all at once and together
the same realm of being, this our world. But they provide distinctions
within this world, different ways of regarding things, different patterns
for psychizing instinct, different modes of consciousness. So, third,
complexes are not assigned either by definition or by nature to specific archetypal patterns. Any complex may at one time or another be
under the aegis of this or that dominant, and any dominant may at any
time take over this or that complex. For example, money may seem to

belong to Saturn's greed, he who coined money, or to Mercurius the trader, or to the hero's booty, or to Zeus who can appear as a shower of gold; or it may be the gold of Apollo, or belong within the Midas constellation; or money may even point a way into the psychic underworld, for Hades' other name was Pluto (wealth). So, too, for sexuality, which takes on altogether different characteristics when Apollonic, Dionysian, Priapian, or in the service of Hera.[20]

Even the puer's orality — seemingly that one complex so certainly belonging to the mother archetype — may be envisioned otherwise. Psychology has surprisingly little to say about taste, food, hunger, eating. All are swallowed up in "orality." Ever since the "oral stage" was laid out by Freud, everything to do with mouth, stomach, with food and cooking and drinking, with hungers of every sort goes back to Mom and her breasts (or bottle). But puer food behavior can show an asceticism, for instance, of a Pythagorean-Orphic sort. It can show a sensitivity in aesthetic flavors that belong (in the magical-astrological tradition of *Picatrix*) to Venus and not the Moon. Or, the puer hunger for more belongs more properly to Saturn and his greed, the wolf, Moloch, Bhoga, a rapacious eating of the world.

The shift of archetypal background to a complex is a common enough experience when a problematic and habitual knot is suddenly released and a wholly new perspective is disclosed. It is as if the complex has been redeemed by the grace, or the viewpoint, of a different God. We are equally familiar with the reverse: when a virtue suddenly is experienced through another archetype and becomes now "destructive" and a "shadow problem." Sometimes this shift from one archetype to another occurs as a breakdown. What previously supported one's ego-complex — say the nymphic anima, or the flaming, inspiring eros, or the conservative self-righteousness of moralistic Saturn — withdraws its domination. Then, a collapse and revolution take place until the complex can recognize its new Lord and find new archetypal sanction.

By giving over any complex to a single archetype, we condemn it to a single view, a diagnosis made too often in analysis. (This is your spiritual animus, your negative father, your neglected child, etc.) This frustrates the movement of the complex among the Gods, fixating it by definition and frustrating its Hermetic possibilities for transformation through movement of perspective. When we fix a complex to only one archetype, only one sort of insight can arise. It is crucially important to view moodiness, for example, not only as typically puer but also as typically anima, typically mother, and also as a power trick of the shadow, and even of the senex. As Eros does not belong only to Aphrodite because there are many kinds of loving, and as fighting can be governed by Ares, Athene, Nike, Apollo, Hercules, and Amazons, and as madness can be brought on and taken away by a variety of dominants, so may any complex be a tributary of the great mother and yet at the same time accord with the puer-senex.

By this I do not intend to deny complex, negative maternal phenomena. The "negative mother" appears in the myths of destructive femininity (Hecate, Gorgo, Kali, Lua, and the other Great Goddesses who consume and lay waste). She is also evident in the barrenness of collective kindness, structures without milk, customs without tradition in a civilization that offers no support, nothing natural. The "negative mother" is visible in the voices of the women with their children, the faces of ugly mouths and flat eyes, the resentment and hatred. It is a wonder anyone survives at all through the early years when mother-love comes with its double, mother-hate. Of course, we live in an age of Moms, for the culture is secular and the ordinary mortal must carry archetypal loads without help from the Gods. The mothers must support our survival without support themselves, having to become like Goddesses, everything too much, and they sacrifice us to their frustration as we in turn, becoming mothers and fathers, sacrifice our children to the same civilization.

The way to "solve the mother-complex" would be not to cut from Mom but to cut the antagonism that makes me heroic and her negative. To "solve the mother-complex" of the puer means to remove the puer phenomena from the mother, no longer viewing puer problems as mother-caused and mother-bound. (For in our civilization what cannot be blamed on the mother?) Rather than separate man and mother, we need to separate the archetypal necessity of their association and to consider puer phenomena in their own right. Then one can turn to each puer aspect and ask it where it belongs, in accordance with the procedure in ancient Greece when consulting an oracle. "To what god or hero must I pray or sacrifice to achieve such and such a purpose".[21] To what archetypal pattern do I relate my problem? Within which fantasy can I insight my complex? Once the problem has been placed upon a relevant altar, one can connect with it according to its own needs and connect to the God through it.

By taking for granted that puer phenomena belong to the great mother, *analytical psychology has given the puer a mother-complex.* Puer phenomena have received an inauthentic cast for which the epithet "neurotic" seems justified. By laying the complex on the altar of the great mother, rather than maintaining its connection with the *senex-et-puer* unity, we consume our own spiritual ground, giving over to the Goddess our eros, ideals, and inspirations, believing they are ultimately rooted in the maternal, either as my personal mother, or matter, or as a causally conditioned contextual field called society, economics, the family, etc. By making spirit her son, we make spirit itself neurotic. By taking the frailties and youthful follies necessary to all spiritual beginnings merely as infantilisms of the mother-complex, we nip in the bud the possibility of renewal in ourselves and our culture. This view of things serves only to perpetuate the neurosis, preventing the reunion of senex and puer. Puer then seems opposite and enemy of senex, and the age seems rightly characterized by what Freud suggested, a universal Oedipus complex, son against father because of the mother.

In individuals, these distortions of the puer show themselves in the personal mother-complex. In society, there are distortions of spiritual goals and meanings, because an ambitiously heroic ego development has been the recipe for resolution of the puer syndrome. To assume that the puer is primarily the same as the son of the great mother is to confirm the pathological distortions as an authentic state of being. The distortion of puer into son is perpetuated by the mother archetype, which prefers the hero myth as the model for ego-development since that model depicts the ego to be primarily and necessarily embroiled with her. Our main Western psychological theories rest on a model that more or less declares the dynamics of the psyche to be derivatives of the family and society, which are the preserve of the mother. Psychology itself is her victim, not only in its therapeutics of ego development, but more fundamentally: the spirit of psychology is lamed by materialism, literalism, and a genetic viewpoint toward its own subject matter, the psyche. The spiritual nature and purposes of psychology never emerge because the puer never emerges from the mother. Or it emerges still bound with a navel-cord, psychology as a heroic mission of the priest-son whose urge is either to spread self through the world or to become self in disdain of the world.

Psychology, as Jung insisted, always reflects our psychic condition.[22] A psychology that sees mother everywhere is a statement about the psyche of the psychologist and not only a statement based on empirical evidence. To advance the psyche through its collective mother-complex, psychology itself must advance in its self-reflection so that its subject, the soul, is no longer dominated by naturalism and materialism, and the goals for that soul are no longer formulated via the mother archetype as "growth," "social adaptation," "human related-ness," "natural wholeness," etc.

Our ideas about the psyche affect the psyche. Ideas can be poisonous as well as therapeutic. Psychological ideas are particularly important since they tell the psyche about itself, giving a mirror in which to view its own events. Psychological concepts can work as liberating transformers, offering a new view of what had hitherto been condemned or misperceived. As Jung wrote: "Psychology inevitably merges with the psychic process itself"[23]— and of course as the psychic process moves it will continue to produce new aspects of psychology. In no other field is the state of the doer more involved with what is done than in psychology. Operator and material are indistinguishable; psychology is alchemy in a new dress. The more complicated and differentiated psychic life becomes, the more anachronistic to go on with simplest accounts in terms of biochemistry, brain physiology, sociology, psychodynamics, family genetics. Moreover, inadequate psychological accounts interfere with psychic differentiation, having a noxious effect on the soul. For this reason, among many others, psychology turns to mythology. Mythic accounts are the most open, most exploratory, most suggestively subtle yet precise, allowing the soul the widest imagination for its complexes.

Yet mythology for all its precision in detail leaves ambiguities about fundamentals, since the figures themselves, like the archetypes, are *dei ambigui*.[24] We find the figures of hero, puer, and son not distinguished as clearly as our monocular minds would want. Myth offers possibilities for perceiving but not facts for building a case to prove that the puer is this and the son or hero is that. Proof is not the aim of myth; it does not set out to display an argument, to explain, or to demonstrate a single line of thought on any theme. Besides, the great mother is everywhere, because pervasiveness is at the essence of that dominant. So it is not independence from mother that separates puer out from son-hero but independence in our *conception* of the puer.

Perhaps the question — puer or son, authentic spirit or mother-derivative — can never be answered in the form of such sharp alternatives which too betray a kind of consciousness that asks questions in terms of swords and sunlight and would codify the psyche into the straight thinking of priestly dogma.

Hero, puer, and son are all the same in one basic respect: *youth*. Youth carries the significance of becoming, of self-correcting growth, of being beyond itself (ideals) since its reals are in *status nascendi*. So it is decisive how we envision this youth, whether embodied in a young person, as a dream figure, or as any young potential of the soul, since this youth is the emergence of spirit within the psyche. Just as there are young Gods and heroes, and young men of genius, who cannot all be understood in terms of the Great Goddess, so there are young men and young figures in our dreams who cannot all be interpreted through the mother-complex. Apollo, Hermes, and Dionysus have many typically puer characteristics that cannot be put down to mother, implying an authentic puer consciousness based on their authenticity as full and distinct Gods. Conversely, there are young men who have true mother-complexes in the sense of modern psychology, yet who do not show authentic puer characteristics. There is no fire, no spirit, no goal; the destructive and renegade tendencies are not present; fantasy is weak, and there is no exaggerated woundedness — distinguishing traits of the puer. So, the ideal therapist of the archetypal persuasion would watch carefully the actual phenomenology. And myth would help him perceive distinctions.

The cosmos in which we place youth and through which we insight youth will influence its pattern of becoming. From the mother's perspective, male youth belongs with the female as a consort, part of her fertility and natural growth, her heroical culture drive, her realm of death. From the senex perspective, male youth is renewal both as hope and as threat, the same and the different in one figure, and a dynamus that calls for order, an innocence asking for knowledge, and a possibility to be realized through time and labor.

Although these two views of youth describe kinds of consciousness, we do not need to make a hierarchy of these kinds, demonstrating that matriarchy is prior to patriarchy or that son, hero, puer reflect levels of development. It is not a matter of which is right in terms of which comes first. We are not concerned with the "origins and history of consciousness" or the origins of son, hero, puer, or of Gods. The search for origins has to lead back to the mother anyway who must always come "first," since genetic analysis, analysis in terms of origins, is an obeisance to her and is determined by her kind of consciousness. It is enough to realize that insight can shift perspective from one archetypal background to another and that phenomena now seeming to be of the son can move elsewhere and offer another kind of psychological movement.

VIII By laying to rest the notion that the puer is only the son of the great mother, we may also abandon former notions of ego-development. Delivery through battle against an overwhelming mother is no longer the only way.[25] The hero of the will — who has been disappearing from drama and fiction, and political history too (if not from action-packed movies) — is not always a viable role for ego, nor must battle be the way. The dragon demands battle and the hero myth tells us how to proceed. But suppose we were to step out altogether from the great mother, from Jocasta and Oedipus and the exhausting, blinding heroics that so often kill the feminine opposite — not just "out there" in the enemy but within the heroic psyche itself.

If Emerson considered the hero to be he who was immovably centered (which can be reversed to mean he who is so fixed on the center that he has lost his mobility), we might define the hero as he who has maimed femininity. In compensation to this, analytical psychology has long concentrated on the anima as therapy for the ego (or persona) identification. But the basic notions of the anima, and the therapeutic sentimentalisms about her, are in turn the result of the same psychology's efforts to strengthen the ego. The anima would not have to carry feeling, femininity, soul, imagination, introversion, subtlety, and what have you if the ego were not so bound to the hero myth, so fixed in its central focus on "reality," "problems," and "moral choice."[26]

Suppose we were no longer to conceive of the ego's relation to its development and to the spirit on the heroic model, achieving through fighting, keeping in shape, trusting in the right arm, overcoming all darkness with the enlightenment of the ego over the id. Is this the only way to consciousness and culture?

Freud defined the intention of psychoanalysis: ". . . to strengthen the ego, to make it more independent of the super-ego, to widen its field of perception and enlarge its organization, so that it can appropriate fresh portions of the id. Where id was, there ego shall be. It is a work of culture."[27] Oedipus, hero and king, determines not only the content of psychoanalysis but also its impetus, its heroism. Analysis, psychological development, becoming conscious are new models of cultural heroism so that the culture hero is the thoroughly analyzed man, sublimated, integrated, whole, conscious. And analysis, as a way of achieving this goal, becomes a suffering pilgrimage or trial by ordeal of the hero. If Freud was right that Oedipus is the stuff of neurosis, then the corollary follows that Oedipus-heroics are the dynamism of neurosis.[28] Heroism is thus a kind of neurosis and the heroic ego is neurotic ego. Creative spirit and fertile matter are there embraced and embattled to the destruction of both. Ego-development that is patterned on the hero will have as part of this pattern the shadow of the hero — estrangement from the feminine and compulsive masculinity — foreshadowing the sterile and bitter senex as outcome of the heroic course.

The wandering loneliness of such figures as Jason, Bellerophon, Oedipus (and perhaps Orestes who lived on to seventy) after their great deeds were done, and their failures, may be seen in two different ways. On the one hand, this wandering loneliness is temporal, belonging to the heroic course which issues into the used-up old king.

(The hero — was he a puer? — of F. Scott Fitzgerald's *Tender Is the Night* slowly falls away, aimless like Bellerophon, wandering to ever smaller towns through the great plains). But, on the other hand, we may regard synchronically this behavior trait as a senex aspect of the puer from the beginning, his steady companion.

The hero and the puer seem to have to go it alone (unlike Dionysus, who sometimes is the lonely stranger but who is usually together with a crowd). Yes, this characteristic shows something renegade, psychopathic, schizoid; however, if it is a senex attribute within the puer figure, the attempt to socialize a young man who is following a puer pattern violates the style of his individuation and the integration of the senex component. Leave it alone, says the style itself. The socializing impetus is again that of the mother, whereas the spirit does indeed blow in gusts, free, where it will, and often where no one else can go along. For the mother this is hard to take because she is "by nature" everywhere and wants no phase, no part off on its own, unconnected, out of touch. As a myth can be read two ways — strung out into successive events or condensed where all parts are present at any one time — so we may look at a life in the same way. Assertive masculinity results in aimlessness, or assertive masculinity results from aimlessness. Owing to the proximity of puer and senex, we cannot tell which comes first.

Assertive masculinity is suspicious. Somewhere we know that it must be reactive to feminine attachment. Mythical levels of the psyche support the suspicion, for there it is recollected that hero and female opponent are inseparable. Although they meet in battle, the hero shouting, they could as well be in bed and groaning, because battle with the mother is a manner of incest. Whether as lover or as enemy, his role is determined by his opposite, his polarity with the mother. When mother determines the role, then regardless how it is played its essence is always the same: son. And, as Jung says of assertive heroism: "Unfortunately, however, this heroic deed has no lasting effects. Again and again the hero must renew the struggle, and always under the symbol of deliverance from the mother . . . The mother is thus the daemon who challenges the hero to his deeds and lays in his path the poisonous serpent that will strike him."[29] As long as psycho-

therapy is conceived in terms of ego development, the development
will never be strong enough and the task will never be done. Rather
than being therapists of psyche, we are therapists (servants and devo-
tees) of mother.

Even the *imitatio Christi* — and especially as it is exhibited in the
contemporary program of Christianity in social action — supports the
heroic ego and keeps it embroiled in the hassle with the archetypal
mother. The "Church in Action" belongs to the myth of the culture
hero, a Herculean absorption of Jesus[30] where Jesus fades into the older archetypal patterns of Gilgamesh, Shamash, and Hercules, losing
the special relation of Father and Son which Jesus' words themselves so
emphasize. Yet, Jesus does bring a sword in the heroic fashion, and this
blade from the beginning of the Christian era until today is plunged
century after century into the body of the dragon, now meaning this,
now meaning that, but always consciousness is defined through this
slaughter. If in traditional Christian heroics the knife slays the evil, in
Greek mythic thought the knife *is* the evil.[31] Have we gone far enough
when we reflect upon our Western history of incredible bloodshed
only in terms of aggression and the aggressive instinct in animals? This
takes evil right out of the psyche and puts it safely into some objective
field. Let us once look closer at the knife (which animals don't have)
and interiorize, psychologize aggression in terms of our *very definition of
consciousness*: the logos sword of discrimination in the hands of the heroic ego in his mission to clean up the mother-benighted world. What
we have taken for consciousness, this too has been determined by the
mother. To be conscious has meant and continues to mean: to kill.

Discrimination is the essential, the sword only a secondary instrument. Consciousness requires discrimination, for, as Jung said, there is
no consciousness without perception of differences. But this perception can use the delicacy of fingers, sensitivity of ear, eye, and taste, a
feeling for values and tones and images. There can be puer aesthetic
distinctions without swords. The puer has this talent for craft in his
background — Joseph the carpenter, Daedalus the inventor;[32] these
fathers put the knife to another use.

Hercules is a primordial figure of assertive masculinity and is the
killer-culture-hero par excellence. His cult was the most widely ob-

served in Greek antiquity, yet his name means simply Glory of Hera.[33] Although this Goddess acts as his enemy before his birth and from his cradle where she sent serpents to kill him, it is this Great Goddess who spurs his deeds as culture hero. In the madness of Hercules described by Euripides, the hero claims he was driven beyond the borders of sanity into heroic extremes by Hera, who plagued his life throughout. Yet, he is explicitly her servant, even coming to her rescue when she had been accosted by Silenus,[34] and he receives as his bride in final reward Hebe, who is none other than Hera herself in her younger, sweeter, seductive form.

Hercules is merely one of the heroes driven by this Great Goddess to perform his deeds for her civilization. Hera sends the Sphinx to Oedipus; she (Juno) is the specific persecutor of Aeneas and is the background to Jason's exploits. Hera, the tales say, mothered the monster Typhon and nourished the Hydra and Nemean lion. She had a part in the persecutions and slaying of Dionysus. Hera is the "Enemy's consort."[35] Her own children are Ares[36] of the battle-rage and Hephaistos[37] the ironworker, the volcano.

We are so used to assuming that the son of the great mother appears as a beautiful ineffectual who has laid his testicles on her altar and nourishes her soil with his blood, and we are so used to believing that the hero pattern leads away from her, that we have lost sight of the role of the Great Goddess in what is closest to us: our ego-formation. The adapted ego of reality is in her "yoke,"[38] a meaning of Hera, just as the words *hero* and *Hera* are taken by many scholars to be cognate.[39] When outer life or inner life is conceived as a contest for light, an arena of struggles, success versus failure, coping versus collapse, work versus sleep, pleasure and love, then we are children of Hera.[40] And the ego that results is the mother-complex in a jockstrap.

My point here is to reverse the usual order: puer is weak and mother-bound; hero is strong and mother-free. If the hero is really the strong son whom the mother wants, then we might look at the puer's weaknesses differently.

The son disguises himself as the hyperactive culture hero of civilization, all of whose conquests, glories, triumphs, and spoils ultimately serve the mother of material civilization. The hero of antiquity was so fond of his trophies. Heroic consciousness must have something to show; the ego must have its concrete proof, for such is its definition of reality. Battle has always been for booty and not only for the fun of fighting and pride of winning. But the loot and spoils soon decorate a city, become the furnishings of domestic life, and the hero begins to accumulate possessions — the culture hero as collector. Hero and puer here differ considerably, since the exploits of the former show a preponderance of civilizing virtues, viz., Hercules, Jason, and Theseus. The puer's task is more an odyssey of the spirit, a wandering[41] that never comes home to any hearth or city.

These considerations of the hero/mother relation must take into account one more essential element in the hero: death. Pointing to any element in heroic psychology as "essential" is always subject to counter-arguments. After all, the hero has been a principal focus for historians of Greek religion and for psychologists, whose writings on this theme reach heroic proportions, as if the theme drives its student into spectacular efforts of mastery. Of the major themes that characterize the hero analyzed and abstracted by Brelich, Farnell, Fontenrose, Kerényi, Nock, Campbell, Harding, Neumann, and Roheim[42] (to extend the list would drive us, too, further into heroics), let us single out *the cult of the burial tumulus* as a central focus of the hero myth. Of course the hero's spectacular mantic and healing powers, his virtue and strength, his cultural deeds, his role as model in initiation and as founder of cult, city, clan, and family should not be overlooked, but most writers agree that the hero cult is bound to a distinct locus and the locus indicated by a burial mound.[43]

When reference is made to a hero in antiquity it is an evocation of something dead; there are no present heroes, no heroes now, living in the present tense. To be a hero (or the hero-in-reverse as antihero) one must be "dead." The hero is dead because he is an imaginal power, a fantasy. The hero is present not in actuality but as a psychic projection through his cult, in his local tumulus where he is buried, and only "after" the events and through legends of them. The hero himself has been translated to the Isles of the Blest, removed, distant, out of it. The hero is a revenant, providing a fantasy for what the complex can do with itself. The hero gives us the model for that peculiar process upon which our civilization rests: dissociation. We worship the drive of the complex and refuse its inertia. The inertia we call unconscious, regressive, dragon, mother; the drive we call consciousness. We all, whose "family" and "city" are founded upon heroic consciousness and whose initiation is modeled upon the hero, are haunted by this revenant spirit that takes the basic element of psychic life, the complex, from one side only, the negentropic upward direction, calling the dynamic movement which it releases "ego." In this manner the complex civilizes itself through achievements, casting off its inertia into unconsciousness. The heroic presents forward marching spirit, active in its questing and transcendent to life (dead) and in the Isles of the Blest.[44] These characteristics may also occur (as we set out in other chapters) as puer themes. Therefore, the puer can be readily caught up in heroics. But there is a difference, and this difference may be conceived in regard to death, the element we have considered central to the idea of the hero.

The son, the hero, and the puer may all die the same death. But I would hazard a suggestion about differences: the son's "death" is for the mother (Attis, say); the hero's "death" is because of the mother (Hercules and Hera, Baldur and Frigg, Achilles and Thetis[45]); the puer's death is independent of the mother. These distinctions are again one of attitude, perspective, not of mythical "fact," and bespeak the place that death holds within the psyche for son, hero, and puer. Where death means sacrifice (the son) or victory (hero) — "death, where is thy sting" — the mother is playing her significant role. Death connected with the senex, its survival, its depression, its penetrating insight, presents another image and emotion.

IX Son and great mother metamorphose into hero and serpent — or do they? Jung says that the hero and the dragon he overcomes are brothers or even one; the man who has power over the daemonic is himself touched by the daemonic.[46] Harrison wrote that the snake as *daimon* is the double of the hero; the early hero had snake form, and even the higher Gods (Ares, Apollo, Hermes, Zeus) have their serpent aspect as did Demeter and Athene.[47] If hero and serpent are one, then the battle turns the hero against his own nature. But what precisely does he turn against, and how does the animal double of his own structure, this daimon or dragon or serpent, become "mother"? Psychology's approach to this motif is usually in terms of development. "Development" has been the master-key to all the locked riddles in modern psychology, just as "fertility" once opened what we did not understand in mythology and archeology. The supposed development of consciousness occurs from a darker level to a lighter one, from only matter to also spirit, from only nature to also culture. This "development of consciousness" supposedly occurs historically in civilizations, phylogenetically in the species and race, and ontogenetically in each individual from maternal attachment to paternal self-reliance. The hero against serpent is thus *the paradigm* for the kernel structure in our personal and collective consciousness.

Were we to be interviewed by an aboriginal anthropologist from Australia for our "dream," our "Gods," and our "cosmology," this would be the story we would tell. We would tell of the struggle each day brings to Ego who must rise and do battle with Depression and Seduction and Entanglement, so as to keep the world safe from Chaos, Evil, and Regression, which coil round it like an oppressive Swallowing Serpent. This gives account to our inquirer of our peculiar irrationalities: why we sweep the streets, why we pay taxes, why we go to school and to war — all with compulsive ritualistic energy so as to keep the Serpent at bay. This is our true cosmology; for Ego, who changes rivers in their course and shoots to the moon, acts not out of hunger or Gods or tribal persecutions, as the inquiring aboriginal might imagine in his savage mind, so inert and lazy, bound to the maternal uroboros, with his "weak ego." No, our civilization's excessive activism is all to keep back the night of the Serpent, requiring a single monotheistic single-mindedness, a cyclop's dynamism of all the Gods which She and Ego have partaken in together at a Western banquet lasting three thousand years and perhaps now coming to its indigestible conclusion as Ego weakens in what we call "neurosis" and the swallowed Gods stir again in the imaginal dark of his shadow and of her belly. Ego and Unconscious, Hero and Serpent, Son and Mother, their battle, their bed and their banquet — this is the sustaining myth we must tell to account for our strange ways: why we are always at war, why we have eaten up the world, why we have so little imaginative power, and why we have only one God and He so far away.

Snake and dragon are *not* one and the same. The snake is a piece of nature and well represents instinctual being, especially the hard-to-grasp movements of introverting libido. But the dragon does not exist in external nature. It is a fantasy instinct, or the instinct of fantasy, which the hero slays, thereby becoming the single-minded ego of will-power. If the snake is the daimon of the instinctual psyche, the dragon, who shoots fire from his tongue and eyes, blazes with color, and controls the waters, who lives below our daily world but could as well with his wings inhabit the sky, is the daimon of our imaginal psyche. The masculine sword of reason in the masculine hand of will kills both snake and dragon, both instinct and imagination in daily combat as Ego enacts our central myth.

Undoubtedly, the dragon has moon associations; and the snake has feminine connotations in mythological and in psychological material and can be found in our culture in association with the Great Goddess. But the snake can as well be found with heroes, kings, and Gods. It is strongly sexual, phallic even, yet transcends gender. It appears in the religion of primordial man. (Adam, too, has his snake.) Like nature, instinct, libido, or the *mercurius* of alchemy — for each of which the serpent stands — it is a primordial form of life, or life in its primordiality, *Ur*-life. *The serpent is primordiality itself*, which can transform into anything, so that we experience it in sexuality, project it backward into ancestors as their ghost, envision it in earth or below it, hear its wisdom, fear its death.[48] It is a power, a numinosity, a primordiality of religion. Its meanings renew with its skin and peel off as we try to grasp hold. (The dragon's many heads say we cannot meet it with one idea alone.) The slippery flow of meanings makes it possible for Great Goddess and daimon to merge, to lose their distinction, so that by means of the serpent (Hera sending the snakes to baby Hercules) the mother gets at the puer and brings his fall into heroism. She tempts him into the fight for deliverance from her. By falling for the challenge he is delivered of his own daimon. Like Beowulf he dies when he kills the dragon. The Dragon-Fight is his undoing.

In the mixture of the three components — man, mother, snake — the snake loses its life, the man loses his snake, but the mother has her hero. This leaves him without wisdom, without chthonic depths, vital imagination, or phallic consciousness, a one-sided solar-hero for a civilization ruled by the mother or by the senex whose snakes have gone into the sewers. By losing chthonic consciousness, which means his psychoid *daimon* root that trails into the ancestors in Hades, he loses his root in death, becoming the real victim of the "Battle for Deliverance,"[49] and ready for Hebe. Because the heroic way to spirit goes against the snake, it is secretly a self-destruction.

By turning against the snake, heroic consciousness also tends to lose the other animals of the mother world, especially the cow of nature. With this goes the warmth, the muzzle and the eyes, the rumination and the slowness, the pastures for the soul, Hera as Hathor, the holiness of life and its rhythm. In the struggle for independence and self-reliance, he can no longer return to the stable without fearing decomposition. (Hercules cleans stables.) So of course heroic consciousness cannot get through, as fairy tales say, without the helpful animal. A consciousness that had not defined itself by refusing the animal in the first place would not be in this predicament of lost animal help, its sureness and knowledge of survival.

Furthermore, heroic consciousness constellates its fundamental opposite as feminine and as enemy. The great figures on whose patterns we build our ego strength — Oedipus and Hercules, Achilles, Hippolytus, and Orpheus — in different ways opposed the feminine and fell victim to it.[50] Could we not turn another way? Could we become conscious without that struggle? Ego development has so long been conceived through the heroics of tough aggression, paranoid misogyny, selfishness, and distance of feeling so typical of the mother's son that we have neglected other paths opened by the puer.

Must the feminine continue to be the primary enemy to be magnified into a magna mater whom one succumbs to, worships, or battles, but with whom one never simply pairs as equal though different? Whenever we are sons of this Great Feminine, the feminine is experienced as "great." Woman is idealized. She is endowed with the divine power to save or destroy. We look for the wonderful woman to be our salvation, which then constellates the other side, betrayal and destruction. Every idealization of the feminine is only a propitiation of her other components: the Amazons, the Furies, the Graeae, the Sirens, the Harpies, Circe, Phaedra, Medea, Baubo, Persephone, Hecate, Gorgo, Medusa. The expectation to be saved by a woman goes hand in hand with the fear of being destroyed by her.

Here we come upon one more difference between puer and heroic son. The magnification of the mother-complex is a sure sign that we are choosing the heroic role whose purpose is less spirit and less psyche than it is the traditional ego, its strengthening and its development. The epic dramas in which the hero is cast with impossible tasks, miraculous weapons, overwhelming enemies, and where mother is a dragon, witch, or Goddess can well make a man forget the ordinary mother in the case. But in many tales the mother is merely human, or a lowly nymph, reminding consciousness of its commonness. By keeping to this personal, ordinary, human mother, her specific pathological lacks and her unique graces, we can keep at our backs as support the sense of human ordinariness given by the limits of our *actual personal* mother-complex, what she passes to us and how we descend from her, for which we have gratitude. She is our history, and it is from her simple lap that we fell (*casus*) as a case. By keeping her in proportion, we can then reserve the *magnificatio* for the puer archetype itself, its narcissism and high-flying ambition to create. The hero's *hybris* (inflation) arises from his hidden identity with the mother; the puer's *superbia* (arrogance) reflects his cocky, narcissistic conviction that he is about his father's business, a child of the spirit, bearing its message.[51]

Released from these mystiques of the son-great mother, the feminine could show other individualities, as in the *Odyssey*. There the feminine plays many roles: Goddess (Athene), Mistress (Calypso), Devourer (Scylla and Charybdis), Enchantress (Circe), Mother-Daughter (Arete-Nausicaa), Personal Mother (Anticleia), Rescuer (Ino), Seductress (Sirens), Nurse (Eurykleia), and Wife (Penelope).[52] With each, man finds individual ways of coming to terms, loving and being furthered. There, the feminine does not threaten the eventual rapprochement of father and son. (But Odysseus, like the King figure in alchemy, is himself *senex-et-puer*.) The feminine in the *Odyssey* works throughout for the reunion of the divided house of Ithaca, giving us a model for the way in which feminine patterns can weave together puer and senex, rather than divide them further through the penchant of the great mother for heroics which magnify her into a man's main concern, literalizing his psychic reality, clouding his puer vision, and distracting him away from his puer necessities.

χ If I could sum up into one main thought the many ideas we have touched upon, it would be this. Jung makes a clear distinction between the role of the mother archetype as regressive and devouring, on the one hand, and as the creative matrix, on the other. He places this duality within the fantasy of another duality — the first and second halves of life. For young consciousness "entry into the mother" is a fatal incest; for old consciousness it is the way of renewal and even that which he calls the way of individuation.[53] We can free this important idea of Jung's from the frame of its presentation. First and second half, young and old, are another way of putting the puer-senex duality. They are structures of consciousness valid *always* and not only as they are divided from each other into first and second halves of life. Because our culture appears now to be in a period when its heroic ego has peaked and where the senex dominant, and so the puer complement, is now of extreme relevance, collective consciousness itself is in what Jung would call "the second half." For anyone in this culture at this time the battle with the mother and the heroic stance of the "first half" cannot but be archetypally wrong, regardless of one's age. This stance is anachronistic in the true sense of being out of tune with time, and every victory over the mother is a defeat for the fundamental task of the present culture: becoming aware of the senex in all its archetypal significance, relating puer phenomena to it, and releasing puer possibilities within it.

Notes

1. [Originally published in Patricia Berry, ed., *Fathers and Mothers: Five Papers on the Archetypal Background of Family Psychology* (Dallas: Spring Publications, 1973).] — Ed.

2. C. G. Jung's main remarks directly on the *puer aeternus* in relation with the mother-complex are in *Collected Works*, vol. 5: *Symbols of Transformation*, par. 393: "The lovely apparition of the *puer aeternus* is, alas, a form of illusion. In reality he is a parasite on the mother, a creature of her imagination, who only lives when rooted in the maternal body." Cf. par. 392, 394, 526 (but also passim in that volume on the mother's son and the hero) and *Collected Works*, vol. 16: *Practice of Psychotherapy*, par. 336 ("provisional life"). In *Collected Works*, vol. 9.1: *Archetypes and the Collective Unconsciousness*, "Psychological Aspects of the Mother Archetype," "The Psychology of the Child Archetype," and "On the Psychology of the Trickster Figure" are important for puer psychology in relation with and distinction from the mother. In *Collected Works* 13, "The Spirit Mercurius" is useful for some puer phenomenology independent of the mother-complex. For classical cases of the mother-complex in the son, see, for instance, *Collected Works*, vol. 7: *Two Essays in Analytical Psychology*, par. 167ff. and also J. Jacobi, "Symbols in an Individual Analysis," in *Man and His Symbols*, ed. C. G. Jung (London: Aldus, 1964), pp. 272ff. This last case might look quite different were it to have been viewed through the eyes of the puer-senex constellation.

Following Jung's early (pre-alchemical) view of the puer would be M.-L. von Franz: "With the concept of the eternal youth, *puer aeternus*, we in psychology describe a definite form of neurosis in men, which is distinguished by a fixation [*Steckenbleiben*] in the age of adolescence as a result of an all too strong mother-bind. The main characteristics are therefore those corresponding with C.G. Jung's elaborations in his essay on the mother archetype" ("Über religiöse Hintergründe des Puer-Aeternus Problems"), in A. Guggenbühl-Craig, ed., *The Archetype* (Basel: Karger, 1964), p. 141 (trans. mine); and J.L. Henderson, *Thresholds of Initiation* (Middletown, CT: Wesleyan University Press, 1967), p. 24: "We may conjecture that when things go wrong with the archetype of the *puer aeternus*, it is because the mother is too demanding or too rejecting, thus frustrating the youth in his normal orientation to the feminine principle as anima-function, or because the youth for some other reason falls into a passive-dependent attitude upon the mother or her substitute." In the same vein: E. Neumann and M.E. Harding, whose works are cited below in the relevant places, and also G.F. Heyer, "*Die Grosse Mutter im Seelenleben des heutigen Menschen,*" *Eranos Jahrbuch* 6 (1938), pp. 454, 474. For intimations of a new view of the puer, this time in connection with Artemis (rather than the mother): R. Malamud, "The Amazon Problem," in J. Hillman, ed., *Facing the*

Gods (Dallas: Spring Publications, 1980), pp. 47–66; T. Moore, "Artemis and Puer," in J. Hillman, ed., *Puer Papers* (Dallas: Spring Publications, 1979).

3. Not all young male figures show the same pattern. For instance: Hercules is threatened by Hera and even complains of being driven mad by her, while Icarus is altogether with the father; Ganymede and Hyacinthus are loved by male figures, Zeus and Apollo. The interest of the mothers in Achilles, Theseus, and Perseus is more protective than erotic, so, too, in the Nordic, Baldur, and in Moses, Jacob, and Jesus. In these latter examples, where protection and pushing the son forward are the mother's concern, the entanglement through incestuous libido is not the paramount theme. Each mythologem tells another story. The differences are more important for an individual destiny than are the generalizations about the "mother-complex."

There are as well differences among the heroes. Various types have been sorted out: messianic hero, culture hero, suffering martyr, trickster, etc. Just as the word "hero" of mythology has become the word "ego" of psychology, so there is a variety of heroic styles as there is a variety of ego styles. What is characteristic of both hero and ego is the central importance of action. Action may be expressed by deeds, by importance of honor and reputation, by a remarkable journey or, in reverse, by desolate, impotent suffering. For action the specific psychological attitude of literalizing is necessary. Both hero and ego — no matter the variety of styles and differences between, say, the Venus-hero and the Mars-hero and the Apollo-hero — require a literalization of the challenge. The maiden must be won, the dragon fought, the culture produced, the death accomplished. Literalism, in my view, is a more fundamental trait of hero psychology than the compulsion to act.

4. Cf. my discussion of this theme in both *The Myth of Analysis* (Evanston: Northwestern University Press, 1972), pp. 169-90, and in *Revisioning Psychology* (New York: Harper & Row, 1975).

5. [Cf. J. Hillman, "Oedipus Revisited," in *Oedipus Variations: Studies in Literature and Psychoanalysis* (Dallas: Spring Publications, 1991)] — Ed.

6. C. G. Jung, *Collected Works*, vol.16, par. 181.

7. Concerning the father (and the senex) as meaning and order, see Chapter 9. See also A. Vitale, "Saturn: The Transformation of the Father," in P. Berry, ed., *Fathers and Mothers: Five Papers on the Archetypal Background of Family Psychology* (Dallas: Spring Publications, 1991) and L. Zoja, *The Father: Historical, Psychological and Cultural Perspectives*, trans. H. Martin (Philadelphia: Brunner-Routledge, 2001).

8. "These are three essential aspects of the mother: her cherishing and nourishing goodness, her orgiastic emotionality, and her Stygian depths," and as Jung goes on to say, *not* "discriminating knowledge" (*Collected Works*, vol. 9.1, par. 158).

9. C. G. Jung, *Collected Works*, vol. 5, par. 199.

10. R.B. Onians, *The Origins of European Thought* (Cambridge University Press, 1954), pp. 349–95.

11. Cf. J. Fontenrose, *Python: A Study of Delphic Myth* (Berkeley: University of California Press, 1959), p. 582, for references to the Venusberg-Siren theme, relevant to the mother-anima contamination.

12. "The Roman ceremonies which were held in Attis's honor during the month of March were divided into two principal parts: the *tristia*, the commemoration of Attis's passion and death, and the *hilaria*, the festivities of his followers, who believed that the god comes to life again after a long winter sleep" (M.J. Vermaseren, *The Legend of Attis in Greek and Roman Art* [Leiden: E.J. Brill, 1966], p. 39). Attis is another of the appearing and disappearing Gods whose cyclical return has been interpreted as the vegetative rhythm and the *tristia* and *hilaria* ultimately as fertility rituals. By substituting "libido" for "fertility," we can transpose the entire pattern from the external and natural to the internal and psychological level. Then the *tristia* and *hilaria* refer to the rhythm of the libido, the discontinuities (comings and goings) of the puer impulse, at whose appearance we rejoice and feel Spring, and in whose absence there is the sadness of Winter, which Attis too represented (i.e., his senex side). These seasons and this fertility are not just "out there" in nature but "inside" experienced as the natural cycle of psychic energy.

13. Curious how the mother archetype has encroached upon areas that once belonged to other archetypes. The earth in ancient Egyptian mythology was Geb, a God (not a Goddess). The sea, taken so stereotypically in the analytical interpretation of dreams as a "symbol for" (hence, "sign of") the collective unconscious as matrix and thus as the maternal element, was once the province of Father Okeanos, who was a source of all things (Homer), and the rivers of life were fathering river Gods, e.g., Achelous, Poseidon (Helikon). Cf. K. Kerényi, "Man and Mask" in *Spiritual Disciplines: Papers from the Eranos Yearbooks 4* (London: Routledge, 1961), p. 158.

In C.G. Jung's English-language *Collected Works*, the only archetype that consistently receives capital letters is the Great Mother, an honoring not offered to the wise old man, anima, animus, or even self; the "gods" and "goddesses" are also written small.

14. [See Chapter 8.] — Ed.

15. C.G. Jung, *Collected Works*, vol. 8: *Structure & Dynamics of the Psyche*, par. 211, 213.

16. The best short treatment of Dionysus in English is that of W.F. Otto, *Dionysus: Myth and Cult*, trans. R. Palmer (Indiana University Press, 1981). The most complete is K. Kerényi, *Dionysos: Archetypal Image of Indestructible Life*, trans. R. Manheim (Princeton University Press, 1976). I have given further literature on Dionysus in my *The Myth of Analysis*, pp. 258–81 and have reviewed how

Jung regards this figure in my "Dionysos in Jung's Writings," in J. Hillman, ed., *Facing the Gods* (Dallas: Spring Publications, 1992, pp. 151–64.

17. E. Neumann, whose main line of thinking (feeling?) is within the mother archetype, of course places Dionysus in her train. He speaks of Leonardo's painting of Bacchus as a portrayal of the puer aeternus: "The relaxed and indolent way in which the hermaphroditic god sits resting in the countryside is wholly in keeping with the ancient conception of Dionysus . . . Leonardo, unconsciously no doubt, portrayed a central figure of the matriarchal mystery world, closely related to the vulture goddess. For Dionysus is the mystery god of feminine existence." He continues this for several paragraphs; his point is that Dionysus is another "divine luminous son of the Great Mother" (E. Neumann, "Leonardo and the Mother Archetype," in his *Art and the Creative Unconscious*, trans. R. Manheim, Bollingen Series [New York: Pantheon, 1959], p. 70). I would not disabuse the reader from Neumann's view: any archetype may be viewed from within any perspective so that Dionysian events may well be seen as matriarchal. I would only disabuse the reader from Neumann's argument, as if it were based on evidence. The vulture has nothing to do either with Dionysus or with the puer; Egypt is only one of many "alien" and "border" areas from which Dionysus and his cult were said to spring; Dionysus did not come "late to Greece" (Neumann) but appears even in the early Cretan culture. Mythical statements about archetypes are anyway to be read mythically, psychologically, and not historically, literally.

There is a significant difference between Jung and Neumann in regard to the puer nature of Dionysus. Although Jung does once place Dionysus (Iacchus/Zagreus) as a *puer aeternus* within the Eleusinian mystery cult, and thus within the mother archetype (C. G. Jung, *Collected Works*, vol. 5, pars. 526–27), he noted already in 1911 (Ibid., par. 184): "The double figure of the adult and infant Dionysus. . . " speaking of him in the context of the "giant and dwarf," "big and little," "father and son." Thus Jung saw what Neumann did not: Dionysus is himself a *senex-et-puer* and can as well be regarded from this perspective as from within that of the mother.

18. Cf. M. P. Nilsson, "The Dionysiac Mysteries of the Hellenistic and Roman Age," *Skrift. Utgv. Svenska Instit. Athen* 8/5 (1957), p. 111.

19. [A lengthy excursion on Leonardo da Vinci and his childhood vision of a kite, with challenges to Freud's and Neumann's interpretations of this event, has been extracted from the text at this point and placed in the appendix.] — Ed.

20. For a more thorough sketch of the mobility of the complex among different archetypal dominants and their perspectives, see my *The Myth of Analysis*, pp. 40–49, where I present the notion (and complex) of creativity as it can be experienced by seven different archetypal structures.

21. H. W. Parke, *Greek Oracles* (London: Hutchinson, 1967), p. 87.

22. C. G. Jung, *Collected Works*, vol. 8, par. 223.

23. Ibid., par. 429.

24. Edgar Wind, *Pagan Mysteries in the Renaissance* (Harmondsworth: Penguin, 1967), p. 196.

25. C. G. Jung's classic work *Symbols of Transformation* (*Collected Works*, vol. 5) provides a full description of the development of consciousness in terms of the hero's struggle with the mother. More or less in the same line are the works of E. Neumann, *The Origins and History of Consciousness*, Bollingen Series (New York: Pantheon, 1954), esp. pp. 44–52, and M. E. Harding, *Psychic Energy: Its Source and Goal*. It is against this background of classic Jungian literature that my critique of the heroic way should be read.

26. See J. Hillman, *Anima: An Anatomy of a Personified Notion* (Woodstock, CT: Spring Publications, 1996).

27. S. Freud, "New Introductory Lectures" in *The Standard Edition of the Complete Works of Sigmund Freud* (London: Hogarth and the Institute of Psycho-Analysis), vol. 22, p. 80.

28. "Oedipus Revisited," in K. Kerényi and J. Hillman, *Oedipus Variations: Studies in Literature and Psychoanalysis* (Dallas: Spring Publications, 1991) [UE 6: *Mythical Figures*].

29. C. G. Jung, *Collected Works*, vol. 5, par. 540.

30. On the Hercules-Christ identifications, see E. R. Goodenough, *Jewish Symbols in the Greco-Roman Period*, Bollingen Series X (New York: Pantheon, 1964), pp. 122–23 with notes, and M. Simon, *Hercule et le Christianism* (Paris: *Publications de la Faculté des Lettres de l'Université de Strasbourg* 2. sér. no. 19, 1955); also, G. K. Galinsky, *The Herakles Theme* (Oxford: Blackwell, 1972).

31. K. Kerényi, "Evil in Greek Mythology can be symbolized by the knife . . . A man desires to kill if he is 'evil,' and that is the nature of the 'evil'" ("The Problem of Evil in Mythology," in *Evil* [Evanston: Northwestern University Press, 1967], pp. 15ff.)

32. C. G. Jung, *Collected Works*, vol. 5, par. 515

33. See P. Slater's *The Glory of Hera* (Boston: Beacon, 1971). The book reviews the major Greek mythical figures, especially heroes, and sees them all from within the sociology of the mother-complex, represented by Hera. The Gods and heroes he treats are ultimately projections of different styles of the mother-complex. His view is not archetypal; that is, he has not learned from Jung that ". . . we are obliged to reverse our rationalistic causal sequence, and instead of deriving these figures from our psychic conditions, must derive our psychic conditions from these figures" (C. G. Jung, *Collected Works*, vol. 13: *Alchemical Studies*, par. 299).

34. K. Kerényi, *The Heroes of the Greeks* (London: Thames and Hudson, 1959), p. 193.

35. J. Fontenrose, *Python*, pp. 256–60.

36. For insights on the psychological importance of Ares, see R. Grinnell, "Reflections on the Archetype of Consciousness," *Spring* 1970, pp. 25–28; and E. C. Whitmont, "On Aggression," pp. 52ff. in the same volume; also R. Malamud, "The Amazon Problem," pp. 50–52, 54. See also my essay "Wars, Arms, Rams, Mars: On the Love of War," in *Facing Apocalypse* (Dallas: Spring Publications, 1987), pp. 117–36.

37. For the psychological importance of Hephaistos, see M. Stein, "Hephaistos: A Pattern of Introversion," in J. Hillman, ed., *Facing the Gods*, pp. 67–86.

38. W. K. C. Guthrie, *The Greeks and Their Gods* (London: Methuen, 1968), p. 70. The Hera of Argos was called the "Goddess of the yoke."

39. J. Fontenrose, *Python*, p. 119, n. 53. Further on the name of Hercules, see M. P. Nilsson, *The Mycenean Origin of Greek Mythology* (Cambridge, 1932), pp. 189ff. Nilsson, however, misses the psychological point that the opposites are one when he writes that the name of Herakles is clearly composed of Hera and *kles* but finds it "forced and improbable" that Hercules should be called "the fame of Hera . . . while this goddess dealt the severest blow to him and imposed pain, grief, and labor upon him."

40. We may read the following description of the hero in the light of psychology's ideals of "ego-strength": "the Homeric hero loved battle, and fighting was his life . . . A hero's activity . . . is concentrated on the most testing kind of action, war . . ." "The hero must use his superior qualities at all times to excel and win applause . . . He makes honor his paramount code, and glory the driving force and aim of his existence . . . his ideals are courage, endurance, strength and beauty . . . he relies upon his own ability to make the fullest use of his powers." "The heroic outlook shook off primitive superstitions and taboos by showing that man can do amazing things by his own effort and by his own nature, indeed that he can almost rise above his own nature . . ." M. Grant, *Myths of the Greeks and Romans* (New York: Mentor Books, 1962), pp. 45–47. This description covers heroic consciousness as such and not only its extraverted manifestations. The same attitudes and the same battle can take place in the confines of a consulting room, as the heroic attitude wrestles introvertedly with "the unconscious" in order to rise above its own nature.

41. [For exploration of the wandering and longing theme, see Chapter 6.] — Ed.

42. A. Brelich, *Gli eroci* (Rome: Ediziono dell'Ateneo, 1958); L. R. Farnell, *Greek Hero Cults and Ideas of Immortality* (Oxford: The Clarendon Press, 1921); J. Fontenrose, *Python*, op. cit.; K. Kerényi, *The Heroes of the Greeks*, op. cit.; A. D. Nock, "The Cult of Heroes," *Harvard Theological Review* 37 (1944); J. Campbell, *The Hero with a Thousand Faces* (New York: Pantheon Books, 1949); M. E. Harding, "The Inner Conflict: The Dragon and the Hero," in *Psychic Energy*, op. cit.; E. Neumann, *The Origins and History of Consciousness*, op. cit.; G. Roheim,

"The Dragon and the Hero," *American Imago* 1, 2, 3 (1940). This list is by no means intended to be complete, especially as it does not extend into the area of heroic literature (epic) or the hero in various sorts of fiction, nor does it refer to the hero figure in nonclassical accounts, e.g., fairytale and folklore and in exotic cultures, etc. For a comparative study of the hero in poetry and the heroic style, see C. M. Bowra's massive opus, *Heroic Poetry* (London: Macmillan, 1961).

43. For more on the underworld affiliations of the hero see my *The Dream and the Underworld* (New York: Harper & Row, 1979), pp. 110ff.

44. Frequently, the hero is translated to the Isles of the Blest without "dying." He simply "leaves the scene," because a God favors him, and is removed into isolation (Cf. E. Rohde, *Psyche*, 8th ed. [London: Routledge, 1925], 64–76). Often it is the mother who raises the hero to immortality — Phaethon by Aphrodite, Telegonos by Circe, Achilles by Thetis, Memnon by Eos, but Hercules from his flaming funeral pyre was borne aloft by Zeus. The Isles of the Blest are ruled over by Kronos (the senex), so that even in this mythologem there recurs the motif of the reunion with the senex, the mother being in these cases the detour (through heroism) and then the necessary helper.

45. The overt cause of Achilles' death is Apollo (or Paris), but the spot hit is the heel, that place where Thetis held Achilles while dipping him into invulnerability. His ultimate cause of death was precisely where she had touched and held him to keep him safe.

46. C. G. Jung, *Collected Works*, vol. 5, par. 575, 580, 593, 671; cf. M. E. Harding, *Psychic Energy*, 259ff. Harding makes the hero-dragon issue excessively moral, as if she were in a Christian version of that myth herself, saying of the kinship between dragon and dragon slayer: "The renegade in man is closely related in its nature to the slothful aspect of the dragon, while the forward-going, heroic element in him is more nearly related to the energy of the dragon. Thus the human being who has conquered the dragon and assimilated its power through tasting its blood or eating its heart becomes a superman." If dragon be translated into "the unconscious," what high hopes, what Nietzschean hopes, analysis bodes the striving ego! If dragon be translated into "imagination" or "vitality" or "Mercurius," what devastation!

47. On the snake forms of the Gods and heroes, see J. Harrison, *Themis*, section "Daimon and Hero"; E. Kuster, *Die Schlange in der Griechischen Kunst und Religion* (Giessen: A. Töpelmann, 1913); J. Fontenrose, *Python*, passim. Artemidorus (*Oneirocriticus* 1, 13) said that the "snake is the symbol of all gods to whom it is sacred, viz. Zeus, Sabazius, Helios, Demeter, Core, Hecate, Asclepius, and the Heroes." On Apollo and snake, K. Kerényi, "Apollonian Epiphanies," in his *Apollo: The Wind, the Spirit, and the God: Four Studies*, trans. Jon Solomon (Dallas: Spring Publications, 1983), pp. 21–45.

48. Cf. "A Snake is not a Symbol" in J. Hillman and M. McLean, *Dream Animals* (San Franciso: Chronicle Books, 1997), pp. 25–29.

49. C.G. Jung, *Collected Works*, vol. 5, part two, chap. 6.

50. See note 52 below for details.

51. [See Chapter 10 for a full discussion of these themes.] — Ed.

52. See W.B. Stanford, Chapter 4: "Personal Relationships," in his *The Odysseus Theme* (Dallas: Spring Publications, 1993). In contrast with ODYSSEUS, let us review the relation to feminine figures in certain other Greek heroes. OEDIPUS belonged to the race Spartoi, "Dragon people," supposedly a matriarchy without paternal principle. He did not recognize his own father because "The child does not know his own begetter, and this is what makes patricide possible" (J.J. Bachofen, *Myth, Religion, and Mother Right*, trans. R. Manheim, Bollingen Series [Princeton University Press, 1967], pp. 180–81). As OEDIPUS is conceived in the line of the Dragons, so is he inconceivable without that complementary mother /dragon, first as Sphinx (sent by Hera, or her fantasy), then as Jocasta. HERCULES' relation with women is summed up by Bachofen (p. 176): "It is characteristic that Hercules alone of all the heroes remained on board the Argo and reproached his friends for lying with the Amazons. . . . In all his myths he is the irreconcilable foe of matriarchy, the indefatigable battler of Amazons, the misogynist, in whose sacrifice no woman takes part, by whose name no woman swears, and who finally meets his death from a woman's poisoned garment." ACHILLES, of the Greek heroes at Troy, was the only one who was a son of a Goddess (K. Kerényi, *Heroes*, p. 347) and was finally overcome by an arrow of Paris, the favorite of Aphrodite and the paramour of Helen. Although a most unheroic and unmilitaristic figure, Paris of "the soft weak ways" (R. Bespaloff, *On the Iliad*, Bollingen Series [New York: Pantheon, 1947], p. 64) is the one who overcomes ACHILLES. Paris is the Achilles' heel of the hero. HIPPOLYTUS was slain through the revenge of Aphrodite whom he had spurned. ORPHEUS, as Vergil and Ovid describe him, shunned entirely the company of women after he had lost Eurydice — or did his misogyny result in her loss to the serpent's bite? (W.K.C. Guthrie, *Orpheus and Greek Religion* [London: Methuen, 1952], p. 31). He let no women in his cult; and thus "in the established tradition it is the women of Thrace who make him their victim" (ibid., p. 32). Aeschylus, who is the earliest source for the legend of his death, presents the Maenads of Dionysus as his slayers. But, as Guthrie points out (ibid., p. 33), other legends tell it differently: the women themselves excluded by Orphic misogyny took their revenge. Furthermore, earlier evidence of vase paintings shows him not torn to pieces (maenad-style), but speared and hacked and stoned by women in a melée of feminine wrath rather than in a Dionysian ritual. However we view it, the point remains: feminine figures were his enemy and did him in. Achilles' son NEOPTOLEMOS ("renewer of war"), also called PYRRHOS ("red-head")

(M. Delcourt, *Pyrrhos et Pyrrha: Recherches sur les Valeurs du Jeu dans les Legendes Helleniques*, Bibl. Faculté Philos. et Lettres, Univ. de. Liége [Paris, 1965], chap. 2), is the one who murders Priam of Troy and the boy infant who would have been the carrier of its line (Euripides, *Trojan Women*). "Vase paintings often combine the death of the old king and that of his grandson at the hands of Neoptolemo" (M.L. Scherrer, *The Legends of Troy* [London: Phaidon, 1964], p. 123). This renewer of Achilles' spirit is the murderer of a senex-puer pair, and he follows the heroic pattern by meeting death at the hands of women: either at the instigation of the Pythian priestess or in the form of a Pyrrhus, King of Epirus, killed by a woman who hurls a tile at him from a rooftop. What comes first: killed by a woman, his woman-killer nature, or his killing the senex-puer pair? Contrast Odysseus!

53. C. G. Jung, *Collected Works*, vol. 5, par. 459.

5

Notes on Verticality: Creation, Transcendence, Ambition, Erection, Inflation [1]

In the general mind the notion of the creative person is strongly colored by puer characteristics. Precocious genius, incredible outpouring of gifts, affliction and early death: Keats and Mozart; van Gogh, Raphael, Schubert, and the brilliant boy mathematicians, chess-masters, physicists. The puer archetype has over-determined the definition of creativity. Who thinks of Hobbes who did all his lasting thinking between the ages of forty and ninety, or Locke who was near to sixty when he published, or the master-painters whose great works come out of late life? Instead we describe creativity in puer terms limiting the idea to joyful magic, original novelty, exquisite beauty, sudden spontaneity, wounded vulnerability, lofty inspiration. [2] The brilliant Harvard psychologist who bore puer traits himself, H. A. Murray condensed these traits into the one hallmark of puer creativity: "ascensionism." [3] Even "genius" refers originally to a daimon or spirit belonging to a world above or below this daily one and, when personified, appears as a winged being or carrying phallic characteristics and announced in symbols of seed, spark, flame, angel.

Characteristic of puer creativity is the envisioned project spurting up from the unknown or alighting out of the blue. Without precedent, acausal, self-generated. The gift depends on no-one, not even on the gifted person who receives it. Shooting in from the dark beyond as inversions of the autochthonous imagination, these little hunches of extraordinary power have been imaged by folklore and myths as inventive elves, dactyls (phallic fingers), kabiroi, dwarves, and as the green sprouts and flowers among which Eros and other pueri appear.

Whether the "place" of origin is above or below, whether angel descending or dactyl emerging, what matters is verticality — the break in and break with the horizontal outlook of the daily world and its incessant continuity. At that intersection a seed is planted, but no home is made on earth. A flash not a foothold, the whisper of a wing, a passing angel, or, as they once said of such breaks in continuity, "Hermes passing." Like a *coup de foudre* when Eros ignites and one falls in love at first sight with a stranger. These moments cannot be constructed, nor deconstructed, no matter how many explanatory elements are said to compose the flash. Consciousness crystallizes into a new and strange, yet nostalgically familiar, structure. The radical has broken the regular. This is the creative effect of the puer.

Because for puer consciousness "transcendence to everything given" becomes ascendance over everything given, upwardness directs all endeavors. The spirit must soar, Eros must flame, insight must produce the overarching view. Icarus would reach the sun, Bellerophon sails skyward on a horse's white wings, Phaethon races the solar chariot through the heavens — all unable to inhibit the upward compulsion. At home in the air, like falcons whirling and sailing among thoughts, schemes, and fantasies of amazing actions. Gawain and Galahad on the aspiring quest of knighthood bore falcon names: "white falcon" and "falcon of summer."[4]

Another hawk of summer's heat when the sun is high in the sky, Harry Hotspur, states his ambitions in vertical terms:

> By heaven me thinks it were an easy leap
> To pluck bright honour from the pale-fac'd moon,
> Or dive into the bottom of the deep,
> Where fathom-line could never touch the ground . . .
> And pluck up drowned honour by the locks.[5]

Limitless verticality is the way of valor. (Different indeed from the puer's *pothos* exemplified in Alexander's longing outward beyond the horizon.[6]) In the passages immediately surrounding Hotspur's speech, his father and his uncle diagnose Harry's condition: "He apprehends a world of figures . . . imagination of some great exploit / Drives him beyond the bounds of patience." Hotspur does "touch the ground" at the end of the play. Dying from wounds, he feels himself caught by time, and slain not by his actual enemy and heroic counterpart, the other Henry, but by the senex (time, Chronos). In his final speech he mourns his own divine youth: "O, Harry! Thou hast robbed me of my youth." Life is "time's fool"; "O! I could prophesy, / But that the earthy and cold hand of death / Lies on my tongue." He is wounded in his "thoughts," he declares, worse than in his "flesh."[7]

Only death seems able to silence puer loquacity, the identification with the outpouring of fiery logos, his thoughts as prophesies, himself as message-bearer. He ends on earth or in earth because death's hand shuts his mouth, ends his boastful speech, and thus the meaning of his life. The earth and its heavy worldly matters is not the scene for this structure, not the place of its reality.

Hotspur's excess derives from a world of "figures," — the imaginal, the Gods — which drive him beyond bounds. The images which his fantasy apprehends apprehend him and carry him off. Another young figure, Ganymede, is carried away by the spirit which comes as a great divine bird, seizing and lifting him to the Olympian Gods whom he then serves far away from earth. This bird is carnivorous. The spirit eats the flesh, driving body beyond its powers and to its death, as with Hotspur, or as an ascending passion of spiritual desire where soul is abused by spirit and the flesh ignored.

Perhaps the earliest cultural image of this great bird of the spirit is the primordial falcon of Horus. He is the supreme exemplar of the vertical compulsion which calls to each puer hero. No sooner is Horus born, this falcon-boy (of whom Isis, his mother, had a dream that he would redeem his patrimony) "soars up into the sky, beyond the flight of the original bird-soul, beyond the stars and all the divinities of olden time."[8]

> I am Horus, the great Falcon. . . My flight has reached the horizon. I have passed by the gods of Nut. I have gone further than the gods of old. Even the most ancient bird could not equal my very first flight. I have removed my place beyond the powers of

Seth, the foe of my father Osiris. No other god could have done
what I have done. I have brought the ways of eternity to the
twilight of the morning. I am unique in my flight.[9]

No doubt his mother propels him, and Isis declares as the birth
begins: "Make way! It is a falcon that is within my body!"[10] Let us here
not miss a subtle clue that the Oedipus complex of psychoanalysis
may blind us to: In the archetypal feeling of Isis, mother of one and
wife of the other, there is no divisive enmity. She favors their union.
Isis does not set son against father, anymore than Penelope comes between Telemachos and Odysseus.[11]

Although the mother complex may drive the heroic component
of the puer, nurse its vulnerability and weep for its agonies, the falcon
-boy[12] depends ultimately on its own force, the puer force, and is
compelled by its own archetypal authenticity. In Horus's case this
force lies in the eye, hence the horror when his eyes are torn out by
his perpetual enemy, Seth, God of storm and confusion, of blind brute
strength, bullying and ballsy. Where Seth's strength comes from the
testicles (which Horus wrenches from him), "Horus's aggressiveness is
in the Eye."[13]

Horus's boast ("beyond the stars and all the divinities of olden
time") reveals much about verticality. Its transcendence has a particular aim: "gods of old." It would redeem the father by surpassing the
father. In the puer is a father-drive — not to find him, reconcile with
him, be loved and receive a blessing, but rather to transcend the father
which act redeems the father's limitations. He must overrule olden
times and old Gods because they are already familiar and institutional-
ized and therefore trapped in time and history. Transcendence aims to
bring "the ways of eternity," a New Age, that is not merely a temporal
progress beyond the old, but is founded in eternity, the timeless and
everlasting. The transcendent drive seeks not improvement, but revolution, a re-founding of the kingdom upon eternal principles. The only
truly new is that which is ever new, beyond ageing, transcendent to
time altogether. Puer rhetoric rails against the old not because it lives
in a simple contrast between the fresh and young versus the worn and
weary, but because the wisdom of the old is worldly, learned from

history, accumulated from time, and this blocks the puer's access to eternity, its source and home, and its goal.

Horus's eye reveals another trait. The puer demand for knowledge has an instinctual fury; it is the demand of a rapacious bird. The sharp insight, the pounce and talons of inquiry are hawk-like, part of the animal compulsion to ascend beyond the heavier manner of Seth by means of knowledge. [14] (The hawk in the *Odyssey* is a swift messenger of Apollo). The upper aspect of instinct urges consciousness toward a mimesis of the higher Gods; consciousness burns to bring to the light of day by experiment and exploration whatever is in the dark. The dark, the unknown, is the challenge of Seth, and the answer to that challenge is the falcon, an all-seeing, never-closing hungry eye, way up high and looking down, enacted in any scientific endeavor and its progressive attempts to go beyond everything known — often killing what it seizes and therefore unconsciously akin to its enemy Seth, one of the Lords of Death. A paradigm shift from a science that kills to a science that serves requires profound re-orientation of the puer struc-ture from transcendence to immanence and from spirit to soul.

Akin to the hawk is the buzzard, [15] ripping into the corpus of "dead" tradition, the old authorities turning the past into a corpse from which the puer steals and upon which his ideas feed with scant acknowledge-ment of what they have offered simply for the taking.

Even as we are considering puer psychology in and of itself, the archetypal forms of existence, like the Gods themselves, never appear alone. [16] They are always incestuous, contaminated one with another, much as our human complexes cannot be captured by denominated definitions, each with its border, each with a set of symbolic represen-tations. That attempt at reductive definition was the cardinal mistake of the earlier phase of psychoanalytic investigation: tracking and at-tributing exactly what belonged to the oral or anal stage of develop-ment, to the mother, the hero, the shadow, and so on. Erich Neu-mann's oversized volume, *The Great Mother* with its excess baggage of symbols remains the *reductio ad absurdam* of this literalization of "who belongs to whom." The pull-out chart of these symbols shows that all becomes everything and the attempt at knowledge dissolves in its own thoroughness, even if his work does bear witness to the amalgamating power of the archetype he is attempting to circumscribe. The Mother can swallow all differentiations into her great maw.

Archetypal contamination, or indefinite borders, means that the puer impetus cannot be restricted to only so-called puer phenomena and persons who exhibit a puer style. Rather, any complex including those with little puer flavor such as anal obsessiveness, motherly tenderness, sensual indulgence, heroic nobility, dutiful bourgeois citizenship can fall prey to the puer daimon, becoming a cause that sets one on the upward path. As soon as we carry a torch, no matter what for, the puer has entered the drama.

‖ We are quick to judge the puer style from the point of view of our ego or of his. But puer ambition is not ego-made, and the satisfaction of ambition is only indirectly an ego-satisfaction. To affirm his point of service to higher principles beyond himself, the puer-man can go to the extreme of sacrificing himself to the cause. Not the ego sends his spirit so high, but the spirit sends his ego there. Ambition precedes its carrier. The ego is pre-patterned by the archetypal drive to ascend. Verticality is embedded in ego structure (not only because what is meant by ego structure is Western, patriarchal, white and male). The differentiated, set apart, individualized and erect *Ich* arises of its own accord, like a vegetable stalk in springtime, like a herm, like the crawling baby pulling itself upright.

As the senex stands behind the ego of the small child claiming its kingdom and defending its demands, so the puer gives the ego its ambitious spirit. Inherent in human nature is the transcendent capacity to rise above and walk at cross purposes with the horizontal world. We can, of course, stand too straight with pride (*superbia*) and fly too high with inflation (*hubris*), but ambition learns little from advice and heeds no caution. It must overreach, catch fire, readily combustible for a risk, a ride, a love, or for an idea. "Flaming youth," "carrying a torch," "consumed by passion," a burning in the breast that concretizes into tubercular consumption that took the lives of poets, composers, writers, painters long before a "mid-life crisis", many not even reaching thirty. The collapse and fall into the world of soul-making as well as the wounds that attend upon puer perfection and high-flying ambition are structurally embedded in the myths. The laming and bleeding, the betrayals, and the depressions in the dark vales can only be mentioned here because they reserve chapters for themselves.

The classical symbols are the hot eye of the sun, the firebird, feathered arrow, flame. The puer ascends with fire because he is "on fire." "Love on, flame on!" writes Michelangelo in one of his love poems, written not by a young man but in the puer gender. "For none can move/ From earth to heaven save upon such wings."[17] Here is Horus again, whose ambition is born from the sun as he is borne sunward, like Icarus, like Phaethon, like the young men (*kouretes*) of ancient Greece who "belonged" to Apollo.[18] This is the verticality of adolescence, the erection of the body, the body in erection, stretching upward.

III The erected penis is therefore a hallmark of puer consciousness. Puer phallicism and puer pornographies demonstrate the special fascination of this organ for this style of existence. This because the organ is not just anatomy, the erection not merely physiology, anymore than the anatomical heart is the seat of love, courage or imagination. A tumescent penis is a transubstantiation into flesh and blood of the archetypal erection: verticality, ascensionism. Erection as miracle, as blatant manifestation of invisible spirits; divinity in the flesh.[19]

Because it lives or dies in accord with the fantasies that ensoul it, erection is a function of imagination, *par excellence*, imagination as physiology,[20] a mystery reducible to neither a material nor a symbolic cause. Hence the central place of the phallus in the mysteries of Eleusis, the worship of Siva, the Tree of the Kabbalah and the cult of Dionysus — none of which, by the way, are exclusively male. The primordial penis-wrapper is the mystery which shrouds it.

Little Dick, Peter, Big Boy, and Jolly Roger, and all its other nicknames personify the daimonic companion, the puer archetype concretized in anatomy announcing his presence, relaying messages, displaying his radical independence. The Freudians have long noted the constellation of psychological factors sharing their life with the penis. This bundle of attributes they have named "urethral erotism."[21] Here belongs ambition, competition and arrogance, and the downfall that follows, sometimes experienced through the abject weakness of impotence and bed-wetting. H. A. Murray's brilliant essay on the Icarus complex elaborates these traits and symptoms in an exemplary case.[22]

Erection combines so many puer qualities — transcendence, spontaneity, verticality, heat, erotic fantasy, creativity, assertive masculinity, insuppressible demonstrativity, sensitive vulnerability — and it is such an especial embodiment of Hermes, Dionysus, Siva, and the Trickster that the erected penis can never be circumscribed by any one account. Its activities are therefore always multifarious and polyvalent.

Though vivid in the iconography and legends of these "pagan" divinities, in the images of Christ whose puer qualities inspire a world religion, erection is notably absent.[23] His genitals are quite out of the picture, displaced or sublimated: erection into Resurrection and the Feast of the Ascension that celebrates the Risen Christ. So markedly absent, so hidden is the penis of the modern adult Jesus that from a pagan and earlier Christian perspective (sensed intuitively by D. H. Lawrence[24]) just here is where to look for Christianity's *deus absconditus*.

A standard Latin word for the phallus was *fascinum*, meaning a state of bewitchment. An erection transposes its bearer and its witness into a symbolic condition, enchanted, fascinated, bewitched. In this moment of magic, spirit and matter are indissolubly joined, concurrently active and utterly dependent on each other. The Victorian students[25] of exotic tribes and curious sexual practices were caught by the *fascinosum* and literalized the magic in their descriptions of fertility rites, phallic cults, fetish objects, charms, cuttings, markings and wrappings. The explanation of these customs, and "perversions," is usually in terms of something else — overcoming castration anxiety, separation from the Great Mother, fertility rituals for crops and offspring — but not in terms of the magic of the erection itself and its transforming enchantment of consciousness. N. O. Brown[26] sees the primitive magician in the phallic cult of the archaic herm and Hermes, but Brown does not accord enough magic to the phenomenon of erection itself.

Curious to note that the phalloi in the tales of Trickster, the statues of the lingam and in most herms are rarely realistic representations of actual genitals. The testicles are often ignored or only rudimentary; they have no luck, no magic, no cult. It is the rhino's horn, the bull's or bear's penis that affords power. Cult images of erection reflect less external nature than the internal consciousness of erection, of erected puer-consciousness and its penis fascination. Freud noticed this over-determination of the penis, writing: "It is remarkable, by the way, what a small degree of interest the other part of the male genitals, the little sac with its contents, arouses in the child. From all one hears in analy-sis one could not guess that the male genitals consist of anything more than the penis."[27]

Besides this overdetermination of the penis, there is also this to observe: The symbolic phalloi usually stand up vertically, whereas (un-less the man is supine as often the case with Siva in his depictions with Sakti) it is the human male (*homo erectus*) who stands vertically, per-pendicular to the horizontal plane, while the usual erection is hardly elevated above that flat line, even if imagination points it skyward. Symbol transforms physiology, and factual reality fades before phallic magic turning our bodies into erector sets of fantasy.

Because the actual generative power resides in that "little sac with its contents," the seeds of strength originate in passivity and tender vulnerability.[28] For puer consciousness, weakness opens immediately into woundedness.[29] To deny this unbearable and fateful lacuna, gen-erative power displaces from sac to erection. It is erection that signifies creation — even if physiology says otherwise. Instead of the sac, the cock; its size, its endurance, its tensile strength.

Erection, *per se;* erectedness as archetypal condition. Not the penis or even a phallus stood as ancient boundary marks or as indications of a God, but simply an upright pile of stones, a pillar, a herm. Hermes takes his name from this form of erectedness,[30] and these peculiar up-right demonstrations bespeak an archaic necessity to confirm vertical-ity, whether at Stonehenge or Easter Island, whether by Mediaeval towers, Gothic spires or New York skyscrapers, all of which in the sad streets of nineteenth-century Vienna were indiscriminately reduced to their lowest common denominator: the penis of a little boy in the mind of a psychoanalyst. Young boys test their "manhood" with com-petitions: whose cock can suspend the most weight, piss the farthest, erect the fastest. Scrotums are *hors de combat.*

For magical thinking the part alters the whole and stands for it; the penis is the man and the man, his penis. It fulfills its true nature, and his, when erect; the flaccid member is ridiculous. Ideally, there would be undying erection, and the social embarrassment over an unheralded erection is a displacement of this wish into a shame. Ideally, unflagging potency, the over-large organ, continuous elevation. Priapism not a symptom but a glory. As he is transformed by its cult, so is it transformed to *baton rouge*, staff of power, mace of office, winged phallus, bird-in-flight. Its will transcends his will: ". . . the focus of the will, i.e., its concentration and highest expression, is the sexual impulse and its satisfaction . . ." [Schopenhauer]. Religious disciplines struggle for mastery of will for which erection is focus. For St. Augustine, an erection was an "insurrection of the flesh."

It is an archetypal mistake to assume creative generation refers only to fertility, to the sac with its contents. In the flat world of physiological function, erection is incidental, merely a penetrating tool to accomplish fertilization, a means of transportation. For the Gods of erection, this same tool is a magical wand, a signifier that changes the world, a means of transport. Because puer sexuality is penis-focused it cannot be confined to the materialistic, moralistic and utilitarian assumptions that sexuality is primarily a fertility function. No; it is primarily a vertical function.

This verticality affects puer eros. An erection serves less to relate lovers than to ride them heavenward in ecstasy. An arrow, not a bridge. It strikes all sorts of far-fetched and disparate pairings — nameless, hap-hazard, opportunistic — into compulsive conjunctions, thereby forming symbols by making unions of impossibles, joining two arrow-struck madnesses by means of its magic, and further joining the human madness with that of the Gods, the bed-chamber a *thalamus* where invisibles cavort. Without the messages that come via physical erections, neither the Trickster, neither Priapos nor Hermes, Eros nor Dionysus would be fully operative. Their signals would not come through.

In order to see more clearly the nature of vertical Eros, and to see past the moralisms about puer eros being unrelated and self-serving, we need to see through the source of these condemnations. The hidden dogma of fertility is based on another archetypal principle, another God or Goddess altogether. The dogma judges all uses of erection other than fertility as renegade — Don Juanism, masculine protest, omnipotence fantasies, exhibitionism, narcissism . . . What is not fertility and/or personal relatedness can be reduced by a diagnosis. But within the vertical cosmos of the puer, erection does not make babies; it makes love. And the love it makes is not necessarily personally related, but fun, inspiring, revelatory, impersonal, imaginative and at moments even heroically redemptive.

Nonetheless, there is some truth lurking in the moralist critiques. Why are the behaviors that clearly show vanity, cold callousness, self-gratification and psychopathy so often penis-focused in one way or another? Why was a traditional sign of the Devil his ice-cold penis and semen? An answer lies in the images we have already seen: that erected pile of stones, the stone statues or herms that were also Hermes.

These effigies place a carved articulated head, sometimes with a beard, on top of an upright slab marked only with protruding genitals. "Such images," writes Eva Keuls of ancient Athens, "stood in front of private houses and in courtyards, and they marked the boundaries of public and sacred precincts. A number of these statues stood in the Agora area, in a section referred to as The Herms."[31] Crucial for grasping the feeling imparted by these statues is neither the head nor the genitals, but the slab between them. Nothing articulated between head and penis — unmarked, untouched, stone cold. *Tertium non datur;* two distinct and separate poles. Though the upper end may enjoy the delusion that it governs the lower and stays on top of it, the autochthonous drive of the genitals may so shape the vision of above that it sees what the erected penis wants to see. Many images from the classical world and elsewhere, including modern dreams, show the meatus of the penis as an open eye.

The moralist critique needs to free itself from its fascination with the phallus as the cause of puer callousness. The critics need to raise their sights from the organ to the slab, which stands tall as a gravestone signifying that here lies something dead and buried. Only a stone-cold blank connects head and genitals. No heart, no breath, no stomach and guts. An absence of inwardness and the presence of innocence. If no body is there, nobody is there, no resonance or reflection brought to behavior from the signals transmitted by the organs as repositories of psyche. This is the source of puer amorality, not the erection itself but the un-awakened body which becomes its appendage, the tail wagging the puer's dogged pursuits.

IV My long harangue on erection has aimed to distinguish yet again the puer archetype from that of the Great Mother's son,[32] specifically here by contrasting the puer's and the mother's sexual codes. Instead of judging the puer from the conventional mother's viewpoint, we can reverse the bias and look at those conventions with the inflammatory, outrageous vision of the puer. My approach, however, is less a senex fault-finding than a puer paen of liberation aiming to free sexuality from the mother's dogmatic restrictions.

The Great Mother on whom fertility depends is today endangered by her own sexual code which demands that coitus serve generation. But literal generation has become over-population, ecologically suicidal, and therefore threatens Mother Nature herself. The Little Old Woman who lives mainly in her shoe of course has so many babies she doesn't know what to do, as the old nursery rhyme said long ago. For her, fertility is a fetish, and the strait-laced eyelets of her perspective never can comprehend puer sexuality which says yes, coitus for generation, not of babies, but generation of soul as the Platonists have long maintained. Therefore, too, homosexual coitus is as valid a conjunction, with as much possibility of generation, as any other. Because erection is primarily a *pars pro toto*, that little lift a microcosmic whisper of the great upward call to generate life on a higher plane, should potency be reduced to fertility and placed in the service of fathering babies, actual erection may immediately flag.

Babies belong to breasts and wombs and mothers — an altogether different archetypal pattern. The puer is neither nurse nor midwife. (Greek midwives had to be themselves mothers.) Even if Hermaphroditos, that roly-poly of sexual possibilities, polymorphic like the original Platonic and Freudian idea of Eros, does preside over some styles of marriages, this mythical figure was never admitted to the birthing chamber.[33] Sex in marriage is one thing, but babies are outside this structure's limits, because the puer-man is himself a divine child who often sees an actual baby as his rival. As babies constellate his own whimpering fragility and omnipotence demand, he may respond to them with a compensatory violence. The terror of pregnancy presents not merely puer irresponsibility, nor are his fears of infection from female bodies, the *vagina dentata*, and his lapses into cool sexual diffidence all disorders to be "overcome." If this kind of consciousness is transcendent and vertical, it will often feel estranged from nature and its fertility cycles. Its very life depends on staying free of the horizontal trap and being yoked to vegetative service. Should the vertical orientation be lost there will be spiritual impotence and castration which the wilted erection and the fears of the feminine attempt to tell him. To succumb means spear into plowshare, a dumb ox toiling in the furrows of the earth.

V In yet another way erection represents puer-consciousness. Plutarch[34] tells of the impetuous tyrant, Alexander of Pherae (369–58 BC) who erected his spear in a temple dedicated to it; he wreathed the spear and sacrificed to it, calling it Tychon. Tychon is a correlative of Tyche, the Goddess of Good Fortune,[35] who appears with a boy-child (sometimes named Ploutos), holding what has generally been read as a cornucopia of "fertility." But Tychon is also another one of the forms Priapos takes, a kind of phallic dactyl. Our theme compounds itself with intertwining motives: priapic penis, good luck, boy-child, cult worship, and erection. For the phallic state of mind erection, good fortune, and spear are interchangeable. The spear too belongs to the sons of the hawk: texts at Edfu in Egypt "show the magical spear of Horus the Falcon."[36] Both spear and falcon appear there as emblematic of Horus — as they do of Hotspur: The cautionary Worcester who diagnoses Hotspur's inflation warns of trying to "o'er walk a current, roaring loud, / On the unsteadfast footing of a spear."

In temples to Mars a standing spear stood — not *for* the God, but *as* the God. By placing erection within the aegis of Ares/Mars, that is by combining both the cult of the spear[37] and the cult of the phallus, the puer's spiritual impetus is reinforced by aggression and sexuality. When that style of consciousness we name puer conflates so many instinctual sources, it has assimilated to itself an overdose of divine force. The transcendent has become immanent. All the Gods are within — within me! So there is no cause to call upon the Gods or beseech them for aid, since the instinctual dominants have lost their externality. The subject, like Saturn, has swallowed the Gods; like Horus has gone beyond all the Gods. Or, they have swallowed and assimilated the reflective subject who is now God — possessed in a conflation of subjective and objective powers, a madness to which the Gods drive a man whom they would destroy. This madness is impiety: the loss of reality about the Gods, a loss of the feeling for archetypal dominants, which govern and a loss of insight into which specific God is now operative. The dominants are no longer sensed as other than "me." Instead, "Its all going my way: strength, joy, good luck, potency. I am one with the flow."

The classic example of these traits is Alcibiades (450–404 BC), brilliant, privileged, exquisitely handsome, notorious libertine, and warrior, who, says the staid (senex) authoritative *Encyclopedia Britannica* (11th edition), "indulged in the wildest freaks and most insolent behaviour." "Superficial and opportunist to the last, he owed the successes of his meteoric career purely to personal magnetism and an almost incredible capacity for deception." Keuls calls Alcibiades "the personification of phallicism;"[38] we would rather say an incarnation of the puer run amok; heroic, megalomanic: "Laugh[ing] at the common ideas of justice, temperance, holiness and patriotism,"[49] Alcibiades neglected the one commandment of Greek polytheistic society: *do not forget the Gods*. In fact, on the eve of the disastrous expedition to expand Athens into Sicily, a fantasy of empire-building he had inspired and was about to lead, he was accused of mutilating (dismembering) the statues of Hermes. Whether historically so, mythically the crime suits the culprit. Hermes, who too was a master of opportunity and had an incredible capacity for deception, was surely his God whom in the madness of impiety, Alcibiades could disdain and even offend.

In Sophocles's play *Ajax*, we find a prime example of "the men of their own power," as Nilsson names this aspect of hubris.[40] The father of Ajax is speaking:

> Son . . . Go out to win,
> But win with God beside you, " "O" said Ajax

With vain bravado, "any fool can win
With God beside him, I intend to win
Glory and honour on my own account."[41]

And earlier he says: "can you not see that I no longer am a debtor to
the Gods?" (Ajax, 589–90). This "terrible boast" says Sophocles "broke
the bounds of mortal modesty." Ajax did not follow the dictum, "God
and my right arm," but made his spear a God. In Seven Against Thebes
(Aeschylus), the youngest of the members, Parthenopais (whose name
can simply mean virgin-boy), who is supposedly a son of Ares and the
Amazon-like Atalanta, is the one whose oath is on his spear.[42]

Ajax of course is punished in the Underworld, but the figure on
whom the Gods take direst revenge is Kaineus, though born a woman, is transformed at her wish into an invulnerable fighter. Poseidon
changed her sex, and she, now he, became King of the Lapiths ("Swag-
gerers") and begot a son. Kaineus erected a spear in the middle of the
market-place to be treated as a God.[43] The Gods then had her/him set
upon by Centaurs who beat Kaineus into the ground with great wooden
logs. The corpse was again female. The Kaineus story reveals another
aspect of identification with the spear. Though transparently a tale of
Freudian penis-envy, there is another reading: within the swaggering
machismo is a concealed female that only comes out when the boasting
is beaten and grounded by a tougher more instinctual force.

To make a cult of the cock, cock as spear, blurs distinctions. Hero
and puer can be kept distinct at least in mind, if not always in life. The
excess of Ajax led to errant foolish rampage, and suicide; of Alcibiades, assassination; of Kaineus and Parthenopais, destruction through
the Gods. The hero ends in glory or tragedy, but these figures end in a
puer fall. The hubris derives less from their vertical heroics, their ambition, than from the spear as its image, as if to warn against an unholy
combination of aggression and ascension. There are, after all, other
modes of ascending — wings, hopes, songs. Ascending by means of
the vertical spear no longer reflects the intentions of Eros, but of Ares,
Lord of Battle. Consciousness still aims at heaven, but now to conquer
it, battling its way to the Gods against the Gods. This phase of verticality was usually called hubris,[44] now psychologized into "inflation."

VI Inflation simply means blown up, puffed out; filled with air, gas; swollen. Psychology uses the term pejoratively, and critics are quick to prick the bubble, flatten. "Inflated" has become a sharp weapon in our sophisticated psychological armory. Diagnosis as accusation. "Neurotic," "paranoid," even "psychotic" are not quite as insulting, for these maladies befall a person; we are not altogether responsible for our genetic substructure or our psychic subconscious. But to be inflated is to be personally guilty, as if we can inflate ourselves, as if there were no intentions of the psyche behind the phenomenon. The converse of inflation, depression, can evoke sympathy and even be encouraged as a path of deepening. But inflation is struck down as juvenile, illusory and dangerous.

Psychotherapy's fear of inflation secularizes the age-old religious awe in regard to breaking the "bounds of mortal modesty" which challenges the Gods to revenge. The Gods are challenged because ascensionism attempts to change the hierarchy of being. The upward drive is an ontological pressure. It aspires toward another and better kind of being, the best of which is heaven. Thus every ascent, every vertical move, every erection, too, has heaven in its fantasy, and every ascent will be *hubris* to the Gods by disordering the levels of place which represent the planes of being. As Augustine said, an erection indeed is an insurrection. But, to puer consciousness, there is no disruption in the order of things, since it does not know its "place;" rather, it believes its place is with the Gods.

The unavoidable necessity of inflation as an end-stage of the creative ascent finds an account in the Chinese *Book of Changes, I-Ching* (Hexagram 1), "The Creative,[45] where "arrogance" is noted, but is regarded as an "absolutely natural result of the situation." An early commentary says: "In harmony with the time, he goes to extremes." Ares belongs within this configuration, for "God does battle in the sign of the Creative" (Hexagram 1). We should therefore not be surprised to find symbols and attitudes — spear, arrogance, heaven, phallus, inflation, extremism — accompanying the ascending creative impulse. The *I Ching* further amplifies this constellation with images of ice-coldness, head, force, hardness, metal, horse and red which are customary features of Ares/Mars as well. Not the individual is at fault for the *hubris*

of battling the Gods, but the God's presentation of its power as battler
makes the battle possible.

The insights gathered in this chapter may be drawn to a conclusion: Puer inflation is neither an escape from harsh reality, nor the omnipotence fantasy of a mother-complexed ego, nor a renegade over-
weaning ambition compensating for failures in the mundane. The solar
drive of Horus is stated clearly in the text quoted earlier: to overcome
the Gods of old and go beyond the father. The puer's call is to re-
found the order of things from heaven downward. The base must be
above existence, a ground of being similar to the *caelum* of alchemy[46]
in which the sky above, the heavens, are imagined to be imagination
itself, a solid blue empyrean peopled with presences that send down
fiery lights.

To reach that ground one must ascend. Ascension offers a further
vision for grounding a different order, a vision that sees with the eye
of the sun looking down onto the world. It must "look down," and that,
to us who walk the mundane plain, is the very definition of arrogance.
The ascensionist pull also explains why this archetypal structure does
not mature, why puer men do not grow up. The cosmos is restored not
through time, but through vision. Dedication, not development, not
experience. Enthusiasm — *en theos*, filled with the wind of the Gods.

"Beyond" — that is the flag under which he sails, whether *horizontally* beyond, as we shall explore in the chapter on Pothos, or *temporally*
beyond which lies in the future and demands ever-increasing acceleration, or *psychologically* beyond, that drive to deliteralize, deconstruct
and see through every limiting denotation, every reductive explanation, every barrier of law, logic and religion. "Beyond" as the unreach-
able *telos* necessitating an infinite progression of ambition and an infinite regression of method. Unending transcendence of the given, so
that the "way" beyond, the *methodos* of transcending cannot help but
also be transgressing. Transgression and transcendence indistinguishable. In the wake lies the waste; the Devil take the hindmost; fare
forward voyager and don't look back.

As the sun is the call, so Seth is the enemy — not the Father; Seth, with the menace of darkness, ignorance, *avidya*, where order becomes repetition of the "same old." And it is this darkness, Seth, who benighted and destroyed the father. Hence the puer's desperate, ruthless knowledge drive: not simply to gain and accumulate knowledge, but as the principal means of overpowering Seth.[47] The motivation is not power, nor to hold the center and replace the sun. The puer is not enemy of the Gods like Prometheus, or partly God like Hercules, or son of God like Christ, but rather belongs among the Gods as their vehicle to raise the cosmos to their level. Throughout, the driving force is not aggression or arrogance or potency for its own sake. The deepest desire is not to combat or defeat the senex, since the senex is already darkened and defeated, and, moreover, gains strength by means of darkness and defeat. The prompting emotions are high: redemption, beauty, love, joy, justice, honor. The flight upward is in respect to the senex, with respect for the senex. It is a spiritual cause; caused by the spirit.

Notes

1. [This essay is published in this present volume for the first time.] — Ed.

2. Cf. "Notions of Creativity" in my *The Myth of Analysis* (Evanston, IL: Northwestern University Press, 1972), pp. 28–49. Cf. Mircea Eliade, "Symbolisms of Ascension and 'Waking Dreams'" in his *Myths, Dreams and Mysteries* (New York: Harper Colophon, 1975).

3. Henry A. Murray, "American Icarus," in A. Burton and R. E. Harris, eds., *Clinical Studies of Personality* II, (New York: Harper & Bros., 1955). Reprinted in J. Hillman, ed., *Puer Papers* (Dallas: Spring Publications, 1979).

4. Robert Graves, *The White Goddess* (London: Faber & Faber, 1948), p. 192.

5. William Shakespeare, *Henry IV*, Pt. 1: I, iii, 201–8.

6. See Chapter 6, "Pothos." [— Ed.]

7. *Henry IV*, Pt. I: V, iv, 76–80

8. R. T. Rundle Clark, *Myth and Symbol in Ancient Egypt* (London: Thames & Hudson, 1959).

9. Ibid., p. 216.

10. Ibid., p. 215.

11. [See Chapter 8 on Odysseus and wounding.] — Ed.

12. For a falcon-boy who struggles to find his own force, see Robert Duncan's exquisite poem "My Mother would be a Falconress."

13. Rundle Clark, op. cit., p. 223. Hathor cures Horus's eyes by bathing them in gazelle milk, p. 204. [On the restorative power of milk and its meanings, see Chap. 13.] — Ed.

14. Seth's ignorance, stupidity, materiality are imaged also by his animal: "Seth is usually associated with the donkey in Egyptian mythology." Jan Assmann, *Moses the Egyptian* (Cambridge: Harvard University Press, 1997), p. 37.

15. On the mythological affinity of hawk/falcon with vulture/buzzard, see W. H. Roscher, "Apollo, X Symbole und Attribute." *Ausführliches Lexikon der griechischen und römischen Mythologie* (Leipzig/Stuttgart: Teubner; Hildesheim, 1965); Graves, loc. cit.

16. "Ficino had already drawn the cogent lesson that it is a mistake to worship one god alone . . . By calling one god, we call his affiliates; and by calling a few, we call them all. Polytheism leads to the Pantheon. *Nimmer, das glaubt mir, erscheinen die Götter / Nimmer allein.* [Friedrich Schiller, "Dithyramb"]. The mutual entailment of the Gods was a genuine Platonic lesson." Edgar Wind, *Pagan Mysteries in the Renaissance* (Harmondsworth: Penguin, 1967), pp. 197–98.

17. Nesca A. Robb, *Neoplatonism of the Italian Renaissance* (London: Allen and Unwin, 1935), p. 261: (Michelangelo, LXI, "E se'l primo suo colpo fu mortale . . .").

18. "Apollo is the patron of young people entering into manhood . . . At his most important festivals it was mainly boys and youths who made their appearance. To him the boy attaining manhood dedicated his long hair." Walter F.

Otto, *The Homeric Gods*, trans. Moses Hadas (New York: Pantheon, 1954), p. 71. Also, Angelo Brelich, *Paides e Parthenoi I* (Roma: Ediz. Dell'Ateneo, 1969).

19. Cf. Eugene Monick, *Phallos: Sacred Image of the Masculine* (Toronto: Inner City, 1987).

20. Regarding "imagination as physiology," cf. Leonardo da Vinci's anatomical observations (sic!) of the penis in cross section showing two urethral passages, one for air (the images that arouse). Also my *The Myth of Analysis*, pp. 222–23. Contemporary potency drugs (e.g. Viagra) also require imaginative arousal prior to physiological erection.

21. S. Freud, *Three Essays on the Theory of Sexuality*, trans. J. Strachey, (London: Hogarth, 1962 [revised]), notes, p. 71, p. 105.

22. H. A. Murray, op. cit.

23. Leo Steinberg, "The Sexuality of Christ in Renaissance Art and in Modern Oblivion," *October 25* (Cambridge: MIT Press, 1983). Further, on the repression of the Biblical God's sexual body see Howard Eilberg-Schwartz, *God's Phallus* (Boston: Beacon Press, 1994).

24. Refers to D. H. Lawrence's late novella, *The Escaped Cock*, which explores Christ's sexual love for Mary Magdalene. A similar theme is encountered in Martin Scorsese's film, *The Last Temptation of Christ*. [— Ed.]

25. H. M. Westropp & C. S. Wake, *Ancient Symbol Worship — The Influence of the Phallic Idea in the Religions of Antiquity* (1875), (New York: Humanities Press, 1972).

26. Norman O. Brown, *Hermes the Thief* (New York: Random House, 1969), pp. 32–35.

27. S. Freud, "The Infantile Genital Organization of the Libido: A Supplement " *International Journal of Psychoanalysis* 5, pp. 125–29. Cf. "Analysis of a Phobia of a Five-year-old Boy," *Standard Edition*, vol. 10 (1909). Cf. Braahm Eily, "Enough of the Phallus," in *Journal of Wild Culture*, Vol. 1, No. 4, 1989.

28. Joseph Cambray, "Fear of Semen," *Spring* 51, pp. 39–54.

29. See chapter 8. [— Ed.]

30. W. K. C. Guthrie, *The Greeks and their Gods* (London: Methuen, [University Paperback], 1968), p. 92: ". . . primeval upright stone from which so much of Hermes' nature seems to have taken its origin."

31. Eva C. Keuls, *The Reign of the Phallus* (New York: HarperCollins, 1985), p. 385.

32. This theme is addressed at length in chapter 4. [— Ed.]

33. H. Graham, *Eternal Eve* (London: Hutchinson, 1960), pp. 38–39.

34. Plutarch, *Pelopidas* 29.8.

35. Good luck, success means for Greek practicality, "right on target," "hitting the mark." Cf. above, chapter 3, "Notes on Opportunism."

36. Jack Lindsay, *The Clashing Rocks* (London: Chapman & Hall, 1965), p. 142.

37. On African spear cults, see "Spear Symbolism" in E. E. Evans-Pritchard *Nuer Religion* (Oxford: Clarenden Press, 1956), chap. IX; also Lindsay, op cit. pp. 135–43 with notes.

38. Keuls, op. cit., p. 384.

39. *Encyclopaedia Britannica* (11th ed.), vol. I, p. 522.

40. Martini P. Nilsson, *Opuscula Selecta* III, pp. 26–31 (Lund: C. W. K. Gleerup, 1960).

41. *Ajax*, 769f.

42. Lindsay, op. cit., p. 162; cf. Graves, *The Greek Myths* I, p. 266.

43. Nilsson, op. cit., p. 27. Cf. Graves, *The Greek Myths* I, p. 78.

44. Nilsson, loc. cit. contradicts the usual view, saying the pejorative "hubris" represents the judgment of a pious bourgeois against an earlier age of individual heroism.

45. Hellmut Wilhelm, *Heaven, Earth and Man in the Book of Changes* (Seattle: University of Washington Press, 1977), pp. 29–51.

46. Cf. my "Alchemical Blue and the Unio Mentalis" in *Spring* 54, pp. 132–48.

47. Seth has another function: "threatening the gods with the sacrilegious discovery of their secrets," (Assman, op. cit., p. 112), i.e., the reduction of mystery to secular explanation, including the reduction of the puer archetype itself to a mother-complex. Of course, Seth, is the puer's true enemy.

6

Pothos: The Nostalgia of the Puer Eternus [1]

The question that shall be engaging us in our wanderings through this chapter is the psychological one of nostalgia. Before setting forth we must be sure to distinguish between the principal and profound experience of nostalgia — an archetypal nostalgia which may itself be a "nostalgia for the archetype" — and all recent manifestations of nostalgia: the attractions for the 1930s and 1940s in films, the longings for romantic sexuality or for pure unpolluted nature, the *nostalgie de la boue* (nostalgia for the mud) of the "honest peasant," or for gypsy clothes and antiques. These are temporalizations of nostalgia into *autre fois* (another time), or a secularization and commercialization of nostalgic values. Such is sociological nostalgia, whereas our eye is on archetypal nostalgia.

I hope we can arrive at a third perspective towards our phenomenon: one that is neither the *dernier cri* of a commercial vogue nor the *premier cri* of primal scream therapy (Janov), a cry for the mother and the past pains in our souls, but a *cri imaginaire*, a cry for the imaginal, the C. R. I. [2] of Chambéry.

To go in this third direction, away from both social and personalistic explanations, we must follow a fundamental principle upon which archetypal psychology is based — the principle of *epistrophé* or reversion. *Epistropé* is a Neoplatonic idea: we find it elaborated best in Proclus' *Elements of Theology*, especially Proposition 29. Briefly, this idea considers all phenomena to have an archetypal likeness to which they can be led back, reverted, returned. All events in the realm of soul, that is, all psychological events and behaviors, have a similarity, correspondence, likeness with an archetypal pattern. Our lives follow mythical figures: we act, think, feel, only as permitted by primary patterns established in the imaginal world. Our psychological lives are mimetic to myths. As Proclus notes, secondary phenomena (our personal experiences) can be reverted to a primary or primordial background against which they resonate and to which they belong. The task of archetypal psychology, and its therapy, is to discover the archetypal pattern for forms of behavior. The assumption is always that *everything belongs somewhere*: all forms of psychopathology have their mythical substrate and belong or have their home in myths. Moreover, psychopathology is itself a means of reverting to myth, a means of being affected by myth and entering into myth. Or, as Jung said: "The gods have become diseases,"[3] so that today it is to our pathologies we must look for finding the Gods.

The particular psychopathological events that attract us specifically here are those of restlessness and wandering, homelessness and homesickness together, the suffering of nostalgia which is at the same time an impetus for search and quest.

Our method has been partly described by Henry Corbin when writing of *ta'wīl*, which he says means: *"reconduire, ramener une chose à son origine et principe, a son archetype."* As he says further: "In *ta'wīl* one must carry sensible forms back to imaginative forms and then rise to still higher meanings; to proceed in the opposite direction (to carry imaginative forms back to the sensible forms in which they originate) is to destroy the virtualities of the imagination."[4] For us, it is the conservation and exploration and vivification of the imagination and the insights derived therefrom, rather than the analysis of the unconscious, that is the main work of therapy.

Turning now directly to our theme, we find that Jung describes the phenomenology of wandering and longing as follows: "The heroes are usually wanderers (Gilgamesh, Dionysus, Herakles, Mithras, etc.), and wandering is a symbol of longing, of the restless urge which never finds its object, of nostalgia for the lost mother."[5] The secret goal of wandering, said Jung in 1912, is the lost mother. There is a piece of libido, which he calls the renegade libido, that turns away from the heroic tasks and incestuously wishes to go back and down to mother.

Blocked by the incest taboo, the libido never finds its goal and so wanders and longs eternally. This dynamic explanation is the early and classical Jungian account of the puer aeternus: the eternally youthful component of each human psyche, man or woman, old or young, that is eternally wandering, eternally longing, and is ultimately attached to the archetypal mother.

We shall not, let me insist, be following this account. And one of our main deviations with the classical Jungian school is just here. For to place all the spiritual phenomenology of the puer eternus motif with the mother archetype is a psychological materialism: a view which attributes spirit to an appendage of maternal matter. To our archetypal view, puer eternus psychology — the wounded hands and feet and bleeding, the high flights and verticality, the aestheticism and amorality, the peculiar relation with Artemesian and Amazonian women, the timelessness which does not age, the penchant for failure, destruction and collapse (*la chute*)[6] — all these events belong to a series of young God-like men or divine youths. These puer events pertain to the phenomenology of spirit. By not grasping this fact as it appears in young men and women today, and in the puer eternus figures in our dreams and fantasies, we miss the epiphanies of the spirit archetype, judging them as something "too young", too weak, sick or wounded, or not yet grown up. Thus does the perspective of the mother archetype prevent the possibilities of spirit as it emerges in our lives. Therefore, we shall be especially wary of attributing wandering and nostalgia to the mother archetype.

However, to go on with the classical position. Norman O. Brown elaborates the same view from the Freudian perspective: "The wandering heroes are phallic heroes . . . All walking, or wandering, is from mother, to mother, in mother; it gets us nowhere. Movement is in space; and space, as Plato says in the *Timaeus* is a receptacle . . . as it were, a mother . . ."[7] Space eventually becomes the female genital, the mother's "yawning pit," or the night-like pit, as Hegel called the imagination. Longing is ultimately for the mother, and when the mother is lost or tabooed the wandering begins, for example Orestes and Alcmaeon slew their mothers after which they wandered, unable to return to their home lands. And Apollo, after slaying Python, suffered nine years in exile.

If we accept this classical position then we must see the journey of the sailor, wanderer, adventurer, neither as a mode of Hermes with a spiritual secret mission, nor as an activity of spiritual quest, but as a prolonged coition with the mother; this world, a double movement of union with her and escape from her. The polytheistic archetypal possibilities of wandering are reduced to one single meaning. The restless urge of puer psychology has been turned into the psychopathology of mother-son incest.

Let us begin again. We may accept the first part of Jung's proposition that wandering is a symbol of longing, but the second we may hold in suspension. Nostalgic longing may not be incestuous at all.

For this new beginning, we follow Odysseus. He is a primordial wanderer — and he detests it. Sitting on the shore of Calypso's island, staring disconsolately, he is filled with nostalgia. "There is nothing worse for mortal man than wandering." Odysseus longs for home. And others long for Odysseus: Antikleia (Bk. 11.202), Telemachos (Bk. 4, 596), Eumaeos (Bk. 14, 144). They pine, long, age, die out of a deep *pothos* or longing for the missing beloved wanderer Odysseus.

Odysseus' longing is not for mother, but for his home and native island. Calypso and Ogygia, after all, could fulfill all the incestuous renegade libidinal longings that a wandering sailor might ever imagine! But Odysseus still pines and suffers for home, the great round bed with Penelope. Nostalgia arises from a separation of halves, a missing conjunction. Our question of wandering has shifted to one of Eros.

The Greek word for this specific erotic feeling of nostalgic desire was *pothos*. Plato defines it in the *Cratylus* (420a) as a yearning desire for a distant object. Its associations in the Classical corpus are with longings for *that which cannot be obtained*: yearning for a lost child, or a beloved (the swineherd, the son, or the mother longing for Odysseus), longing for sleep and for death. *Pothos* also applies to a kind of flower placed on graves (blue delphinium or larkspur), to a white asphodel or hyacinth-like flower, and also to a clambering travelling plant that never stays in one place and is always seeking new attachments. As late as the Church Father, Gregory of Nazianzus, *pothos* was described as a striving power in plants.[8] It is the "vegetable love," a *vis naturalis* of which Andrew Marvell has written, or "the force that through the green fuse drives the flower drives my blood" of Dylan Thomas.

The greatest exemplary of pothos in antiquity was Alexander the Great. He is said to have himself invented the phrase "seized by pothos" to account for his indescribable longing for something beyond, a longing that carried him beyond all borders in a horizontal conquest of space, a true "space man" of ancient times. Alexander had merely to sit upon a river bank or before his tent and look into the distance when he would be seized by pothos and urged to go farther. Space and distance became the visual image that released his yearning. (I forego the tempting diversion of elaborating the puer eternus characteristics of Alexander the Great: early death, mythical divine father, wounded foot, intoxication, etc.[9])

Pothos was not only a concept and a feeling; he was also a divine personification, an actual figure, for example sculpted by Skopas (395–350 BC), which has been described as a "youngly ripened boy's body." This figure has been brought into association with Dionysus, Apollo, Attis and Hippolytos, and with phallic Hermes. According to Pliny, the main cult figures on Samothrace were Aphrodite and Pothos.

Let us look for a moment at this Aphrodite-Pothos relationship before setting forth to Samothrace. There are three portions or persons of Eros that have been classically differentiated: *himeros* or physical desire for the immediately present to be grasped in the heat of the moment; *anteros* or answering love; and *pothos*, the longing towards the unattainable, the ungraspable, the incomprehensible, that idealization which is attendant upon all love and which is always beyond capture. If *himeros* is the material and physical desire of eros, and *anteros* the relational mutuality and exchange, *pothos* is love's spiritual portion. *Pothos* here would refer to the spiritual component of love or the erotic component of spirit. When *pothos* is presented on a vase painting (fifth century, British Museum) as drawing Aphrodite's chariot, we see that *pothos* is the motive force that drives desire ever onward, as the portion of love that is never satisfied by actual loving and actual possession of the object. It is the fantasy factor that pulls the chariot beyond immediacy, like the seizures that took Alexander and like Odysseus' desire for "home."

Pothos here is the blue romantic flower of love that idealizes and drives our wandering, or as the Romantics put it: we are defined not by what we are or what we do, but by our *Sehnsucht*: Tell me for what you yearn and I shall tell you who you are. We are what we reach for, the idealized image that drives our wandering. Pothos, as the wider factor in eros, drives the sailor-wanderer to quest for what cannot be fulfilled and what must be impossible. It is the source of "impossible love", producing the Tristan complex that refuses *himeros* and *anteros* in order to maintain the transcendence of pothos. This side of eros makes possible living in the world as a scene of impossible mythical action, mythologizing life. This component of eros is the factor, or the divine figure, within all our senseless individuation adventures, the phallic foolishness that sends us chasing, the mind's mad wanderings after impossibilities, our forever being at sea, and the fictive goals we must set ourselves — all so that we may go on loving.

||| We come to another island — and our Greek topology is a topology of islands, of sailors and travelers, of nostalgia for Ithaca, and of winds and wind-Gods that blow one off course, a topology that is like that of the individuation adventure through unconscious waters — Samothrace (Samothraki). The cult of the Kabiroi on Samothraki was perhaps the most important, after Eleusis, of all mystery initiations of the ancient world. A series of rituals there took place. The acts and the mythic contents are understood even less than those of Eleusis. We have only conjectures by Bengt Hemberg,[10] Karl Lehmann,[11] and Karl Kerényi.[12] Legends say that wandering heroes stopped on this island for initiation: Jason and the Argonauts, Hercules, Odysseus. Prometheus — who was also a wanderer — is associated with the Kabiroi cult;[13] and Alexander indirectly, for legends say that his parents, Olympias and Philip, fell in love there while they were undergoing the initiations — as if Alexander was conceived in the place of pothos, his life becoming its embodiment and a demonstration of its power. The heiron of Samothraki was sacred to the Dioskuri because of shipwrecks and for the protection of sailors. It was, in other words, a haven for wanderers; if one could enter into some relation with pothos, there was protection against "shipwreck."

Let us look at a few of the other relevant phenomena conjectured by classical scholars and archeologists about Samothraki, the Dioskuri, and the Kabiroi mysteries in order to understand something more about wandering in relationship with nostalgia, and about pothos in relationship with the archetype of the puer eternus. But let us at the same time bear in mind how speculative and fantasy-filled all scholarship must be in this area. As Farnell has written about the Dioskuri: "The study of these twin-personalities of cult presents more perplexing problems than perhaps any other chapter of Greek religion."[14]

First, there is the perplexing mystery of the Mighty Ones or *Megalo Theoi*. The Kabiroi were called The Mighty Ones. The initiation seemed to have involved a ritual activity in regard to a *pair of unequal male figures*, perhaps a male parallel to the mother-maiden pair at Eleusis. Who was this pair of Gods? Perhaps a brother pair: Prometheus-Hephaistos? Perhaps the Dioskuri Twins? Or was it, as Kerényi seems to believe, a bearded God-figure together with a *pais* or younger boy-figure: Pothos, perhaps?

The pair of unequal male figures is one of those archetypal themes that releases extraordinary speculations. They have been imagined to be mortal and immortal, or divine and human, or age and youth, or initiated and uninitiated, or cultural and natural. This unequal pair even appears in the published letters of Freud and Jung,[15] where Freud (Letter 274F) considers the theme to refer back to primal memories: the mortal brother of the Dioskuri pair is nothing else in Freud's letter than the placenta, the short-lived afterbirth, the twin companion with which each human is born.

The pair on Samothraki — where our interest centers because there the Skopas' statue of Pothos held such prominence and because there the cult was for wanderers, sailors and adventurers — are further complicated by the discovery of a statue of a blind old man. It has been suggested that this old man was Teiresias, which fits in with Lehmann's theory that part of the Kabiroi cult was a journey through the underworld. Others have imagined the statue to be of Homer; others, Aristotle. As Teiresias was Odysseus' teacher, Aristotle played old man to Alexander, and Socrates did for the notorious Alcibiades. Kerényi believes the older male figure to be central to the entire mystery and that this older figure was Dionysus-Hades. So much for the unequal male figures and who they might have been: a boy and an older man, puer and senex.

Second, there is an erotic and phallic aspect of the Kabiroi world. On Samothraki a phallic Hermes was identified with Pothos; the Kabiroi themselves were phallic figures such as are familiar from vase paintings. Moreover, Pliny says that Skopas's statue of Pothos together with Aphrodite were the main cult figures on Samothraki. There is the later association of Priapos (son of Aphrodite) with wanderers, sailors and fishermen. Again, Aphrodite, in her form as Helen, has a special relation with the twin Dioskuri.

This collection of erotic and phallic motives seems to give mythological depth to Jung's and Norman O. Brown's vision of wandering as a renegade phallic activity in nostalgic search of mother. Pothos would then be the figure of the boyish urge to come home and be safe in the harbour of Aphrodite. Aphrodite would be image of what the puer in us each longs for, the Helen-Paris conjunction arranged by Aphrodite, the face that launches a thousand ships daily in our erotic fantasies. Kerényi interprets the Kabiroi mysteries similarly: according to his fantasy, the renegade or primordial phallic force was tamed by bird-like women and placed in service of civilized generation.

Beyond these two major fantasies of Samothraki (which I have condensed and abstracted), the one about unequal male figures and the underworld, the other about sexual initiation and Aphrodite, scholarship can penetrate no further. The secret of the mystery still remains closed.

IV If we know so little of what the place of Pothos is within the Kabiroi mysteries, perhaps our ignorance is due to a psychological lack and not only to historiographical lacunae. Archeological digs cannot help us if our psychological awareness cannot penetrate to equal depths. Sometimes we can refine this awareness through reflection upon comparative psychological events. What the texts don't tell us, we may be able to reconstruct through the context of archetypal experience. At the level of myth and archetype, time does not matter. Samothraki is also an eternal island of the imaginal psyche, of psychological geography.

Therefore at this point in our discussion we shall return to the psychological, even psychopathological, face of the archetype. Just as we can illumine psychology through mythology, so we can substantiate mythology through psychopathology. The double movement between mythology and pathology is the basis of our archetypal work. Just as myths move our pathologies into a wider field and deeper background, away from personalistic and literalistic reductions, so pathologies are the means by which myths enter our lives and become corporal. Then they are no longer stories in an illustrated book; the story is taking place in our lives and we are its illustration.

The idea we follow here is that each archetype has its style of pathology. The *pathos* of the archetype, our being moved by it, is as essential to it as its *logos*, its significance. Myths tell us not only about archetypal psychodynamics but also about archetypal psychopathology.[16] In our pathologies we enter myths and myths enter us; pathologies are ways we imitate, are mimetic to, divine patterns.[17]

In our pathological lives the puer eternus appears as a specific style of prolonged adolescence, lasting sometimes until forty — and sometimes ending with sudden violent death. The puer would be the figure within Sartre's remark: "La jeunesse? C'est une maladie bourgeoise" — no, not a social reflection but the archetypal background to it, an archetypal reflection: *une maladie archétypique*, as are all pathologies.

In Part I above I sketched a few characteristics of this figure. Let me review them again: woundedness (hypochondria, wounds of hands and feet, lungs, bleeding); ascensionism (verticality); proclivity for fire and water (Icarus); aestheticism (flower-people, Hyacinthus, Narcissus); timelessness (unable to enter time or to grow old, or a curious antiquarianism); self-destructiveness (desire to fail, to fall, to die in cataclysm); amorality or super-morality; exaggerated parental constellation (the divine figure's inability to live in a human situation without divinizing or demonizing the actual parents). Finally, for our purposes here, the puer eternus is that structure of consciousness and pattern of behavior that (a) refuses and struggles with the senex — time, work, order, limits, learning, history, continuity, survival and endurance — and that (b) is driven by a phallicism to inquire, quest, travel, chase, search, to transgress all limits. It is a restless spirit that has no "home" on earth, is always coming from somewhere or going to somewhere in transition. Its eros is driven by longing; psychologists condemn this spirit as unrelated, autoerotic, Don Juanistic, even psychopathic.

It is these last two traits — erotic phallicism and the puer-senex division — which are particularly focussed, and focussed together, on Samothraki. There we found the concatenation of puer motifs: wanderers, sailors and adventurers; old man and young boy; beautiful youthful body of Skopas' statue of Pothos; phallicism (Kabiroi).

Let us imagine: perhaps the Mighty Ones initiated the wanderer into the archetypal source and significance of his restlessness, revealed to him the *telos*, "that for the sake of which" we are so driven. Perhaps the cult was a mythic enactment for the sake of teaching *pothos* about itself, giving a ritual account of the psychopathological drivenness of the renegade libido that eventually leads to "shipwreck" (the *scheitern* of Jaspers) unless some transformation of awareness brings sight to our blindness. Blind Teiresias and blind Homer bring insight, by taking the boy in the man into the underworld, into psychic reality, leading to a consciousness of depths about one's driven windblown wandering across surfaces. The unequal male pair tell us that at Samothraki puer and senex rejoin, as they do in the person of Odysseus. Young spirit finds its cautionary counterpart that teaches survival; bearded man finds the *pothos* of eros again, the awakened heart. He can set sail again, go on journeying. If there Hermes was identified with Pothos, then the signs of *pothos* in us — the nostalgic longing to move, the erotic yearning, the driven urge to transgress — have a hermetic quality. These feelings are from Hermes, Guide of Souls. These movements refer to the relationship between *soul and space*, offering psychological possibilities to the horizontal puer, and possibilities to a psychology of space other than Cartesian materialism. It was space, we remember, that released Alexander's pothos; and *pothos* is the emotion equivalent to the experience of space as a spiritual phenomenon, such as described by Plato in the *Timaeus*: the formless, incomprehensible, existential condition that is the ground of all becoming, the space and spaced-outness in which all humans are puer wanderers, guided by the goals of our longing.

V   The initiation which we imagine taking place at Samothraki
    brings puer consciousness to an awareness of its *essentially double
nature*. It is this double nature that we imagine to be at the root of its
pothos, its nostalgic longing and wandering in search of the lost or
missing other. The pair of Mighty Ones and the Dioskuri and all the
other couplings point directly at a *double structure of consciousness*. We
do not need to qualify the doubleness as this or that pair of opposites
— old-young, mortal-immortal, male-female. Nor must we make a
grand philosophy, a senex principle, of binarism (Lévi-Strauss) as the
fundamental mode of all myth. Nor is it necessary to concentrate our
focus only on the pair as witness to the spiritual aspect of all erotic
longing and the erotic aspect of all spiritual quests.

   These precisions of the pair tend to literalize too narrowly the
fundamental idea: *puer consciousness is a twin consciousness; and awareness of
this doubleness of individuality is precisely the initiation*. Unlike Eleusis, the
Samothraki cult was for individuals. One went through it alone. It was
for freeman and slave, for Greek and barbarian, for man and woman.
It had therefore to do with transformation of consciousness in regard
to one's individuality, one's individual daimon spirit or angel and one's
destiny in relation to it. The initiation transmits an awareness that
individuality is not essentially unity but a doubleness, even a duplicity,
and our being is metaphorical, always on two levels at once. Only this
twofold truth, *gloria duplex*, can offer protection against shipwreck by
teaching us to avoid foundering upon the great monolithic rocks of
literal realities. Eleusis told much the same thing: Mother and Daughter are always each other. Wherever one is, there is always an "other"
by means of whom we reflect existence and because of whom we are
always "more," "other," and "beyond" what is here-and-now.

   In our lives the presence of otherness feels like self-estrangement,
self-alienation. I am always somehow a stranger to myself and can never know myself except through discovering the other which I fantasy
to be somewhere else — so I wander in search of him or her. In my life
this is felt as ambivalence, dissatisfaction, restlessness. Self-division or
the divided self of modem psychiatry is the primary condition and not
a result, mistake or accident. Self-division is not to be joined or healed,
but to be reflected through an archetype which initiates conscious-

ness into the significance of the pathology. The unequal, the asymmetrical, pair of Samothraki states that no individual is whole-hearted and single-minded, at one with himself and in at-one-ment with the Gods. This initiation does not make us whole; rather it makes us aware of always being in a syzygy with another figure,[18] always in a dance, always a reflection of an invisible other. Whether the other be senex. to puer, female to male, mother to child, death to life in whatever form the other is constellated from moment to moment — *it is beyond reach,* though we travel to Ogygia or with Alexander beyond the Indus. The other is an *unattainable image,* referring not to *himeros* and *anteros,* but to *pothos.* Or rather, the other is an image that is attainable only through imagination.

Moreover, singlemindedness or the onesidedness of unity of personality is the condition *before* initiation. Oneness is not the goal, but the pre-condition. Jung has considered "onesidedness" to be the widest definition of neurosis, that is, pathos without logos. The initiation through the Mighty Ones (*Megalo Theoi*) is an initiation by the *two.* And an *asymmetrical* two! The mighty image of necessary doubleness and asymmetry teaches us about both the driven compulsions of onesidedness (uninitiated condition of literal-mindedness) and about the significance of our eternal sense of disbalance. The Mighty Ones are an epiphany of *ontological inequality* which gives an archetypal image to the disharmonies we feel as longings. Metaphorical man, unlike literal man fixed in his certainties, is always at sea, always en route between, always in two places at once. The Samothraki mystery as we have imaginally reconstructed it in the soul does not resolve tension and assuage longing; but it does provide their archetypal context.

Thus we are left at the end with a source of nostalgia other than the mother and other than eros. The only response which is as limitless as the limitlessness of pothos is the imaginal itself. Our wandering and our longing is for the very archetypal imaginal figure that instigates the longing, the *puer aeternus* in his personification as *Pothos.* Our desire is towards the image that initiates the desire; it is an epistrophé, a desire that would return desire to its source in the archetype. And this archetype of the puer eternus is, as Henry Corbin has often said, the figure of the angel, the wholly imaginal reflection of ourselves, who makes us realize that we are metaphors of him.[19] Not Freud's placenta was lost at birth, but Corbin's twin likeness, our sense of doubleness. Not Jung's renegade libido that would go "back" home to mother, unless home is the womb as metaphor (the Receptacle of the *Timaeus*) for the "place" where our original doubleness is imagined to be "originally" located and contained. Ultimately, then, our pothos refers to our angelic nature, and our longings and sea-borne wanderings are the effects in our personal lives of the transpersonal images that urge us, carry us, and force us to imitate mythical destinies.

Notes

1. [This paper was first delivered in French in 1974 in Chambéry. It was then published in the original English in J. Hillman, *Loose Ends: Primary Papers in Archetypal Psychology* (New York/Zurich: Spring Publications, 1975).] — Ed.

2. This is the acronym for the hosts of the conference: Centre de Recherche sur l'Imaginaire.

3. C. G. Jung, *Collected Works*, vol. 13: *Alchemical Studies*, par. 54.

4. H. Corbin, *Avicenna and the Visionary Recital*, trans. W. R. Trask (London: Routledge & Kegan Paul, 1960); H. Corbin, *Creative Imagination in the Sufism of Ibn'Arabi*, trans. Ralph Manheim (Princeton University Press, 1969).

5. C. G. Jung, *Collected Works*, vol. 5: *Symbols of Transformation*, par. 299.

6. [The theme of wounding is discussed in Chapter 8, "Puer Wounding and Odysseus' Scar;" the theme of flight and verticality is discussed in Chapter 5.] — Ed. See Gilbert Durand, *Les Structures anthropologiques de l'imaginaire* (Paris: Presses Universitaire de France, 1963), pp. 111–16.

7. Norman O. Brown, *Love's Body* (New York: Random House, 1966), p. 50.

8. Pauly-Wissowa, "Pothos," in *Realencyclopädie der classischen Altertumswissenschaft* (Stuttgart: 1953); W. H. Roscher, *Lexikon der griechischen und römischen Mythologie* (Leipzig: B. G. Teubner, 1909/1965); "Pothos," Liddell and Scott, *A Greek-English Lexicon* (Oxford: Clarendon Press, 1968).

9. V. Ehrenberg, "Pothos," in *Alexander the Great: The Main Problems*, ed. G. T. Griffith (Cambridge: Heffer, 1966).

10. Bengt Hemberg, *Die Kabiren* (Uppsala: Almquist Wiksells, 1950).

11. Karl Lehmann, *Samothrace* (New York: Bollingen, 1958).

12. Karl Kerényi, "Mysterien der Kabiren," *Eranos-Yearbook* 11 (1944) [engl. transl. in *The Mysteries* (New York: Bollingen, 1955)]; K. Kerényi, , "Das Theta von Samothrake" in *Geist und Werk: zum 75. Geburtstag Daniel Brody* (Zurich: Rhein-Verlag, 1958); K. Kerényi, *Symbolae Osloenses* 31 (1955), pp. 141–52.

Karl Kerényi, "Theos und Mythos" in *Griechische Grundbegriffe* (Zurich: Rhein-Verlag, 1964).

13. Karl Kerényi, *Prometheus* (New York: Pantheon, 1963).

14. L. R. Farnell, *Greek Hero Cults and Ideas of Immortality* (Oxford: The Clarendon Press, 1921).

15. W. McGuire, ed., *The Freud/Jung Letters* (London: The Hogarth Press and Routledge & Kegan Paul, 1974).

16. [See James Hillman, "Essay on Pan" in *Pan and the Nightmare* (with W. H. Roscher, [New York/Zurich: Spring Publications, 1972]) and his long chapter on Dionysus in *The Myth of Analysis* (Evanston, IL: Northwestern University Press, 1972). Both elaborate in great detail the relation between mythical figures and pathological styles.] — Ed.

17. [At this point in the original text the reader is reminded of some of the mythic figures bearing typical puer traits: "Attis, Adonis, Hippolytus, Bellerophon, Icarus, Jason." He continues: "But there are puer aspects as well in Horus, in Dionysus, in Hermes, in Jesus. Students of literature would find the puer perhaps in Saint-Exupéry, in Shelley, Rimbaud, in Rousseau; Shakespeare's Hotspur is an example; Herman Melville has at least five such beautiful sailor-wanderers."] — Ed.

18. [For another examination of this "other" as *daimon* see J. Hillman, *The Soul's Code* (New York: Random House, 1996).] — Ed.

19. H. Corbin, op.cit. See also my *The Soul's Code*.

7

Betrayal[1]

There is a Jewish story, an excruciatingly twisted Jewish joke. It runs like this: A father was teaching his little son to be less afraid, to have more courage, by having him jump down the stairs. He placed his boy on the second stair and said, "Jump, and I'll catch you." And the boy jumped. Then the father placed him on the third stair, saying, "Jump, and I'll catch you." Though the boy was afraid, he trusted his father, did what he was told, and jumped into his father's arms. Then the father put him on the next step, and then the next step, each time telling him, "Jump, and I'll catch you," and each time the boy jumped and was caught by his father. And so this went on. Then the boy jumped from a very high step, just as before; but this time the father stepped back, and the boy fell flat on his face. As he picked himself up, bleeding and crying, the father said to him, "That will teach you: never trust a Jew, even if it's your own father."

This story — for all its apparent anti-Semitism — has more to it than that, especially since it was told me as a Jew and by a Jew and is a well-known Jewish story. I believe it has something to say to our theme, betrayal. For example: Why must a boy be taught not to trust? And not to trust a Jew? And not to trust his own father? What does it mean to be betrayed by one's father, or to be betrayed by someone close? What does it mean to a father, to a man, to betray someone who trusts him? What has betrayal to do with initiation of a boy by an elder? To what end betrayal at all in psychological life? These are our questions.

We must try to make a beginning somewhere. I prefer in this case to make this beginning "In the beginning," with the Bible, even though as a psychologist I may be trespassing on the grounds of theology. But even though a psychologist, I do not want to begin at the usual beginnings of psychologists, with that other theology, that other Eden: the infant and its mother.

Trust and betrayal were no issues for Adam, walking with God in the evenings. The image of the garden as the beginning of the human condition shows what we might call "primal trust", or what Santayana has called "animal faith," a fundamental belief — despite worry, fear, and doubt — that the ground underfoot is really there, that it will not give way at the next step, that the sun will rise tomorrow and the sky not fall on our heads, and that God did truly make the world for humankind. This situation of primal trust, presented as the archetypal image of Eden, is repeated in individual lives of child and parent. As Adam in animal faith at the beginning trusts God, so does the boy at the beginning trust his father. In both, God and Father the paternal image is reliable, firm, stable, just, a Rock of Ages whose word is binding. This paternal image can also be expressed by the Logos concept, by the immutable power and sacredness of the masculine word.

But we are no longer in that Garden. Eve put an end to that naked dignity. Since the expulsion, the Bible records a history of betrayals of many sorts: Cain and Abel, Jacob and Esau, Laban, Joseph sold by his brothers and their father deceived, Pharaoh's broken promises, calf-worship behind Moses' back, Saul, Samson, Job, God's rages and the creation almost annulled — on and on, culminating in the central myth of our culture: the betrayal of Jesus.

Although we are no longer in that Garden, we can return to it through any close relationship, for instance, love, friendship, analysis, where a situation of primal trust is reconstituted. This has been variously called the *temenos*, the analytical vessel, the mother-child symbiosis. Here, there is again the security of Eden. But this security — or at least the kind of *temenos* to which I refer — is masculine, given by the Logos, through the promise, the covenant, the word. It is not a primal trust of breasts, milk and skin-warmth; it is similar but different, and I believe the point worth taking that we do not always have to go to Mother for our models of the basics in human life.

In this security, based not on flesh but on word, primal trust has been reestablished and so the primal world can be exposed in safety — the weakness and darkness, the naked helplessness of Adam, the earliest man in ourselves. Here, we are somehow delivered over to our simplest nature, which contains the best and least in us, the million-year-old past and the seed ideas of the future.

The need for security within which one can expose one's primal world, where one can deliver oneself up and not be destroyed, is basic and evident in analysis. This need for security may reflect needs for mothering, but from the paternal pattern within which we are talking, the need is for closeness with God, as Adam, Abraham, Moses, and the patriarchs knew.

What one longs for is not only to be contained in perfection by another who can never let one down. It goes beyond trust and betrayal by the other in a relationship. What one longs for is a situation where one is *protected from one's own* treachery and ambivalence, one's own Eve. In other words, primal trust in the paternal world means being in that Garden with God and all things *but Eve*. The primeval world is pre-Eve, as it is also pre-evil. To be one with God in primal trust offers protection from one's own ambivalence. One cannot ruin things, desire, deceive, seduce, tempt, cheat, blame, confuse, hide, flee, steal, lie, spoil the creation oneself through one's own ambivalent nature, betray through one's own left-handed unconsciousness in the treachery of the anima who is that source of evil in Eden and of ambivalence in every Adam since. We want a Logos security where the word is Truth and it cannot be shaken.

Of course, a longing for primal trust, a longing to be at one with the old wise Self, where I and the Father are one, without interference of the anima, is easily recognized as typical of the *puer aeternus* who stands behind all boyishness. He never wants to be sent down from Eden, for there he knows the name of everything in creation, there fruit grows on the trees and can be had for the picking, there is no toil, and long interesting discussions can be carried on in the cool of the evening.

Not only does he know; he expects to be known, totally, as if God's omniscience is focussed all upon him. This perfect knowledge, this sense of being wholly understood, affirmed, recognized, blessed for what one is, discovered to oneself and known to God, by God, in God repeats itself in every situation of primal trust, so that one feels only my best friend, my wife, my analyst truly understands me through and through. That they do not, that they misperceive and fail to recognize one's essence (which can anyway only be revealed through living), feels a bitter betrayal.

It would seem from the Biblical tale that God recognized that He is not help enough for man, that something other was needed more meet for man than God Himself. Eve had to be created, evoked, pulled out of man himself, which then led to the break of primal trust by betrayal. Eden was over; life began.

This way of understanding the tale implies that the situation of primal trust is not viable for life. God and the creation were not enough for Adam; Eve was required, which means that betrayal is required. It would seem that the only way out of that Garden was through betrayal and expulsion, as if the vessel of trust cannot be altered in any way except through betrayal. We are led to an essential truth about both trust and betrayal: they contain each other. You cannot have trust without the possibility of betrayal. It is the wife who betrays her husband, and the husband who cheats his wife; partners and friends deceive, the mistress uses her lover for power and vice versa, the analyst discloses his patient's secrets, the father lets his son fall. The promise made is not kept, the word given is broken, trust becomes treachery.

We are betrayed in the very same close relationships where primal trust is possible. We can be truly betrayed only where we truly trust — by brothers, lovers, wives, husbands, not by enemies, not by strangers. The greater the love and loyalty, the involvement and commitment, the greater the betrayal. Trust has in it the seed of betrayal; the serpent was in the garden from the beginning, just as Eve was pre-formed in the structure around Adam's heart. Trust and the possibility of betrayal come into the world at the same moment. Wherever there is trust in a union, the risk of betrayal becomes a real possibility. And betrayal, as a continual possibility to be lived with, belongs to trust just as doubt belongs to a living faith.

If we take this tale as a model for the advance in life from the "beginning of things," then it may be expected that primal trust will be broken if relationships are to advance; and, moreover, that the primal trust will not just be outgrown. There will be a crisis, a break characterized by betrayal, which according to the tale is the *sine qua non* for the expulsion from Eden into the "real" world of human consciousness and responsibility.

For we must be clear that to live or love only where one can trust, where there is security and containment, where one cannot be hurt or let down, where what is pledged in words is forever binding, means really to be out of harm's way and so to be out of real life. And it does not matter what is this vessel of trust — analysis, marriage, church or law, any human relationship. Yes, I would even say relationship with the divine. Even here primal trust would not seem to be what God wants. Look at Eden, look at Job, at Moses denied entrance to the Holy Land, look at the newest destruction of His "Chosen People" whose complete and only trust was in Him. [I am implying that Jewish primal trust in God was betrayed by the Nazi experience, requiring a thoroughgoing reorientation of the Jewish attitude, of Jewish theology, in terms of anima, a recognition of the ambivalent side of both God and of man.]

If one can give oneself assured that one will come out intact, maybe even enhanced, then what has been given? If one leaps where there are always arms to take one up, there is no real leap. All risk of the ascent is annulled—but for the thrill of flying through the air, there is no difference between the second step, the seventh or the tenth, or ten thousand metres up. Primal trust lets the puer fly so high. Father and son are one. And all masculine virtues of skill, of calculated risk, of courage, are of no account: God or Dad will catch you at the bottom of the stairs. Above all, one cannot know beforehand. One cannot be told ahead of time, "This time I won't catch you." To be forewarned is to be forearmed, and either one won't jump, or one will jump halfheartedly, a pseudo-risk. There comes that one time where in spite of a promise, life simply intervenes, the accident happens and one falls flat. The broken promise is a breakthrough of life in the world of Logos security, where the order of everything can be depended upon and the past guarantees the future. The broken promise or broken trust is at the same time a breakthrough onto another level of consciousness, and we shall turn to that next.

But first let us return to our story and our questions. The father has awakened consciousness, thrown the boy out of the garden, brutally, with pain. He has initiated his son. This initiation into a new consciousness of reality comes through betrayal, through the father's failure and broken promise. The father willfully shifts from the ego's essential commitment to stand by his word, not to bear false witness by lying to his son, to be responsible and reliable come what come may. He shifts position deliberately allowing the dark side to manifest itself in and through him. So it is a betrayal with a moral. For our story is a moral tale, as are all good Jewish stories. It is not an existentialist fable describing an *acte gratuite;* nor is it a Zen legend leading to liberating enlightenment. It is a homily, a lesson, an instructive piece of life. The father demonstrates in his own person the possibility of betrayal in even the closest trust. He reveals his own treacherousness, stands before his son in naked humanity, presenting a truth about fatherhood and manhood: I, a father, a man, cannot be trusted. Man is treacherous. The word is not stronger than life.

And he also says, "Never trust a Jew." Why not trust a Jew? Because the father is locating his fatherhood within the widest possible context, the fatherhood of Jahweh. A Jewish initiation like other initiations reveals a mystery of the divine, in this case the mystery of God's nature. The father's statement to his son is an archetypal lesson, not a nasty anti-Semitic sociological lesson. Yet, it teaches the boy something profound abut the anti-Semitism he is likely to encounter in his life: you are maligned for a characteristic you share with your God and essential to your God's nature, that most untrustworthy Lord who must be continually praised by psalm and prayer as patient, reliable, just, and propitiated with epithets of stability — because he is so arbitrary, emotional, ruthless, unpredictable. The father says, in short, I have betrayed you as all are betrayed in the treachery of life created by God. The boy's initiation into life is the initiation into adult tragedy.

|| The experience of betrayal is for some as overwhelming as is jealousy or failure. For Gabriel Marcel, betrayal is evil itself.[2] For Jean Genet, according to Sartre, betrayal is the greatest evil, as "the evil which does evil to itself."[3] When experiences have this bite to them,

we assume an archetypal background, something all-too-human. We assume that we are likely to find a fundamental myth and pattern of behavior by which the experience can be amplified. I believe the betrayal of Jesus offers this archetypal background, which may give us further understanding of the experience from the point of view of the betrayed one.

I am hesitant to talk about the betrayal of Jesus. So many lessons may be drawn. But that is just the value of a living symbol: from it can be drawn an endless flow of meanings. And it is as psychologist in search of psychological meanings that I again trespass on theological grounds.

In the story of Jesus we are immediately struck by the motif of betrayal. Its occurrence in threes (by Judas, by the sleeping disciples, by Peter) — repeated by Peter's betrayal thrice — tells us of something fateful, that betrayal is essential to the dynamics of the climax of the Jesus story and thus betrayal is at the heart of the Christian mystery. The sorrow at the supper, the agony in the garden, and the cry on the cross seem restatements of a same theme, each on a higher key, that a destiny is being realized, that a transformation is being brought home to Jesus. In each of these betrayals he is forced to the terrible awareness of having been let down, failed, and left alone. His love has been refused, his message mistaken, his call unattended, and his fate announced.

I find that our simple Jewish joke and that great symbol have things in common. The first step of betrayal by Judas was already known beforehand. Forearmed, Jesus could accept this sacrifice for the glorification of God. The impact must not yet have fully hurt Jesus, but Judas went and hanged himself. Peter's denial was also foreknown, and again it was Peter who went and wept bitterly. Through the last week, the trust of Jesus was in the Lord. "Man of sorrows," yes, but his primal trust was not shaken. Like the boy on the stairs, Jesus could count on his Father and even ask His forgiveness for his tormentors — up until the last step; he and the Father were one, until that moment of truth when he was betrayed, denied and left alone by his followers, delivered into the hands of his enemies, the primal trust between himself and God broken, nailed to the irredeemable situation. Then he felt in his own human flesh the reality of betrayal and the brutality of Jahweh and His creation, and then he cried the twenty-second Psalm, that long lament about trust in God the Father:

> My God, my God, why hast thou forsaken me? Why art thou
> so far from helping me, and from the words of my roaring? O
> my God, I cry in the daytime and thou answerest not; and in
> the night . . . Yet thou art holy . . . Our fathers trusted in thee:
> they trusted, and thou didst deliver them . . . They trusted in
> thee, and were not confounded . . . Thou art He that took me
> out of the womb: thou didst make me trust when I was upon my
> mother's breasts. I was cast upon thee from my birth: thou art
> my God from my mother's belly. Be not far from me; for trouble
> is near; for there is none to help . . .

And then come these images of being set upon by *brutal* bestial forces:

> Many bulls have compassed me, strong bulls have beset me
> round. They open wide their mouth against me as a lion . . .
> the dogs have compassed me. The company of evil-doers have
> inclosed me: they pierced my hands and feet . . .

This extraordinary passage affirms that primal trust is in the paternal power, that the cry for rescue is not a cry for mothering — in fact God has delivered him from the mother's breasts — but that the experience of betrayal is part of a masculine mystery.

One cannot help but remark upon *the accumulation of anima symbolism constellated with the betrayal motif.* As the drama of betrayal unfolds and intensifies, the feminine becomes more and more apparent. Briefly, may I refer to the washing of the feet at the supper and the commandment to love; to the kiss and the silver; to the agony of Gethsemane — a garden, at night, the cup and the salty sweat pouring like drops of blood; to the wounded ear; to the image of the barren women on the way to Golgotha; to the warning from the dream of Pilate's wife; to the degradation and suffering, the gall and bitter sop, the nakedness and weakness; the ninth-hour darkness and the abundance of Marys; and I refer especially to the wound in the side at the helpless moment of death, as Eve was torn from Adam's side. And finally, the discovery of the risen Christ, in white, by women.

It would seem that the message of love, the Eros mission of Jesus, carries its final force only through the betrayal and crucifixion. For at the moment when God lets him down, Jesus becomes all too truly human, suffering the human tragedy, with his pierced and wounded side from which flows the water and blood, the released fountain of life, feeling, and emotion. (This blood symbolism has been amplified extensively in the work of Emma Jung and M.-L. von Franz on the Grail.[4]) The puer quality, the position of fearless safety of the miracle preacher, is gone. The puer God dies when the primal trust is broken, and the man is born. And the man is born only when the feminine in him is born. God and man, father and son no longer are one. This is a radical change in the masculine cosmos. After Eve was born from sleeping Adam's side, evil becomes possible; after the side of the betrayed and dying Jesus was pierced, love becomes possible.

III The critical moment of the "great let down", when one is crucified by one's own trust, is a most dangerous moment of what Frances Wickes would call "choice."[5] Matters may go either way for the boy who picks himself up from the floor; his resurrection hangs in the balance. He may be unable to forgive and so remain fixated in the trauma, revengeful, resentful, blind to any understanding and cut off from love. Or he may turn in the direction which I hope to sketch in the rest of my remarks.

But before we turn to the possible fruitful outcome of betrayal, let us stay awhile with the sterile choices, with the dangers which appear after betrayal.

The first of these dangers is *revenge.* An eye for an eye; evil for evil; pain for pain. Revenge is natural for some, coming immediately without question. If performed directly as an act of emotional truth, it may be cleansing. It may settle the score without, of course, producing any new results. Revenge does not lead to anything further, but counter-revenge and feuding. It is not psychologically productive because it merely abreacts tension. When revenge is delayed and turns into plotting, lying low and waiting your chances, it begins to smell

of evil, breeding fantasies of cruelty and vindictiveness. Revenge delayed, revenge refined into indirect methods can become obsessional,
narrowing the focus from the event of betrayal and its meaning to the
person of the betrayer and his shadow. Therefore, St. Thomas Aquinas
justifies revenge only when it is against the larger evil and not against
the perpetrator of that evil. The worst of revenge, psychologically, is
its mean and petty focus, its shrinking effect on consciousness.

The next of these dangers, these wrong though natural turns, is the
defense mechanism of *denial*. If one has been let down in a relationship,
one is tempted to deny the value of the other person; to see, sudden and
at once, the other's shadow, a vast panoply of vicious demons which
were of course simply not there in primal trust. These ugly sides of the
other suddenly revealed are all compensations for, an enantiodromia
of, previous idealizations. The grossness of the sudden revelations indicates the previous gross unconsciousness of the anima. For we must
assume that wherever there is bitter complaint over betrayal, there was
a background of primal trust, of childhood's unconscious innocence
where ambivalence was repressed. Eve had not yet come on the scene,
was not recognized as part of the situation, was repressed.

I mean by this that the emotional aspects of the involvement, especially the feeling judgments — that continuous stream of evaluations
running within every connection — were just not admitted. Before
betrayal the relationship denied the anima aspect; after betrayal the
relationship is denied by the anima resentments. An involvement that
is unconscious of the anima is either mostly projected, as in a love af-
fair, or mostly repressed, as in an all-too-masculine friendship of ideas
and "working together." Then the anima can call attention to herself
only by making trouble. Gross unconsciousness of the anima is simply
taking the emotional part of a relationship for granted, in animal faith,
a primal trust that there is no problem, that what one believes and
says and "has in mind" about it is enough, that it works all by itself, *ça
va tout seul*. Because one failed to bring overtly into a relationship the
hope one had for it, the need for growing together in mutuality and
with duration — all of which are constellated as ultimate possibilities
in any close relationship — one turns the other way and denies hopes
and expectations altogether.

But the sudden shift from gross unconsciousness to gross consciousness belongs to any moment of truth and is rather evident. And so it is not the main danger.

More dangerous is *cynicism*. Disappointment in love, with a political cause, an organization, a friend, superior, or analyst often leads to a change of attitude in the betrayed one which not only denies the value of the particular person and the relationship, but all love becomes a Cheat, causes are for Saps, organizations Traps, hierarchies Evil, and analysis nothing but prostitution, brainwashing, and fraud. Keep sharp; watch out. Get the other before he gets you. Go it alone. I'm all right, Jack — the veneer to hide the scars of broken trust. From broken idealism is patched together a tough philosophy of cynicism.

It is well possible that we encounter this cynicism — especially in younger people — because enough attention has not been paid to the meaning of betrayal, especially in the transformation of the *puer eternus*. As analysts we have not worked it through to its significance in the development of feeling life, as if it were a dead end in itself out of which no phoenix could arise. So, the betrayed one vows never to go so high again on the stairs. He remains grounded in the world of the dog, *Kynis*, cynical. This cynical view, because it prevents working through to a positive meaning of betrayal, forms a vicious circle, and the dog chases its own tail. Cynicism, that sneer against one's own star, is a betrayal of one's own ideals, a betrayal of one's own highest ambitions as carried by the puer archetype. When he crashes, everything to do with him is rejected. This leads to the fourth, and I believe main, danger: self-betrayal.

Self-betrayal is perhaps what we are really most worried about. And one of the ways it may come about is as a consequence of having been betrayed. In the situation of trust, in the embrace of love, or to a friend, or with a parent, partner, analyst, one lets something open. Something comes out that had been held in: "I never told this before in my whole life." A confession, a poem, a love-letter, a fantastic invention or scheme, a secret, a childhood dream or fear — which holds one's deepest values. At the moment of betrayal, these delicate and very sensitive seed-pearls become merely grit, grains of dust. The love-letter becomes silly sentimental stuff, and the poem, the fear, the dream, the ambition, all reduced to something ridiculous, laughed at boorishly, explained in barnyard language as *merde*, just so much crap. The alchemical process is reversed: the gold turned back into faeces, one's pearls cast before swine. For the swine are not others from whom one must keep back one's secret values, but the boorish materialistic explanations, the reductions to dumb simplicities of sex-drive and milk-hunger, which gobble everything up indiscriminately; one's own pig-headed insistence that the best was really the worst, the dirt into which one casts away one's precious values.

It is a strange experience to find oneself betraying oneself, turning against one's own experiences by giving them the negative values of the shadow and by acting against one's own intentions and value system. In the breakup of a friendship, partnership, marriage, love-affair, or analysis, suddenly the nastiest and dirtiest appears and one finds oneself acting in the same blind and sordid way that one attributes to the other, and justifying one's own actions with an alien value system. One is truly betrayed, handed over to an enemy within. And the swine turn and rend you.

The alienation from one's self after betrayal is largely protective. One doesn't want to be hurt again, and since this hurt came about through revealing just what one is, one begins not to live from that place again. So one avoids, betrays oneself, by not living one's stage of life (a middle-aged divorcee with no one to love) or one's eros (I'm through with men and will be just as ruthless as they) or one's type (my feeling, or intuition, or whatever, was all wrong) or one's vocation (psychotherapy is really a dirty business). For it was just through this trust in these fundamentals of one's own nature that one was betrayed. So we refuse to be what we are, begin to cheat ourselves with excuses and escapes, and self-betrayal becomes nothing other than Jung's definition of neurosis: *uneigentliches Leiden*, inauthentic suffering. One no longer lives one's form of suffering, but through *mauvaise foi*, through lack of courage to be, one betrays oneself.

This is ultimately, I suppose, a religious problem, and we are rather like Judas or Peter in *letting down the essential thing*, the essential important demand to take on and carry one's own suffering and be what one is no matter how it hurts.

Besides revenge, denial, cynicism, and self-betrayal, there is yet one other negative turn, one other danger, which let us call *paranoid*. Again, it is a way of protecting oneself against ever being betrayed again, by building the perfect relationship. Such relationships demand a loyalty oath; they tolerate no security risks. "You must never let me down" is the motto. Treachery must be kept out by affirmations of trust, declarations of everlasting fidelity, proofs of devotion, sworn secrecy. There must be no flaw; betrayal must be excluded.

But if betrayal is given with trust, as the opposite seed buried within it, then this paranoid demand for a relationship without the possibility of betrayal cannot really be based on trust. Rather it is a convention devised to exclude risk. As such it belongs less to love than to power. It is a retreat to a logos relationship, enforced by word, not held by love.

One cannot re-establish primal trust once one has left Eden. One now knows that promises hold only to a certain point. Life takes care of vows, fulfilling them or breaking them. And new relationships after the experience of betrayal must start from an altogether different place. The paranoid distortion of human affairs is serious indeed. When an analyst (or husband, lover, disciple, or friend) attempts to meet the requirements of a paranoid relationship, by giving assurances of loyalty, by ruling out treachery, he is moving surely away from love. For as we have seen and shall come to again, love and treachery come from the same left side.

IV I would like now to leave the question of what betrayal means to the son, the one betrayed, in order to return to another of our earlier questions: What might betrayal mean to the father? What it meant to God to let His son die on the cross we are not told. What it meant to Abraham to lead his son to sacrifice we are also not told. But they performed these actions. They were able to betray, just as Jacob the patriarch entered into his estate by betraying his brother. Could it be that the capacity to betray belongs to the state of fatherhood? Let us look further at this question.

The father in our story does not merely show his human imperfection, that is, he does not merely fail in catching his son. It is not merely weakness or error. He consciously designs to let him fall and cause him pain and humiliation. He shows his brutality. The same brutality is shown in the treatment of Jesus from his capture to his crucifixion, and in the preparations of Abraham. What happens to Esau and to Job is nothing else than brutal. The brutality comes out again in the animal skin Jacob wears to betray Esau, and the great beasts God reveals to Job as the rationale for his torment. Also, in the images of Psalm 22 as we saw above.

The paternal image — that just, wise, merciful figure — refuses to intervene in any way to ameliorate the suffering which he himself has brought about. *He also refuses to give an account of himself.* The refusal to explain means that the explanation must come, if it comes at all, from the injured party. After a betrayal one is in no position to listen to the explanations of the other anyway! This is, I believe, a creative stimulus in betrayal. It is the betrayed one who must somehow resurrect himself, take a step forward, through his own interpretation of what happened. But it can be creative providing he doesn't fall into and stay in the dangers we have sketched above.

In our story, the father does explain. Our story is after all a lesson, and the action itself is educative as an initiation, whereas in the archetypal tales and in much of daily life betrayal is not explained by the betrayer to the betrayed, because it happens through the autonomous left side, unconsciously. In spite of the explanations, our story still shows brutality. *The conscious use of brutality would seem a mark common to the paternal figures.* The unjust father reflects unfair life. Where he is impervious to the cry for help and the need of the other, where he can admit that his promise is fallible, he acknowledges that the power of the word can be transcended by the forces of life. This awareness of his masculine limitations and this hardheartedness imply a high degree of differentiation of the weak left side. Differentiation of the left side would mean the ability to carry tension without action, going wrong without trying to set things right, letting events determine principles. It means further that one has to some extent overcome that sense of uneasy guilt which holds one back from carrying out in full consciousness necessary though brutal acts. (By conscious brutality, I do not mean either deliberately perverse brutality aimed to ruin another, or sentimental brutality as found sometimes in literature and films and the code of machismo.)

Uneasy guilt, tender-mindedness, makes acts double-binding. The anima is not quite up to the task. But the father's hard heart is not double-binding. He is not cruel on the one hand and pious on the other. He does not betray and then pick up his son in his arms, saying, "Poor boy; this hurt me worse than it hurt you."

In analysis, as in all positions of trust, we are sometimes led into situations where something happens that requires a consciously brutal action, a betrayal of the other's trust. We break a promise, we are not there when needed, we let the other down, we alienate an affection, betray a secret. We neither explain what we do, nor pull the other off his cross, nor even pick him up at the bottom of the stairs. These are brutalities — and we do them, with more or less consciousness. And we must stand for them and stand through them, else the anima renders our acts thin, listless and cruel.

This hardheartedness shows an integration of brutality, thereby bringing one closer to nature — which gives no explanations of itself. They must be wrested from it. This willingness to be a betrayer brings us closer to the brutish condition where we are not so much minions of a supposedly moral God and immoral Devil, but of an amoral nature. And so we are led back to our theme of anima-integration, where one's cold-heartedness and sealed lips are as Eve and the serpent whose wisdom is also close to nature's treachery. This leads me to ask whether anima-integration might not show itself not only in the various ways we might expect — vitality, relatedness, love, imagination, subtlety, and so on — but whether anima-integration might not also show itself in becoming nature-like: less reliable, flowing like water in the paths of least resistance, turning answers with the wind, speaking with a double tongue — conscious ambiguity rather than unconscious ambivalence. Supposedly, the sage or master, in order to be the psychopompos who guides souls through the confusion of creation where there is a fault in every rock and the paths are not straight, shows hermetic cunning and a coldness that is as impersonal as nature itself.[6]

In other words, our conclusion to the question: "What does betrayal mean to the father?" results in this — *the capacity to betray others is akin to the capacity to lead others.* Full fatherhood is both. In so far as psychological leading has for its aim the other's self-help and self-reliance, the other will in some way at some point be led down or let down to his own level, that is, turned back from human help, betrayed into himself where he is alone.

As Jung says in *Psychology and Alchemy,*

> I know from experience that all coercion — be it suggestion, insinuation, or any other method of persuasion ultimately proves to be nothing but an obstacle to the highest and most decisive experience of all, which is to be alone with his own self, or whatever one chooses to call the objectivity of the psyche. The patient must be alone if he is to find out what it is that supports him when he can no longer support himself. Only this experience can give him an indestructible foundation.[7]

V What then is trustworthy in the good father or psychopompos? What in this regard is the difference between the white magician and the black? What separates the sage from the brute? Could we not, by means of what I have been presenting, justify every brutality and betrayal that a man might commit as a sign of his "anima-integration," as a sign of his attainment to "full fatherhood"?

I do not know how to answer this question other than by referring to the same stories. We find in all of them two things: the motif of love and/or the sense of necessity. The Christian interpretation of God's forsaking Jesus on the cross says that God so loved the world that He gave His only Son for its redemption. His betrayal was necessary, fulfilling his fate. Abraham so loved God that he prepared to put the knife to Isaac in offering. Jacob's betrayal of Esau was a necessity already announced in the womb. The father in our story must have so loved his son that he could risk the broken bones and broken trust, and the broken image of himself in his son's eyes.

This wider context of necessity or love leads me to believe that betrayal — going back on a promise, refusing to help, breaking a secret, deceiving in love — is too tragic an experience to be justified in personal terms of psychological mechanisms and motives. Personal psychology is not enough; analysis and explanations will not do. One must look to the wider context of love and fate. But who can be certain when love is present? And who can state that this betrayal was necessary, fate, a call of the Self.

Certainly a part of love is responsibility; so too is concern, involvement, identification — but perhaps a surer way of telling whether one is closer to the brute or the sage is by looking for love's opposite: power. If betrayal is perpetuated mainly for personal advantage (to get out of a tight spot, to hurt or use, to save one's skin, to gain pleasure, to still a desire or slake a need, to take care of Number One), then one can be sure that love had less the upper hand than did the brute, power.

The wider context of love and necessity is given by the archetypes of myth. When the event is placed in this perspective, the pattern may become meaningful again. The very act of attempting to view it from this wider context is therapeutic. Unfortunately, the event may not disclose its meaning for a long, long time, during which it lies sealed in absurdity or festers in resentment. But the struggle for putting it within the wider context, the struggle with interpretation and integration, is the way of moving further. It seems to me that only this can lead through the steps of anima differentiation sketched so far, and even to one further step, towards one of the noblest of religious feelings: *forgiveness*.

We must be quite clear that forgiveness is no easy matter. If the ego has been wronged, the ego cannot forgive just because it "should," notwithstanding the wider context of love and destiny. The ego is kept vital by its *amour-propre*, its pride and honor. Even where one wants to forgive, one finds one simply can't, because forgiveness doesn't come from the ego. I cannot directly forgive, I can only ask, or pray, that these sins be forgiven. Wanting forgiveness to come and waiting for it may be all that one can do.

Forgiveness, like humility, is only a term unless one has been fully humiliated or fully wronged. Forgiveness is meaningful only when one can neither forget nor forgive. And our dreams do not let us forget. Anyone can forget a petty matter of insult, a personal affront. But if one has been led step by step into an involvement where the substance was trust itself, bared one's soul, and then been deeply betrayed in the sense of handed over to one's enemies, outer or inner (those shadow values described above where chances for a new loving trust have been permanently injured by paranoid defenses, self-betrayal, and cynicism), then forgiveness takes on great meaning. It may well be that betrayal has no other positive outcome but forgiveness, and that the experience of forgiveness is possible only if one has been betrayed. Such forgiveness is a forgiving which is not a forgetting, but *the remembrance of wrong transformed within a wider context*, or as Jung has put it, the salt of bitterness transformed to the salt of wisdom.

This wisdom, as Sophia, is again a feminine contribution to masculinity, and would give the wider context which the will cannot achieve for itself. Wisdom I would here take to be that union of love with necessity where feeling finally flows freely into one's fate, reconciling us with an event.

Just as trust had within it the seed of betrayal, so betrayal has within it the seed of forgiveness. This would be the answer to the last of our original questions: "What place has betrayal in psychological life at all?" *Neither trust nor forgiveness could be fully realized without betrayal.* Betrayal is the dark side of both, giving them both meaning, making them both possible. Perhaps this tells us something about why betrayal is such a strong theme in our religions. It is perhaps the human gate to such nobler religious experiences as forgiveness and reconciliation with this enigmatic labyrinth, the creation.

But forgiveness is so difficult that it probably needs some help from the other person. I mean by this that the wrong, if not remembered by both parties — and remembered as a wrong — falls on the betrayed. The wider context within which the tragedy occurred would seem to call for parallel feelings from both parties. They are still both in a relationship, now as betrayer and betrayed. If only the betrayed senses a wrong, while the other passes it over with rationalizations, then the betrayal is still going on — even increased. This dodging of what has really happened is, of all the sores, the most galling to the betrayed. Forgiveness comes harder; resentments grow because the betrayer is not carrying his history and the act is not honestly conscious. Jung has said that the meaning of our sins is that we carry them, which means not that we unload them onto others to carry for us. To carry one's sins, one has first to recognize them, and recognize their brutality.

Psychologically, carrying a sin means simply recognizing it, remembering it. All the emotions connected with the betrayal experience in both parties — remorse and repentance in the betrayer, resentment and revenge in the betrayed — press towards the same psychological point: remembering. Resentment especially is an emotional affliction of memory which forgetting can never fully repress. So is it not better to remember a wrong than to surge between forgetting and resenting? These emotions would seem to have as their aim keeping an experience from dissolving into the unconscious. They are the salt preserving the event from decomposing. Bitterly, they force us to keep faith with sin. In other words, a paradox of betrayal is the *fidelity* which both betrayed and betrayer keep, after the event, to its bitterness.

And this fidelity is kept as well by the betrayer. For if I am unable to admit that I have betrayed someone, or I try to forget it, I remain stuck in unconscious brutality. Then the wider context of love and the wider context of fatefulness of my action and of the whole event is missed. Not only do I go on wronging the other, but I wrong myself, for I have cut myself off from self-forgiveness. I can become no wiser, nor have I anything with which to become reconciled.

For these reasons I believe that forgiveness by the one probably requires atonement by the other. Atonement is in keeping with the silent behavior of the father as we have been describing him. He carries his guilt and his suffering. Though he realizes fully what he has done, he does not give account of it to the other, implying that he atones, that is, self-relates it. Atonement also implies a submission to betrayal as such, its transpersonal fateful reality. By bowing before the shame of my inability to keep my word, I am forced to admit humbly both my own personal weakness and the reality of impersonal powers.

However, let us take care that such atonement is not for one's own peace of mind, not even for the situation. *Must it not somehow recognize the other person?* I believe that this point cannot be overstated, for we live in a human world even if victims of cosmic themes like tragedy, betrayal, and fate. Betrayal may belong within a wider context and be a cosmic theme, but it is always within individual relationships, through another close person, in immediate intimacy, that these things reach us. If others are instruments of the Gods in bringing us tragedy, so too are they ways we atone to the Gods. Conditions are transformed within the same sort of close personal situation in which they occurred. Is it enough to atone just to the Gods alone? Is one then done with it? Does not tradition couple wisdom with *humility*? Atonement, as repentance, may not have to *be expressis verbis*, but it probably is more effective if it comes out in some form of contact with the other, in full recognition of the other. And, after all, isn't just this full recognition of the other, love?

VI May I sum up? The unfolding through the various stages from trust through betrayal to forgiveness presents a movement of consciousness. The first condition of primal trust is largely unconscious and pre-anima. It is followed by betrayal, where the word is broken by life. For all its negativity, betrayal is yet an advance over primal trust because it leads to the "death" of the puer through the anima experience of suffering. This may then lead, if not blocked by the negative vicissitudes of revenge, denial, cynicism, self-betrayal and paranoid defenses, to a firmer fatherhood where the betrayed can in turn betray others less unconsciously, implying an integration of a man's untrustworthy nature. The final integration of the experience may result in forgiveness by the betrayed, atonement by the betrayer, and a reconciliation — not necessarily with each other — but a reconciliation by each to the event. Each of these phases of bitterly fought and suffered experiences which may take long years of fidelity to the dark side of the psyche, is also a phase in the development of the anima, and that has been, despite my emphasis upon the masculine, the main theme of this chapter.

Notes

1. [From *The Guild of Pastoral Psychology*, Guild Lecture No. 128 (London, 1964); also in *Spring* 1965, pp. 57–76. Reprinted in J. Hillman, *Loose Ends: Primary Papers in Archetypal Psychology* (New York/Zurich: Spring Publications, 1975).] — Ed.

2. Gabriel Marcel, *Being and Having* (London: Collins, 1965), p. 47.

3. Jean-Paul Sartre, *Saint Genet: Actor and Martyr* (New York: The New American Library, 1964), p. 191.

4. Emma Jung and M.-L. von Franz, *The Grail Legend* (New York: Putnam, 1971).

5. Frances Wickes, *The Inner World of Choice* (New York: Harper and Row, 1963).

6. "Heaven and Earth are not humane
They regard all things as strawdogs
The Sage is not humane
He regards all people as strawdogs."
(*Tao-te ching*, no. 5)

7. C. G. Jung, *Collected Works*, vol. 12: *Psychology and Alchemy*, par. 32.

8

Puer Wounds and Odysseus' Scar[1]

He was nuts, he was a psychopath. He was crazy, nearsighted, always
having trouble with women. He was very talented, very sensitive, very
clinging. There were gaping wounds in him.

— Elia Kazan on James Dean[2]

Mythological figures of young Gods and Heroes often show laming,
crippling, bleeding, and sometimes castration. The motif of laming
has been examined in some detail from a Jungian perspective by Sas.[2]
I would concur with his findings that the crippled one is also the creative one (Hephaestus as paradigm). He interprets the laming as a
one-sided standpoint. But even if the lamed foot and wounded leg
express the one-sided unbalance supposedly necessary to creativity,
and even if this notion is symbolically reinforced by the sexual implications of the foot and the devilish associations of limping, we have
yet to uncover its deeper ground.

There has got to be more to it than that. That word "creativity"
dulls and blunts the spirit of inquiry; it covers over more than it reveals, and is, in fact, a most uncreative word. The usual misty-eyed
reverence with which it is spoken is an invocation to the fresh, spontaneous, unreflecting and beautiful, though tortured, spirit; that is, it
refers us back again to the puer which it is supposed to explain. When
we account for puer woundedness with "creativity," we have become
redundant and circular.

Why does the puer spirit require such massive wounds and crippling distortions? We must inquire into the specifics of laming, placing
it within puer woundedness. Here again, it will be difficult to discern

puer from hero, since the wound itself seems to identify the puer spirit with heroic destiny. Therefore, this chapter will have to go where puer consciousness is embodied in heroic configurations. We can't keep them apart until we have discerned the necessity of the spirit's entrapment in the wounds of heroism. Our aim is to recover mythical images that lose the hero but save the wound.

Modern psychology tells us that parents can be the wounders. Everyone carries a parental wound and has a wounded parent. Today we go to therapy for healing the parental wounds. Ancient myths tell of wounding parents in various stories. Pelops is chopped up by his father, Tantalus, who served his son boiled to the Gods to eat.[4] Pelops, however, regenerated, except for a shoulder. Is Pelops that young man who must shoulder his father-complex, and yet cannot because this same complex deprives him of his capacity to shoulder? Or is his mode of shouldering aesthetic: the ivory prosthesis replacing the irrecoverably missing part?

Other tales tell of other parental woundings: when maddened by Dionysus, Pentheus' mother cuts off her son's head[5] and Lykourgos cuts off his son's extremities.[6] The boy Odysseus is wounded while he is with his grandfather, and by a "parental" boar.[7] The soft spot in Achilles (and in Baldur) comes from the Mother. Achilles is held by the heel and dipped into the bath to make him invincible — except for where she held him. His fatal wound is precisely where his mother touched him under the guise of protecting him.[8] One wound of Hercules occurs in a battle with a Father and Sons (Hippocoon and his sons).[9] This father-son conflict wounds Hercules in the hollow of his hand; and in another tale Hercules kills his own children.

The wound-in-reverse, or the wounded parent, is shown by Aeneas who totes his lame father on his back, and by Perseus who, with a discus, accidentally wounds his grandfather Akrisos in the foot.[10]

The mythical image of the wounding or wounded parent becomes the psychological statement that *the parent is the wound*. Literally, we hold our parents responsible, but metaphorically the same statement can mean: that which wounds us can also parent us. Our wounds are the fathers and mothers of our destinies.

LAMING. Puer wounds always occur in specific images within specific stories, and more: they are local wounds to specific bodyparts:
Achilles' heel, Pelops' shoulder. In Adler's terms, puer psychology is
marked by quite specific organ inferiority; first of all by wounds to the
lower extremities. Achilles' heel, Oedipus (swellfoot), Hercules (the
crab at Lerna),[11] Alexander the Great (wounded in the ankle),[12] Odysseus' leg, Jason's single sandal,[13] Philoctetes, Bellerophon who limps
— all these are marked in the foot.[14] Does the fact that every human
descended from Eve shall be bruised in the heel by the serpent say that
each human being is susceptible to the puer?

The wounded foot (and its reverse, the winged feet of Hermes
and the seven-league flight boots) says something basic about the puer
condition. His stance, his position is marked in such a way that his
connection with *res extensa* is hindered, heroic, and magical. The spirit
does not fully reach downward into this world, since at that place of
contact with the world, the puer figure is deathly weak. This consciousness cannot walk and thereby extend itself step by step. It is unable to be in the world with both feet on the ground, as if the transcendent seems unable to posit itself fully as human. Even the incarnated
Christ, whose mission was to bring Heaven down to earth, himself was
wounded in the feet and crucified above our heads, in the air. When
transcendent, Heaven's Son, the puer, is superb — like Bellerophon
on Pegasus piercing through illusions; but when fallen onto earth, like
Bellerophon the spirit limpingly drags itself around Aleion, the "plains
of wandering."[15] How important shoes then become — Maine boots,
Guru shoes, earth sandals, thicksoled, thinsoled, holes, cleated, or air-
filled with luminous heels: ritualizations and magic of the feet.

If the deeper implication of laming is the verticality of the spirit,
we may expect to find images of laming as an advantage or achievement. The one-legged dance of a Shaman[16] is just such an example of
unnatural distortion representing supernatural power. Another example
is the alchemical image of the hermaphroditic uniped.[17] The double
standpoint of left and right is unified into a single pivot. Movement no
longer shuffles along, back and forth, now this side, now that; instead,
consciousness has to hop and skip about. The left-right rhythm that
steadies one with the mutual self-corrections of thesis and antithesis

is off-balance, and with it, man's relation to the earth as walker who paces the dimensions of reality, taking its measure with his footsteps and his tempo. Instead of steadiness, there is the gift of leaping about in discontinuity and then being wholly identified (at one with) wherever one lands. And wherever one has landed, at once becomes the center so that one's motion is no longer locomotion but a self-turning on one's own axis. In this condition consciousness is single, centroverted, and also in precarious balance, which does imply that the exceptional state of wholly centered consciousness is less stable than we like to believe. Perhaps the uniped shows a state of continuous discontinuity, in which the alchemical achievement is less a solid-state stone than the wonky wobble, always teetering, susceptible to falling. Consciousness leaps to the center of things, is identified with its standpoint, but cannot stand there. Nor can it even observe itself since there is no longer any one foot in and one foot out. We are now into the genius and pathology of fusional states, the single standpoint of identification.

Whereas alchemy represents one-footedness as an accomplishment, usually this virtue — if such it is — of being "singled" out through the foot does not feel like an achievement. He who has it experiences its onus and usually not its blessings. At best the marked foot represents a condition of being singled out by an abnormal standpoint. Jason's absent sandal meant that he was pledged with one foot (the left) to the Underworld. Mopsos, the prophet whose "special skill in divination was concerned with birds. He could understand their language," was snake-bitten in the left foot.[18] (The odd relation between the marked foot and prophecy is brought out further in Melampus = "Black Foot," the earliest legendary prophet of Greek myth.)[19] The cost of sight into the divine (divination), and thus foresight into time, is a marking in relation to this normal world of here and now. To soar one must hobble, too. The marked foot is also a laming, a limiting hindrance, a frustration and a wound. The complex through which we gain our profoundest insight is also our greatest hindrance. The native sensitivity through which we receive the Gods also continually hurts and may kill us.

In a sense the heroic puer is uniped, as Emerson suggests in his definition of the hero as the one "who is immovably centered." He is tied
to the Immovable Point or World Navel, "for the hero is himself the
navel of the world, the umbilical point through which the energies of
eternity break into time."[20] The wound represents the immobility, the
limits of destiny nailing one to the spot so that through one's wound
these energies of eternity can flow. Or, at least so it feels. The hurt
leg or foot then keeps one eternally bound to the archetypal realm
by one's very immobility. One never has to descend from the cross.
So, heroic puer-consciousness that releases energies is itself paralyzed
— almost senex-like, stuck forever to and by its own eternality.

Furthermore, the wounded leg or foot calls for a crutch. We need
someone to lean on, special inclines, footstools, wheels. Winged and
frail as the puer figure may be, he still can dominate through the power
of his neediness.

Laming also expresses the weakness and helplessness at the beginning of any enterprise. The initial moment is also the most vulnerable;
first steps are tentative and uncertain. The whole project stands or falls
with the first stroke since everything after that is but a further development of the initial act. We may improve, rectify, or transform, but
always the source is that first sketch or draft tossed off initially by puer
inspiration. This is the motif of "difficulty at the beginning," of youthful foolishness or fantastic bravado; here we experience the fragility of
the spirit. The wounded puer personifies the spirit's structural damage
and, maybe, damaging structure.

‖ MAIMED HANDS. Sometimes the damage shows in the hands that
cannot take hold, grasp the tools, comprehend the problems,
seize the issues. Then, puer consciousness complains that it cannot
"manage." The hands may be clever and manipulative, but there is difficulty at hanging-in or hanging-on to the "matter at hand" so that it
can be resolved. Knots are sliced open with a brilliant stroke, rather
than carefully sorted out strand by strand.

The inabilities of the hands are sometimes repaired in dreams by
surgical operations. A slug-like worm is pulled out of the metacarpus
of a woman who feels herself slow at grasping ideas. A surgeon oper-

ates painstakingly, seemingly for hours, at the base of a young man's right fingers, as if careful slowness is the operation itself, giving a base to the patient's deft but fluttery fingers that drop everything too soon. A young potter's hand is cut open down to the bone. He is horrified and fascinated by the sight. The dreamer can now see that his hand which forms is itself formed by deep, hard, ancient structures and that the shapes he makes have a preformed interior pattern. The dream has released an archetypal sense of what he is doing.

To the hands belong two distinct spiritual functions: creative and authoritative, the wand and the mace. The creative function appears in the conception of the fingers as independent forces, the little gnomic phallic *daktyls* who fashion new shapes in their spontaneous play. Inventions are fantasies of the fingers. The spirit plays with things, pries them open with curiosity, picks them apart analytically, puts the incongruous together into symbols. Jung[21] associates the fingers directly with the *puer aeternus*, so that a wounded or maimed finger strikes directly at the archetype itself. At the fingertips we are at the growing edge, reaching into the unknown. "The hand reacts quicker than the arm, the arm quicker than the shoulder."[22] As we move outward into the extremities, the expansive, experimental vitality of the individual comes into play. Here, too, the unconscious spirit presents itself by doodling, automatic writing, free-hand drawing — and writer's cramp. Scratching, picking, drumming with the fingers, fondling stones, worry-beads — the fingers must be busy. Even masturbating may be as much for the sake of idle hands as for the claims of the genitals. To lose one's fingers is to lose one's creative fantasy and one's childlike vitality. It is a loss which may signify the sacrifice of "newness."[23] These imaginative and playful activities of the hands can be distinguished from their other spiritual function: the fist of will and oath, handling, seizing, and comprehending the world.

The two spiritual meanings of the hands, imaginative and executive, pull against and may even damage each other. After all, the fingers disappear into the fist and must serve its punch, just as the fist is gone once the fingers come into play. The gifts of the puer-man may be in his hands yet these same hands may be the place where he lets go of his own gifts. Perhaps, the executive hands must be wounded;

perhaps the imaginative function of the hands wounds their executive capacity. The gift both blesses and curses. The talent placed in my hands does not necessarily become mine. To seize the talent may realize it, but it also may make the talent vanish. The man whose life-style follows the puer and lives from the spirit shows wounded hands when he cannot handle his gifts or manage that spirit which comes and goes of its own accord. His handicap reminds him of his limits, keeping him to the fingers of fantasy rather than the fist of control.

Perhaps, the puer spirit may not be meant to manage but to imagine. In the hands of the puer are shapes and gestures, and the puer touch, but not the reins of will. The desultory execution, the indecision that cannot grasp the sword-hilt and slash a way forward may be symptomatic not only of what is wrong. It may also hint at something right: that one way forward is not via action but fantasy, the way of imagination. If maiming puts everything active out of reach, only fantasy remains. And fantasy is not wildly inspirational only. It has its laws and will, its intrinsic intelligibility of forms that the hands follow in each of the crafts. The strict demands of craft — that fantasies be crafted with precision into shapes — provide discipline and an ethic for an imaginal ego. By staying true to the puer archetype and its transcendent function, we work at our crippling from within the imagination.

A primary method for the crafting of fantasy is what the French call *bricolage*, pottering about with bits and pieces that are given.[24] The wound reduces one to an "occupational therapy," that is, making something of one's complexes *as they are*. We recombine them into new fantasies by becoming a handy-man who can make-do with the limitations of his psychic complexity. Here, the wound is a teacher to which one apprentices one's puer ambition. It is forced into the concrete, for *bricolage* is the "science of the concrete." One can take hold of only small things, one at a time, try this with that. This *bricolage* gives one the feel of the complexes, their blunt places and sharp edges, and above all, how they fit into each other. The wounded hand is clumsy, and the healing of the puer's messy concrete life begins in the experience of one's clumsiness. (So long as we are soaring, we have no notion of the mess we leave behind.) Moving around in this way among the complexes, becoming more crafty because one is so clumsy, holds up the impulse towards idealized abstractions. The straight line of puer ambition is tamed by the wounded hand. And, because fantasy itself is wounded, that is, kept limited by its own inability, the wound saves puer consciousness from higher flights and worse falls.

The autonomous hand extends to manipulate the world and make all things its tools. *Orexis*, the most embracing Greek term for appetite or desire, etymologically means the extension of the hand, its reach and greed. Puer nightmares show autonomy of the hands and the fear of their strangling or stabbing. Sometimes suicidal wrist-slashing seems to attempt a self-cure by the autonomous hand of its own independence: if I offend thee, cut me off. The self-wounding act may be read less in terms of bleeding and more in terms of the hands themselves. Although the fear of the Autonomous Hand may pervade a puer person, the same puer consciousness worships this autonomy as creativity, believing himself or herself an artist.

Let us remember that our fingers let us fly. Phylogenetically our hands compare with birds' wings. The ascensional possibility in the hands is expressed by Darwin in literalistic fantasies; Darwin considered humankind's verticality to be the result of its hands.[25] We have pulled ourselves up from the bestial floor by our hands. In them lies our freedom; they are our wings.

So far we have discussed the two spiritual functions of the hand, the fist and the fingers,[26] suggesting that for the same hands to perform both functions — talent and the control of this talent—may be more than human. In fact, it may be devilish, since only by shaking hands with the devil can one have the creative spirit in one's own hands to do with as one likes. As long as we are driven both by the hand of will and by the hand of imagination, there must be wounds. Left hand has need to ring its fantasy with wedding bands, seals and signets, and right to relax its fist. Until the power of ambition and the power of imagination rest their struggle, they mutually cripple each other.

The healing of the hand depends therefore on bringing into play a third function of the hands, their soul aspect. Now we are speaking of the hand as healer, the flat of the hand, its palm, which is the etymological root of our word *feel*. All kinds of powers pass through the palms: soothing, blessing, warming, caressing, weighing, slapping,

begging.[27] Here, in the palms, are the lines of our fate, and here we are
nailed. Also here, we are naive, open-handed, bare.

So, another way of envisioning the three functions of the hand
— fingers, fist, and palm — is in terms of puer, senex, and anima. This
suggests that wounds in the palm go to the soul, both its peaceful
simplicity and its crisscrossed complexity. Here the wound affects our
grip on things and our handle on the world by means of tools. With
the awakening of the anima through suffering the flat of our hands,
we have to let go of the utilitarian connection. There is nothing more
we can *do* about things (fist) or to things (fingers). Instead we learn
about maintaining and holding — just keeping in touch. This the puer
has least of all. His wounded hand betrays a structural inability of the
spirit — or a charismatic superability — to handle what is today called
"human feeling." He may show a sign, point a way, but can he give us
a hand? He may brilliantly grasp, but can he hold on? Nonetheless,
that same wounded palm opens the soul of the hand, making it excruciatingly aware of giving and receiving. Swift-footed boy, mimetic to
Hermes, hitherto all cap and phallus, God of exchanges, commerce
and *Handel*, may now experience by means of his hurt that what actually passes through his hands are values.

We begin to see that the wounded hand is a saving grace, because
it keeps the puer spirit human. Were it not for this inadequacy, every
puer-person would long ago have built his way to heaven and would
never have let slip the reins of his sun-frenzied horses. The maimed
hands are the necessary correlate of puer giftedness. The wound is a
consequent of the gift; the gift wounds; the gift is a wound.

The wound may also be a gift. To construe maiming in only symptomatic terms is to miss its necessity within an archetypal pattern. The
feet that walked the waters had to be nailed but the legs left unbro-
ken at Christ's final descent into humanity. The same foot that made
Achilles the "swiftest" also carried that flaw which made him mortal.[28]
Wounds contain a blessing as well as the evident curse. To assume that
the curse can be cured — by exercising will power, by taking a grip to
overcome a weak ego — without at the same time affecting the blessing is naive. It is also irreligious, i.e., neglecting the archetypal structure. The religious or spiritual must be kept foremost in mind when

dealing with puer consciousness, since that is the archetypal substrate of every puer problem. What happens in ego-consciousness is only derivative of something transcendent. Thus organ inferiority cannot be adequately met with ego compensations in the Adlerian sense. Organ inferiority is indeed a ground of the weak ego, but the "weak ego" is merely pathology's way of stating that the ego is only human. Organ inferiority is the human condition, our liability to be bruised at the heel, our mortality. The ego is weak because it is mortal, with its specific lacuna or privations, deprived of ideal and abstract good by its complexes. These complexes keep us continually wounded, that is continually limited to our inferiority, our mortal condition. Every wound is a mortal wound, the realization of mortality. The crippling is indispensable for the puer, who, had he the gift without the wound, would be altogether inhuman. His handicap compensates his omnipotence, making his archetypal structure viable for human existence. His viability lies just in his vulnerability. The wound brings the senex virtue of limitation to an unlimited reach.

Ordinary psychologists, whose weight is upon analyzing the unconscious and strengthening the ego, berate the puerman for his fragile adaptation. He is so vulnerable to break-downs. In reply to them we shall remember that through the lacuna of the wound not only "the eternally pubescent individual"[29] shows, but also mortal man who is Wounded Man enters life. This "infantile, childlike individual" whom Jacobi berates is none other than the archetypal Child, chrysalis of the puer. The wound that makes adaptation so special or impossible also makes possible a new fate. A new spirit emerges in weakness, and through our holes the unexpected comes out. Hans Castorp's lung with its *petite tache humide* makes him unable for life. He has to go and live it on the *Magic Mountain*, where, through the little hole of his wound, the immense realm of spirit enters. A wound has this spiritual logos quality. It is a learner and a teacher both, and has been compared with a mouth (*Julius Caesar*, III, 1; *Henry IV*, Pt. II, I, 3). It has a message.

One meaning that speaks particularly through the wounded hand has to do with gestures. Imaginal reality, which informs puer consciousness, gives to acts and deeds a fantasy quality of gestures. Puer consciousness can transform the acting-out of the complexes into gestures, giving another style to a complex, a style that has been called fantastic and irresponsible, even hysterically theatrical. Yet, for puer consciousness, whatever role is played, however the hands are used, life itself is a gesture of the spirit; life as *mudra*, a significative gesture.

Damage to the hand discloses the fate of one who is purely and only puer: life as broken gesture, unachieved, a fragment that points beyond itself. At the same time, this damage offers the very possibility for moving from this fate into a human world where handicaps give soul.

Our hands are exposed to all the risks of daily life. They are our first touch with the concrete, how we defend ourselves, how we express ourselves, what we give each other. In them lies our sensitivity. Little wonder that the puer's hands break at this direct contact. Because hands are particular to the human species, playing a special part in shaping each destiny which we can never really read, we turn to hands to read fate. Their lines, like the prints at each finger-tip, are unique, as personal and changing as those on our faces. Yet, they are also indelible and inherited. So the wound to the hand is a wound in fate and the fate of woundedness, the fuller meaning of which we are trying to place within the phenomenology of the puer archetype.

||| BLEEDING. Another aspect of woundedness is bleeding. Here we may recollect Baldur, and the Near Eastern figures of Attis, Tammuz, and Adonis,[30] also the dismembered Osiris and the dismembered Dionysus, and Jesus, too. Why must the young god bleed? Why does he bleed to death? What does bleeding to death signify for this kind of consciousness?

On the face of it bleeding would seem to signify castration. The sons of the Magna Mater are emasculated, die of their hemorrhaging, and from their blood comes the flowering of nature. Their male substance fertilizes mother earth. By losing their external sex and bleeding from the genitals as women, they are transformed back into the female body from which they came. They are re-absorbed into nature, becoming "gardens," *kepos*,[31] another name for the vulva in Greek. Castration and subsequent bleeding states a primary identity of the son with the mother: one makes oneself one with her by making oneself into her. As such, castration bleeding is more appropriate to the son of the Great Goddess.[32]

Another aspect of bleeding, however, is more authentically puer. With Jesus, Baldur, certain saints, knights, and heroes, bleeding is primary, as if before the wound, as if the wound releases and reveals essence. Let us focus upon the continuous bleeding that cannot be stopped. Of course, this image has been given overwhelming religious significance through Jesus. The bleeding stigmata and the bleeding heart and the relics associated with the blood stir the most profound emotions of Christianity. It is said that the bleeding of Christ tells of love, of compassion, of suffering and of the endless flow of the divine essence into the human world, and of the bond through blood kinship and blood mystery of the human world with the divine. The bleeding of Jesus is a transfiguration of a basic puer motif onto a theological plane.

What does this specific form of woundedness say about the psychology of the puer? His bleeding reveals his archetypal structure in several ways. *First*, it is an image for vulnerability in general, the skin too thin for real life, the sensitivity to every pointed instrument of attack, the defenselessness of youngly naive and open truth. The bleeding tells of the puer propensity for victimization, for the constellation around him of the psychopathic attackers: Loki, Hagen, the Roman soldiers, the crowd of arrows into Sebastian.[33] He draws the assassins to himself, a hero-in-reverse, noble for his martyrdom, remembered finally less for what he does than for what is done to him. The bloodthirsty aggression that comes to him from the outside belongs to his fate, but he is unaware that it belongs to his character too. He points up the ancient idea that "character for man is destiny,"[34] so that the insights arising from the complexes composing our character also tell us about our fate. (*Amor fati* thus also means loving one's complexes.) To draw blood or to have it drawn is part of the same constellation of bloodletting. As the hero, i.e. puer, cannot stop his manic seizure of slaughter (Achilles abused Hector's corpse for twelve days), so the hero-in-reverse cannot staunch his own bleeding. He has no tourniquet partly because his bleeding is so beauteous.[35] Why stay such blood, a blood that is latent with flowers? Myths tell us again and again that from slain pueri spring wondrous blooms.[36] The puer is transfigured by his wounds into glory. It is as if he does not sense his broken vessels, cannot smell blood, only flowers. Aestheticism can defend one even against pain. Parsifal has only to ask Amfortas "What ails him?" but the question of the wound never occurs to this beautiful young man, single-minded on his quest for the grail. So Amfortas's wound continues to suppurate — ailing is all in the King, the senex; there is none in the pure young knight.

There are other wounds, suppurating and bitter, leading neither to death nor cure, serving instead as focus of psychic complexity. Prometheus' liver is always being torn at; Hercules burns in his poisoned shirt; Philoctetes' foot is continually infected. No flowers here, but rather the stuff for reflection for thousands of years in myths, dramas, and poems. These bitter wounds hurt; they stink and give rise to continual complaint, and, in Philoctetes' case, the complaint gives the dignity of an individualized destiny.

It might be well to relate complaining to woundedness, rather than to a search for mothering and a childish inability to take the hardships of life and "be a man." Complaint then may be regarded as part of woundedness, a first realization of imperfection. The shield is pierced, life is seeping away in a process of decay. A touch of Saturn. Sometimes with the puerman the wound is evident only in the complaint betrayed in the voice or posture. The breakdown begins in a cry. "I broke down and cried." The invulnerable spirit becomes human just by feeling miserable. To wail is *the* human sign, as the first emotion of the infant is crying, as the last statement of Jesus was his complaint on the cross.

Human existence is wounded from beginning to end, and the puer complaint reminds that physical nature, life of the body, the only-natural perspective is not enough. The puer body is broken through; his is an opened *physis*. The complaint, like the so-called accident that suddenly ends a promising sports career, states that consciousness is no longer contained by only the physical mode of experience. The "accident" disengages puer from the heroic carrier who has anyway been accidental to the essential puer fate which is beyond the heroic. Puer comes into his own, but complainingly. The complaint tells of separation from nature and announces the call of spiritual destiny. Mistakenly, we who hear a puer complaining consider him calling out to mother, whereas his cry is over a fate that now announces Mother Nature gives us no support and the body's life is not enough.

Bleeding also expresses the outpouring dynamus of the puer. We see it in inflation and enthusiasm. The vitality of the puer spreads and stains like the red tincture of the alchemist's *lapis*. His bleeding is a *multiplicatio*, the infectious giving out of essence for the sake of transforming the world around. The archetypal structure of the puer insists on gushing forth, hyperactive, charismatic, sacrificial. So Hotspur, for the honor of Mortimer would "empty all these veins, / And shed my dear blood drop by drop . . ." The magic touch of the puerman is not spurious; it is his life-blood that he puts into his projects and his friends. He pours out his heart despite himself.[37] His bleeding seems mere display, but it is an enactment of those god figures whose bleeding is the emanation of their essence, the exteriorization of creative vitality. Through this enactment of them he participates in them and so has superabundant energy; his bleeding seems never to exhaust him. Through their wounds these god figures are recognized as divine, so that entry into the god's love is through the divine wound, a mimesis of the archetypal infirmity, which paradoxically gives power, as the Christian mystics so triumphantly declared. A superhuman power emanates through the open wound and through being wounded. Thus puer consciousness by continually giving out and spilling forth keeps in touch with his style of power.[38] Thus, too, the puer man, mimetic to "suffering Jesus" may be playing a power game, dominating by means of his disregard for himself. His egoless generosity and self-sacrifice keep him high on his cross.

But, *third*, he has no clotting instinct. Giving becomes spilling, a psychic hemophilia. The inhibiting senex factor does not function or overreacts; both sudden borders and no limits. Here we touch upon the puer difficulty with eros. Because the heart's blood can flow so freely, the puer structure makes a man tend to draw back, to protect himself, closing off and trying to control the seepage with ego strictures of the senex. He never feels able to contain his life energy or eros: it pours through him and out of him, or he stops it up, unlovingly cold. It is an all-or-nothing phenomenon, beyond human intervention. He does not know how to feed on himself, to partake in his own essence, as the pelican could nourish its own children from its wounds. Through his wounds the puer may feed others, but may himself be drained thereby. There is a curious fault in his love for himself. Modern attempts to deal with this condition, such as Kohut's psychology of narcissism, tend to miss a main point. An archetypal force has no true care for its human incarnation. A power beyond the ego demands such immense service that we must bleed for it. Were we able to supply ourselves with enough narcissistic counsel, of course we would not be wounded, nor would we be dominated by the puer archetype, that demonic angel.

To find that caring love of self, puer often constellates — not senex and the instinct of survival — but the nurse. Myths show divine-child figures each with special nursing attendants. In the individual puer person, nursing plays a subtle role, now one's sustenance, now one's doom. Indeed the spirit needs nursing, from the milk which philosophers drink from Sophia to the glass at night for a burning stomach. But with milk may come the Great Mother and the decline of the puer spirit into whimpering for physical aid and pampering with concrete solutions. Milk has many sources, and one can be nursed in various manners. Dionysus, too, brings milk.[39] The Dionysian nurses are *daughters* of the spirit, followers, a troupe of participants, enjoying and serving spirit as their mode of mothering it. They drink, dance, and bring humor. Puer spirit, when nursed through the maiden-maenad-daughter, is no longer forced into the role of child of the mother, but instead becomes the troupe's "father." The daughter-nurse reconnects senex and puer.[40]

IV LEAKING AND CONTAINING. *Fourth* — which sums it all — is the problem of the vessel. Socrates in Plato's *Gorgias* refers to an Orphic tale which says the soul of "foolish uninitiated being" is like a leaky vessel (493b). The uninitiated are the most unhappy in the Hades depths of the psyche because there they are undergoing a process of senseless repetitive compulsion: they carry water in a sieve and pour it into a perforated jar.[41] The uninitiated have no proper vessel; they are unsealed and unretentive, says Plato. They are filled with eagerness for more because they do not hold what they have. When everything passes through, the person himself is only passing through, without substance. The open wound may here refer to the *unbuilt psychic body* which originally, in Plato, is the guard and keeper (not imprisoner) of the soul. Then the rush of life energy bursts the thin bag of psychic skin and the reddening comes too fast which, as the alchemists said, shows that the work was spoiled.

Thus, what is fundamentally missing in the puer structure is the *psychic container* for holding in, keeping back, stopping short, the moment of reflection that keeps events within so that they can be realized as psychic facts.[42]

Let us regard this vessel as a womb which — for two thousand years from Hippocrates until Charcot — was considered to be the special cause of hysteria. When this feminine vessel, the uterus (*hystera*) was out of place (wandered) it caused that leaking, dripping, out-pouring of substance, or hysteria. Without a proper feminine vessel, we can gestate nothing, nourish nothing, bring nothing to complete birth. Through the same unstoppered vessel out of which one pours oneself, one is subjected to the invasion of influences. Or, as Plato puts it, the leaky soul "can be swayed and easily persuaded." These souls are sieves that cannot close on themselves and so worship at springs (continually bubbling forth) and riversides, trusting in flow. The worship of flow, however, means also to be continually flowed through, provisional, suggestible, receptive to sinking into any surrounding. Now we meet another danger to puer consciousness: dissolution into water, oblivion. Nothing ever really happens. The virginal Yes that is both continual renewal and indiscrimination, all wet. Wide eyes, open mouths, ready laps.

The proposition that the wound is an opening further proposes that the wounded one is *afflicted by openness*. Puer openness appears as innocence, which means literally "without hurt," free of noxiousness, out of harm's way. The wound that is so necessary to initiation ceremonies ends the state of innocence as it opens one in a new way at another place, making one suffer from openness, bringing to a close the world as wonder. Now it hurts, and I must protect myself. I am no longer unharmed and harmless. So, the puer impulse will force a car-crash or a ski-spill, not merely for risk or the penchant for destruction, but as well because these adolescent accidents may move the soul into a harmed and initiated body. It is as if the soul can find no path out of innocence other than physical hurt.

This lets us look again at castration, so usually imagined to be the root problem of puer states. The usual view considers puer wounded-ness reducible to castration: he has been weakened by the mother or become her hystericized ineffectual son because of the father. Let us start from the usual view, although revisioning it anew. Let us imagine that puer castration is indeed a return to the mother — but less as her son than as a disembodied wandering spirit searching for one's *hystera*, one's internal "mother" as the womb has been called.[43] The return to the womb is to find shelter and enclosure for one's leaky, hysterical suggestibility. In other words, like cures like: my very sickness shows the mode of its healing. Hysterical regressions to the mother reveal my profound vulnerability, how utterly exposed I am, like an exagger-ated wound, and I enter into my woundedness so that it may mother me. Instead of hysterically fleeing castration I am initiated by it. Here, the fantasy is wound = womb. Now, the womb is in the right place, inside the deep belly, no longer wandering in hystericized wounded-ness, seeking a little help from friends, love in a restaurant, straws in the wind.

When wound = womb, then castration is the very ground and carrier of fecundity. One's weakness bears one's future; one's inability is the place of one's potential. So often we read this truth in the lives of sickly, hystericized young persons whose "castration complex" is precisely the locus of their genius. So, we may consider the puer's cas-tration (how he is cut off from his phallic force and seminal thoughts) as a mutilated and desperate recognition of the need for a womb-like soul that can gestate his embryonic values. My self-castrations may be my mother teaching me how to mother; they are attempts at holding myself in. Rather than wounded bleeding into the world, there is in-ternal, rhythmical bleeding like a womb, moving more easily between openness and secrecy.

Openness and secrecy — so puer! The bleeding puer reveals his naked life and his soul is a sieve. It is all there for anyone to come and look; he will tell you all about himself. The puer influence in any com-plex lays out its wares in public, and passers-by are amazed that any-one can be so open, so unpsychological. This public display is enacted by writers, painters, performers, whose complexes compulsively insist on being widely published, hung upon the wall, or shown to applauding audiences.

Together with this openness, a counter-movement of paranoid anxieties begins to cloud over. A peculiar secretiveness darkens the innocence. One feels that emotions can be shared with only a few; whom can one really trust, on watch for betrayals. To be open only leads to hurt. These anxieties initiate a sense of isolation, enmity and separation — cunning, exile and silence — in contradistinction to the charmingly naive defenselessness. Paranoid worries come as answer to over-exposure; they are self-protective and indicate closure. This happens, however, only when openness begins to hurt — hence betrayals[44] are so important for moving consciousness from the only-puer condition.

As wounds heal, they close in on themselves. Paranoid anxieties, therefore, may be therapeutic for the innocent puerman. By sealing up in secretiveness, he moves toward initiation; he has a secret without which there is no separate individuality. The secret that seals one off has often to do with the paranoid anima: a secret fantasy, a secret love, a secret goal. Curled inside the paranoid suspicion is the chrysalis of one's special individualized soul. My soul wants something unique from me. Anima is one meaning and one cure of puer-woundedness.

The paranoia of the enclosed anima in its reaction to puer openness can go to extremes. Interior life is sealed up tight, like those images of Mary, the Closed Gate, Enclosed Garden, *Semper Virgo*. The virginal anima that has not been pierced to the emotions by the experience of *physis* (which we literalize as sexual and physical experience) keeps puer persons youngly innocent while offering another way of denying woundedness.

Moreover, the eternal virginity of Mary in soul constellates a Christ identification in action. There is let loose a fresh round of bleeding into the world that never really stains one's interior life. This version of the Christian mother-son drama plays itself like a routine repertoire, season after season, in the psyche of those mimetic to this particular pattern of the puer. Yet from all that repetition little awareness comes since the anima remains *virgo intacta* and the man remains crucified by spiritual questions — the relations of spirit and flesh, God and world, ego and self, east and west, one and many — never moving past the psychological age of thirty-three. (Fortunately there are other images of Mary and other modes of the Mary-Jesus tandem, and even other less literal modes of being in the *semper virgo* pattern.)

Building the psychic vessel of containment, which is another way of speaking of soul-making, seems to require bleeding and leaking as its precondition. Why else go through that work unless we are driven by the despair of our unstoppered condition? The shift from anima-mess to anima-vessel shows in various ways: as a shift from weakness and suffering to humility and sensitivity; from bitterness and complaint to a taste for salt and blood; from focus upon the emotional pain of a wound — its causes, perimeters, cures — to its imaginal depths; from displacements of the womb onto women and "femininity" to its locus in one's own bodily rhythm.[45]

Whatever is necessary and missing gains in importance, so anima assumes grotesque, compulsive and mystical proportions in puer-consciousness, receding only as this consciousness takes on its own wound that is its container. But the opus of woundedness is counterculture. It must move Western history itself. For we stem from adventurers, missionaries, and especially crusaders. The crusading impulse that laid cities to sack and stormed through centuries of our heroic history — and still sets sails in our heroic hearts — was in grotesque search of a mystical Grail, the Crusader's noble Quest for a Vessel to contain the endlessly flowing blood of an uncontained Christ-modelled puer consciousness. To recognize that the soul is this grail returns puer consciousness to itself. In the chalice of the wound is soul. This means that psyche is the aim of our bleeding love and that the wound is a grail. The opus is not in Jerusalem; it is right here in our own wounds.

V WOUND CONSCIOUSNESS AND DIONYSUS. Although the wound may be experienced through a symptom, they are not the same. A symptom belongs to diagnosis, pointing to something else underlying. But the wound, as we have been imagining it, takes one into the archetypal condition of woundedness and gives even the smallest symptoms their transcending importance. Every symptom would turn us into its fantasy, so that skin spots make us lepers, diarrhea makes us little babies, and a sprain turns us into old has-beens on the bench.

The *magnificatio* that wounding brings is a way of entering archetypal consciousness: an awareness that more is going on than my reason can hold. One becomes an open wound, hurting all over, as consciousness is transfigured into the wounded condition. We experience affliction in general, afflictedness as a way of being-in-the-world. The wound announces impossibility and impotence. It says: "I am unable." It brutally brings awareness to the fact of limitation. The limitation is not imposed from without by external powers, but this anatomical gap is an inherent part of me, concomitant with every step I take, every reach I make.

Because limitation is so difficult and painful for the puer structure, its statement, "I am unable" is exhibited by the painfulness of the wound. He stands before you, still radiant and cheery, as innocent as ever, all the while grossly demonstrating his incapacity by the thick plaster cast on his leg. Puerman hides his wound, since it reveals the secret that weakens this mode of consciousness. It fears feeling its own inability. For, when the wound is revealed at the end of the story, it kills one as a puer. Each complex has its symptom, its Achilles' heel, its opening into humanity through a vulnerable and excruciatingly painful spot, be it Samson's hair or Siegfried's heart.[46]

Therapy must touch this spot; it must move from the beautiful wounded condition into the actual present hurt. The archetype generalizes, because archetypes are universals. So drive the nail home! Go into the crippling, maiming, bleeding; probe the specific organ — liver, shoulder, foot, or heart. Each organ has a potential spark of consciousness, and afflictions release this consciousness, bringing to awareness the organ's archetypal background, which, until wounded, had simply functioned physiologically as part of unconscious nature. But now nature is wounded. The organ is now inferior. Deprivation of natural functioning gives awareness of the function. We realize for the first time its feeling, its value, its realm of operations. Limitation through the wound brings the organ to consciousness, as if we know something only as we lose it; as if the knowledge death gives is the knowledge of what a psychic thing is in itself, its true meaning and importance for the soul. A "dying" consciousness is released by the wound.

This dying awareness or awareness of dying may heal the wound, for the wound is no longer so necessary. In this sense, a wound is the healing of puer consciousness and, as healing takes place, the wounded healer may begin to constellate. We must admit, after all, to a curious connection in fact between puer persons and the vocation to therapy.

The "wounded healer" does not mean merely that a person has been hurt and can empathize, which is too obvious and never enough to heal. Nor does it mean that a person can heal because he or she has been through an identical process, for this would not help unless the process had utterly altered consciousness. Let us remember that the "wounded healer" is not a human person, but a *personification* presenting a kind of consciousness. This kind of consciousness refers to mutilations and afflictions of the body organs that release the sparks of consciousness in these organs, resulting in an *organ or body-consciousness*. Healing comes then not because one is whole, integrated, and all together, but from a consciousness breaking through dismemberment.[47]

The moments of localized consciousness are the healers in the wounds. This is a dismembered, dissociated consciousness, one that speaks now from the heart, now from the hand, now from the feet that are hurt and can't walk. It is a wounded consciousness that is always sensitively inferior. And, this dismemberment and dissociation allows conversation between two persons to go on through the wounds. My wounds speak to yours, yours to mine. Wounded consciousness is less threatened by decomposition fantasies of decaying parts (aging, cancer, circulatory disorders, psychosis) because it is itself built upon specifically localized wounds and has emerged from the decay into parts. When disintegration anxiety is no longer paramount, the compensatory emphasis upon ideals of wholeness, order, and union can fade into the thin spiritualized air that is its jinn.

The archetypal root of this dying consciousness that is brought on by wounds may be found in the Dionysian aspect of dismemberment. The tendency of the puer to hysterical dissociation may refer to the vital life-force breaking into bits of consciousness as occasional, multiple insights. Dismemberment is thus not only a matter of passion and of being pulled apart by opposites. For such would be to place Dionysus upon the Cross and to formulate with ego conceptions movements on the vital level. Rather, dismemberment refers to the decomposition or decentralization (and thus decerebralization) of consciousness into primordial regions of organs, complexes, and erogenous zones. Through dismemberment we may also contact the sensuousness of the complexes and not only their suffering. Sometimes, and especially for the puer, the sensuousness comes through suffering, i.e., the first discovery of the body complexes is through a craving skin, straining rigid back, thin breathing, cramped anus, and neglected arches in cold feet. The puer structure often shows this peculiar mixture of suffering and sensuousness. There is both narcissistic body-love and masochistic body-pain, both hypochondria and heroic disdain for the fleshly aspect of the complex. Yet, just this is constellated by the wound which joins in one the psyche and the libidinal body. A wound may be a mouth that speaks spirit, but the spirit is in the flesh.

Dionysus was *zoé*, the divided/undivided life force, what we might today call the libido (a cognate of Dionysus's Roman counterpart, Liber) at that psychoid or genetic level where information and living matter are difficult to distinguish. Dionysus is a consciousness that occurs in "loosened," "democratic," uncontrolled and disintegrative states. As systematic integration decays and the organs are liberated into differentiated experiences, we feel wounded. And we are wounded by the profound body-consciousness that Dionysus brings, for "Dionysus and Hades are one."[48] The experience of the Dionysian body is also a death of our own habitual physical frame. Woundedness is initiatory to meeting Dionysus. It starts us into the subtle body.

VI ODYSSEUS' SCAR. Still another Greek figure bears on our theme — Odysseus, Ulysses. One derivation of Odysseus' name (Latin, *Ulixes*) is *oulos* = wound and *ischea* = thigh.[49] Evidently his wounded thigh is essential to his nature if it has given him his name.

A singular difference between Odysseus and the other wounded heroic figures we have mentioned is that Odysseus does not die from the goring. His wound becomes a scar. "It was a common form of royal death to have one's thigh gored by a boar, yet Odysseus had somehow survived the wound."[50] *Somehow?* Evidently there is a specific quality in his character allowing him to survive. On the one hand, like the others, he is a puer — always leaving for another place, nostalgic and longing, loved by women whom he refuses, opportunist and tricky, forever in danger of drowning. On the other hand, he is father, husband, captain, with the senex qualities of counsel and survival.

The story of Odysseus' wounding is revealed toward the close of the *Odyssey*. As his old nurse washes his feet, she espies the scar and almost gives him away.[51] We are even told in this scene that Odysseus' name derives from the incident of his wounding. As Auerbach[52] points out, this tale is suddenly introduced, and thereby the whole fate of Odysseus is revealed. This is not only a stunning literary denouement, but the revelation of his psychic essence: he is the one of the wounded-thigh.

The sexual symbolics of the wound, and by a boar, especially to the groin or thigh, has already been discussed above. In the case of Odysseus, the wound suggests that he had been violated and opened while still a youth. His wounded thigh is a symbolic vulva, like the thigh of Zeus that brings forth Dionysus. Moreover, this wound is there before the story begins; he comes on the scene wounded, not in the history of the tale but in his nature or essence. The others, like Achilles, begin invulnerable and thus must be wounded. In other words, Odysseus is never innocent and this shows in the *Odyssey* as his being continually in harm's way.[53] He is not innocent (*innocere*) because of his inherent wound which is also the symbolic incorporation of female fecundity.

Odysseus is the one hero — if we must call him that — who had differentiated relations with many female figures and Goddesses, relations which furthered his journey making survival possible.[54] It is hard to point at any one of these figures — Wife, Mother, Queen, Nurse, Mistress, Enchantress, or Goddess Athene — as most telling. ("He recognized all these women," concludes Book 22.) There is, however, a subtle sea-change in Odysseus after the encounter with Nausicaa, who bears traditional traits of what Jung calls "anima." After bathing in her stream Odysseus is renewed.[55]

I would suggest that his multiple relations with anima, implied by the scar and the suffering that lie in his name, is the secret of his epithet, *polytropos*, "of many turns," or "turned in many ways" by which he is described in the very first line of the epic.[56] Odysseus is not locked into opposites. He does not suffer from one-sidedness. In him there need be no conflict between senex and puer. His is an "anima" consciousness, which also helps account for his successful descent to the Underworld.

We see an easy commerce between young and old in his special relationship with Nestor (called *senex* in Latin versions) and also with the son of Achilles (called *puer*); as well, there is remarkable love between him and his father and him and his son, Telemachos. Odysseus is emotionally bound in both directions. Only Aeneas, at the beginning of Vergil's *Aenead*,[57] who leads his little son by the hand and carries his lamed father on his back, can be compared to the senex-puer integrity in Odysseus. The very last page of the book has the new day dawn with Odysseus rising and, together with his son, going to join his father.

Of course, it is Athene who helps maintain this integrity. But so does Penelope. For instance, Telemachos says: "My mother says I am his son, I myself do not know: no one of himself knows his own father." Penelope could have told another tale to turn son against father. Instead, she acted as did the mother of Horus, encouraging the son's search for the father's redemption. "One general feature emerges from the study of Odysseus' more intimate personal relationships. He seems to have met none of the suspicion and distrust of his male associates among the women who knew him well."[58] Little wonder that a theory has been put forth that the Odyssey was written by a woman.

It has been said that Odysseus is the most human of the heroes. He certainly does not fit within the divine pattern of the puer or into that of the senex — yet both are present in an array of traits. What "humanizes" the archetypal configuration is the scar. He cannot be only unblemished or bleeding puer. Nor can he be deformed and crippled senex, for the wound has healed. He has been spared by his thigh from the perfections of archetypal identification. Thus, he says flatly that he resembles no God but is like only to mortal men.[59] He refuses divinization. When Calypso offers to make him immortal and ageless, he chooses the usual path.[60] "No, I am not a God. Why liken me to the immortals? But I am your father," he says to Telemachos.[61]

A scar is a blemish, a weakness, and from the outset we meet Odysseus as weak. He is no usual hero. The senex qualities of judgment, sobriety, prudence, patience, deviousness, isolation, and suffering are reinforced by yet one more character trait that separates him from the heroes. He is a man of little power. He has no massive army like Achilles, Agamemnon and Menelaus; he contributes but one ship. Nor has he the strength of Ajax and Diomedes. Often, it seems, he'd rather eat than fight. He is not past feigning madness to avoid going to war. It is as if Odysseus proceeds by means of depression. When we first meet him, disconsolate on the shores of Calypso's isle, he broods in melancholy like Saturn and yet with the *pothos* of the sailing wanderer. His most usual disguise is outcast of the islands, ragged beggar, connected with dogs. (Yet as direct descendent of Autolykos and Hermes, he has a slippery kind of puer blood in his veins.) Even his pale alter-ego or double, Telephos, who is also wounded in the thigh, is a man of counsel and does not fight owing to his relation to his wife.[62]

With all this in mind we may turn again to the scene of the nurse washing Odysseus' legs and feet, understanding now this moment of recognition-through-disguise as revelation of essence. The scar by which he is known is the mark of soul in the flesh. It is the seal of anima, the somaticized psyche. His flesh has become wound, just as our flesh "hurts all over" when we enter wounded consciousness. Now, we can see that this generalization of a symptom into the pathologized condition of complaining pain is an attempt at giving full body to the wound by letting the body be fully sensitized by the wound. Odysseus, the pained one, is the personification of pathologized consciousness — like Christ in his way and Dionysus in his. The wounded body has become the embodied wound; and, as embodied, as built into his existence in the leg that carries him and walks with him, his woundedness is also his hidden understanding and grounding support.

A clue to the nature of this understanding is to be found in Montaigne, who wrote: "So I do not want to forget this further scar, very much unfit to produce in public: irresolution, a most harmful failing in negotiating worldly affairs. I do not know which side to take in doubtful enterprises. 'Nor yes nor no my inmost heart will say'(Petrarch)."[63] The scar reminds consciousness of its wobbling uncertainty, the dark vulnerability in the heart of its light.

VI CONCLUSION: THE UNION OF SAMES. As we have been elaborating, the open wound belongs with the puer structure; the scarred wound, however, suggests the person whose soul can care for him, the person whose life-blood circulates through his complexes, feeding and washing them, a self-contained eros. Healing is not expected to come from somewhere else. It emerges from the wound's depth and leaves a scar, a scar that is always visible to one's own nurse.

In Odysseus the senex urge to persist and endure takes care of the puer spirit that is always ready to risk and die. Healing and wounding alternate, or, as healed wound, tender scar, they present the complex image of weak-strength, of soft-hardness. The scar remaining is the remainder, the soft spot recalling the body to its tenderness. The scar acts as a *memento mori*, recollecting the Grandfather and oneself as a Hunting Boy. That scar gets Odysseus through twenty years of unparalleled dangers, like a talisman of dying consciousness, keeping remembrance of death. "Few in the *Iliad* are as conscious as Odysseus of why they are at Troy, and death [to the others] is a recurrent surprise."[64]

This scar could have become a deformity. It could have meant lameness, which characterizes the only-puer or only-senex onesidedness of the archetype. Then the scar would have been that deformity which, as Jung writes,[65] separates father and son, man and boy, large and small. Odysseus, however, is not deformed by onesidedness in as much as he signifies the twice-born man: father-with-son, male-with-female, body-with-soul. This initiated consciousness has been discussed elsewhere in regard to *pothos* and the mysteries of Samothrace where Odysseus was said to have been initiated.[65]

Initiation refers to the transition from only-puer consciousness, wounded and bleeding, to *puer-et-senex* consciousness, opened and scarred. It is experienced as well in the transition from the sense of oneself in a story to the sense of oneself as an image, all parts inherent and present at once. Heroic puer consciousness enacts its story, racing forward with its narrative into its denouement. This kind of consciousness can remain invulnerable because the mode of story can put off wounding until the end. Moreover, puer consciousness remains "at the beginnings" because the end is only the puer's sudden undoing and his conversion into the opposite — failed, crippled, ashen. Story tells puer and senex into beginnings and endings, first half and second, keeping green and gray apart. Odysseus' scar, however, builds the wound in all along the way. It belongs to the image of Odysseus, necessary to his very name, and therefore it is not a fatal flaw that brings his fall.

The heroes — Ajax, Theseus, Philoctetes — nursing their hurts have fallen for their stories. Even in the underworld where they are sheer images, they are still stuck in their stories, as if it is essential to the heroic mode never to realize *oneself as imaginal* even when undergoing the most prodigious exercises of imagination. A separation of puer from hero takes place when one's account of oneself moves from history and epic destiny to imaginative fantasy. Our fiction changes from epic and tragic to comic or picaresque. Simply by moving out of its story, consciousness may move out of the heroic mode.

We might extend this thought further by saying, along with Patricia Berry and David L. Miller,[67] that story consciousness will set us up as heroic *pueri*, fatefully leading us into the woundedness which is inherent to the story but which comes at its end. "Ourselves as epic stories" might well be a good way of defining the puer neurosis. Then we must go to therapy to "reversion"[68] the story, that is, to integrate the symptoms by discovering their inherent necessity. This discovery takes us out of story and into image, for we realize that the wound, like that of Odysseus, has been inherent to us all along, a realization which turns wound into scar. In other words, image consciousness heals. The sense of ourselves as images in which all parts belong and are co-relatively necessary keeps ends and beginnings together,[69] like the wound remembered by the scar.

"Much in the *Odyssey* suggests that it is an old man's poem. Its analogue is Shakespeare's *Tempest* . . . a world shared, so to speak, between the old Prospero on one side and the young lovers and the beauty of nature on the other . . . The battered Odysseus has sympathy for old people who have endured as much as he . . . but the young Telemachus and Nausicaa give freshest renewal, and the green islands of his travels confirm nature's persisting youth . . . It is the old and the young who jointly effect the marvel of life made new, as if Homer were conscious of the transformation and in some part saw himself now in Odysseus."[70] The sea, ever-renewing and freshening, yet the oldest father, Okeanos, is background to both the *Tempest* and the *Odyssey*, and finally from this sea will come Odysseus' death.[71] The sea, the great long poem, Homer, Odysseus, are each "ever young yet full of eld" (Spenser). Is this why that figure, Odysseus, "thigh-wound," continues to shape himself again and again in our Western imagination?[72]

There are many reasons for the imaginal power of Odysseus, but surely a major part of his greatness is that Odysseus resolved a morbid division fundamental to the Western psyche. The major genealogical myth of Uranos, Kronos, and Zeus the youngest son — leaving aside the Biblical patriarchs and their sons — is present in all the wrenching horror of the father-son, puer-senex struggle.[73] Our torturing battles with our fathers and with our sons was raised by Freud to the central explanation of our culture and our soul. That this struggle between senex and puer is at the heart of our culture has also been attested to by Christian doctrine, which insists that recognition of the unity of Father and Son is the way of redemption. But that very union of sames is threatened by the Son's last words on the cross, perhaps a residue of puer consciousness not joined with the Father.[74]

Odysseus is not in this dilemma, and the entire *Odyssey* holds senex and puer together, as at the end in the most obvious and heroic climax Odysseus and Telemachos battle side by side against the common enemy who would take Penelope from them. But the union of sames is also more subtly woven through the whole text. It gives us Homer's answer — or is it Odysseus' answer — to this unbearable psychic affliction.

The last scene of rejoining Odysseus with his home takes place with old Laertes, his father, wearing a tattered tunic and goatskin hat, hoeing alone in a briar patch: Saturn, the gardener, squalid and in mourning. Until now, Odysseus had always been father, and Telemachos, the son, in search of the father. But now at the end,[75] facing Laertes so perfectly sketched in his outcast senex condition, Odysseus is son, remembering the wound, the hunt, and the garden of his youth. And by these signs he is known.[76] As *senex-et-puer* Odysseus comes home, and his odyssey tells the tale of the diversified, polytropic process of homecoming.

Notes

1. [Originally published in J. Hillman, ed., *Puer Papers* (Dallas: Spring Publications, 1979). Reprinted in *Dromenon* 3 (1981).] — Ed.

2. As quoted by Mary Blume, *International Herald Tribune*, December 13–14, 1969.

3. Stephan Sas, *Der Hinkende als Symbol* (Zurich: Rascher, 1964); on foot symbolism (mainly as sexual) see Aigremont, *Fuß- und Schuh-Symbolik und Erotik* (Berlin, 1909). Cf. Murray Stein, "Hephaistos: A Pattern of Introversion," *Spring* 1973.

4. Pindar, *Olympic Ode* 1; Apollodorus, *Epit.* 2, 3.

5. Euripides, *The Bacchae*, 1170–1330.

6. "Lykourgos," W. H. Roscher, *Lexikon der griechischen and römischen Mythologie* (Hildesheim: B. G. Teubner, 1965), 11, 2, 2194.

7. On "parental" boar symbolism, See E. Neumann, *The Origins and History of Consciousness* (New York: Pantheon, 1954), pp. 77ff., p. 94f.; J. Layard, "Boar Sacrifice and Schizophrenia," *Journal of Analytical Psychology*, 1:1 (1955); "Identification with the Sacrificial Animal," *Eranos-Yearbook* 24 (1955). Other boar deaths include Osiris by Typhon and Hackelbrand in German mythology.

8. The stories concerning Achilles' bath of invulnerability vary. Apollonius of Rhodes (IV, 869) says he was bathed in ambrosia; or he was bathed in fire (*Schol. Ilias* XVI, 37), or dipped in the Styx (*Quint. Smyrn.*, 111, 62). Cf. C. M. Bowra, *Heroic Poetry* (London: Macmillan, 1961), Chap. III; on Achilles' death, Karl Kerényi, *The Heroes of the Greeks* (London: Thames and Hudson, 1959), p. 353. The heel (ankle) as spot of vulnerability is given witness in a sixth-century BC vase painting: M. R. Scherrer, *The Legends of Troy* (London, 1964), p. 99.

9. Pausanias III, 15, 5; 29, 7.

10. "Perseus," Roscher, op. cit. III, 2, 2011.

11. Kerényi, *The Heroes of the Greeks*, p. 144.

12. On Alexander's wound see, J. R. Hamilton, "Alexander and his 'So-Called' Father," in G. T. Griffith, ed., *Alexander the Great: The Main Problems*, (Cambridge: Heffer, 1966), p. 236ff.

13. On Jason *monosandalos*, see Kerényi, *The Heroes of the Greeks*, p. 248.

14. Paris, who hit Achilles in the heel, is himself mortally wounded in the ankle by Philoctetes, whose insufferable wound was in the foot (Graves, *The Greek Myths* (Harmondsworth: Penguin, 1960), vol. II, p. 326). Philoctetes' father, Poeas, shoots Talos, the winged, heroic, bronze Guardian of Crete, in the ankle (Roscher, op. cit., V, 29). In Talos the bleeding and the foot motifs coincide: his single long blood canal from neck downwards came unstoppered through the wound in the ankle and all his blood poured out. On five versions of how Philoctetes was wounded, see Graves, II: pp. 292–93. Ajax's

vulnerable place was the armpit; Cycnus, son of Poseidon, the head. Hercules' son Telephos is wounded in the upper thigh.

15. Kerényi, *The Heroes of the Greeks*, p. 84. For more on puer wandering, see Chapter 6.

16. On the one-legged Shaman: see his dance on the stick or hobbyhorse in M. Eliade, *Shamanism* (New York: Pantheon, Bollingen series, 1964), pp. 467ff.; also J. Lindsay, *The Clashing Rocks* (London: Chapman Hall, 1965), pp. 197, 200, 332–33. The broomstick of the witch can also carry one off into the verticality of spiritual flight.

17. C. G. Jung, *Collected Works*, vol. 14: *Mysterium Coniunctionis*, par. 720.

18. H. W. Parke, *The Oracles of Zeus* (Oxford: Blackwell, 1967), p. 14f.; Cf. "Mopsos," Roscher, op. cit., II, 2, 3207f. This seer, one of the heroes of the Argonauts, was called by some a "son of Apollo." He was a wanderer, colonizer, and a conqueror of Amazons (perhaps a different "Mopsos"?).

19. Parke, *The Oracles of Zeus*, pp. 165ff.

20. J. Campbell, *The Hero with a Thousand Faces* (New York: Pantheon, Bollingen Series, 1949), p. 41.

21. C. G. Jung, *Collected Works*, vol. 5: *Symbols of Transformation*, par. 180–84.

22. N. Vaschide, *Essai sur la psychologie de la main* (Paris: M. Rivière, 1909), p. 478. For a fuller phenomenology, see J. Brun, *La main et l'esprit* (Paris: Presses Univ. de France, 1963).

23. The finger lost may have been given up for the social good, preventing anything new being formed that may disturb the archaic conservatism of tribal law. Among the Hottentots, but also in tribal societies in South Africa, America, the Pacific Islands, India, and in ancient Palestine, fingers are dedicated for sacrifice and mourning. Fingers have been found in graves with Goddess figures, which recalls Attis whose little finger still lived even after his death (cf. M. J. Vermaseren, *The Legend of Attis* [Leiden: E. J. Brill, 1966] and *Cybele and Attis* [London: Thames and Hudson, 1977], p. 91). A relation between the Finger Tomb of Tantalos (who chopped up his son Pelops) and the phallic creative daktyl (= finger) is mentioned by Jane Harrison in *Themis* (London: Merlin Press, 1963), pp. 402–3. Orestes (Eumenides) bites off his finger in his madness, which may point to the sacrifice of a puer impulse (unlike Attis) and a dedication to a new, limited way of being. Cf. R. Levy, *The Gate of Horn* (London: Faber and Faber, 1948), pp. 17, 49, 93; J. Lindsay, pp. 191–92; R. B. Onians, *The Origins of European Thought* (Cambridge: Cambridge University Press, 1953), pp. 496–97, where the fingers are associated particularly with the child.

24. Cf. E. Wind, *Art and Anarchy* (London: Faber and Faber, 1963), p. 160; C. Lévi-Strauss, *La Pensée sauvage* (Paris: Plon, 1962), pp. 26–47; N. and S. Schwartz, "On the Coupling of Psychic Entropy and Negentropy," *Spring* 1970, pp. 77–80. Perhaps the earliest image of the *bricoleur* was "Eros the Car-

penter," an image found already in Etruscan times. (R. Klibansky, et al., *Saturn and Melancholy* [London: Nelson, 1964], p. 308, with illustration). The figure of Eros is surrounded by joiner's tools, making quite practical and on the level of a craft the usual high-blown notions of Eros (as a cosmogonic force of unions, lord of fantasy and emotional upheavals). This sober aspect of Eros shows the joining function not within the cosmos of Aphrodite, but perhaps in connection with Athene. "Hesiod uses the periphrasis 'Athene-Servant' for a carpenter" (N. O. Brown, *Hermes the Thief* [New York: Vintage Paperback, 1969], p. 66). Daedalos, too, can be taken as a primordial *bricoleur*. He made new things out of what was at hand. From within the "Daedalos complex" the attempt to gain a wider perspective (Talos) or to soar above what is at hand (Icarus) ends in ruin. *Bricolage* seems to limit ambition, glory, wings.

25. This subject is examined beautifully by Brun, *La main et l'esprit*, ch. 2.

26. The distinctions between fist and fingers (will-power and fantasy) have often been literalized into right-versus left-handedness to the detriment (in our culture) of left-handed persons and to the bafflement of ethnologists who try to establish the right/left distinction universally (e.g., Hertz, *Death and the Right Hand* [Aberdeen: Cohen and West, 1960]). But see Fritsch, *Left and Right in Science and Life* (London: Barrie and Rockcliff, 1968), who brings evidence contrary to the idea that left must be imaginative, hence sinister and gauche.

27. Cf. Brun, *La main et l'esprit*, ch. 10, "La main et la caresse." Contrary to the palm's feeling is the "back of the hand' — an expression for insulting dismissal.

28. In Greek thought, the main difference between humans and Gods is that all men are mortal; whereas Gods are *athnetos* (im-mortal).

29. J. Jacobi, *The Psychology of C. G. Jung* (London: Routledge and K. Paul, 1951), p. 40.

30. Every year in Lebanon, it was said, the river Adonis turns red, flowing to the sea stained with the blood of the beautiful slain lover ("Tamuz," Roscher, op. cit., V, 62.).

31. Liddell and Scott, *A Greek-English Lexicon*; compare Latin *hortus* (garden) a term for female pudenda; further, J.J. Bachofen, *Myth, Religion, and Mother Right*, trans. R. Manheim, Bollingen Series (Princeton University Press, 1967), p. 131. The most complete study is by M. Detienne, *The Gardens of Adonis: Spices in Greek Mythology*, trans. J. Lloyd (London: Harvester Press, 1977). Detienne works from J. G. Frazer's Adonis section of *The Golden Bough*, but radically revisions the cult so that, in Detienne's words (p. 122): "Adonis is not a husband or even a man: he is simply a lover, and an effeminate one . . . an image of seduction."

32. [This theme is discussed in Chapter 4.] — Ed.

33. An example closer to our times of one who draws the psychopathic attacker is J.J. Winckelmann, the great classicist, who "invented," in the eigh-

teenth century, the modern fields of archeology, the scholarly art museum, and an aesthetics based on classic models. His life is rife with puer phenomena: logos obsession in childhood, out of obscurity to fame by following his childhood fantasy, idealized homosexuality, falling in love with an idealized idol (Apollo Belvedere), dedication to aesthetics, and finally bleeding to death in 1768 from brutal knife wounds suffered at the hands of a thief-homosexual psychopathic liar named Arcangeli.

34. Heraclitus, D.K., Frg. 119.

35. The beauty of the bleeding wound evokes a love that is more than compassion for the sufferer. The bleeding calls to the lover, not only to the nurse. Greek paintings of young men of the Trojan war binding the wounds of comrades and the love expressed in the act continues as a theme in war films today. The bleeding heart of Christ stands as a central icon of the beauty inciting the most passionate love.

36. Cf. Paul Kugler, *The Alchemy of Discourse: An Archetypal Approach to Language*, (Lewisburg, PA: Bucknell University Press, 1982), for phonetic relations between "blood" and "bloom."

37. A. Ulanov (*The Feminine in Jungian Psychology and in Christian Theology* [Evanston: Northwestern University Press, 1971], p. 236) misses this point when assuming that a young man's pouring out and spilling over derive from an anima not yet separated from the "maternal instinct." Readings in terms of the Mother always miss the spiritual authenticity of puer phenomena, in this case a phenomenon as important as love.

38. See my *Kinds of Power* (New York: Doubleday, 1995), "Charisma."

39. W. F. Otto, *Dionysus* (Bloomington, IN: 1965), p. 96.

40. [See Chapter 13 below on milk and the daughter.] — Ed.

41. A full discussion of the leaky vessel can be found in Eva Keuls, *The Water Carriers in Hades* (Amsterdam: A. M. Hakkert, 1974).

42. Compare Socrates' self-reflection and his use of the image of the vessel in regard to his own soul, *Phaedrus* 235c.

43. On the implications of hysteria for the psyche, see my *The Myth of Analysis* (Evanston: Northwestern University Press, 1972), Part 3.

44. [See Chapter 7 below.] — Ed.

45. For a discussion of anima and bleeding, see Penelope Shuttle and Peter Redgrove, *The Wise Wound. Menstruation and Everywoman* (London: V. Gollancz, 1978), "Animus, Animal, Anima."

46. Ajax's wound is said by Graves to be in the armpit. Does this not tell us something about the vulnerable place of the man of mighty arms, that he is wounded in the underside of his very strength? Maybe it also tells us about our heroic obsessions with deodorized armpits, especially in view of the relation between sense of smell as the preferred sense in the underworld of soul (as discussed in my *The Dream and the Underworld* [New York: Harper and Row, 1979]).

47. I have elaborated on the theme of " wounded" and "disintegrated" consciousness in several other places: "Dionysus in Jung's Writings," *Spring* 1972, pp. 199–205; "On the Necessity of Abnormal Psychology" *Eranos-Yearbook* 43 (1974), pp. 91–135; *Healing Fiction* (Putnam, CT: Spring Publications, 1994), Part III; *Re-visioning Psychology* (New York: Harper and Row, 1975), ch. 2, "Pathologizing."

48. Heraclitus, DK 15.

49. Cf. Robert Graves, 2:170.10.

50. Ibid.

51. *Od.* 19:276ff. There is an ambiguity concerning exactly where the wound is. Is it in the foot or ankle which the nurse washes, or is it higher in the thigh which she sees while crouching below Odysseus, washing his feet? The ambiguity discussed by scholars need not be univocally settled, inasmuch as his foot wound (puer hero) is also a thigh scar (puer-et-senex).

52. E. Auerbach, *Mimesis* (Princeton University Press, 1968), ch. 1, "Odysseus' Scar."

53. Cf. G. E. Dimock, Jr., "The Name of Odysseus," in C. H. Taylor, Jr., *Essays on the Odyssey* (Bloomington: Indiana University Press, 1963). Dimock derives the name from odyne "to cause pain, and to be willing to do so." Odysseus thus becomes the sufferer, the pained one, and the one who brings suffering and pain. Dimock also suggests the name "Trouble" for Odysseus; others have suggested the "Odd-Man-Out" or "Oddball," "Man of odium" (hated or angry one), etc.

54. [This aspect was discussed in Chapter 4.] — Ed.

55. *Od.* 6: 216f.

56. Cf. W. B. Stanford, *The Odysseus Theme* (Dallas: Spring Publications, 1992), p. 99.

57. For more on the puer-senex in the Aenead, see S. Bertman, "The Generation Gap in the Fifth Book of Vergil's Aenead," in *The Conflict of Generations in Ancient Greece and Rome*, ed. Stephen Bertman, (Amsterdam: Grüner, 1976).

58. Stanford, *Odysseus Theme*, p. 65.

59. *Od.* 7: 208f.

60. *Od.* 5:81, 135, 203-24; 23:335

61. *Od.* 16:187

62. Graves, *Greek Myths*, 2:160.

63. Translated from Montaigne's Essay "Of Presumption," by Philip P. Hallie, *The Scar of Montaigne* (Middletown, CT: Wesleyan University Press, 1966). Cf. pp. 130–33, "The Scar."

64. J. H. Finley, *Four Stages of Greek Thought* (Stanford: Stanford University Press, 1966), p. 15.

65. C. G. Jung, *Collected Works*, vol. 5, par. 184.

66. [See Chapter 6.] — Ed.

67. Cf. Patricia Berry, "An Approach to the Dream ("Narrative") *Spring* 1974, pp. 68–71; David L. Miller, "Fairy Tale or Myth," *Spring* 1976, pp. 157–64.

68. "Reversioning" is a term I have borrowed from E.S. Casey's phenomenological investigation of memory. Cf. my "The Fiction of Case History," in *Healing Fiction*.

69. According to the ancient Pythagorean physician, Alcmaion of Croton: "Men die because they cannot join the beginning to the end."

70. Finley, *Four Stages*, pp. 11–12.

71. Odysseus does not die in the *Odyssey* but the post-Homeric tradition, especially in the Latin Middle Ages, told the Trojan legends mainly according to the version of Dictys of Crete (in *The Trojan War*, trans. R.M. Frazer (Bloomington, Indiana: Indiana University Press, 1966). In these tales, Odysseus has a dream of death coming from the sea which is fulfilled by the arrival on the shores of Ithaca of his son (by Circe) Telegonos, who then in an unwitting battle between father and son kills Odysseus with a special spear.

72. W.B. Stanford and J.V. Luce, *Quest for Odysseus* (London: Phaidon, 1977).

73. For listings and discussions of these struggles see: Bertman, *Conflict of Generations*, pp. 22–23 *et passim*. On the relation of the classic myths to Freud, there are interesting comments by M.D. Altschule, *Roots of Modern Psychiatry* (New York/London: Grune and Stratton, 1957), p. 162.

74. Matthew (27:46) and Mark (15:34) attest that the last words were the cry of being forsaken by the Father; Luke (23:46) does not mention this cry, but instead re-unites Father and Son: "Father, into thy hands I commend my spirit." It is noteworthy that the ambiguity about the Father-Son relation is itself reinforced by the variant accounts of the last words.

75. Cf. Dorothea Wender, *The Last Scenes of the Odyssey* (Leiden: E.J. Brill, 1978).

76. *Od.* 24:327ff.

Part Three

Senex

9

On Senex Consciousness [1]

Senex is the Latin word for old men. We find it still contained within our words *senescence, senile,* and *senator.* In Rome the time of the senex was from the latter half of the fortieth year onward. It could apply to old women too. But as we shall inquire into this idea, senex will come to mean more than old person or old age. The imaginal notions condensed into this short term extend far beyond whatever personal ideas we might have of oldness, beyond our concerns with old age, old people and the processes of time in personal life. Perhaps, however, at this first level, where the senex affects our lives and ageing we can grasp its import most easily.

The discussion that follows makes two assumptions: first, the senex is an archetype; second, this archetype is the one most relevant for the puer. By this we mean that the senex is a *complicatio* of the puer, infolded into puer structure, so that puer events are complicated by a senex background. Although these two archetypal structures are intertwined, we shall draw the portrait of the senex away from the puer in sharpest relief and contradistinction in order to reflect the psychological tension between them. Nevertheless, the senex archetype is more than something "psychological," not merely a derivative of experience, an aspect of man and his behavior, an icon foisted upon life by man's idolatrous imagination. Rather, the senex is one of the crystallizations of monotheism's God, one of his *numen multiplex,* or, the senex is itself a god, a universal reality whose ontological power is expressed in nature and culture and the human psyche.

As natural, cultural and psychic processes mature, gain order, consolidate and wither, we witness the specific formative effects of the senex. Personifications of this principle appear in the holy or old wise man, the powerful father or grandfather, the great king, ruler, judge, ogre, counsellor, elder, priest, hermit, outcast and cripple. Some emblems are the rock, the old tree, particularly oak, the scythe or sickle, the time-piece and the skull. Longings for superior knowledge, imperturbability, magnaminity express senex feelings as does intolerance for that which crosses one's systems and habits. The senex also shows strongly in ideas and feelings about time, the past, and death. Melancholy, anxiety, sadism, paranoia, anality, and obsessive memory ruminations reflect this archetype. Moreover, the main image of God in our culture: omniscient, omnipotent, eternal, seated and bearded, a ruler through abstract principle of justice, morality and order, a faith in words yet not given to self-explanation in speech, benevolent but enraged when his will is crossed, removed from the feminine (wifeless) and the sexual aspect of creation, up high with a geometric world of stars and planets in the cold and distant night of numbers — this image depicts a senex god, a god imaged through the senex archetype. *The high God of our culture is a senex god; we are created after this image with a consciousness reflecting this structure.* One face of our consciousness is inescapably senex.

Because this archetype expresses all that is old, ordered and established, it has particular bearing upon our culture and its supposedly dead or dying God. The breakdown of structure is the death of this particular structure, who is the Principle of Structure; if this central fixation of our religious consciousness has aged into remote transcendence, there to wither and die, then the image in which we have been cast, reflecting this main god, is also passing away. A kind of consciousness departs. The "de-struction" of culture and the breakdowns in individual lives result from this transition of the senex dominant which has also been a senex dominance: *the usurpation of one God over many,* of one archetypal form over others, of one kind of consciousness pressing others into unconsciousness. Although the theology of our culture gives witness to the death of the senex God by proclaiming reform and loosening principle, an archetypal power does not "die" in the sense of emptied out, inoperant and still. It continues in the imaginal realm through which it influences our fantasy and emotion and continues to receive its due worship through the psyche in ways we shall discover as these notes proceed. Although fading as an icon, an image "out there" with a name and an observance, it catches us from within, through its immanence in the fantasy levels of the psyche. What the Greeks called Kronos, and the Romans Saturn, our tradition has worshipped as "Our Father which art in Heaven." But gone from Heaven, and Heaven gone too, the senex now can be best encountered indirectly, through a psychological phenomenology.

SENEX CHARACTERISTICS IN SATURN.[2] In piecing together the major characteristics of the senex, one basic text on which we rely is the Warburg Institute's study *Saturn and Melancholy*.[3] The double nature of the senex we have already mentioned. This duplicity must be kept in mind as we read through his qualities; one characteristic is never safe from inversion into its opposite. We shall never encounter the good wise old man without recognizing him as an ogre at the same time, nor come upon one destructive trait that cannot be saved into virtue by turning it upside down.

As addressed in Chapter One the temperament of the senex is cold, which can also be expressed as distance. Senex-consciousness is outside of things, lonely, wandering, a consciousness set-apart and outcast. Coldness is also cruel, without the warmth of heart and heat of rage, but slow revenge, torture, exacting tribute, bondage. As lord of the nethermost, Saturn views the world from the outside, from such depths of distance that he sees it all "upside down," and to this view the structure of things is revealed. He sees the irony of truth within the words, the city from the cemetery, the bones below the game of skin. Thus the senex view gives the abstract architecture and anatomy of events, plots and graphs, presenting principles of form rather than connections, inter-relations, or the flow of feeling.

The senex emblem of the skull signifies that every complex can be envisioned from its death aspect, its ultimate psychic core where all flesh of dynamics and appearances is stripped away and there is nothing left of those hopeful thoughts of what it might yet become, the "final" interpretation of the complex as its end. The end gives the pessimistic and cynical reflection as counterpart to puer beginnings.

As complexes can cloud themselves with puer-illusions, senex-consciousness penetrates these illusions with its fantasy of "bitter truth" and "cold reality," of seeing through all exteriors. The fantasy of "laying bare," is a favorite one of the philosopher, like Jeremiah the Prophet or Diogenes the Cynic, exposures of truth to the bone, "where it hurts." The fantasy of this consciousness is that a complex can be dissolved by concentration upon itself, penetrating to a self-knowledge, a truth which can be known and is unpleasant. Ultimately this fantasy turns into a life-style of permanent cynicism for all complexes, the seeing through of everything; vanity, all is vanity.

The skull also refers to the concern of senex-consciousness with structure and intellectual abstraction. In Mediaeval and Renaissance imagery Saturn was often depicted together with instruments of geometry and astronomy. Structure and abstraction point yet deeper: to the principle of order itself. Kronos-Saturn as original governer of the universe is the *nous* — an idea that can be traced back to Plato.[4] Hesiod's Kronos ruled at the beginning of things. The senex provides the original designing mind, its ideal form, the foundations, principles and axioms upon which a state is built. He promulgates its law and its order. The state and its government are also the state of the complex and that ruling fantasy by which it is governed. The structure of the complex, the rules by which it abides, making it repetitive in responses and so difficult to dismantle or even argue against except in the terms of its official, habitual logic — this is the senex aspect of the complex.

Senex fantasies, such as the longing for law and order, for return to a golden age where there might be contentment in agrarian simplicity under patriarchal solidity, can be found in Greece and in Rome in connection with the festivals of the senex, the Cronia and the Saturnalia. Then, the senex power was honored with anarchy and propitiated from hardening into its despotic tendency. The rigid structure of the complex cured itself, so to speak, by providing for its own de-struction. Its order included anarchy; the festivals of Kronos and Saturn provided for a fantasy of leisure, peace and bounty, food and drink without toil, an end of slavery and property. Western culture no longer uses these homeopathic cures. Instead we attempt to break down the senex power from without, introducing violence to topple the structure.

These attacks upon it merely reinforce the ruling complex by increasing the rigor of its law and the vigor of its order. When the senex forgets its form of renewal through its own asocial and anarchic fantasy, it loses one side of its structure, becoming one-sided. By banning breakdown, breakdown is ensured.

Within the individual psyche we find the same senex fascination with order. We want to get the complexes into order in accordance with the first principles of what complexes are, their rules of behavior, their analysis through association experiment plotted by means of time on graphs, so as to discover their laws and to master them through these laws. Whenever we make order we ask the senex to enter. And he enters through every fantasy of structural analysis, and therefore has his place in this book and its fantasy.

Saturn and his attributes show many ways in which order can be brought about: through time, through hierarchy, through scientific system of measurements. Order may be brought also by setting limits and exclusions, by the logical thought of negation and contradiction, through establishing and extending power, by conserving what exists and fulfilling duty. Saturn's order may also be made by relating events to the fixity of the earth and the definition of shape that earth gives. Order may also refer to a spiritual order and a spiritual discipline which requires inwardness, isolation and reflection. Those virtues too belong to Saturn. To grasp the senex at work in our lives is to watch the way in which we order our lives. Habit is the movement of Saturn through our days; so too is counting; so too is remembering. Our relation to the clock, the calendar, and the passing years show Saturn. The principles by which we live, the limits we set ourselves and the world around us, the scale of values (less the values than their hierarchy) and, above all, the order brought through control, self-control and control over others, express this senex nature.

The senex makes order particularly through boundaries. Senex-consciousness draws division lines: your kingdom and mine; conscious and unconscious; body and mind. Also, as Norman O. Brown exhibits with his characteristic brilliance, our idea of the ego and its notion of order require a boundary between real and fantasy, between inner and outer. Boundary is necessary for properties and possessions, for territory and ownership. One's own is within one's boundaries. The idea of a self, an enclosed and individual *proprium*, requires boundary and boundary is made by the senex.

But boundaries are set — and here Brown is silent — for religious reasons, too. *Fanum* and *temenos* mark off the sacred. The boundary differentiates districts of being; it permits ontological distinctions and the possibility of symbols. Senex-consciousness, by maintaining the wall and law against something which does not like a wall and a law, makes possible the psychological region of the borderline and a host of symbols whose existence requires boundaries. Without boundaries there would be no container and no preserves; without boundaries, what sense in gates, doors, openings, barricades, exits and entries, secrets, initiations, election, esotericism. Saturn draws the lines and therefore rules both sides: the exaltation of holiness and the degradation of the profane, the city and the outcast, the king and the slave, the ego and its repression.

Slow, heavy, chronic, leaden — these analogous qualities referred to Saturn. Lead was especially important for the alchemical work of redemption. The work could not be begun nor be completed without lead, so Saturn in some alchemical systems was the beginning and the end. A senex quality was required to give realization through time and dense corporality. The alchemist's accomplishment came through his own leadenness, his chronic patient labour and the accompanying depressed states of mind. Lead was not merely a metal; it was a quality of consciousness which the alchemist had to have inherently present in order to do his work with the metal. He and the substances had to correspond. The lead remained to the end as a necessary ingredient of the Stone, so the depressed state of mind survived to the end, reflecting a consciousness that survives through and by means of depression. It was not all done away with, all transmuted into shining gold. The poisonous lead, its turpitude and its dullness, were the curse of the work, yet necessary to it.

From early Greek to late Roman times superstitious curses were inscibed on leaden tablets (*defixiones*). These curses (*katadesmoi, katadeseis*) literally mean "bindings." They were left in tombs or buried for the spirits of the underworld. Evidently in popular imagination Saturn had a special relation with the spirits beyond the grave and the black art of manipulating these spirits. The same charge in another language is brought against senex-consciousness today for its affinity with what is dead and buried and its binding curse upon present life through manipulation of past history. For some critics of senex-consciousness, institutions such as the law courts and banks, the medical profession, university instruction and parliamentary government are "black arts" that bind the soul. The laws and prescriptions written by these institutions are, for some, tablets of lead, *defixiones*, curses of the senex. The mixture of knowledge with power and the magical use of it for evil seem one propensity of senex-consciousness. This archetype bridges to lower powers, as Saturn-Dis at the *imum coeli*, as Hypete the gravest note and longest chord, as lead the heaviest of the classical metals. Below is the place of the dead and the uncanny; it is also in our tradition the locus of evil.

For this reason, extreme inwardness (involution) and downwardness (dejection of melancholia, from the Greek word for black bile, Saturn's humor) have been met with especial suspicion. Of all psychic disorders the melancholic has long been regarded not only as seriously ill but as particularly sinful. The black color associated with Saturn, besides standing for winter, night, death, distance, also evokes decay and evil. Hildegard of Bingen combines the theological and medical condemnation of this aspect of senex-consciousness in her *Of Causes and Cures*. The *humor melancholicus* originates in Adam's sin and the Fall of Man; it is a direct poisoning from the bite of the apple at the suggestion of the devil, and as such an incurable hereditary taint. Our resistance to depression, including the radical methods of shock and pep, continue to exhibit the fear of those black extremes to which senex-consciousness can penetrate through its melancholy.

From another regard, the lead of Saturn is the downward and inward pull of gravity into subjectivity. The plumb-line drops ever deeper, straight to the grave, and below, to time past and the underworld spirits. The inward and downward pull into oneself and one's death implies that the senex is the chief force at work in some Jungian descriptions of individuation. The end-goal is often presented in senex imagery: isolation, unity, stones, cosmic systems and geometric diagrams, and especially the structured mandala and the Wise Old Man. Even "wholeness through integration" can reflect Saturn who ate all the other Gods, swallowing his children.

Furthermore, the method of arrival at these goals is also determined by senex fantasies: depression (not inflation), suffering (not laughter) and introversion and imagination require turning away from the world. At the same time the ego is to be stable, ordered and strong. There is a distinct stress on numbers as archetypal root-structures, a belief in compensation as a psychic law (karma, retribution, revenge, and the balance of opposites belong to Kronos-Saturn), and a profound oc-cupation with archeology, history, religion, prophecy and outcast or occult phenomena. Part of the discipline, in this description of the way, is the intellectual study of abstract subjects, a scrutiny of dreams and oracular procedures (*I Ching*), prolonged and constant loyalty to the analysis of the unconscious. Natural man, as peasant, woodchopper or stonecutter, is idealized. Here we find a parallel in Marsilio Ficino who believed that one became a child of Saturn by turning to those occupa-tions and habits that belonged to Saturn: ". . . hence, by withdrawal from earthly things, by leisure, solitude, constancy, esoteric theology and philosophy, by superstition, magic, agriculture, and grief, we come under the influence of Saturn." The senex archetype profoundly affects Jungian collective consciousness and, as we shall come to later, equally affects the Jungian judgements against the puer.

Slow, heavy, chronic, leaden: these qualities produce weight. Senex-consciousness ponders; it weighs things, as did the scales in the Roman temples to Saturn and the long history of the balance image as-sociated with melancholy and Saturn. The voice of this consciousness carries weight, sometimes felt as lead-weight, too pessimistic and dry and altogether untimely, as if from a perspective that is both outmoded and prophetic. The weight represents congealing and coagulation, for Saturn is the personification of the *coagulatio* as it was called in alchemy. Coagulation makes things stick and hold together, becoming solid, trustworthy and time-worthy, but also dense and immobile.

The experience of coagulation is classic to depression, the inhibi-tion and congealing of all psychic reactions, to the degree of static inertia, a dry hunk of wood, a block of stone. This condition was once called the sin of *acedia* — only partially rendered by our *sloth.*[5] The main affliction was less of the body and its members, than of the spirit and its expression. Although the heaviness shows particularly in the head — the melancholic is usually depicted with his head held up by a hand or dejectedly thrown forward onto a table — it is the voice that is "rendered mute, like a spiritual aphonia, a true 'extinction of the voice' of the soul . . . Interior being closes in on itself in its mutism and refuses to communicate with the outside. (Kierkegaard will speak of *hermetism.*)"

When Ficino refers to "leisure" and the "withdrawal from earthly things," or the Jungians speak of introversion as dominating behavior, or the alchemists of the hermetic vessel, or the clinician of depressive inhibition, we find the background to these manifestations of *acedia* to be senex-consciousness. As long ago as the Mediaeval period, a treatment for involutional withdrawal was work, since work (and prayer) were precisely what *acedia* was preventing. Treatments for depression through work and occupational therapy are prefigured in these older cures for the sin and disease of sloth. Work is the enemy of the devil; and again the senex provides a cure within its own archetype in accord with its own kind of consciousness, which includes toil and prayer as well as sloth and spiritual inertia. The recipe of work for "curing the puer" of course will not have the same success because work is not rooted in the puer's own structure.

The pattern of two-sidedness continues through the collection of traits, thereby affecting especially the moral attributes of this consciousness. They become two-sided, dubious. Saturn presides over honest speech — and deceit; over secrets, silence — and loquacious slander; over loyalty, friendship — and selfishness, cruelty, cunning, thievery and murder. He is the just executioner *and* the executed criminal; the prisoner *and* the prison. He is retentive but forgetful; slothful and apathetic but rules the vigil of sleeplessness. His eyes droop with depression, apathetic to all events, and they stare inconsolably open, the super-ego eye of God taking account of everything. He makes both honest reckoning and fraud. He is god of manure, privies, dirty linen, bad wind — and he is cleanser of souls.

Senex duality presents moral values inextricably meshed with shadow; good and bad become hard to distinguish. Because of the inherent antitheses, a morality based on senex-consciousness will always be dubious. No matter what strict code of ethical purity it asserts, in the execution of its lofty principles there will be a balancing loathsome horror not far away, sometimes quite close. Torture and persecution are done in the best of circles for the best of reasons: this is the senex.

SATURN'S SEXUALITY AND FERTILITY. We recall that the relation of Saturn to sexuality is also dual,[6] being both patron of eunuchs and celibates — dry, cold and impotent — yet represented by the dog and the lecherous goat. Certain kinds of sexual disorder could be controlled by means of lead, according to Albertus Magnus: "The effect of lead is cold and constricting, and it has a special power over sexual lust and nocturnal emissions . . ." Here, the senex constricts; yet it also imagines with the inordinate goatish desire of the "dirty old man." In either case, sexuality is at its extremes, transcending the conventional and expected, so that these characteristics no longer refer to actual sexuality but to a fantasy of it. The dog and goat describe the impersonality of the desire, its commonplace and uninhibited earthiness, all eros-sentimentality shed. Impotence, on the other hand, prevents even the dog and goat level of connection, isolating the person and the drive itself to purely imaginal happenings. Impotence, like castration, is a pathological disturbance only when one expects sexuality to perform in the normative sense of generation and intercourse, sexuality in the service of life and love. But these are only two of its possible fantasies; sexuality may also be impotent for life and yet have potency in other aspects.

We must ask what is implied when sexuality is powerless to move externally, when it is contained altogether within; what is a man who is not a male, a force without an issue, a lifelessness of that which is generally considered the creative. Impotence as a death in the midst of life opens another avenue of sexual exploration so that senex consciousness offers the complex another kind of sexual possibility, another way of coming to terms with the meaning of its sexuality and of creativity. Without the senex and his inhibiting impotence, sexuality would exhaust itself in exteriority, the copulative delights, the cease-less generations.

That senex consciousness is associated with extremes of irrational and thus ungovernable sexuality is an idea that can be traced back to the *Problemata* attributed to Aristotle. This idea has been summed up in *Saturn and Melancholy*:

> Melancholics followed their fancy entirely, were uncontrolled in every respect and were driven by ungovernable lust . . . They were greedy, and had no command over their memory, which re-fused to recall things when wanted, only to bring them to mind later and unseasonably. All these weaknesses . . . came from the immoderate irritability of their physical constitution, so that neither could love give them lasting satisfaction nor gluttony alter their congenital leanness. In both cases they sought enjoy-ment not for its own sake but simply as a necessary protection against an organic failing; for just as their sexual craving came from excessive tension, so did their greed spring from metabolic deficiency . . .[7]

"Especially to visual images" were they susceptible so that in sum one could say they were characterized by an "exaggerated irritability of the '*vis imaginative*'."[8]

The "excessive tension" as well as the excess of libido have their source — according to the Aristotle of the *Problemata* — in an "excess of pneuma." The sexuality of the senex is given a pneumatic source. Its disorders, whether in the form of lechery or of impotence, become ultimately accountable through the *heightened power of imagination*. Senex consciousness presents a sexuality of the *vis imaginativa*, an apprecia-tion of sexual behavior itself as one more form of fantasy. Impotence and lechery are aspects of the imagination first of all; they find their expression in sexuality but in other areas too. So we can look again at the castration of Uranos by his youngest son Kronos, not merely as an emblem of sexual impotence where the old king is dethroned when his fertility is replaced by the usurping heir. The tale tells as well that the reign of the old sky God as a myth maker and creator of imaginal possibilities is over when the sexual aspect of the *vis imaginativa* no longer functions.

If lechery and impotence both originate in the heightened imagination, we may detect in these apparently dissimilar phenomena a latent identity. Commonly, because old men are impotent they, of course, have dirty thoughts. Dirty thoughts are, commonly, inferior substitutes for the "real thing." But turned the other way around "real" sexuality dwindles in order to stimulate dirty thoughts. These fantasies are the sexualization of consciousness, the needed erotic stimulation to fertilize the imagination. The transition to a lecherous spirit and an impotent body is the transition from the normal to the *noetic*, where impotence may become the precondition for a potent imagination. A similar transition can occur through senile memory loss which opens the way from the normal to the noetic memory, to the remembrance via early childhood of the archetypal as described in Plato's *Meno* and *Phaedo*.

To be filled therefore with lecherous fantasies means Saturn is near, and depression too; these fantasies offer access to this archetypal perspective and to all the complications that come with this senex structure. So, too, with impotence: Aphrodite may not want it, nor Zeus, nor Pan, but its appearance demands that sexuality be re-imagined now through the senex. As senex pertains not only to old people but to a structure of consciousness, so senex sexuality refers not only to the sexual behavior of old people but to a kind of sexual consciousness, which provides the imaginal background for both impotence and lechery.

Despite the impotence, Saturn retains the attributes of Kronos; he is a fertility God. Saturn invented agriculture; this God of the earth and the peasant, the harvest and the Saturnalia, is ruler of fruit and seed. Even his castrating sickle is a harvesting tool. It would have to be Saturn who invents agriculture: only the senex has the patience equaling that of the soil and can understand the soil's conservation and the conservatism of those who till it; only the senex has the sense of time needed for the seasons and their chronic repetition; the ability to abstract so as to master the geometry of ploughing, the essence of seeds, the profitable counting, the dung, the loneliness and the affectionless, objectified sexuality.

III THE SENEX AND THE FEMININE. According to Hesiod, in the Golden Age when Kronos ruled, there were no women. The lore of Saturn in the astrological-magical texts continues the tradition of an estrangement between the senex and the feminine.

The original Saturn figure of Rome was not married (even if his Greek parallel, Kronos, had his sister-wife, Rhea). His feminine counterpart in Republican Rome was principally Lua (goddess of the spoils of war, the plundered fields, the booty) who had the power of working evil (lues) on women, crops and harvest. Crops were spoiled or became the spoils of war. In later imagery of which Dürer's *Melancolia* is the paradigm, Saturn's feminine aspect is Dame Melancholy. The mood of depression, with Saturn's usual attributes including the signs of wisdom, is now carried by the *anima tristis*. In a sense, Dame Melancholy is the senex vision of Sophia: senex wisdom may be depressing; senex depression may be wise.

Despite the disregard for women, senex-consciousness may keep the feminine imprisoned in secret, a secret soft spot or a secret mistress. Like the Old King with the Princess in the keep, he does not let out his feminine side, warding off with cruelty and wiles anyone trying to rescue it. Or, the femininity of the senex may be an enactment of Dame Melancholy. Then the feminine side of the negative senex is a moody consort with whom no one can get along. It is not merely the anima-complex turned sour, bitter, resentful, complaining; the moody consort emanates like an atmosphere from any moribund complex, giving it the stench of Saturn.

For complexes when they lose their life, putrefy. Putrefaction belongs to Saturn as God of agriculture, dung and dying. Putrefaction in alchemy was natural disintegration necessary for change. Such putrefaction is ferment, decomposition into elements through the release of "sulphuric" aggressive fumes which assault and insult one's sensibilities. Its purpose is a re-ordering of "matters." But when the senex has lost its child, then the rot is stagnation, nothing flowing in, nothing flowing out. One turns around and around in one's own mess. Matters do not change. A dying complex infects all one's psychic life. It can be recognized by grief and helped with mourning; therewith we acknowledge the fact of decay. But when ignored it spreads to the life of others.

We become old witches, old devils, old monsters that the world would put away because of the death spread by the old dying complexes. In our delusions of strength and power we refuse to bear witness to our decay.

Saturn's female partner, Lua, shows growth gone wrong through Saturn's aggrandizement, the materialism and the greed. Without awareness of the *anima tristis* component of Saturn, Lua's reign may extend. Thus though senex-consciousness intends benevolence, wisdom and order, senex-unconsciousness in the control of the feminine counterpart spreads like *lues* (the plague) and looks for battle to gain spoils. We may also read Lua as a goddess of decay and pollution, for Saturn is also named the Lord of Decrease. Senex growth is inward and downward, or backward; its force can come through shrinkage, his power manifest in the last stage of processes, in their decay. He rules over the spoiled, the filth and the refuse of society not only owing to sordid anality and repression, but because senex consciousness finds its awareness in the underside of the complex and as it decays. So accustomed are we to growth and to what T. S. Eliot calls "superficial notions of evolution / Which becomes, in the popular mind, a means of disowning the past" ("The Dry Salvages") and to the Positive Great Mother doctrines of milky-way philosophy, onward and upward with Teilhard de Chardin, that we miss Lua, the spoiler, the consciousness that is possible through the natural process of decomposition. "Decay is inherent in all composite things," says the last dictum o the Buddha, so what we work at is not our growth, but the modes of our rot.

Dame Melancholy may also appear as the embodiment and vision of depression, where she brings wisdom, as she did to Boethius, who was betrayed and thrown into prison when not yet forty. There his suicidal melancholy conjured the feminine figure of Wisdom, who dictated to him his *Consolation of Philosophy*. Depression and the awakening of one's genius are inseparable, say the texts. Yet for most of us there is much depression and little genius, little consolation of philosophy, only the melancholic stare — what to do, what to do.

Psychological clichés claim that senex-consciousness is "cut off" from the feminine. But Kronos has mother and wife and daughters (Demeter, Hera, Hestia). Rather than dissociated femininity, this archetype shows a female counterpart — Lua, Dame Melancholy — which mirrors, and is thus indistinguishable from Saturn himself. His mother Gé (Mother Earth) repeats in his sister-wife Rhea, so that Saturn's agricultural, fertility and material functions are reflected by these feminine mirrors. The urge to "build cities" and "mint money," the deep-seated concretization of the senex impulse may very well be taken as an attribute of this mother-sister-wife complex. The *complicatio* of these earth goddesses in Kronos involve the senex in earthiness. Thus senex preoccupation with property, with the things and matters of the established order, its hoarding and its greed, derives not from the "excess of pneuma" and the "exaggerated irritability of the *vis imaginative*," that is, Saturn's own native spirit, but rather from the feminine side of this structure, the earth and its materialism to which its ties are reinforced in triplicate.

By showing saturnine traits, senex femininity presents unpleasant, even maleficent, aspects of the anima. Here we meet her mad moodiness, her peculiar fascinations with the occult, or with power and possessions, or with the "way out" things of prisons, sewerage and magic. A state of mind occurs that seems obsessive, not anima and not feminine as we prettily conceive these notions. Senex femininity seems rather the crone side of the mother archetype. As if as we grow older not only do we whine and need helping, but use our infirmity for power. The old man has cut off not his mother, but his father; his mother he has married; they have become one. The senex anima can be so objectionable to ruling consciousness that a life may be, so to speak, dragged into the senex state. One turns against the moody consort and her materializations, attempting indeed to "cut off" the feminine, negating her effects by clinging to the relics of male authority, refusing the natural decomposition of the complexes, refusing that decay emanating through the earth-crone and depression, the senex bride and sister.

Or, to re-awaken the puer aspect, the feminine may re-appear as an object for complex-compelled falling-in-love. Enter: the girl of our dreams; exit: old woman, the decay and depression. Falling-in-love is a phenomenon not only of old age, but of an old attitude. It may occur at any time of life and be occasioned by the loss of any puer

aspect. Then one is "ripe for it." It is less a *coniunctio* fantasy, nor even
the renewal of the feminine, as much as it is prompted by the lost child
and the re-connecting to the puer in oneself. So, the woman becomes
Pandora — the first female brought into the all-male Kingdom of Kronos — a magical, beautiful box of fantasies and hope for the complex
to be rejuvenated, *senilis* to *juvenilis*. The fantasies bring forth Venus
from the sea of unconscious emotions, suddenly ebbing and flooding
again. Her birth is closely tied with the senex; she is his progeny, his
sole creation. Without Kronos and the senex-despair of the complex,
Aphrodite and her illusions might never float in off the foam. Venus
rose from the sea after being conceived there from the genitals of Uranos which Kronos-Saturn, his son, cut off with his left hand and flung
away. A senex act creates her of the seminal stuff of the father. The
hidden connection between falling-in-love with the dazzling seduction of foam-borne Aphrodite and the seed and scythe of old senex
is not easy to discern. But how else account for the terrible cruelties,
the vicious eat-or-be-eaten fights that break out of the most translu-
cently lovely love affairs? And, when Venus departs, Saturn returns
with brooding melancholy, devastating loneliness feelings of ugliness
— even psychic crippling or suicide.

But these genitals are of the sky-god. They are the "upper" aspect
of sexuality, sexuality's fantasy power. So Venus is born from imaginal
froth, the sea-foam of unconscious fantasy. When one attacks sexuality with senex-repression, severing the fathering fantasies of one's own
loins, throwing it away left-handedly, dismissively into unconsciousness, it does not cease creating. Sexual fantasies inseminate below the
waves, returning in the shape of Venus. Cut-off sexuality goes on living. The images return as the father's daughter: sweet, alluring, aphro-
disiacal fantasies bred of the union of sexuality's "upper" genitals and
the emotional depths.

Kronos' act fathered other daughters besides Aphrodite; her sisters were dark indeed: the Moira and the Erinyes. The latter — even
called "daughters of Kronos" — were death-dealing dieties; the former,
goddesses of death, chthonic powers of the fate portioned to all humans. These mythical sisters of Aphrodite (like the mythical servants
of Aphrodite: Custom, Grief, Anxiety) reflect their parentage in senex-

consciousness and its underworldly, otherworldly associations. Even the feminine delights that might be promised the old man through a young love come to him sternly and take him to his grave. Oedipus' daughters at the end bring not refreshment and renewal but ease his parting. The complex in its senex phase is inescapably doomed to its fate and the revelation of its psychic essence through the anima of death which however does have, as its sister in inseparable *complicatio*, the joy and beauty of Aphrodite. Only when we would have Aphrodite alone, her sisters ignored, that they come pursuing like the Erinyes snarling with endless complications the portions of inheritance, the retributions and recriminations of a mess left behind and passed like a fateful karma to next generations.

IV SENEX CONSCIOUSNESS IN CHILDHOOD AND MIDLIFE. If the senex as archetype is there a priori, "from the beginning," we must expect it in a person's life from the beginning. We must expect a show of the archetype already in childhood, the old man in the little boy. And there we do find it when the small child says " I know" and "mine" with the full intensity of his being. There is senex, too, in the child's loneliness; a sense of utter abandonment, isolation and helplessness that may not come again until old age. The senex gives that ontological loneliness, a removal from human existence, in the special world set apart for the old, the mad and small children. The child's loneliness is part of that misery we call "ego-development." We conceive the ego as having boundaries, separated and able to withstand isolation. It must be able to go it alone. Part of the heroic initiation is exposure and loneliness. Loneliness gives the ego a vision of the world from the exile of childhood where one is outside like the senex, in another state of being. The ego is a superstition born of solitude, a magical way of entering the world of full human being. Call it an enacted omnipotence fantasy.

The small child shows its senex when it is the last to pity and the first to tyrannize, when it enjoys destroying what it has built, spurs its will with envy, keeps its secret, relishes detail, performs its esoteric superstitions, carries its grief, and in its weakness produces oral omnipotence and anal sadistic fantasies, or defends its borders and tests the limits set by others. The child can be solemn and ceremonious like old men. The child is obsessed with the limitations imposed by the body, tiny sores, afflictions and complaints. Its compulsion is like that of the aged: once obsessed it cannot let go until it suddenly forgets. The senex traits are there; we need but see them for what they are. Childhood is governed not only by the archetype of the child, and by the mother. The senex is there too, just as Saturn is in the birthchart, constellating its effects from the beginning. Seneca put it like this: "Ere the Child has seen the light, the principle of beard and grey hairs is innate. Albeit small and hidden, all the functions of the whole body and of every succeeding period of life are there."

Although the senex is there in the child, the senex spirit nevertheless appears most evidently when any function we use, attitude we have, or complex of the psyche begins to coagulate past its prime. It is the Saturn within the complex that makes it hard to shed, dense and slow and maddeningly depressing — the madness of lead-poison — that feeling of the everlasting indestructibility of the complex. It cuts off the complex from life and the feminine, inhibiting it and introverting it into an isolation. Thus it stands behind the fastness of our habits and the ability we have of making a virtue of any vice by merely keeping it in order or attributing it to fate.

The senex of the complex appears long before a person has himself put on his *toga senilis*. Michelangelo and Voltaire complained of old age around 40 though they lived long into their 80s. Dante's four ages of man (adolescence, youth, *senecte* and *senio* (senility) placed at least two of them directly under the influence of the senex. Shakespeare considered a man of forty old. Erasmus wrote "On the Discomforts of Old Age" while still 39. Tasso who died at fifty wrote his autobiographical essay on his infirmity and old age when he was 41. Another representative of the Renaissance, Thomas Eliot, in his *Castle of Health* (1534) declared that *senectus* begins at age forty. The awareness of the senex archetype through depression, complaint and limitation, the sense of time and death, of decay and the *anima tristis* has been fundamental in the kind of awareness we attribute to the creative person. Rembrandt, yet in his twenties, painted old people; Plato, we conjecture, devoted his early dialogues to the dying of a wise old man. There is, according to Jacques, a "mid-life crisis" in regard to death which determines the course of artistic work in later life. From what we know of the senex archetype, a crisis is brought on by its demand for entry. It brings a re-orientation of consciousness — in this case, in terms of senex structures.

The need for a "second beginning" is often put in creation myths. The first start is wiped out, and the world begins again, after the flood. Gods and heroes have a second birth (Osiris, Dionysus) or two tales are told of their origin, and mystical man is twice-born. Psychology has taken this ontological image about two levels of being and two structures of consciousness and laid it out in terms of progressive time: first-half and second-half of life. But these "halves" are less biological or psychological fact as they are a *mythical description of the two levels on which we live.* Some men and women live from a "twice-born" state early in their youth; others go through a mid-life crisis moving from one to another; others may repeatedly live now one, now the other in alternations. First-half and second-half pertains to kinds of consciousness, not to periods.

So the senex may appear in dreams while we are still very young. It manifests as the dream father, mentor, old wise man or knowing crone, to which the dreamer's consciousness is pupil. When accentuated it seems to have drawn all power to itself, paralyzing elsewhere, and a person is unable to take a decision without first taking counsel with the unconscious to await an advising voice from an oracle or vision. Though this counsel may come from the unconscious, it may be as collective as that which comes from the standard canons of the culture. For statements of sagacity and meaning, even spiritual truths, can be bad advice. These representations — elders, mentors, analysts, and old wise men and women — provide an authority and wisdom that is beyond the experience of the dreamer, "helping" to keep him helplessly dependent. Therefore it tends to have him rather than he it, so that he is driven by an unconscious certainty, making him "wise beyond his years," ambitious for recognition by his seniors and intolerant of his own youthfulness. According to some research the senex figure comes more frequently in the dreams of women than those of young men, further indicating the distance between puer and senex in our present culture. Crucial in this discussion is that senex consciousness may be constellated at any age and in regard to any complex.

Notes

1. [First published in *Spring* 1970. Reprinted in Patricia Berry, ed., *Fathers and Mothers* (Dallas: Spring Publications, 1990).] — Ed.

2. [See Chapter 1 for accompanying descriptions of the senex. As this present chapter was at one time an extended version of the material contained in Chapter 1, there are some minor revisions and omissions from the original version.] — Ed.

3. R. Klibansky, E. Panofsky, and F. Saxl, *Saturn and Melancholy* (London: Nelson, 1964).

4. *Laws*, IV, 713b–14a.

5. See S. Wenzel, *The Sin of Sloth* (Chapel Hill: University of North Carolina Press, 1967).

6. [Refer to descriptions of the senex in Chapter 1.] — Ed.

7. *Saturn and Melancholy*, p. 34.

8. Ibid., p. 35.

10

Negative Senex and a Renaissance Solution [1]

> Men perish because they cannot join the beginning to the end.
>
> — Alkmaeon of Croton

From the preceding chapter we learned two essentials of senex consciousness. First, there is an "excessive tension" deriving from an "excess of pneuma," a description going back to Aristotle's *Problemata*.[2] This basic characteristic is also referred to as an "exaggerated irritability of the imaginative powers." In other words, the senex is particularly subject to the effects of mental images which it elaborates, and suffers, in a manner that is "pneumatic," i.e. mental, intellectual, spiritual. Second, "excessive tension" also refers to the extreme duality of this particular figure.

Many Greek Gods have their dualities. They both chastise and bless, destroy and aid. In none of them, however, is this duality so fundamental as in Kronos. His nature is dual not only with regard to its effects in the outer world of events, but in regard to his own personal destiny — the excessive tension of his suffering, and our melancholy. Because duality is so sharply marked in Kronos, he might fairly be called The God of Opposites.[3]

In descriptions of the senex figure we find again and again the antithetical aspects contrasted by the words positive and negative, beneficent and maleficent. When he appears, so does the problem of opposites; when opposites appear as a *problem*, so does senex consciousness.

Jung recognized and warned about this inherent duality in the senex:

> ... whenever the "simple" and "kindly" old man appears, it is advisable for heuristic and other reasons to scrutinize the context with some care ... the old man has a wicked aspect too, just as the primitive medicine man is a healer and helper and also the dreaded concoctor of poisons. The very word. *pharmakon* means "poison" as well as "antidote" ...[4]

With this defining duality in mind let us turn to questions of senex negativity.

SENEX DESTRUCTIVENESS

> Turn of mind into melancholy and frequent madness and extravagance from the Turn of Life — the top of the Hill — at 35 to 40 — different in different men.
>
> — Samuel T. Coleridge[5]

Because duality lies so entwined in this structure, how can we know which way it may turn in our lives? And is there a way out at all? Which is really more destructive — to be the executioner or the executed; to be the dried melancholic staring voiceless into space, or a king on his throne to the end, fist-clenched and dotty? The images are not cheerful. They are not among those described by the Founding Fathers in their pursuit of happiness. (But then those fathers had a puer fantasy — life, liberty, and a declaration of independence from the Old King.) Is there a way out of the saturnine convention so that we are not eaten by the senex complex?

Identification with the senex occurs subtly; we learn the role slowly. It is a chronic disease, creeping upon us unnoticed. We seem to recognize lost youth first in the flesh and fight the senex in the body. But shriveling (blackening) of the mind goes apace and often precedes actual ageing in years. The child of the imagination may die long before our body's aging begins. How does the old king in my habits and attitudes change? How can all that I have learned and now know become wisdom used with charity? How do I admit the new and its error, disorder and nonsense within my borders? How can I die right? The manner in which we turn over these issues within ourselves affects the historical transition. We are each makeweights in the scales of history, as Jung said. Perhaps our psychic weight increases in these scales as we fantasy upon the heaviest of all problems, the senex.

By pulling back these issues into ourselves we relieve history of having to carry them for us. After all, the problem of ageing begins in the psyche. It emanates from the individual into civilization, destructive as radiation, a fall-out onto society from complexes we have not the lead enough to encase. Pollution begins in the undigested portions of our personal history that we release into the body politic. History out there is loaded with greed, passions, regrets that we have not come to terms with in ourselves. If we refuse to admit that an urge to suicide and disintegration are equally basic to the same structure that would make order, how can we prepare a future. How can we speak of plenty if the same drive of our consciousness has appetite for decay and negation.[6] Unemployment, depression, energy crises, and isolation are psychic phenomena. If we do not understand the archetypal nature of our reactions in the areas belonging to Saturn, our reactions become stereotyped. Push the same button, get the same response. History is obliged to repeat itself simply because we will not look at what makes history.

The transformation of history begins in the soul as a destruction of what time has wrought. It is an operation of the senex upon the senex: the *nigredo* experience of the depression and rottening of the mind filled with accumulated time. Alchemy says how this work proceeds: "The divine organ is the head, for it is the abode of the divine part, namely the soul . . ." and the philosopher must "surround this organ with greater care than other organs."[7] In the *nigredo* the brain turns black. Thus a Hermes recipe cited in the *Rosarium* says: "Take the brain . . . grind it up with very strong vinegar, or with boys' urine, until it turns black." The darkening or benightedness is at the same time a psychic state called melancholia (black bile). In the *Aurelia occulta* there is a passage where the transformation substance in the nigredo state says of itself:

> I am an infirm and weak old man, surnamed the dragon; therefore I am shut up in a cave, that I be ransomed by the kingly crown . . . A fiery sword inflicts great torments upon me; death makes weak my flesh and bones . . . My soul and my spirit depart; a terrible poison, I am likened to the black raven, for that is the wages of sin; in dust and earth I lie . . .[8]

From the senex viewpoint, our complexities cannot altogether be elucidated, led into light, even if therapy believes that the process of individuation gradually increases consciousness. That our complexities become clearer may mean that we have lost touch with their darkness, the fundamental impenetrability of the other side at their core. The antidote is not extracted from poison, since the poison and the antidote are one and the same thing. The snake that heals is the same snake whose bite kills; there are no "good" snakes and "bad" snakes; there is but one snake, even in Paradise. Besides, with every extraction of kindliness from wickedness, of light from darkness, the old residual stuff becomes denser. In alchemy the poisonous portion of the complex remaining after its goodness had been separated out became the new nigredo, the substance for the next transformation. The new work was on the old remainder, the lead, the raven, the black sludge left over. If alchemy is a "therapy," then the focus to which its operation returns again and again is the senex component of the complex. Here, is the stubborn poison.

Therapy in this sense becomes a working on Saturn, a depressive grinding of the most recalcitrant encrustations of the complex, its oldest habits, which are neither childhood remnants nor parental introjections but senex phenomena, that is, *the structure and principles by which the complex endures.* Fundamental in this structure is its double nature, so no experience can possibly be only beneficial. Even the moments of kindly and benign wisdom concoct a new toxin. The fear of the poison and the wickedness of the old wise man is not only a heuristic caution.

This fear is also a true recognition of the nature of wisdom, its Saturn aspect.

For the alchemical operations on Saturn the operator and the material operated upon must be in sympathetic rapport, i.e., under the same archetypal constellation. One works on the blackened mind with the sour vinegar and residual salts of youth left behind. *Depression would be the prerequisite for working on anything belonging to the senex.* Consciousness itself must be blackened before one can approach this *nigredo.* Insoluble problems can be adequately met only with an attitude of hopelessness that gives them their due and mirrors them truthfully. Hatred, envy, grinding meanness become tools of insight. They provide ways of darkening the light and cutting deeply into psychological truth. By dimming the brightness and by hiding and cloaking the head, depression also wraps and cares for the soul. If the substance worked upon is the "old man" in the complex, then this work cannot take place without the old man, who is our weakness and infirmity and the dragon-like monstrosity of our destructive power that devours everything into its bad mood.

Senex destructiveness confronts us more dangerously than we realize — particularly when we fasten attention on destruction elsewhere, e.g., the violent and aimless chaos of youth. The danger from the senex lies just in the fact that we are unaware of it as dangerous. We are so used to the institutions of order into which we mold our society, our lives and conceptions, we do not see that these institutions and images are patterned after a senex God and are conditioned by senex forces. We are so used to our complexes and their odors that we do not realize their decay.

The fantasies we have had for coping with the historical issues betray the senex behind the fantasies: the hope for peace and plenty and full-employment; security through settled boundaries and financial accords; urban-planning as panacea; longevity; the extension of law and of knowledge; unification into monopolies and ever-larger systems, or the reverse into individualistic isolation, one man, one gun, one family, one bomb-shelter; computers and their basis on the either/or of contradiction, memory-storage and retrieval; and, finally, the paternal world organization with rational policing of disorder.

So, too, our hope for the Great Individual, a creative wise-man, scientist or leader, who can lay the problems at rest. The sage[9] who stands above the street but close to the earth is just another anthropomorphic image of the same senex God. As Jung himself pointed out in that passage referred to above[10] the old wise man is no solution, for the antidote and poison are inseparable. So withdrawal from the scene to go about the Father's spiritual business — solitude, reflection, wisdom — may only produce more blackening of the brain, more of the dragon. Withdrawal will not do it since the psyche does not move in isolation; the soul requires involvement and emotion, even if the spirit may ascend its mountain all alone.[11] *"C'est une grande folie de vouloir être sage tout seul,"* said La Rochefoucauld, which may mean that wisdom of the lonely sage is folly. In considering the old wise man and any of the "Paths to Wisdom," from Zen to Blavatsky, as the solution to the senex problem, it would be advisable to keep in mind the ambivalence of the images we have been considering. A consciousness that chooses wisdom, also chooses the senex; choice of the senex means destruction in one style or another. The archetype does not permit the ego to select from it the sweeter parts.[12] Mimesis implies myth lived into its consequences.

The senex and its anima, Lua,[13] tend to materialize and exteriorize issues away from the psyche. Without the possibility of psyche in today's events they become unavailable to human reflection. We may think and plan, but our thinking and planning will not be reflective upon the subjective factor. The thinking and planning will be itself a reflection of the archetypal drivenness which created the problem that calls for these thought-out constructed solutions. The anti-psychological aspect of so much that is constructed by thinkers and planners betrays Saturn, not in his prophetic furor and imaginative insight, but in his obsessions with order.

Within ourselves the senex fights to maintain order by laying down the law or projecting some new system to end conflict. We do not want the turmoil which the senex-puer struggle within ourselves releases. So Saturn self-perpetuates by pretending issues are not psychological, but are real, economic, political, practical. Whenever we use these reasonings, whenever we take a position that is anti-psychological or anti-eros it is the senex speaking. Saturn is "never in favour with woman or wife."[14] He prevents the connection between eros and psyche.

One of the main subterfuges to prevent this connection is again the old dog's concretizing of eros into sexuality, so that even pornography can be said to be ruled by Saturn. Pornographic eros that has no soul in it, differs hardly from the dried, profaned, and loveless psyche of academic psychology, another preserve of the senex. The dry calls up lubricity; denial invites pornography. We create the concretistic psychopathic age by defining consciousness as reality-oriented, forgetting that *psychic* reality is primary and that primary in psychic reality are the fantasies, feelings, and values of eros.

Psychopathy means unwavering, unreflected, irremediable acting-out. The sociopath puts his pathology and his psychology out into society. Society is to blame for his lot and society is the place where it can be undone — so he insists. The model of thinking in sociopathy does not differ greatly from that in sociology: both attribute to society the cause and cure of psychic affliction. When the reality of the psyche is second to real reality "out there," then what else but act out in the streets. The senex has decreed that that is where the action is, and the puer, trying to change society, is unwittingly caught by his father's belief. Thus he is swallowed as he castrates, unable to bring real change. Real change means archetypal change, a change in the mythic dominants of our perceptions.

For it is the senex, too, who creates the generation problem and the generation gap. The senex conceives in terms of time,[15] succession, and the patriarchal vision of fathers and sons. When we use this language we are again under senex dominion. Despite the blessings it offers of patronage and patrimony, castration is inherent in the generational model; Kronos who castrated his father has castrated his fatherhood.

"Father" and "son" are not only a succession in time, but various ways of incarnating the ancestral archetype. There is the father form of being myself and the son form, the grandfather and the little boy — they are ways of enacting my family myth. "Youth" and "age" are symbolic manners of expressing certain psychic realities through personifications. I need not be trapped in one of these personifications so that my consciousness cannot be the little boy when I am in the shape and figure of an old man, or vice versa. The literalness of the Saturn mind would keep us defined by our skins [16] and their wrinkles, whereas consciousness can play many parts of the family drama, including the ancestral figures and perhaps those not yet born. The generation fantasy, and the war between them, is essential to the Uranos-Kronos-Zeus pattern. And to the Bible, a patriarchal book devoting pages and pages to generational descent.

The age of psychopathy threatens with continual possibility of immediate destruction. But the enemy is not as before: an enemy with a plan, schizoid dreams of world rule, paranoid plots. There is no master plan; the assassins among us are already in uniform on duty or are those out for but a bit of loot. Destruction comes from a kid who has nothing better to do some sunny afternoon. Or, possessed by the puer the assassin becomes its explosive force, a living torch that would cleanse the world of its senex rot. The time bomb he sets was put in his hand by the old King. Senex consciousness when split from the puer offers this chronic invitation to destruction. Senex devotion to its own definition of order leaves open only one way out: obliteration. Even here the extreme and inherent contradiction of Saturn, upholder and negater, is operative. Besides the senility, the obsessive, paranoid, and melancholic streaks, we may add schizoid ambivalence to the diagnostic categories of senex consciousness. Destruction is one of its defenses.

Could not this destructiveness of the senex, which the senex itself has constellated, begin from within? Could not the establishment be dismantled and melted through insight? The monuments may remain; but their pretentious dignity need not be taken at their own level of seriousness. The self-destruction of senex consciousness could begin with insight into that consciousness — suicide through mimesis.

The Saturnalia provided a destruction of hierarchy, law, order, and time. It brought back the Golden Age. All borders down, lust released, denials and cautions to the wind — within the limits of the "game." The Saturnalia reincorporated the puer, his dream of freedom and his world outside time. But the Saturnalia, too, is an interior phenomenon, in that we can see through civilization *and ourselves* with the same Saturnalian vision. When I see myself as the caricature that I also am, the

Saturnalia has begun, and the appearance of my craziness begins to shine through the system I had built against it.

The Greeks made fun of Kronos, who was a "symbol of dotage and imbecility."[17] Kronos was full of antiquated phrases, Polonius-like platitudes, a ridiculous old man who passed his time in the wanton foolery of senility to be driven off his throne by his son. Even the prophetic gift was shadowed with references to the dim sight of rheumy eyes. Wise he may be, but he is also dotty.

Part of dismantling the power of Saturn may be a gift of his own brand of humor — even if loss of the "mirth reaction" is supposedly a clinical sign of depression. Scurrile jokes to do with latrines, underwear, and bad wind — which classically "belong" to Saturn — return the schoolboy puer to the constellation. Here, seeing through "from below" becomes a dirty joke.

Satire, too, belongs to this dismantling operation. Elliott[18] has written on the relations between the Saturnalia and satire, showing that the literary form is a way of turning things upsidedown. This too saves the senex from his own seriousness, yet, at the same time maintains his superior rule. For if one can be satirical about the complexes, see them like Swift and draw them like Daumier, grotesquely, one comes to believe that one is endowed with a penetrating consciousness that can see through human foibles. It's a way of being God, another inflation of the wise old man. This kind of insight does not show psychological results, remaining still within the senex perspective that would dominate through brain power, even a blackened one. Satirists notoriously do not deepen psychologically; they merely polish their style, resharpening the same pointedness.

Whatever the instrument, the point of all is to see through this style of consciousness, to destroy its destruction with insight.

For the senex is not "out there" in institutions of society any more than the old God is "up there" in heaven. It has all fallen down and in. We find the senex in our solitary taking account, sorting through, figuring out; alone behind the wheel on the way to work; head under the shower, under the dryer; alone at the kitchen table looking down into black coffee, in bed staring into night — the senex mind tying together the unravelled fringes of the day, making order.

Here is our melancholy trying to make knowledge, trying to see through. But the truth is that the melancholy *is* the knowledge: the poison is the antidote. This would be the senex's most destructive insight: our senex order rests on senex madness. Our order is itself a madness.

The old king is crazy old King Lear, and the old wise man, a man mad as the prophet and the geometer,[19] with his obsession of motionless Parmenidean order, mad as the old Board Chairman with his tables of organization and charts of aggrandizement, as the senex General with his weapons called "toys." As we get older we get crazier, but the senex in our complexes has the foresight to see the mad outcome of each complex. "All true insight is foresight," said Coleridge (in *On the Constitution of the Church and State*).[19a] Thomas Browne put the progressive madness in the complex in moral language:

> But age doth not rectify, but incurvate our natures, turning bad dispositions into worser habits, and (like diseases), brings on curable vices; for every day as we grow weaker in age, we grow stronger in sin . . . The same vice committed at sixteen, is not the same . . . at forty, but swells and doubles by the circumstances of our ages . . . Every sin the oftner it is committed, the more it acquireth in the quality of evil; as it succeeds in time, so it proceeds in degrees of badness . . . like figures in Arithmetick, the last stands for more than all that went before it.[20]

Against the foreknowledge of its madness, and against the madness too, senex consciousness builds its establishment of order, system, knowledge, and justice, which again and again breaks down in actuality, for it too is a fantasy of the complex against its accumulating twisted "incurvature." Puer consciousness does not see the madness of the archetype. It moves among the Gods like beautiful Ganymede, serving ambrosia, carrying their messages but not reading the horror between the lines. (How long it takes the puer in us to learn to suffer, to stink and shrivel, to find his acid, salt, lye, lead, and dung.) The prophet in senex consciousness, and the measurer, does know what proportions the Gods can take and to what madness the archetype can lead with its excess and its infirmity. The establishment is refuge: the realm of ego, of Caesar and senex consciousness, a keep of sanity, and sanity too is a fantasy. The only protection is the dissolution of this fantasy of sanity and, in Joseph Conrad's language the recipe is "immersion in the destructive element" and knowledge of the "horror, the horror," which in this case is Saturn's own special madness, his melancholy. To penetrate the riddle of senex destruction means to go to the heart of darkness.

If wisdom is the most we long for and destruction the worst we fear, and if both are "children of Saturn," then how to further the former and escape the latter? Since one face or the other of the senex rules our time and fate, is there no way out?

‖ SENEX INCURABILITY. One "way out" — besides the Saturnalia and its pranks and black humour leading to the recognizing insight into melancholy through melancholy — is abandoning the notion of a way out altogether. This notion is anyway a puer reaction to the senex, whose consciousness prefers the hemlock within the prison walls, the cure of death.

Senex images of the hour-glass and Father Time, the Reaper and the Old Man with the White Beard, and the like, are not only shorthand emblems for the time process taking place inside or outside of us. They refer to the ancient identity, spoken of by Plutarch for instance, between the Kronos of Hesiod with Chronos, Time. The emblems state that the archetypal structure is concerned not so much with quantitative amounts of time, nor even with temporal process, time passing, as with time itself as an ontological real. Thus leisure and sloth are ways of "finding time" or "making time," and the withdrawal from the flux of the world is a way of occupying oneself with the eternal, and thereby being occupied or possessed by it. Constancy, grief, lethargy, and solitude do not mean only slowing things down or drawing things out; they are ways of experiencing the senex essence of Kronos-Chronos, where time is a quality that verges on endlessness (the fidelity of friendship, the return of the seasons, the protracted grief of mourning) without process or alteration of any kind, a state of being where becoming has been crowded to the edge.

In this sense, senex-consciousness is particularly temporal, structuring its vision in terms of the chronic. It eyes the eternal, since that lasts longest; and its judgement is based on truth in terms of durability, not whether it awakens insight, moves the heart, or brings beauty. Beauty, itself, is defined in terms of unalterable criteria of form or meaning, the eternal verities, whereas the proof of love is not ardor but constancy. The Yiddish maxim is a senex maxim: "Love me little but love me long." So if things are to last they will be connected to the senex archetype, and if a complex endures, it tends towards stabilizing itself, congealing into a usual part of one's psychic establishment, and finally, through sheer intractability transforming from a burden to hide in to a habit to wear. In senex consciousness time is the "cure," in the sense of tanning, leathering, hardening, weathering through dry air, salt, smoke, or alum.[21]

For senex consciousness a complex needs to remain true to itself. Through this constancy and suffering, the vice eventually regards itself as a virtue. Endurance (Saturn as *tenax*) is the key, so that any complex lasting long enough begins to set the standards for psychic life in general. The psyche becomes dominated by its most stable element, its most habitually continuing complex which, because it can endure, influences other attitudes to choose the same path. Its values are in terms of time — time as history, as slowness, or as resistance to alteration. If a habit or symptom has enough personal history, or can be connected to a historical idea or symbol, then it becomes acceptable. "I was always this way." If a compulsion can be realized in detail and over a long period (in a relationship, a long analysis, a piece of "creative" work), it is *ipso facto* part of one's style. Or, again from the viewpoint of senex consciousness, if a matter cannot be altered at all, recalcitrant and obdurate to every treatment, by the very virtue of its durability it must be true and good. The fixedness of things is evidence of their superior place in the scale of values. Thus does the senex make things last, hard to shed, ourselves coagulated in this or that rigidity, and by gradually extending its stoic reign, adds layers of character armor to our psychic establishment. The senex keeps us in protracted pain and the protracted treatment for the pain, ourselves as time's serf and victim, chronically caught in occupations we would quit, in marriages we would leave, in habits no New Year's resolution can ever dent. Ripeness is all has come to mean tenacity is all.[22]

REPRESSION AND NEGATION

For there is falsehood in our knowledge, and darkness is so firmly planted in us that even our groping fails.

— Albrecht Dürer [23]

We are used to negative namings of the archetypes in Jungian psychology where "negative mother," "negative animus," "negative attempts at restoration of the persona," and "negative feelings" have become conventions of the language. Negative senex is the same kind of epithet, and it too will not do.

First, let us make clear that because the negative senex is not an ego fault it cannot be altered by the ego. It is not merely a matter of moral admonitions (as if the ego should do better, be more modest, or humble or "conscious"). Nor is it a problem of updating ideas (as if the ego should "keep moving"). Travel, in order to change ideas by new impressions and thus make the coagulation come unstuck, was a cure for depression recommended by the psychiatry of the nineteenth century, its antecedents going back to Celsus. [24] Nor is the root of this hardening merely the decline of biological vitality (as if the ego should keep its body fit and active). These problems in the ego are consequents rather than causes; they reflect a prior disorder in the archetypal ground of the ego. That the negative senex is not the result of the ego is clear enough in those desperate states of *acedia* [25] where the causes are placed outside the ego. Psychiatry speaks of endogenic or metabolic depression and recommends physical treatment, as if to say such states are altogether outside the influence of will and reason.

So, we must inquire more closely into the negativity of senex consciousness. Those phenomena anciently called maleficent and related to Saturn also will require "saving" if we are to be consistent in method. By leaving one side of senex phenomenology in the shadow of a negative judgment, all the phenomena subsumed under this rubric — silence, decay and filth, the focus on morbidity and penury, apathy, paranoid rigidity, impotence, and psychic pain — are stopped short, their meanings kept from further fantasy, condemned. Fantasy is imprisoned by the structure of consciousness it is fantasying about.

For instance: the most notorious of senex crimes, the one commented upon faithfully from its first appearance in Hesiod, through Sallust, to Goya — Kronos eating his children[26] — by belonging to the "negative" senex, thus has but a negative meaning, such as, the swallowing of youth by age, joy by depression, freedom by form, imagination by intellect, innocence by experience, etc. That very same negativity we attribute to the senex, catches us in the negative senex. We become one of his children, our fantasy swallowed by the position archetypally forced on us through the imagination, and we cease imagining. We have let the basic dualism of the structure force us into taking a stand, the familiar ego stance of a positive or negative position. *It is this division itself*, and not what we judge to be positive or negative, *that puts us into senex consciousness*. All such judgments about an archetype are from the ego, who takes from the archetype what it wants for its own self-preservation, rejecting as "negative" the other side and thereby building up compensatorily yet more negativity. In making this "negative" judgment it is guided by the senex. Negativity seems necessary to the senex. Why?

We have seen that this structure suffers from an "excessive tension," which it tends to overcome by a compulsion to order. On the one hand, antithesis is given with Saturn as with no other God, so that this consciousness is self-destructively ambivalent and irrational. On the other hand, it is the principle of long-lasting survival through order and therefore compelled archetypally *to deny its own conflicting nature*. Although "lord of opposites," Saturn is not "lord of ambiguity," which the internal opposition and ambivalence of his essence would lead one to suppose. Rather than ambiguity, Saturn is the patron of deductive precision and measurement, whose order denies ambiguity. One and the same senex nature expresses itself in pairs of coinciding opposites (harvest and spoiler, truth and deceit, protector and ogre) and also must repress the symbolic paradox of opposites through a separative, rational order. This is its tension.

Moreover, in the very tension the antitheses continue: the senex that carries extreme tension is the same principle that seeks to return to a Golden Age and to remove internal tension (Freud). The same principle builds a universe on reason and also finds the structure of its reason to rest upon incompatible antinomies (Plato in the *Parmenides*, Nicholas of Cusa, Kant). The same principle that, on the one hand, insists on the concrete, literal, and logical also, on the other, goes to those depths of mind expressible by what Empson calls the seventh type, or ultimate, ambiguity.[27]

The ways of making order[28] are various and we have summarized many of them. The final triumph of the compulsion to order is ego formation, and essential to this formation are its epistemological habits. Senex builds ego by excluding the middle, by keeping the opposites in extreme tension, especially through its rules and laws which maintain borders, categories, walls.

These habits of thinking have been worked out in the logic of Aristotle, the axioms and proofs of Euclid, the classifications of Linnaeus, the antinomies of Kant. And these habits follow Plato's Stranger who says: "We must go on as before, dividing always and choosing one part only, until we arrive at the summit of our climb and the object of our journey" (*Statesman* 268d–e).

Particularly important in senex consciousness is the law of contradiction. Opposites, such as that of puer and senex, become contradictions. "Opposition," writes C. K. Ogden[29] in his essay on this subject, "is not to be defined as the maximum degree of difference, but as a very special kind of repetition, namely of two similar things that are mutually destructive in virtue of their similarity." But contradiction freezes the destruction into mutual exclusion: the either/or of negation. Upon the principle of negation rest all the judgments of positive and negative in whatever sphere — moral, aesthetic, psychological. Even the "un"-conscious has been named in this senex way, thereby we miss its similarity with consciousness and instead experience it as a negative opponent. The ego, too, in Freud's later writing was defined through the senex influence of negation.[30]

Negation, according to Freud, is repression: "A negative judgment is the intellectual substitute for repression; the 'No' in which it is expressed is the hall-mark of repression."[31] Here Freud moves negation from philosophy to psychology. He saw it as an equivalent of repression.

But still, why this sort of repression? Kant answers: "The peculiar province of negative judgments is solely to *prevent error*."[32] In other words the sort of repression we call negation is aimed particularly at maintaining an ideal and perfect vision of truth and order, the senex cosmos.

As long as consciousness means ordering, and ordering by means of negation, then repression is necessary. Other archetypal perspectives — Lunar, Hermetic, Heroic, Apollonic, etc. — organize the world with different logics creating different ego styles. But the senex ego thrives on repression and derives its energy from the strength of its boundaries. Lift repression and the ego weakens — not at all the case, say, in a Dionysian cosmos. But lift repression for the senex and the ego loses its role at central control. Deprived of its archetypal support in the senex, it is "invaded," becomes "unconscious," a dethroned king, wandering like Lear and looking for love, and whose deepest expression of love comes at the end, over death, as "Never" (V, 3). Psychoanalysis that lifts repression was not originally intended for the ageing. Repression is inherently necessary to senex consciousness, flowing consequently from its internal antitheses.

Repression in our culture has long been associated with anality. Freud attributed to the anal character three main traits: "They are exceptionally orderly, parsimonious, and obstinate."[33] These traits, together with those later elaborated (inhibition, sadism, and a special obsession about time), seem a description in psychoanalytic language of the classical senex. The relationship between anus and melancholy has a long history. A specific treatment for melancholy, until Pinel raised a humane and authoritative voice against it, was a most violent purge, hellebore.[34] By means of it one hoped to deliver the melancholic of his excess black bile. The black stools (actually internal bleeding) were mistakenly taken as evidence of its success. As far back as the Hippocratic writings, the re-establishment of hemorrhoids was a favourable prognostic sign in melancholy: anal bleeding meant calling forth excess and poisoning humour. Esquirol at the beginning of modern psychiatry and Calmeil in 1870 still found coincidences between the reappearance of anal bleeding and the cure of melancholy.[35]

Norman O. Brown has written the definitive piece on repression and anality.[36] So many senex qualities and functions are discussed in his chapters that they are a contemporary appendix to the material presented in *Saturn and Melancholy*, showing the consistency of the archetype. For Brown, anality and repression belong together, so that the end of repression (the *telos* of his own writings) means the end of the anal character and its repressive civilization. Then, too, would end the kind of ego which we have come to call civilized, but which for him, who never loses sight of the negation of this kind of consciousness, is sadistic, avaricious, paranoid, and suicidal.

To carry Brown's thought onward requires, first, distinctions between three terms — senex consciousness, repression, and anality both as symbol and as body-zone.[37] We shall first have to free repression from its anal focus and its reduction to the anal character. In order of comprehensiveness, the sequence should read: senex archetype, then repression, then anality. As the senex includes repression as an attribute, so repression in turn includes the anus. Repression is primary to the senex; anality is secondary. (Meaning and truth, ageing, melancholy, and the host of other qualities we have noted cannot all be attributed, even in the widest psychoanalytic system, to anality). Anality is not the basic Western condition, but senex consciousness, which has focussed repressively upon the anus in order to draw what libidinal energies it can from there.[38]

The main trouble in Brown's position in that book is his commitment to the materialistic hypothesis that puts body prior to psyche. Therefore psychic traits such as repression and negation become secondary to the actual libidinal zone of the anus. When psychic events derive from body, body becomes something different from psyche and a field on which we can "rely" for "solid ground," something older, more universal and objective. Body begins to take on another kind of reality, no longer the experienced body of the imagination. It becomes a set of concepts based on external observations and composed of ontological and moral contents. I would be the last to join what Brown considers to be the neo-Freudian desertion from "the primal psychoanalytical insight into the bodily base of all ideological superstructures."[39] But let us keep body and soul together, regarding neither as primary to the other, neither as more real, basic, or valuable. As soon as we fantasy the body as a "base" we have created a biological object of another order separate from what it carries. The inherent antithesis within all thought means that whenever we put something up we put it down at the same moment. Whenever we have to insist upon body we have begun to lose touch with it.

By freeing repression from its reduction to a body focus, we may also free this focus, the anus, from the repression of senex consciousness. Were Aphrodite to reign there, it would be a region of libidinal joy and sexual love; for the trickster, a realm of irresponsible play and jokes; for the heroics of Hercules (who tends to serve the old king), a cleaning job, a cultural task; for Demeter,[40] to whom digestion also belongs, a shameless part of the growth and decay cycle. In other words, an archetypal psychology can imagine body zones and functions through various perspectives. Another "excremental vision" (Brown) is possible if senex consciousness and its repression are no longer fixated upon anality. Repression precedes the anal stage and makes possible the infantile organization of libido through stages; repression precedes and permits civilization itself. Because repression belongs to the senex as archetype, it has an archetypal not an anal source.

Freud noted that "the repressed remains unaltered by the passage of time."[41] What has been repressed neither decays and disappears — nor does it develop. But since the ego does develop, repression causes one's inner time to be out of joint, parts moving and parts standing still. Let us however give a purposive inversion to Freud's observation and say "in order to conserve complexes unaltered by time, repress them." Saturn is the great conserver who would take all things into timelessness in one manner or another. Repression and negation serve this purpose. Hitherto we have regarded repression as an evil, an activity of the ego, a defense mechanism that generates neurosis. Could repression be regarded anew, could this phenomenon also be "saved"? What is its necessity?

If repression takes psychic events out of time, it takes them back into timelessness. From the ego's regard this is regression. But the ego is a hopped-up dynamism, heroically projecting itself forward, exhaust pipes trailing pollution and the unmuffled roar of history to the rear. The ego craves time and never has enough of it. To take things out of time ends their movement in history, their growth and their becoming. When repressed out of time, complexes re-approximate the timelessness of the archetypal world. Of course, this means that the infantile component of the complex stays untouched by the clock. But the infantile component is also the childhood of the complex, its child aspect, its primordiality.

If, following Freud, we may speak of a "primordially repressed," then repression is primordial. Although Freud places repression in the ego, stating that "we never discover a 'No' in the unconscious",[42] it is more accurate to say that repressions (like projections) *happen* before the ego is formed and, more, that repression makes the ego as we know it. Because repression is given primordially with the Id, it is archetypal and necessary. It belongs to the archetypes, especially the senex.

We can imagine archetypal repression like this. The order of the primordial powers requires boundaries[43] between them. The consciousness of one tends to exclude the consciousness of another. A mutual repulsion between their perspectives is the counter-tendency to their mutual entailment.[44] "One God keeps another in check."[45] Each represses the others. Repression establishes their limits and reflects a senex aspect that makes order through the archetypal world by negations which prevent any power from overstepping its necessity.

As repression affirms the boundaries within the archetypal, so by repressing we affirm the boundaries of the patterns we live. The roles we enact fit into the skin of this or that archetypal pattern. To lift repression is also to lose boundaries and to blur the distinctions between the modes of existence. The polytheistic background to existence requires a continual repulsion of energies between forms, like between negative poles of two magnetic lodes. The Gods, who swear by the Styx (hatred), keep each other out and do not trespass into the preserves of another. And each God has its specific style of exclusion, so that when we repress, it is always in one or another style. Repression can be differentiated by means of myth: who is excluding whom? There is no global act of general repression unless our style be modelled on a monotheistic principle that starts off by excluding all others, i.e. no other God whatsoever. An accurate description of the collective unconscious notes the multiplicity of sparks which cannot be formulated through syncretism, pantheism, or unitarian monotheism. Each of these "isms," by amalgamating and unifying, loses the distinctions given by repression.

The imaginal realm too calls for fixed boundaries, otherwise there can be no imaginal geography. It is not just inner *space* that matters, but inner *places*, a precision of *topoi*, each archetypal figure in the well-defined context of its landscape, its clime.[46] If the Golden Age is the utopia where Kronos-Saturn rules (not *when* he ruled), then the Golden Age is the topology of the primordially repressed, where repression continually makes distinct places for distinguishing among primordial images.

Our human repressions conserve psychic life from developing away from primordiality. Yes, they keep the complexes infantile, i.e. in their infancy — but does this not also mean: close to the imaginal? Primordial repression can invert to mean *repressed for the sake of primordiality*, the return to the repressed, that transcendent vision of this earth called "the golden age." To return to this place of imagination is Kronos' fundamental purpose and a continuing intention within senex consciousness. It represses to restore perfection. Its consciousness is Utopian. Only there are the contradictions overcome.

If we ask *what* is repressed, the answer emerges both from Freud and from myth. The repressed is infantile, the children of Kronos who are the other archetypal varieties of imagination. The swallowed children are the infantilities which nourish fantasy life and which Freudian psychodynamics saw as neurotic and regressive. The displacements, distortions, symbolizations, fantasies are the children fermenting within, producing the excess of pneuma and exaggerated imaginative powers of the senex.

In senex consciousness the child must be swallowed. This belongs to the myth. It is not "negative." For Neoplatonism (Sallust) eating the children reflects introverted self-fertilization where "swallowing denotes a union with one's own substance"[47] — one's own seed and the cultivation of that seed.[48] From the perspective of senex consciousness, as long as the children remain inside they are in the right place; swallowing keeps them alive.

Trouble breaks out when they break out. For Saturn is driven as much by the urge to realize concretely as by his far-out mind. He lives in two houses side-by-side, Capricorn and Aquarius. The urge to material-ize abstractions and images turns the child back into an objective stone, the materialized, literalized thinking so characteristic of the senex.

So we see that it is the very same archetype that both contains and breaks the containment. The fermentation gets out because Saturn has such hunger for the concrete. He makes his vessel so literally. When the vessel for psychic fermentation is defined by the senex, we set down priestly codes and heavy laws of techniques for alchemy, for spiritual practices, for psychotherapy, sealing the vessel with literal prohibitions — and thus the vessel must break, and Saturn self-destruct. Senex con-sciousness takes hermetic secrecy literally as Saturnian repression. Mys-tery becomes mutism; *No*, the ever-necessary defense.

By starting from a fantasy of primordial repression — rather than from the repressive acts reflected in the ego — we can see the neces-sity of repression in psychic life. We envision it as a way the Gods may turn their backs on each other in mutual respect. They keep themselves perpetually in connection with Saturn and limited by his bounded or-der. And as he fathers Zeus, so the principles of exclusion, repression, negation, and limitation are father to creative acts.

The limitations which Saturn at the outer rim of the spheres im-poses upon the other Gods and which senex consciousness imposes upon the psyche may be seen as a modified form of negation. There remains a real value in the Saturnian ego informed by the senex spirit of limitation. Know-thyself becomes know-thy-limits, beyond which are powers that do not belong to any human. The ego can then no longer be a do-er and maker, a creator, or any of the romantic expectations the hero asks of us. Ego becomes a conserver, a guardian figure, or a witness at the frontiers of a weak kingdom, who dozes at the edge of star-filled madness in continual relation with what's "out there."

A consciousness of limitation both rules and is in exile. It drifts among the complexes, a watchman in the night of their fantasies, keeping time by the measure of images traversing the inner sky, an astrologer of constellations. The heroes gone under, his rule is through depression and sacrifice; for limitation means serving Saturn, the God of sacrifice: Moses and Abraham, patriarchs, demanding the entirety, "costing not less than everything," so close to Moloch. The kingdom shrinks; decrease is on the ascendant; what is not sacrificed will any-way decay. But sacrifice, which is depression in another guise—and is limitation too — is not a one-time gesture. Through prolongated depression, sacrifice becomes chronic; one keeps up the sacrifice and perpetuates limitation into a mode mimetic to the senex God.

 IV   A RENAISSANCE SOLUTION

> The speculative intellect thinks nothing that is practical and makes no assertions about what is to be avoided or pursued.
>
> — Aristotle, *De Anima*, III

How to come to terms with the archetype in its entirety was the issue faced by Marsilio Ficino (1433–99), the profoundest psychologist of the Renaissance:

> . . . he himself was a melancholic and a child of Saturn — the lat-ter, indeed, in particularly unfavorable circumstances, for in his horoscope the dark star in whose influence he so unshakably be-lieved stood in the ascendant, and as it did so, moreover, it was in the sign of the Aquarius, Saturn's "night abode." It is unusually illuminating to see how Ficino's notion of Saturn and melan-choly sprang from this personal, psychological foundation, for there is no doubt that fundamentally, despite all his familiar-ity with Dante and ancient Neoplatonism, he regarded Saturn as an essentially unlucky star, and melancholy as an essentially unhappy fate, so that he attempted to counter it in himself and others by all the means of the medical art which he had learnt from his father, perfected by his own training, and finally firmly based on Neoplatonic astral magic. [49]

The result of his undertaking was three volumes, *De Vita Triplici* (1482–89) [50] on the symptoms and therapy of senex consciousness. In this work he allows himself the fullest identification with his subject; opus and operator are affected by the same constellation:

Ficino's system — and this was perhaps its greatest achievement — contrived to give Saturn's "immanent contradiction" a redemptive power: the highly gifted melancholic — who suffered under Saturn, in so far as the latter tormented the body and the lower faculties with grief, fear and depression — might save himself by the very act of turning voluntarily towards the very same Saturn.[51]

The redemptive power of senex contradiction is discovered by turning to the contradiction itself. The antitheses of its nature release healing insight. The insight is a function of thought; contemplation, speculation, music, mathematics, and especially imagination become the *via regia*. Problems are taken to their extremity where they no longer are living realities but have become fantastic, reflecting their source in imaginal reality. The world is taken back into its *logos*, the end into its beginnings in *nous*. Issues are removed from the narrowed field of personally particularized depression and expanded into a melancholic contemplation of impersonal and imaginal universals. The *acedia* of silence and the turning inward by refusing to blame anyone but oneself and one's stars lead to the interior space, *memoria*.

Crucial to this inward move is realizing that interiority must be black and must be empty, otherwise the antidote cannot appear in the poison. Rigid self-centered focusing without escape into future hopes is precisely the melancholy method, a process of archetypal self-correction.

The very agitation and circling thoughts that accompany the narrowing solitude and interior imaginal monologue are the peripheral activities that go along with every centering. The contradictories of center and circumference appear in the paradox of "agitated depression" — hand-wringing, pacing, insomnia. The intensely focussed desert saint is assailed by chattering distractions; the Old King wanting to be left alone to his books at the same time is out busily defending his far-flung borders. (It's only when we are in a centering fantasy that we worry about "the ten-thousand things.") The structure obsessively works at its inner opposition. The body-symbol is still the head.[52]

In the old medical doctrine (Hippocrates): "Fatigue of the soul comes from the soul's thinking";[53] the new view of Ficino turns this upside down. Now, mental exertions restore the soul. Its fatigue is the gateway. Apathy, *acedia*, depression are not merely symptoms of something wrong to be cured, but indications of what the soul is naturally seeking, i.e., a full realization of the *vis imaginativa*. *Similis similibus curantur*. The senex is its own inherent possibility of transcending its "excessive tension." The archetype, infirm and hindered though it might be, like the Neoplatonic Gods, who are immortal, is self-perpetuating; its energy does not run down. It finds methods for its own revivification. Some of these methods of revivification we have already seen: the pedophagy where the child is consumed to keep fermenting within the father; the ancestor worship (which is "archetype" worship) of the aged who reflect backwards, seeing their ancestors in their grandchildren; the melancholic furor where the silent black rages churn the soul; the depression that sucks energy from the surroundings; the retardation for the sake of perpetuation; the Cronia or Saturnalia through which a reversal of values restores the rule of the God. Each of these are ways the archetype maintains itself.

When a psychotherapist finds it beneficial for a depressed person to not resist the depression, or for older people to occupy themselves with thoughts, visions, and the strange otherness in their dreams, he is expressing what Ficino, child of Saturn that he was, presented as a cogent method. Senex consciousness is finally at rest in the imaginal realm of the *archai*, which are *dei ambigui* of endless complications and contradictions. Melancholy drives us to where we can think and imagine no further, to the inmost void which is also the furthest limits of the mind. These are the borderlands, a borderline condition of emotional ambivalence which, as Freud wrote, is a root factor in melancholia.[54] But now, from what we gather of Ficino's approach to what might be regarded as the psychotic bottom of depression, there is no rage to end the internal contradictions by choosing one or the other. The opposite impulses present themselves as indistinguishable. At this border, one side is the same as the other. Fantasy here transcends the opposites as a problem. *Images are merely themselves*, not arraigned for judgments, positions and oppositions. There is nothing to affirm or deny, for, as Aristotle said: "Phantasia is distinct from assertion and negation . . ."[55]

From this perspective the earth of Saturn and the chthonic spirits with which he is associated, Lua the spoiler, the destruction of all existence as the blackening of the brain and the leaden curse, may be understood anew. They refer to a decay and sinking below the earth and its actualities to the *imum coeli*, to the hidden God (*Deus absconditus*) and the land of *nous*, a hidden earth. The hidden earth is the Islamic "terre celeste" in the language of Corbin,[56] or the Buddhist "terre pure" in the words of Paul Mus.[57] Saturn's sacred art of geometry would be the art of this land. Not the physical world which shows no visible points, no straight lines, no true circles, but the abstract structures of fantasy the likeness of which do not exist on this earth. Melancholy expresses the nostalgia of the spirit for this territory, where melancholy is beauty and beauty melancholic.[58] Sadness[59] takes one there; so can death, and music.

Music occurs frequently in connection with Saturn, especially in the Renaissance and humanist accounts. (The opposite is there too: Saturn is deaf.) This music belongs to the interior earth, a "music beard so deeply / That it is not heard at all, but you are the music / While the music lasts."[60] When one of the daughters of Catherine de Medici felt the approach of death she sent for her musician: "Julien, prenez votre violon et sonnez-moi toujours jusqu'à ce que vous me voyez morte." Baldassare Castiglione, one of the great masters of intellectual education of his time, denied that music was appropriate only for women. For him, as for senex consciousness, "the world is composed of music, that the heavens make harmony in their moving, and that the soul, being ordered in like fashion, awakes and as it were revives its powers through music."[61] Music was another entrance into death and provided revivification of the archetype. Music was the perfection and proportion of number manifested in sound; like geometry it bridged two worlds, attuning the soul to its function of bridge to the hidden.

It also bridged to the visible world. Ficino's systematic attempt to heal his melancholy through music consisted in working out laws for preparing astrological songs. On the analogy of microcosm/macrocosm the music of man touched the harmony of the spheres, and specifically, individual planets were addressed through music. As each planet ruled provinces of life and of man's body, soul, and actions, the constellated planet could then activate the microcosmic man through the effect of music on emotion and through astral-magic influences. In Ficino's system, senex melancholy is the consequent of mental exertion, the mind's wrestling with its excessive tension. The exertion extracts vital spirits from the blood, leaving it dry, dense, and black, i.e. melancholy. By relating with astrological songs to the beneficent planets (Jupiter, Sun, and Venus) the melancholy would be alleviated.[62]

Cure of sorrow through music was not Ficino's discovery. But to him belongs credit for connecting it with the Neoplatonic system through which he elaborated an idea that we find in many authors fully reported on by Burton.[63] By means of Neoplatonism, the cure for sorrow was transposed to the transformation of Saturn, i.e., Ficino presents us with a system of *archetypal therapy*. The cure of sorrow through a musical relation with the archetypes was known to Homer and to Hesiod:[64]

> . . . for though a man have sorrow and grief in his newly-troubled soul and live in dread because his heart is distressed, yet, when a singer, the servant of the Muses, chants the glorious deeds of men of old and the blessed gods who inhabit Olympus, at once he forgets his heaviness and remembers not his sorrow at all . . .
>
> (*Theogony*, 97ff.)

Music alone is not enough, since music has innumerable modes. For music to serve in attuning the soul, it must sing the right "astrological songs" of the Heroes and the blessed Gods; that is, its content and structure must provide the archetypal bridge to the hidden earth.

The weight and reality of this other earth compares with the great weight of the abstract elephant of the Vissudha Chakra in the Kundalini Yoga system. This is the region of the upper earth, where the elephant is white, his reality now more imaginally realized. Its locus is the throat, area of song, speech, and silence. (The voice's *acedia*[65] as well as the afflictions of the region of the other darker concrete elephant,[66] Muladhara in the anal zone, we have already discussed.)

Other Saturn symbols for bridging the two earths also have two poles: the compass and the balance. By means of these instruments the world here is made mimetic to the other. They are precision tools. The exact in the matter of this earth is equivalent to the perfect of the hidden earth of the mind. The senex obsession with precision may be referred to anality, paranoia, and the power of boundaries and negation. But it is also a utopian vision of reconstruction. The model is perfection: to restore the terrestial earth to the celestial earth by means of measurement, order, number, music, and prophetic furor. Here we uncover the latent idealism and extraordinary compulsion of the exact sciences; the torment of extremes between concrete and abstract are here resolved.

The planning and building of senex consciousness — its loyalty to the concrete, its laws and justice, its fortifications and minting of money for the cities of mankind — belong to the ideal of replicating a vision. It is a vision of the New Jerusalem. The city is God's.

But the peculiar twist which senex consciousness adds to utopian vision is the emphasis upon the role of depression and solitude for discovering the vision and for measuring it out. The vision is not of a brotherhood of man, of redemption through love, nor even through senex work, law, knowledge, justice, or prayer. It is a speculation, a mirroring for the sake of nothing; hence the central significance of negation. And this *terre pure*, in a senex imagination of it, is reached through a vision that comes from the afflicted outcast, the man whose feet [67] no longer can walk on this earth; only he can see through the illusions of this earth by which he has been dejected and disowned.

Exile gives the imagination its power to perceive with the instruments of the senex structure. Exile reflects the idea that human life itself is cast out of its origins in Kronos' Golden Age, the lost *terre celeste* of archetypal forms. We are each in exile; but senex consciousness cooped in its cabin of winter desiccation bridges beyond by spatial imagination, by measure and music, or with a "dying" awareness of decline. It sees through, sees out with insight. The melancholy temperament, never bled nor purged, never transformed, is nonetheless satisfied by seeing to the end where impenetrable darkness is penetrated by the darkening intellect[68] and blackened psyche of a "being whose thoughts have reached the limit."[69]

Such is our vision of Ficino's vision. His solution in the Renaissance is worth our contemporary notice, since he resolved a question for each of us struggling with the "negative senex" not only in our natures, but also in our culture. The inbuilt contradiction and the inherent need in senex consciousness for negation were transmuted by him into a profound process of soul-making. His work on the senex archetype made his own soul and had effect on the psychic constellation of his time. This time was the Renaissance. Does that word not bear upon our revivification?

A history of Ficino in relation to the *psyche* of the Renaissance is yet to be written. Nevertheless we cannot refrain from drawing lessons from the movement in his psyche.[70] He arrived at the place where transmuting melancholy comes about through communication with one's genius in its depressive weakness, into its woundedness. The orientation of this movement was generally governed by avid intellectual curiosity, by imaginal contemplation mainly in terms of the classic ideas and Gods, and by a particular devotion to Eros and to soul. The net which held his ideas was Neoplatonic, that is, his personal survival depended upon the revival of the Platonist fantasy of the psyche. This fantasy and these dominant themes which it interwove are also propensities of puer phenomenology.

In Ficino and the world around him the puer archetype played an extraordinary role. We need but read for instance the love lyrics of old Michelangelo, or let Renaissance beauty and its anima fantasies dazzle us, watch the daring young men launch their incredible ventures in the midst of vicious shadows or hear their tributes to reputation, to understand that the same tension then in different historical dress was moving in the psyche of that time. Yet, they came through, maybe because in their radical experimentation with everything established, they carried age with them (the Venetian Doges, the ponderous Church, and all the old men like Michelangelo, like Titian going on to 99, etc.), always looking back toward antiquity and down into their souls through melancholy. The senex was the inseparable dark background for their brilliance, their haste slowed, their maxim: *festina lente.*[71]

Notes

1. [First published in *Spring* 1975.] — Ed.

2. R. Klibansky, E. Panofsky, and F. Saxl, *Saturn and Melancholy* (London: Warburg Institute/Nelson, 1964), pp. 33–36 and notes. The *Problemata* is included in the second volume of the revised Oxford translation of *The Complete Works of Aristotle*.

3. *Saturn and Melancholy*, pp. 134–35; see also a prayer of Agrippa of Nettesheim where Saturn is invoked "by a series of antitheses more numerous than anywhere else," p. 354.

4. C. G. Jung, *Collected Works*, vol. 9.1: *Archetypes and the Collective Unconscious*, par. 414.

5. Note by S. T. Coleridge on flyleaf of his copy of A. Weishaupt's *Apologie des Missvergnügens und Übels*, quoted by K. Coburn in *Inquiring Spirit* (London: Routledge and Paul, 1951).

6. "To whom increase and decrement belong": Thomas Taylor's 1824 translation of "To Saturn" in *The Mystical Hymns of Orpheus* (London: Kessinger Publishing, 2003), p. 40.

7. C. G. Jung, *Collected Works*, vol. 14: *Mysterium Coniunctionis*, par. 732; see *Collected Works*, vol. 13: *Alchemical Studies*, pars. 95, 101; *Collected Works*, vol. 11: *Psychology and Religion*, par. 350. Hades wore a special dogskin head covering; Saturn's head was cloaked: R. B. Onians, *Origins of European Thought* (Cambridge: Cambridge University Press, 1954), p. 424

8. C. G. Jung, *Collected Works*, vol. 14, par. 733.

9. For a beautiful and thorough, even if wrong-headedly anti-Jungian, description of the sage, wise-old-man, or "positive senex" in Western literature from the Greeks through the Renaissance, see Alarik W. Skarstrom, *"Fortunate Senex": The Old Man, a Study of the Figure, his Function and his Setting*, diss. (Yale University, 1971); Ann Arbor: University Microfilms, 1972).

10. C. G. Jung, *Collected Works*, vol. 9.1, par. 413–15.

11. On differences between soul and spirit, see the extended discussion in chapter 3. Also my *Re-Visioning Psychology* (New York: Harper & Row, 1975), pp. 68–70.

12. See A. Guggenbühl-Craig, *The Old Fool and the Corruption of Myth* (Dallas: Spring Publications, 1991).

13. W. W. Fowler, *The Religious Experience of the Roman People* (London: Macmillan, 1933), pp. 481–82; Roscher, *Lexikon* 11, 2, "Lua" Leglay, (n. 26, inf.), 1, 457, considers Lua to be the first name of a combined name, *Lua Saturni*, in which the prefix refers to a lower attribute of the higher power of Saturn. Lua then becomes a specific genius or force within the Saturn complex, having two particular functions — agricultural and military — coupled through the idea of spoiling. Cf. G. Dumézil's discussion of "Lua Mater" in *Déesses latines et*

mythes vediques, Coll. Lat (Bruxelles: 1956), pp. 99–107. He concludes that Lua (who corresponds with the Vedic Nirrti) belongs within a basic Indo-European constellation that emphasizes the primary importance of order (in Roman as in Indian thought, but unlike Greek where there is no corresponding figure). Lua thus represents the balancing opposite to order, as "Mother Dissolution" and the idea of disintegration (Dumézil, p. 114). See also Chapter 9, section III on the senex and the feminine.

14. [Quoted in Chapter 1.] — Ed.

15. E. Panofsky, "Father Time," *Studies in Iconology* (New York: Harper Torchbook, 1962).

16. Skin belongs to the boundaries ruled by Saturn, as in mediaeval lore he ruled the pelts of animals, bark of trees, rinds, crusts, peels, and shells, i.e., concrete limits.

17. A. O. Lovejoy and G. Boas, *Primitivism and Related Ideas in Antiquity* (New York: Octagon, 1965), pp. 77ff.; H. Oeri, *Der Typ der komischen Alten in der griechischen Komödie* (Basel: B. Schwabe, 1948).

18. R. C. Elliott, "Saturnalien, Satire, Utopie," *Antaios* IX (1967): 412–28. "Very little is known from early authors of the Greek Cronia," Lovejoy and Boas, op. cit., p. 65, but they present relevant materials, pp. 65–70.

19. For Saturn and geometry, see *Saturn and Melancholy*, pp. 312ff., 327ff.

19a. Samuel Taylor Coleridge, *On the Constitution of the Church and State* [1830] (London: J. M. Dent, 1972), p. 52.

20. Thomas Browne, *Religio Medici* (London: Everyman, 1964), p. 47.

21. For examples of cures for senex troubles (stiffness of the joints, gouty and rheumatic pains, piles, skin troubles) by means of actual lead, see Mr. Goulard, *A Treatise on the Effects and Various Preparations of Lead, Particularly of the Extract of Saturn* (London: P. Elinsly, 1773). The extract is made, according to the appendix by G. Arnaud, with the strongest vinegar that can be procured.

22. Ripeness or completion is one of the conjectured root meanings of the word Kronos (H. J. Rose, *A Handbook of Greek Mythology* [London: Methuen, 1964], p. 69 n.). When we confuse ripeness with tenacity or endurance, then we are repeating the mythical confluence of Kronos with Chronos (Time); then endurance refers back to its root meaning of dure, "hard." Senex logic then says: what is ripe in us is that which is fully coagulated, a stone. A Dionysian logic of ripeness might take only what is sweet and full of moisture, like the grape, as ripe.

23. *Saturn and Melancholy*, p. 365; K. Lange und F. Fuhse, *Dürer's schriftlicher Nachlass* (Halle: Max Niemeyer, 1893), p. 222.

24. J. Starobinski, *Geschichte der Melancholiebehandlung von den Anfängen bis 1900* (Basel: Documenta Geigy, 1960), pp. 67ff. The travel-for-depression therapy suggested by Calmeil seems to have been aimed at a revival through rediscov-

ering antiquity, a "Renaissance," i.e., "the museum replaced the hospital" and the route of the trip was through the classical world, Florence, Rome, Naples, Athens. An attempt was made to reconnect quite literalistically with the images of antiquity. The patient together with his tutor-guide-therapist actually performed archeological digs. Cf. "Lypemanie" in *Dict. encycl. des sci. med.*, vol. III (Paris: 1870). (Lypemanie was the nineteenth-century term, from Esquirol, for *tristia* without delirium.)

25. Siegfried Wenzel, *The Sin of Sloth, Acedia in Medieval Thought and Literature* (Chapel Hill: University of North Carolina Press, 1967).

26. The fantasy of Kronos eating the child is taken literally by Robert Graves (*Greek Myths* I [Harmondsworth: Penguin, 1960], p. 42), who seriously writes that "in backward districts of Arcadia boys were still sacrificially eaten even in the Christian era." Here, Graves becomes himself a "child of Saturn," taking concretistically a past age when children were eaten. He locates an archetypal Greek fantasy in geographical and historical Greece. However, the North African cult of Saturn did include actual child sacrifice as late as the second century A. D.; according to M. Leglay, *Saturne Africain*, 3 vols. (Paris: Arts et Métiers Graphiques, 1961–66), 1:317, five hundred children were supposed to have been offered in one large rite. The purpose seems to have been the re-invigoration of the father with the new life of the child, a ritual which guaranteed the health of the God, and so of the community. Augustine, who came from this district where Saturn ruled (and who attacked Saturn in his writings), says the Romans did not adopt this rite. According to Leglay, child sacrifice is not a Graeco-Roman practice, but belongs to Molk (Moloch), and therefore within the Punic/Phoenician/Carthaginian/African religious mode. Leglay gives full documentation. For additional references to the fantasy of child-eating, see my *The Myth of Analysis* (Evanston: Northwestern University Press, 1972), pp. 276–77. On Saturn as Moloch, see Lovejoy and Boas, op. cit., 74f; Klibansky, p. 135n. I believe that the compulsive eating habits of youth, including its anorexia, as well as those of old age need to be explored in terms of the senex-puer mythologems.

27. William Empson, *Seven Types of Ambiguity*, rev. ed. (London: Chatto and Windus, 1947), esp. pp. 192–97, 232–33.

28. The way of ordering particularly favored by much Jungian theory is through number (traditionally a province of Saturn, though sometimes attributed to Minerva, and Mercurius). Jung, in his old age, turned particularly to number as "the archetype of order" (C. G. Jung, *Collected Works*, vol. 8: *Structure & Dynamics of the Psyche*, par. 870). Jung's interest has been subsequently worked out by M.-L. von Franz in her *Number and Time* (Evanston: Northwestern Univ. Press, 1974) where we find many images and concepts, and concerns, of senex consciousness. A. Plaut, "The Ungappable Bridge: Numbers as Guides to Object Relations and to Cultural Development," *Journal of Analytical*

Psychology 18/2 (1973), also attempts a fundamental ordering of the psychic world by means of numbers. The number fantasy appears within a context of antithetical opposites (the ungappable bridge between subjects and objects, or between physics and psychology [von Franz]) as a way of uniting them.

29. C. K. Ogden, *Opposition, A Linguistic and Psychological Analysis* (Bloomington: Indiana University Press, 1967), p. 41.

30. In *Beyond the Pleasure Principle* (1920) (London: The International Psychoanalytical Press, 1950), Freud's description of the ego seems a formulation of senex consciousness, as if Freud were a "child of Saturn" when he wrote this essay. He writes that psychoanalysis "had first come to know [the ego] only as a repressive, censoring agency, capable of erecting protective structures and reactive formations" (pp. 69–70). He makes "a sharp distinction between ego instincts, which we equated with death instincts, and sexual instincts, which we equated with life instincts" (pp. 71–72). The death instinct, using the ego as its instrument of repression, shows itself in sadism and hate. The ego opposes the conjugation of entities (Eros), thus implying that the ego is the separating and isolating factor of the psyche. Above all, for our emphasis upon Freud's Saturnian formulation, the death instinct seeks "to remove internal tension" (p. 78) and "to restore an earlier state of things" (p. 79). The "compulsion to repeat which first put us on the track of the death instincts" (p. 79) accords with the "most universal endeavor of all living substance — namely to return to the quiescence of the inorganic world" (p. 86). We recall Saturn's inclinations for inorganic symbols and abstractions. That the ego in Freud's conception belongs to the senex appears yet more strongly in his paper "Negation," *Collected Papers* V (London: Hogarth Press, Institute of Psycho-Analysis, 1950), p. 185: "Affirmation . . . belongs to Eros; while negation . . . belongs to the instinct of destruction . . . This view of negation harmonizes very well with the fact that in analysis we never discover a 'No' in the unconscious, and that a recognition of the unconscious on the part of the ego is expressed in a negative formula."

31. Freud, "Negation," p. 182.

32. The passage appears at the beginning of Part I of the Transcendental Doctrine of Method, in *The Critique of Pure Reason*, trans. J. M. D. Meiklejohn (London: Everyman, 1934), p. 407: "Negative judgments — those which are not so merely as regards the logical form, but in respect of their content — are not commonly held in especial respect. They are, on the contrary, regarded as jealous enemies of our insatiable desire for knowledge; and it almost requires an apology to induce us to tolerate, much less to prize and to respect them. All propositions, indeed, may be logically expressed in a negative form; but in relation to the content of our cognition, the peculiar province of negative judgments is solely to prevent error." For the necessity of error, see my essay "On the Necessity of Abnormal Psychology," *Eranos* 43, 1974 and for

a discussion of error and errancy (wandering, phantasia), see my *Re-visioning Psychology*, Chapter 3.

33. Freud, "Character and Anal Erotism," *Collected Papers* II (London: Hogarth Press: Institute of Psycho-Analysis, 1953), p. 45.

34. Hellebore (black root), though used often in connection with melancholy, was not a specific; it was employed in other mental disorders and in physical ones, too. For a description of its violence see "elléborisme," *Dictionnaire des sciences médicales* (Paris: 1815); also the article by Pécholier, *Dictionnaire encyclopédique des sciences médicales*, Vol. 12 (Paris: 1886). As long as melancholia was taken literalistically as a disease of the black bile, then whatever could purge the gut of its blackness or of its accumulations of blood was consequently a therapeutic agent. The usual relief of the lower body took place through menstruation and hemorrhoidal bleeding. See E. Fischer-Homberger, *Hypochondrie* (Bern: Huber, 1970), p. 23. The black anger, black moods, and black spirit of the saturnine disposition finds its forerunner in classical Greek texts, see F. Kudlien, "Die Urgeschichte der griechischen Begriffe 'Schwarze Galle' und 'Melancholie'," in *Der Beginn des Medizinischen Denkens bei den Griechen* (Zurich/Stuttgart: Artemis Verlag, 1967), with notes.

35. Starobinski, op. cit., p. 18.

36. N. O. Brown, *Life Against Death* (New York: Vintage, 1959), Part V, "Studies in Anality."

37. Other body parts and afflictions traditionally associated with Saturn are: spleen, black bile, bones and head, bladder, skin and body hair, the right ear (and deafness), dizziness, all slow diseases (rheumatism) and fevers, chronic conditions, any inhibition of function (laming, speech defect, impotence), waste products (feces, gallstones; urine, rheum from the eyes and nose): cf. "*Picatrix*" *das Ziel des Weisen von Pseudo-Magriti*," trans. H. Ritter and M. Plessner (London: Warburg Institute, 1962).

38. See Freud, "On the Transformation of Instincts with Special Reference to Anal Erotism," *Collected Papers* II, p. 164: " . . . each one of the three qualities, avarice, pedantry and stubbornness, springs from anal-erotic sources — or to express it more cautiously and more completely—draws powerful contributions from these sources." In the Kundalini Yoga system the consciousness associated with Muladhara, that body center "located" in the anal-genital-coccygeal region, does not have a specifically anal or genital character, even if it may draw contributions from anal and genital archetypal sources.

39. *Life Against Death*, p. 203. Support for the hypothesis of a "bodily base for all ideological superstructures" comes from some theories of language, e.g., O. Jespersen (*Negation in English and Other Languages*, 2nd ed. [Kobenhavn: A. F. Høst, 1966], p. 6ff.) who writes: " . . . the old negative *ne*, which I take to be together with the variant *me*) a primitive interjection of disgust, accompanied by the facial gesture of contracting the muscles of the nose . . . This natural

origin will account for the fact that negatives beginning with nasals (n, m) are found in many languages outside the Indo-European family."

40. Diogenes Laertius VI, 69 on Diogenes the Cynic: "It was [Diogenes'] habit to do everything in public, both the works of Demeter and those of Aphrodite."

41. Freud, *New Introductory Lectures on Psychoanalysis* (London: Leonard and Virginia Woolf at the Hogarth Press, and the Institute of Psycho-analysis, 1933), p. 99. See *Beyond the Pleasure Principle*, p. 33; and *Life Against Death*, pp. 274–77.

42. Freud, "Negation," loc. cit. sup.

43. N. O. Brown, "Boundary," in *Love's Body* (New York: Random House, 1966).

44. See my *Myth of Analysis*, p. 264.

45. H. Usener, *Götternamen* (Frankfurt: Verlag G. Schulte-Bulmke, [1895] 1948), p. 348.

46. On archetypal topography, see E. S. Casey, "Toward an Archetypal Imagination," *Spring* 1974. The locus of the image is particularly important in the art of memory, and in the geography of the imaginal in Corbin's writings.

47. C. O. Muller, *Introduction to a Scientific System of Mythology* (1825), trans. J. Leitch (London: Longman, Brown, Green, and Longmans, 1844), p. 308; Sallust's discussion is in his *Concerning the Gods and the Universe*, A. D. Nock, ed. (Cambridge: The University Press, 1927), par. 4. The Uranos-Kronos-Zeus tale has drawn innumerable, especially Neoplatonic, commentaries. Compare F. Bacon, *Cogitationes de scientia humana* (1605), Sp. III, p. 86; Sp. VI, pp. 723–25. This and other myths "explained" by Bacon are given in P. Rossi, *Francis Bacon* (London: Routledge and K. Paul, 1968), pp. 73–134. Vico gives a more sociological hermeneutic (T. G. Bergin and M. H. Fisch, *The New Science of Giambattista Vico*, Book II, par. 587 [Ithaca, NY: Cornell University Press, 1968], p. 213). For an elaborate sexual fantasy presented as a scholar's "interpretation" of the mythologem, see G. S. Kirk, *Myth*, Sather Lectures, (Cambridge and Berkeley: University of California Press, 1970), p. 218: " . . . the myth seems to convey an underlying message, that excesses and unnatural acts in the realm of sex and childbirth give rise to counterbalancing and deterrent excesses in the other direction." For another, archetypal, perspective to this myth, see Murray Stein, "The Devouring Father," in Patricia Berry ed., *Fathers and Mothers* (Zurich: Spring Publications, 1973).

48. See "On Seeds," Appendix III, in Skarstrom, op. cit.

49. *Saturn and Melancholy*, p. 256. In a letter to his friend Cavalcanti, Ficino gives his horoscope as follows: "Saturn established in the middle of Aquarius, my ascendant, receiving the influence of Mars in the same place; Moon in Capricorn . . . the Sun and Mercurius in Scorpio, another catastrophic house of heaven. Venus in Libra and Jupiter in Cancer have perhaps offered some resistance in that which concerns my melancholic nature." ("Lettres sur la Connaissance de soi et

sur l'astrologie," trad. et ann. par A. Chastel, in *La Table ronde* [n.d.]). The translation from French to English is mine; original Latin in the Basel edition (1576). See *Saturn and Melan-choly*, p. 256ff. with notes, for English and Latin versions of many letters.

50. See Thomas Moore, *The Planets Within: The Astrological Psychology of Marsilio Ficino* (Great Barrington, MA: Lindesfarne Press, 1990); *Marsilio Ficino's Book of Life*, trans. Charles Boer (Dallas: Spring Publications, 1980).

51. *Saturn and Melancholy*, pp. 270–71. In a letter to the Archbishop of Florence, Ficino describes his depression which reduced him utterly. After a favor for which he asked had been withdrawn, he says, "I was strongly astonished and I searched with the greatest care for the reason in this series of disorders. Not finding the reason on earth, I found it in heaven." Chastel suggests that this was the beginning of Ficino's "obsession saturnienne" ("Lettres," p. 200).

52. *Saturn and Melancholy*, p. 286, "The Motif of the Drooping Head." See E. Goodenough, *Jewish Symbols in the Graeco-Roman Period*, Vol. 10 (New York: Bollingen, 1964), p. 58, on lead issuing from the head of the fallen Gayomart in "The mysticism of the seven metals"; Rob. Burton, *The Anatomy of Melancholy*, 3 vols., (New York: E.P. Dutton and Co., Everyman edition, 1932) I: 409; II: 235; also vol. I, pp. 300–30 on melancholy as an affliction of intellectuals; on Kronos-Saturn as *nous*, Plotinus, *Enn*. V, 1, 4; see *Saturn and Melancholy*, pp. 153, 155.

53. *Saturn and Melancholy*, p. 84.

54. Freud, "Mourning and Melancholia," *Collected Papers* IV, pp. 161, 168ff.

55. Aristotle, *De Anima* II, 9, 432a, 10–12.

56. H. Corbin, *Spiritual Body and Celestial Earth*, trans. Nancy Pearson (Princeton: Princeton University Press, Bollingen Series, 1977).

57. P. Mus, "Traditions asiennes et Bouddisme moderne," *Eranos-Yearbook* 37 (1968), pp. 226–33.

58. On beauty and melancholy, see A. Vitale, "Saturn and the Transformation of the Father" in *Fathers and Mothers*, p. 9; see also essays in *Arcipelago Malinconia*, ed. Biancamaria Frabotta (Rome: Donzelli, 2001).

59. "Sad" corresponds with *gravis* in Latin, and both words have gone through a parallel development which reflects the myths of Saturn appearing within etymological history. Words too carry archetypal messages. One meaning of *gravis* (from which we have our "grave") is "heavy," "weighty," and rather like "solid" and "full of import," even pregnant (gravid). "Sad," too, once meant "full." "Anglo-Saxon *saed* (plural *sade*) is brother to Old Norse *saddr* and cousin to Latin *satur*, and all three words have originally the same meaning: gorged, full (of food), replete." (C.S. Lewis, "Sad," in his *Studies in Words* [Cambridge: Cambridge University Press, 1967], p. 77.) Again, the motif of Saturn and devouring. But also there is the implication that in one's sadness there is a fullness, even a pregnancy.

60. T. S. Eliot, "The Dry Salvages," *Four Quartets*.

61. W. Kaegi, "The Transformation of the Spirit in the Renaissance," in *Spirit and Nature* (Papers from the Eranos Yearbooks) (New York / London: 1955), pp. 280–81. Cf. G. Bandmann, *Melancholie und Musik* (Cologne: Westdeutscher Verlag, 1960); E. E. Lowinsky, "Music in the Culture of the Renaissance" in *Renaissance Essays*, ed. P. O. Kristeller and P. P. Wiener (New York: Harper and Row, 1968), pp. 337–81 and his "Music of the Renaissance as viewed by Renaissance Musicians," in D. O'Kelly, ed., *The Renaissance Image of Man and the World* (Columbus: Ohio State, 1966).

62. See *The Planets Within*, pp. 85–-90, 193–208; D. P. Walker, "Ficino's Astrological Music" in *Spiritual and Demonic Magic* (London: Warburg Institute Studies, 1958), pp. 12ff., 230ff.; also his "Ficino's 'Spiritus' and Music," *Ann. Musicol.* I (1953) (Paris), pp. 131–50; P. Ammann, "*Musik und Melancholie bei Marsilio Ficino*," dissertation, C. G. Jung Institut, 1965, with relevant passages from *De Vita Triplici* of Ficino. Ficino loved to sing and to improvise to the accompaniment of his lyre in the circle of the academy. (Yet he complains in a letter, ["Lettres," 204] that the bitterness of his state is not calmed or sweetened by his playing.) While there was in the Renaissance in general an almost magical faith in music and its role in "sanctification of the soul," Ficino worked the notion into a theory and practice. Because his influence on other musicians, however, was slight, we may take his ideas primarily on a psychological level as a music therapy rather than as a theory of composition.

63. *The Anatomy of Melancholy*, vol. II, pp. 115ff.

64. See P. Lain Estralgo, *The Therapy of the Word in Ancient Antiquity* (New Haven: Yale, 1970), on song as therapy.

65. See *Saturn and Melancholy*, pp. 34, 50 on stuttering and lisping. The blocked fragmentary expression may have to do with Saturnian insight into two-fold truth, the ambivalence and contradictoriness of all statements. Theophrastus, supposedly the first to have devoted to melancholy an entire book, now lost, said that Heraclitus, "owing to melancholy left most of his work unfinished or lost himself in contradictions." (Ibid., p. 41, with note.)

66. Other animals, besides the usual raven, dog, and goat, traditionally associated with melancholy in iconography and lore, and which therefore represent ways in which one can be depressed, are: the "gloomy elk," the lamb, and the swan (which, though sacred to Apollo as the bird that sings its death, is also melancholic); see *Saturn and Melancholy*, pp. 378, 105ff. Lore places the tortoise and the snail under Saturn, and the camel and donkey. The former are slow and withdrawn behind their thick borders; the latter are carriers of burdens, tenacious and able to withstand aridity. On the elephant, see *Saturn and Melancholy*, p. 204; on the pig, ass, and bear as images of *acedia* (slothful depression), see Wenzel op. cit., pp. 106–8. The dog particularly represented senex consciousness not only for its sexual associations and its

sloth (ibid., p. 106 and notes), but also because it had a traditional reference to the underworld where Saturn relates with Hades, Lord of the chthonic spirits, ancestors, dead souls, and prophetic wisdom. Of his three sons, Zeus, Poseidon, and Hades, it is with the last that Kronos ultimately resides after his dethronement. In Rome, Saturn was *Dis Pater*, ruler of the underworld, whose entrance is guarded by the dog (as Kronos was associated with Anubis in Egypt).

67. Damaged or chained feet, paralysis, and lameness belong to Saturn; hence travel and moving about were supposed to cure melancholy. *Acedia* was linked especially to the feet (Wenzel, op. cit. p. 108), even to Christ's wounds in the feet. See also Chapter 8.

68. See *Saturn and Melancholy*, p. 338.

69. Ibid. p. 345.

70. I have pointed to the relevance of Ficino for archetypal psychology in *Re-visioning Psychology*, part 4, and in "Plotinus, Ficino, and Vico as Precursors of Archetypal Psychology" in *Loose Ends: Primary Papers in Archetypal Psychology* (New York/Zurich: Spring Publications, 1975).

71. "*Festina lente* (make haste slowly) became the most widely cherished Renaissance maxim," wrote E. Wind in *Pagan Mysteries in the Renaissance* (Harmondsworth: Penguin/Faber, 1967), p. 98.

Part Four

Old and New

11

Coda: A Note on Methodology [1]

The acorn theory of biography [2] seems to have sprung from and to speak the language of the *puer eternus*, the archetype of the eternal youth who embodies a timeless, everlasting, yet fragile connection with the invisible otherworld. In human lives he accounts for the precocious child and the undeniable call of fate, such as we saw in Menuhin and Garland. He appears especially as the dominant archetype in those visionary figures who make their mark early, disturb the commonplace, and vanish into legend, like James Dean and Clyde Barrow and Kurt Cobain, like Mozart and Keats and Shelley, like Chatterton and Rimbaud and Schubert, like Alexander the Great (dead at thirty) and Jesus (dead at thirty-three), like that brilliant boy Alexander Hamilton, at eighteen already a Founding Father of a revolution and an idealized new nation. Charlie Parker was gone at thirty-five, Bunny Berigan at thirty-three, Jimmy Blanton at twenty-three, Buddy Holly at twenty-two; and think of the dead young painters like Jean-Michel Basquiat and Keith Haring. Any of us could make a list — and not only of the celebrated and notorious, but of those elemental young men and women who touched our lives with their promise and then were gone.

And of course the *puer eternus*, as archetype, is beyond gender: Jean Harlow, dead at twenty-six, Carole Lombard at thirty-three, Patsy Cline at thirty. Janis Joplin, Eva Hesse, Moira Dryer, Amelia Earhart . . .

These figures of fame find backing in figures of myth: Icarus and Horus, who flew higher than their fathers; fleet Atalanta; young Lancelot and Gawain; marvelous Theseus; St. Sebastian, pierced through the breast; boy David, sweet singer of psalms; Ganymede, cup-bearer of ambrosia on Olympus; and all the luminous lovers: Adonis, Paris, and Narcissus.

Colloquial speech calls bright young stars "geniuses." Especially relevant to this connection of genius with puer, of glans with acorn, is the Roman primary identity of the *genius* with procreative phallic power so that the spontaneity of the penis represents, *pars pro toto*, the *genius* itself.[3] For this reason a man may speak of his member as having its own intuitive eye, its own will, and feel that it plays a major role in his fate. Men may fetishize the organ, conferring upon it the mysterious motions of an invisible divinity. This delusional, narcissistic, obsessive, overvalued idea of the penis (in the terms of conventional therapy) can best be accounted for by placing this style of puer phallicism against a background in myth.

The puer figure — Baldur, Tammuz, Jesus, Krishna, Attis — brings myth into reality. The message is mythical, stating that he, the myth, so easily wounded, so easily slain, yet always reborn, is the seminal substructure of all imaginative enterprise. These figures, like myths themselves, seem not "real." They feel insubstantial; tales of them say they are quick to bleed, fall, wither, vanish. But their devotion to the other world — they are missionaries of transcendence — is never forsaken. Somewhere over the rainbow. *"La lune, c'est mon pays,"* says the white-faced clown in the film *Les Enfants du Paradis*. Looney and lonely, lovely and pale — this is the puer, touching earth tentatively, and of course promiscuously by the glans of the penis, wanting to be received by the ground.

The devotion to an altered state of mind propels puer fantasy toward altering the mind of the state by setting fires of rebellion. The calling from the eternal world demands that this world here be turned upside down, to restore its nearness to the moon; lunacy, love, poetics. Flower power, Woodstock, Berkeley, the cry of the students of Paris '68: "Imagination au pouvoir." No gradualism, no compromise because eternity doesn't make deals with time. Inspiration and vision are results in themselves. But then what happens? Immortal ideals fall to mortality: Kent State; then baby boomers and business. "Golden girls and lads all must, / As chinmey-sweepers, come to dust." Manolete, bleeding in the sand.

Not only a biography can be touched by an archetypal figure. There are archetypal styles of theories as well. Any theory that is affected by the puer will show dashing execution, an appeal to the extraordinary, and a show-off aestheticism. It will claim timelessness and universal validity, but forgo the labors of proof. It will have that puer dance in it, will imagine ambitiously and rebel against convention. A puer-inspired theory will also limp among the facts, even collapse when met with the questioning inquiries of so-called reality, which is the position taken by the puer's classical opponent, the gray-faced king or Saturn figure, old hardnose, hardass, hardhat. He wants statistics, examples, studies, not images, visions, stories. Knowing about these constellations and how they affect what we read and how we react to what we read helps readers find where they are on the archetypal map — at one moment entranced by the revolution in ideas, at another thoroughly skeptical of the bullshit.

This kind of self-reflection belongs to psychological method. Unlike the methods used by other disciplines when positing their ideas, an archetypal psychology is obliged to show its own mythical premises, how it is begging its first question, in this case the myth of the acorn. Because theories are not merely cooked up in the head or induced from cold data, they represent the dramas of myth in conceptual terms, and the drama is played out in arguments over paradigm shifts.

Having uncovered the puer in our method, let us go on with the acorn. Galen, the learned and prolific medical writer (129 to 199 A.D.), confirms the ancient belief that acorns are a primordial food, which is a mythical way of saying that you feed off your inner kernel. Your calling is your psyche's first nourishment. Galen said that the Arcadians were still eating acorns even after the Greeks had learned to cultivate cereals. This is another way of saying that the support of the acorn precedes the practical civilizing effects of your natural mother, the mother world of Demeter-Ceres, the nourishing civilizing Goddess after whom cereal is named. The acorn is a gift of nature before nurture, but a nature that is mythical and virgin (that is, never known, never grasped); so acorns, according to Sir James George Frazer's compilations, belonged to the realm of Artemis, who presided at childbirth.

Then, and up into modern times in French and English poetry and painting, this Arcadia of the ur-acorn was the imaginal landscape of primitive nature, similar to Eden or Paradise, where the untrammeled natural soul lived in accord with nature. Therapy has transplanted

Arcadia to childhood; the natural being, feeding on acorns, therapy has christened the inner child. Replacing the Garden of Eden, filled with animals and serpents and sin and knowledge, as well as replacing the Arcadia of rough acorn-eaters with an abused and idealized inner child is an abuse itself. For the pagan mind you did not go "back to childhood," nor did you idolize innocence to recover the idylls of free being; you went to Arcadia, an imaginal terrain where we are cared for by our genius.

In the acorn lies not only the completion of life before it is lived but the dissatisfied frustration of unlived life. The acorn sees, it knows, it urges — but what can it do? This discrepancy between seed and tree, between the spindle in the lap of the Gods in heaven and the traffic in the lap of the family on earth, packs the acorn with the fury of incapacity, of reach without grasp. The acorn is like a tiny child empurpled with rage because it cannot do what it imagines.

Although the inner taste of the acorn may be nourishing, and communion with the angel sweet, the acorn is also bitter. It is astringent and tannic. It shrinks back; says no, as Socrates' daimon only cautioned negations. Maybe that's why actual acorns must be soaked and leached, boiled and blanched again and again, undergoing long softening before their meat can be ground into palatable flour. As the recipes say: "You'll know they're done when they no longer taste bitter." Inside the beautiful puer is a terrifying, even toxic, bitterness. See it in the gestures of Basquiat, the sounds of Cobain, Hendrix, Joplin, the suicidal desperation that can't wait into the time of the oak. Theories, too, are afflicted with shadow. The acorn theory and the extraordinary lift to life that it offers — vision, beauty, destiny — is also a tough nut to swallow.

This coda proved to be a necessary and final excursus on method. It tied the acorn theory with its founding image and tied the founding image yet further out to a mythical configuration called *puer eternus*. By means of this excursus I was able to show how one can transplant an organic metaphor from its usual pot in a philosophy of organicism, which would have confined our acorn theory in a developmental model of human life.

Life is not only a natural process; it is as well, and even more, a mystery. To account for life's occluded revelations by analogies with nature commits a "naturalistic fallacy," that is, assuming psychic life obeys only natural laws as described, for instance, by evolution and genetics. Humans ever and again try to crack the soul's code, to unlock the secrets of its nature. But what if its nature is not natural and not human? Suppose what we seek is not only something else, but somewhere else, in fact, having no "where" at all despite the call that beckons us to search. There is, therefore, nowhere to look beyond the fact of the call. It seems wiser to attend to the call than to avoid it by searching for its source.

The invisibility at the heart of things was traditionally named the *deus absconditus*, the "concealed god," that could be spoken of only in images, metaphors, and paradoxical conundrums, gems of immense worth buried within giant mountains, sparks that contain the flammable force of wildfire. The most important, said this tradition, is always the least apparent. The acorn is one such metaphor, and the acorn theory draws upon this tradition that goes back to Blake and Wordsworth, to the German Romantics, and to Marsilio Ficino and Nicholas of Cusa in the Renaissance.

As the acorn is one such metaphor of smallness, so, too, are the daimon and the soul metaphors. They are even smaller than small because they belong among the invisibles. For the soul is not a measurable entity, not a substance, not a force — even if we are called by the force of its claims. Nothing corporeal at all, says Ficino, and therefore the daimon's nature and the soul's code cannot be encompassed by physical means — only curious thought, devotional feeling, suggestive intuition, and daring imagination, each a mode of puer knowing.

In keeping with the specific archetypal figure of the puer, this theory is meant to inspire and revolutionize, and also to excite a fresh erotic attachment to its subject: your subjective and personal autobiography, the way you imagine your life, because how you imagine life strongly impinges upon the raising of children, the attitudes toward the symptoms and disturbances of adolescents, your individuality in a democracy, the strangeness of old age and the duties of dying—in fact, upon the professions of education and psychotherapy, upon the writing of biography, and the life of the citizen.

Notes

1. [Excerpted from J. Hillman, *The Soul's Code*, (New York: Random House, 1996).] — Ed.

2. [On this theory, at the beginning of *The Soul's Code*, Hillman writes: "The acorn theory proposes and I will bring evidence for the claim that you and I and every single person is born with a defining image. Individuality resides in a formal cause — to use formal language going back to Aristotle. We each embody our own idea, in the language of Plato and Plotinus. And this form, this idea, this image does not tolerate too much straying. The theory also attributes to this innate image an angelic or daimonic intention, as if it were a spark of consciousness; and, moreover, holds that it has our interest at heart because it chose us for its reasons." (pp. 11–12)] — Ed.

3. Jane Chance Nitzsche, *The Genius Figure in Antiquity and the Middle Ages* (New York: Columbia University Press, 1975), pp. 7–12.

12

Old and New: Senex and Puer[1]

LAURA POZZI: *In reading all you have written one hardly ever reads references to what is modern: you hardly ever report on your cases, and in speaking of culture, your models come always from the old humanistic classical culture. The old culture has the upper hand. Why?*

JAMES HILLMAN: The old culture has the upper hand because I think it's more important! One reason — you are looking for reasons — is that living in America I see the danger of connecting everything to what is immediately topical. America is a complete immersion in what is happening; it's a Now culture, utterly Now. So, involvement with the past should be seen as a way of stepping out of the Now, rather than making social comments on it. Of course, that step is already a comment because you can't really step out of where you are. There is nowhere else to step to. The Renaissance is not another place or another time. It's a mode of being in Now or looking at Now and talking about it. But it means that my comment doesn't have to be stated in Now language. The very fact that I talk in mythical and historical terms is my comment on Now. Those are fantasy landscapes by means of which you can see the Now or save the phenomenon from being lost in Now.

LP: *So the reason you moved to the Renaissance in your latest books . . .*

JH: . . . It's evident that in a culture that is floating and lost I'm making the same move that people made at other times; they went back. In the Renaissance — and they were lost then, too — they went back. This is a move made by artists, by thinkers, by cultures, the move of going back so that one stands somewhere . . .

LP: *More solid? The past better than the present?*

JH: No, not solid: but one has an eye that has been trained by stepping back. . . .

LP: *The eye of the old?*

JH: Yes, the old eye, the call of the old, and it may be the essential eye. It is to gain essence, not time: it's to train the eye to read and the hand to make the right move and not simply because it's old. I think that calling it "old" is already a prejudice of the Now. The Now is not a matter of time. The Now is simply the unreflected, the naturalistic perspective, the way things happen, the "forgetful" as the phenomenologists say. "Now" means here, close, appearance; therefore distance, depth, and essence are given by the old.[2] Now-consciousness doesn't understand that the old has nothing to do with time. The old doesn't belong to the senex in some sterile dusty way. If you see the Renaissance as old, you are in Now-consciousness. I don't see the Renaissance as old, I see the Renaissance as having been concerned with the same things, but more essentially. I don't see tradition as historical, I see tradition as contemporary, as informing what we do, what we feel. What is it that still makes people so interested in Greek temples, pyramids, Riace's bronzes or Altamira caves? It is not history: that's only the first level of it, people asking themselves, "Oh, my goodness, people did this four thousand years ago, isn't that extraordinary, they could build these pyramids without modern cranes?" That's the first level of the reaction. But after that first impact, which begins to break down the Now, the level and the quality change and one gets in touch with something essential. Essential doesn't necessarily mean that it has to have been there for a thousand years. But in some way, being in a Greek temple or seeing the pyramids or seeing the graffiti on the walls of a cave in Spain evokes the eternal, essential images of the soul. It does not have to be the actual pyramid that I am seeing: that is the literalism of it. You are seeing the ancient images, the archetypal images, not merely the pyramids themselves: but seeing the pyramids evokes the archetypal sense that there are eternal images, and those give you a sense of essence.

LP: *What do you mean exactly by eternal images, archetypal images?*

JH: What makes us able to be in touch with what we are given, the forms of recognitions, the basis my knowledge is founded on, everything that I sense of being right or being off, doing it right or wrong, the governing bodies of my imagination — those are the essential images. And they are essentially human; they are what make me human and deepen my compassion for human history, let me understand things, feel into things way beyond the limits of my personal education and personal experience. You see, by opening up the essential imagination we also expand our compassion.

LP: *That is the old argument of the humanists, too: the belief that culture expands the heart and makes it more sensitive, "human."*

JH: It's how I understand "morality," too. If you don't have those governing bodies of imagination, if you don't have an eternal, archetypal sense in the midst of the Now, then you don't have any sense of where you are going, what structure you are in, and your animal response is off. Instinct. Jung said that instinct and images are the same thing. When you lose that sense of the essential images, then instinct is off and you build ugly buildings, and you overeat, you become obese, and your whole structure is disoriented. You become immoral. I mean irrelevant, without any instinct, sort of anesthetized. I go back more and more to old places, not because that is where essence *is*, but because it evokes the *sense* of essence. So I definitely do not mean that you "have to know history": it's not history, but a sense of essence, and that deliteralizes history. That is very important because history is such a big burden when it's taken as a senex thing . . .

LP: *It kills everything. . . .*

JH: It kills everything, absolutely. History is nothing at all in itself — just a statue in the park for pigeons. Only as an avenue for seeing the Now in perspective is it valuable. You can't see up close; everything flattens out. You don't have to make history relevant, because once you have a historical sense then it gives relevance and sorts out the trivia in events by giving perspective.

LP: *"Perspective" appears again and again in your writings. You speak of the Gods as perspectives and that myths give us perspectives, so that we can see events differently. Could you say more about your notion of "Perspective"?*

JH: I'd like to come at it in terms of something I've been thinking about recently. Old and new, or what we've been calling essential and Now, can be seen in terms of foreground and background in Gestalt psychology. Whatever you focus on becomes a foreground, that is, really *seen*, if there is a background. Take any event that's obsessing us, some item of Now — some symptom, some topic in the news, some argument in psychology like narcissism — it's just utterly, immediately up-close and literal. But the moment we bring in the Renaissance or Egypt or Greek myth, the moment we introduce a phrase from Shakespeare or Keats, we see it as a foreground phenomenon. It's tied into a background; it can resonate. It's still up-close and blown up, but it has become suddenly relativized; because it has background, it is *only* foreground. The Now becomes only now and not the whole gestalt. It becomes an image and not just an event. It's the same way with cases. They are only cases, utterly literal real people with real problems until we get an essential perspective, some kind of background, an archetypal fantasy, if you like. Then the cases become images. But be careful here, not images of the archetypal myths or fantasies—that's to get into a Platonic argument — but images as foreground phenomena because there is a background. History is one way of making a gestalt: historical references, figures from the past release the foreground event from being stuck in only what it says it is.

LP: *But this is also a rhetorical* topos, *the past as a "topos" that makes sublime everything that is being talked about, whereas the present is used as a way of trivializing the argument . . .*

JH: That's of course senex — the perspective of Saturn, the old established wisdoms: the past deepens, makes more valid, becomes proof. You know, this is a classical, Latin way of proving something: "Truth stands the test of time." But if one is at the opposite pole of this senex mode of consciousness, if one is in the archetype of the child, if a puer, youthful myth is dominating, as is often the case when you are fourteen and even when you are much older, then you throw out every reference to the past as out of the question. History and time would ruin your position completely. The puer never learns with time and repetition: he resists development and is always unique. No precedents, no past — that's how it feels to him. A culture in that archetype, like our culture, cannot help but be radically against the past, against what has already become and therefore is not unique. This shows in every aspect of the culture. For example, an American textbook in sociology, psychology, anthropology, even history, cannot be more than three years old or it will not be listed in the catalogs . . . three years old and the book has to be revised. Instant revision! Only the newest is valid.

LP: *When you introduced the idea of "re-visioning" you didn't mean "up-dating" or modernizing. You meant rather looking again, gaining a new vision based on going back. Is your book* Re-visioning Psychology *a new psychology or an old one?*
JH: Why ask that question? What difference does it make? It keeps us paralyzed in the puer-senex: new or old. The main thing is to recognize that the really new is not the Now. It's more like re-new. What matters is the little syllable "re" — that's the most important syllable in psychology: remember, return, revision, reflect . . .

LP: *. . . recognition, which is a knowledge coming from what is already in the soul and in the culture.*
JH: Yes, and response. Responding to what's right there.

LP: *React . . .*
JH: Yes, re-act, both as repeating and responding . . .

LP: *Repetition would be a way of "going back."*
JH: These are the important words — even repent and remorse — religious words.

LP: *Religion itself has been explained to mean "re-ligion": linking or tying back . . .*
JH: . . . or connecting again. Of all these "re" words, maybe the most important is re-spect, which means to look again. Did you know that? And that's all that psychology does, that's the whole thing in a single word. That's what our dreams are doing and our memories: bringing us to respect ourselves — not *in*spect with guilt — to re-gard what

happened yesterday, what happened in childhood and re-spect it. We look again at what was forgotten or repressed, we even look again at the mechanisms of forgetting and repressing, and whatever we look at again we gain a new respect for — whether in ourselves or the culture. But to do this, you have to let it be as it is and not try to up-date it, make it new. Just the looking again, the respect, renews it. The up-dating process is constantly wiping out history; nothing in our culture is more hated, more repressed than the old. There is a desperate fear of the senex, as if he were old George III — senex turned into ogre. But the senex is also the old wise man, the old whale, the old ape. And if you stick only with the new and the future, you only have the bluebird or the mosquito: no whale, no old ape. We still are all positivists; we believe you move forward by turning against the past, whereas in the Renaissance we move forward by looking backward — that was a favorite maxim. *Philosophia duce regredimur* . . .

LP: *Aren't you now doing exactly what I said a moment ago: using the rhetorical topos of the past, or let's say, the senex, in order to ennoble the old?*
JH: Oh, sure! The puer could come along and say: historical references to the Renaissance deaden an argument while references to *Star Wars* make it lively, relevant, immediate. This teaches us that we are always in one or another archetypal style of rhetoric. You can't open your mouth without an archetypal perspective speaking through you. Rhetoric doesn't mean just the art or system of persuasive argument; by rhetoric I mean that all speech is rhetorical in that every archetype has its own mode of rhetoric, its way of persuading you.

LP: *Again, the Renaissance, especially the Italian Renaissance. . . . Why?*
JH: I do not talk of the Renaissance as a "philologue" or as anyone knowledgeable about the culture . . . I don't regard myself in any way to be a scholar of Greece or of the Renaissance or of history. I don't see myself as an historian, but I feel that these materials are our roots, our Western historical roots, and they have been locked up by the academics, put into universities, put into museums, so we citizens, you and I, have been cut off from our roots by the academics who claim they are educating people to have culture, but who actually cut us off from culture because they've made it a preserve of the academic. You have to

go through decades of scholarly brainwashing in order to work on the Renaissance. It needs to be opened up again for the citizen to reclaim his own culture . . . We live in a terrible split. Maybe the Renaissance did, too, but they had maxims for healing the split, like *gloria duplex*, keeping the consciousness of both sides. The danger lies in splitting the duplex into only senex or only puer. Exclusive. One turned against the other. We had one-sided puer in the sixties, and now that chaotic style of destruction is giving way to programmed style of senex destruction — political repression, armaments, CIA — in the name of economics and security, which are senex ideals. If *gloria duplex* sounds too old-fashioned, too Italian for you, then what about our little syllable "re"? It takes the old and gives it a puer twist. It turns things back and turns things upside down at the same moment.

LP: *How else can you imagine the re-union of senex and puer?*
JH: I think first we have to watch out for anything simple. Simplifications are already part of the rhetoric of one or another side of the split. *Gloria duplex* means complicated answers, not many single answers lined up as alternative scenarios. A string of alternatives is not what I mean by "poly" which is always complex. The Renaissance, as Edgar Wind depicts it, for instance, spoke of *complicatio* instead of *explicatio* or *simplicitas*. When we complicate in the right way we begin to force imagination to work. Simplification stops the imagination . . . as we imagine the world, as we imagine our historical problems, they begin to be interiorized, they begin to be psychological. But it isn't we who make those complications — it's the psyche, the anima. That's what anima does — messes things up, blurs the edges. She gets things tangled — isn't that what "plicated" means, folded? So the beginning of a puer-senex reunion means letting the anima get at both sides, letting the dried-out senex feel soul again, little bits of moisture, little gipsy fantasies, and letting the high-flying, fire-eating puer feel inferior and moody and confused. A little lonely and outcast and misunderstood like the senex. It's so hard to realize that big pathological problems can have fuzzy solutions, pathological solutions. The only difference between the dangerous old admiral and the wise old whale is that anima connection.

LP: *Then there is a great difference between your devotion to the old as a mode of giving value and essence and simply being caught in the senex as a conservative or a patriarch — tradition glorified for its own sake and used to suppress the young.*

JH: The main task for me is to keep in touch with the senex in all its different facets. The senex slips in unawares — not just in depressions and cruelties. It's very easy to become unconscious of the senex as a *psychological* factor because it tends to concretize its perspective as "real," "hard," and "out there". . . economics, for instance . . . Saturn as fixations into literalisms and materialized abstractions.

LP: *This seems to be again a lack of concern for the concrete world and its laws, so common with the Jungians. . . .*

JH: Isn't that the senex speaking right there in your sentence? I'm not at all unconcerned with the concrete world, the world of matter, just the contrary! I'm writing on all sorts of material questions, even chemistry and bus transportation and downtown buildings. But one particular *view* of matter — call it scientific, economic, sociological — is killing our civilization slowly. Or it will kill it fast by setting up the puer in his exclusive one-sidedness . . . then the puer will react and kill the world-view of the senex quickly, anarchically, the fire of apocalypse. So the job of psychology is to keep senex always in some sort of psychological context, to keep Saturn from becoming paranoid, antisocial, which is potential in his nature. That's why I struggle so with monotheism: I see Saturn in it, his dangerous "singleness of vision." That senex intolerance and blindness could wipe us all out. By blindness I mean particularly soulless concreteness.

LP: *Your approach to the material world — even if it is concrete, is not soulless. Isn't that what you mean when you call for concrete immediacy, for instinct and instinctual attention to the actual material world?*

JH: Exactly! My approach to the world is via the *anima mundi*, as a world ensouled. The senex, as we have been talking of it just now, is fixated literally on the concrete — economics, power politics, energy, whatever — without any psychological, without any anima overtone. The world for the senex, as we have been speaking of it, is not an expression of soul; it is the countervalence of soul. And this soulless concretism dominates both the N-bomb project and the terroristic attitude, and this shows that they share the same archetypal reality, the same insanity. Both think what is most real are the physical and external structures. Soulless concretism. I think what's most real are the structures of consciousness, of imagination, so that when ideas move, when the mind moves, when the images move, then the other things also move. By attacking and defending the same concrete and institutional structures both sides reinforce the very conflict. The Old Guard and the Red Guards only make each other stronger and don't conserve anything or renew anything. The soul isn't really touched so nothing moves. The anarchic, the terrorist vision is to my mind very old-fashioned, an early-nineteenth-century vision of reality that we have to see through and let go of — prepsychological, premeta-phorical, prephenomenological. On the other hand psychoanalysis needs more dissidents, more even than Laing and the antipsychiatric movement; it needs its own "terrorists of soul" in the sense of a radical seeing through and destabilizing its fixed investments in profession — its dues and insurance and case management; its ethics tribunals; its associations of bureaucracy — to return soul to the world.

LP: *This sounds messianic, like the rhetoric of the puer again.*
JH: Why not — for a moment at least! Doesn't that just show how the puer breaks through when one fantasies on the old. The archetype of old and new can't really be separated. It seems better to me to focus carefully, painfully on the old and let the puer break in spontaneously as it just did now to us, rather than to focus on the new so literally that the senex absorbs it and makes it concrete and soulless in the same old dried-out patterns.

LP: *This topic of old and new, of age and youth, is so very old itself, such a basic topos in literature, and it repeats in psychoanalysis in* Oedipus *and in* Totem and Taboo, *the fathers versus the sons; and yet it is always new. Expressing it with Latin terms deliberately keeps it old, and in our culture gives it a new sound. We can hear or see the questions differently. Conflicts of generations, renewal of civilization, conservatism versus radicalism — even arguments about style in art, architecture, and literature — can be conceived within this archetypal pair and thought about so as to enlighten conflict, making it more psychological, rather than merely to go on in the same old ways that are always presented as new ways.*

JH: Enlightening conflicts means nothing more than making them psychological, remembering that the two, senex and puer, have to appear together. You can't have one without the other somewhere near.

LP: *The terms themselves, senex and puer, illustrate so very well just what we have been talking about: the value of going back to the Italian Renaissance, which at the same time brings something fresh into psychology.*

Notes

1. [Reprinted from Hillman, *Inter Views: Conversations Between James Hillman and Laura Pozzo On Therapy, Biography, Love, Soul, Dreams, Work, Imagination and the State of Culture* (New York: Harper and Row, 1983). Reprinted: Woodstock, CT, Spring Publications, 1996.] — Ed.

2. See my *The Force of Character and the Lasting Life* (New York: Random House, 1999), especially chapter 3, "Old."

13

Of Milk . . . and Monkeys [1]

There is a tale of Pero and Cimon (or Micon) of the *caritas romana* derived from a text of Valerius Maximus which was depicted frequently during the High and Late Renaissance, and by such major painters as Caravaggio, Rubens, Ribera, Panneels, and Murillo.[2] In a cell lies a bearded old man, his arms bound, his feet chained, dying. A young matron, his daughter, suckles him with her milk. Although this profane subject from a profane source had a moralizing purpose, showing both filial piety and Christian charity (feeding the hungry and visiting the prisoner), it has as well a psychological depth of mythical proportions.

Another picture, said to be part of *Aurora consurgens*, shows two old men kneeling before *mater sapientia* and drinking from her breasts.[3] The picture is entitled *de processu naturali* and the inscription says that the milk is *prima materia* as "beginning, middle, and end." The old man bound hand and foot, unable to move, unable to do, Saturn the senex in his dual nature, cut off from life, bound by the ligatures of his obligations and locked in the constructs of his own systems, lies on the ground exhausted and thirsting: from power to helplessness.[4] So too was Boethius, the King's advisor, betrayed and deposed from power, thrown into prison where in despair and aged beyond his actual forty years he longed for his end.[5] But his end in power was his beginning in wisdom, for he too was visited by a thirst-quenching feminine form who reminds him that he has been nourished on her milk and who now meets his need with "the consolation of philosophy" which opens with a song.

Milk as "beginning, middle, and end" connects our polarities of senex and puer. They both require milk. As beginning, milk is the *prima materia*, where we start at the breast. As end, milk is a *prima materia* that is also the *sapientia* that revivifies the old man by means of her breasts.[6] Beginning and end of the process conjoin in milk which dissolves in weakness the old physical man and coagulates in wisdom the new spiritual man.[7] The world begins out of the milky churning sea; or as another alchemical text tells us, milk precedes even the blood and water as the first of firsts.[8] So man at the breast is beginning, middle, and end: suckling, lover, and dotard. At the breasts of the sister are to be found all fruits "new and old" says the "Song of Songs."[9] When man is both beginning and end, puer and senex together, then woman is daughter, mother and sister, nurse as nourisher — all merge into the "tutelary madonna" who teaches us at her breast. One learns at the breast; what does one learn at the breast? What can we be taught by milk?

But there is a necessary condition to be fulfilled before we can turn to this question. First the milk must appear, and this requires thirsting and longing, the deprivation of Saturn, the Saturn of the *Picatrix*, "weak and weary."[10] First the thirsting, then the quenching. The perfect and powerful on their thrones have no need of milk, wisdom and song. First the desire and need for milk — then, "Little David, come play on your harp," says old mad King Saul. The self-sufficient are self-enclosed, whether puer or senex. Both deny their need and defend their borders. But helplessness and thirsting as a continuous need is the open-mouthed condition which draws forth the milk as a process in nature, indicating that the prerequisite of renewal is acceptance of dependency and need. Jung discusses these pre-conditions for renewal in that same passage from *The Undiscovered Self* with which we began:

> A human relationship is not based on differentiation and perfection, for these only emphasize the differences or call forth the exact opposite; it is based, rather, on imperfection, on what is weak, helpless, and in need of support — the very ground and motive for dependence. The perfect have no need of others, but weakness has . . .

And again: "It is from need and distress that new forms of existence arise, and not from idealistic requirements or mere wishes." And Jung, in writing his conclusion on the deepest meaning of the transference phenomenon, says: "What our world lacks is the *psychic connection*; and no clique, no community of interests, no political party, and no State will ever be able to replace this."[11]

The need, the distress, and the longing point to a form of existence that is longed for. The thirst points to its object, to what will satisfy it: the primordial food which transubstantiates one into the primordial condition nourished by primordial knowledge, before history and the split of sames, the Tao as "infant" and "weakness." Milk restores the psychic connection with others and with oneself by feeding the primordial levels of the soul. At these milky levels all connect and age differences dissolve in psychic agelessness. The old man is a little boy and the little boy wise with *sapientia*, for "out of the mouths of babes and sucklings . . ."

The negative reciprocity of puer and senex, their *lack of psychic connection*, their differentiation and independence, their tensions which maintain the ego in its active searching, its ordering and defenses — all falls down. Time itself, and history with it, has a stop. Who I was, what I shall be — my case is closed. But my soul is opened by admitting my weakness and my need, for these needs make me a human creature, dependent in my creatureliness upon the creation. Or, to say it another way: as Tao is "weakness," so the way (Tao) to Tao is through our needs, our continual state of dependency.[12] And we cannot meet these needs ourselves, self-enclosed, tight-lipped. Abandoned child and abandoned old man together, in need of nursing *caritas* and the consolation of philosophy, find that love for which they long only when control and knowledge are laid away.

When ablution is achieved through nutrition (or imbibition) it has another meaning than dissolution. I take the milk into my body rather than its taking my body into itself and dissolving me in the oceanic bliss of the mother. Nutrition is not regressive because the "I" remains and I am changed from within, from the interior outward. The milk of wisdom enters me, my mouth, and runs over my tongue into my belly. So first, what is learned at the breast is immediate physical knowledge, concrete knowledge, which melts the constructs and abstractions and ordering systems in which Saturn lies dried and caged. The milk is "tasted knowledge" and its taste (*sapor*) produces the *sabrosa* of the true *sapientia*. Thus is a first need answered: a need for substantial food that assuages a gut-hunger for knowledge of the immediate reality of things, their direct taste, which is a first of firsts.

As the milk is primordial *sapientia* and not merely dissolution into the maternal, so then the breast cannot be only "mother." The breast has too often been taken as a Freudian *pars pro toto*, only as an udder of the Great World Cow. But it is not a sign meaning but one thing to be interpreted in but one way. The breast is a symbol, a ritualized object of adornment and concealment, of longing and delight. The breast is a revelation of tenderness and the *caritas* of human feeling. It belongs not only to mothers, but to the sister and beloved, to the nurse and daughter. When we are sons to its milk, then the breast is mother; when we are lovers of its milk, then it belongs to the sister-beloved; or as Old King, weak and weary, then the milk comes from the daughter as that life within one that one has oneself fathered, but with which one has only tenuous psychic connection. Redemption through the milk of the daughter suggests a different and renewed relationship to the soul. The daughter-anima restores the "old" man by bringing to his distress other considerations and other qualities than what has gone before in a man's life with the nurse-mother and with the sister-beloved. With the daughter, mutuality, reciprocity, and erotic intimacy all give way to the *futurity* of the anima. The daughter represents the independence of the soul from the ego; her milk expresses the dependency of the ego on the anima for its life. [13]

The eyes of the Holy Old King, a mystical image of God in the *Zohar* of which Professor Scholem told us here at Eranos, are bathed in milk:

> For when the *Gevurah* extends itself, and the eyes shine with a red color, *Atika Kadisha* illuminates its own whiteness, and it shines in the mother, and she is filled with milk and suckles everything, and all the eyes bathe in the mother's milk, which flows forth perpetually. [14]

The streaming milk may be the tears of his caring and the eyes bathed in milk may be the *collyrium philosophorum*, which washes away all that one has seen, all the enraging events of history, restoring vision to its child-like origins in archetypal remembrance.

Each drink from the vessel of milk presented to the Prophet by an angel, the Prophet interpreted as if he had it while dreaming.[15] The milk of knowledge, the *sapientia* or *connaissance du soi*, came as if in a dream state. Perhaps each drink of milk is a dream and the vessel of milk the vessel of dreams. Thus, what one learns at the breast is knowledge of ourselves as we are in essence, as we are upon entering the world and leaving it, "*sans* teeth," defenseless, a kind of "imaginal animal" in continuous open-mouthed need of primordial dreams as the necessary substance from which we live, ourselves as always ageless children of the eternal. For "We are such stuff / As dreams are made on, and our little life/Is rounded with a sleep."[16] From that sleep we come into life and go back to it at the end, remembering it intermittently in dreams. Before we are *homo faber, homo ludens,* or *homo sapiens,* puer or senex, we are first dreamers in psychic reality, imaginers, living in psychic connection with the eternal milk of an imaginal cosmos: the milky images of childhood, the ecstatic images of loving, and the prophetic images of old age.

Is not this flowing stream of substantial knowledge, are not these dreamings, just what alchemy describes as the "lunar moisture," or rejuvenation from "the white tree"? These dreamings soothe, cool, and sweeten. And are not these dreamings on another level the milk prescribed by Avicenna[17] as the humectant food for the aged because it restores to them the psychic connection? This psychic connection — so necessary according to Jung — perhaps the very thing which may tip the scales, what really is it? At least we know it is not mere relatedness between people, old and young. A psychic connection depends on the psychic factor, that is, it is a connection arising spontaneously from the archetypal view of things. So it is a connection via the primordial world which is ageless, which obliterates the viewpoints of age and youth so that all "see" the same imaginal essence of things in the same way. As such, milk is also the way to a psychic *Anschauung.* This way of milk is direct, as taste to the tongue; immediate, physical, not abstracted into systems of senex or puer formulations. It connects us together as humans, as the first food of all humanity, because it connects us to the core of human nature: the psyche. Milk thus opens the gates of the psychic realm, or that "Kingdom" promised by Joel [18] and repeated by Peter at the Pentecost, [19] where all agelessly participate: "your sons and your daughters shall prophesy, your old men shall dream dreams, your young men shall see visions."

Milk finally "represents'" the original connection to and continual thirst for the world we long to "remember.'" Through remembering the original, memory can be cleansed of history. The Golden Age of old Kronos and of the Young God can return as images. History may thus be redeemed by psyche through its connection with the primordial, thereby allowing Clio, the daughter of archetypal remembering, again to record history as a celebration of the psychologically meaningful. In that thirst for that kingdom we are neither puer nor senex but prior to that split, "sucking at the breast of Tao," [20] where we learn that *primordial image is identical with immediate essence*, that the imaginal meaning is also the taste and sweetness of the physically real, that *caritas* and *sapientia* are the same substance, and that all knowledge and all cognition derives from the "a-ha" experience of a-historical recognition. This understanding of the milk reflects the mother-complex redeemed and is the secret of prophet, poet, mystes, messiah, king, child, culture, hero, priest, and sage — images of archetypal forms of living, ambivalent and not split into polarities, and for whom according to the evidence of comparative religion the required food is milk.

As the way of the milk takes us down and back into humble intimacy with our natures, healing our division, and at the same time clear out of all divisions into a cosmic Milky Way, so too does the way of the monkey. Again, we begin our amplification of a mythical image through a painter.

In the nineteen-thirties, C. G. Jung observed that Pablo Picasso was depicting an ancient chthonic force in the psyche. This shadow force, as buffoon, as harlequin, with Dionysian undertones, was leading the way inward and downward in a *katabasis eis antron*. Through the years since Jung's observation, an ape returns again and again in the work of Picasso as he, *senex-et-puer*, grows older and older.

It has been complained by socialist critics that as Picasso grows older he becomes emptier, without historical message, and that in his old age he has not produced transfigured canvases as did Rembrandt and Titian; that the ape is self-revelatory, an expression of his antics without sense, the ugliness and sensuousness of "the dirty old man." But Jung foresaw the significance of the ape in the work of Picasso when he wrote: "The journey through the psychic history of mankind has as its object the restoration of the whole man, by awakening the memories of the blood."[21]

The memory of the blood and the restoration of the beast in man is a dangerous way, and a way that especially the generation of the 1930s and 1940s has lived through, so it matters not a little *how the assimilation takes place*: whether it be for the sake of humanity or for bestiality. As with the milk: do I take it into myself, or does it assimilate and dissolve me? The memory of the blood, which by remembering and recognizing Adam resurrects him. The memory of the blood is also the milky memory, that memory of primordial images, the messages that precede history where the angel of man merges with his pre-historical ape. For Adam, the whole man as first man, puer of God and senex of mankind, Talmudic and other European legends tell us originally had a tail like a monkey. Jung and Hoyle told us at the beginning of this work that it is upon the "essentially primitive creature" that the *kairos* depends,[22] and that the metamorphosis of the Gods — and all the Gods are within, said Heinrich Zimmer — is "the expression of the unconscious man within us who is changing."[23] The "unconscious man," the "essentially primitive creature": is he the ape? If "God is dead," in what form will He be born again? Or, as Yeats asks in "The Second Coming," when falcon and falconer divide, when things fall apart and the centre cannot hold, " . . . what rough beast, its hour come round at last,/Slouches towards Bethlehem to be born?"

"The wisest man is an ape compared to God, just as the most beautiful ape is ugly compared to man," said psychology's favorite professor, Heraclitus.[24] We, mankind, are in the middle, neither ape nor angel. Can we tell in this moment of transition when ends and beginnings merge, which is the way backward and which the way forward? Or do the two ways themselves merge? For if Adam had a tail, and Adam was created in the image of God and is God's likeness, what does this tell us of the *Imago Dei*? Perhaps we need reassess our conceptions of the divine angel, our twin. Perhaps there is a first and second ape or an ape below us and an ape above us. Again, C. G. Jung:

> Zarathustra is an archetype and therefore has the divine qual-
> ity, and that *is always based upon the animal*. Therefore the gods
> are symbolized as animals; even the Holy Ghost is a bird, all
> the antique gods and the exotic gods are animals at the same
> time. *The old wise man is a big ape really*, which explains his peculiar
> fascination. *The ape is naturally in possession of the wisdom of nature*,
> like any animal or plant, *but the wisdom is represented by a being that is
> not conscious of itself*, and therefore cannot be called wisdom. For
> instance, the glow-worm represents the secret of making light
> without warmth; man doesn't know how to produce 98% of light
> with no loss of warmth but the glow-worm has the secret. If the
> glow-worm could be transformed into a being who knew that
> he possessed the secret of making light without warmth, that
> would be a man with an insight and knowledge much greater
> than we have reached; he would be a great scientist perhaps or a
> great inventor, who would transform our present technique. So
> the *old wise man*, in this case Zarathustra, *is the consciousness of the
> wisdom of ape*; it is the wisdom of nature and that is nature itself,
> and if nature were conscious of itself, it would be a superior be-
> ing of extraordinary knowledge and understanding.[25]

Upon this image of natural wisdom has been projected the repressions of our human shadow. The primitive darkness that we bury in-
wards or cast behind in our climb to the light looks too much like the
monkey, so that which lies at the threshold — too hairy, too embar-
rassing, too tricky, and too wise — is carried for us by the monkey.

But Chinese and Hindu stories of the monkey (Sun Hou-tzu and
Hanuman) place him above us, winged, at the tops of mountains, with
the sun and the wind and the sky. For all his mercurial shiftiness remi-

niscent of the puer, he is at the same time of the earth and the peasant, most alive on the popular levels of the collective psyche where monkey cults and worship of this figure still exist in the villages. He is a God and a Helper of the Gods. In ancient Egypt, Dravidian India, and southern Africa, the monkey is "above" as the clever one, poet, scholar, philosopher. An identity of monkey above and monkey below is reflected also in the classic story of Sun Hou-tzu, who is prone to all evil, yet is twice immortal; who relishes his meat and drink, yet becomes Buddha at the end of the tale. In Chinese astrology, the monkey is placed in the ninth position where the West has Sagittarius, the centaur: at one end wild and animal, at the other tutelary guide of heroes and father of music and medicine.[26]

The main strands of our culture have combined against the ape: to the Jew he was image for Egyptian darkness;[27] to Greek antiquity he was ugliness and unreason; for the Christian the epithet "ape" was applied "to all the enemies of Christ, whether pagan, apostate, heretic, or infidel."[28] And already in Rome his appearance in dreams was an evil omen and could be an oracle of madness. At least until the thirteenth century in our culture, the monkey was mainly a *figura diaboli*. In his *superbia* he aped man as man apes God: the simian, *similitudo hominis, simia Dei*. He gathered onto himself all that was "only human" in a theological age: in the Middle Ages the monkey with apple was Eve the temptress, fond of the fruits of sin, and in the Renaissance a manifestation of Dionysus because of his pleasure in the grape, the sense of taste, and in dance and music.[29] The ape is sinner, and folktales from other parts of the world re-state it:[30] monkeys were once men (as men were once angels), and monkeys are cursed men, degenerated devolved men who are "prone to all evil": folly, vanity, idleness, avarice, stupidity, sensuousness, curiosity, hypocrisy, depravity — that "polymorphous perversity" of the pleasure principle for which the ape often stands in dreams today. Even Orpheus could not charm him, for the ape sits confronting him, playing his own instrument — a parody and mimicry, say the interpreters of allegory, further evidence of his deviltry. But perhaps the ape does not succumb to the higher order of Orpheus because he makes his own kind of music, which never loses the primary throb. For the monkey in us comes out, according to a Jewish legend, at the end state of drunkenness: "Then (man) behaves like a monkey, he dances and sings, talks obscenely, and knows not what he is doing." [31]

He knows not what he is doing. Reason is lost, consciousness eclipsed. is this *abaissement du niveau* the wisdom of nature, or is this madness? Is there light in this shadow which we cannot see because we stand in the dazzle of our own light? And *our* light — is it light or shadow, is it wisdom or madness? What would the monkey say to that? In this monkey, old man and boy merge; they are the same in their monkey tricks and deceit and vanity, their foolishness, their mute pathetic helplessness as not-yet and has-been devoluted deformed men: silly old man, silly little boy; dirty old man, dirty little boy; greedy old man, greedy little boy. Perhaps the formula of Heraclitus, "ape is to man as man is to God," may be given another turn: "man is to God as man is to ape" — *above and below are one, so that restoration of the fallen man into his original divine likeness depends upon a prior reunion with the fallen ape.* Resurrection into the Second Adam would then require restoration of the First Adam, since this image with the tail, which is a likeness of God, indicates a helpless devoluted mute aspect of divinity.

To this ape, carrier of our sins and fallen aspect of the divine, we owe much. This deepest shadow of prehistorical man, our antic selves, is untouched by time, undivided into polarities of senex and puer, both wise and foolish and not a little mad. On what happens to him the *kairos* depends. What happens to us depends on what happens to him. If our fortune is at least partly in his hands, then he is indeed at least partly our protective angel. Perhaps we must even look up to him for help. Our ailing consciousness is like the "sick lion" in the perennial symbolism of animal lore of Pliny, the *Physiologus*, and later compendia, who searches for monkeys to eat because a diet of apes is his healing. The integration of the ape cures the "king."

The ape that is both above and below takes us deeply into *the essential ambivalence of the shadow.* Our values are turned upside-down, which is the same as a metamorphosis of the Gods. (Did we not begin this work with a quotation from Jung describing this hour of history as a time of the metamorphosis of the Gods?) Perhaps it is a *kairos* of the archetypal shadow? Yet by entering this place of the shadow we may heal the split between the puer and senex and their mutual projection of shadow. If we leave the ape below unrestored, where he has so long been in our culture, we leave to him the symbols he holds in his hands — they too are lost to what is human. The dancing monkeys and the monkey musicians in so many times and cultures must be playing something for us. Are the instruments of music to be left there unresurrected so that ape-music becomes the sound of social discord and the shadow's revolt? A new generation comes in with a new song;[32] yet the puer-senex split makes us hard of hearing and we miss the transitions of sound and movement that go on at the deepest level. This deepest level because it is psychoid has an "upper" aspect, so that the music in the blood and the music of the spheres may be in harmony. The grape and the apple cannot be only moral errors; they too have an "upper" aspect, as the peach which Sun Hou-tzu eats bestows on him immortality. And that mirror into which the monkey has been staring through centuries of iconography cannot be only vanity and mimicry. It, too, has an "upper" aspect. One first becomes self-preoccupied in order later to become self-conscious. That fascination with "how one looks," the phenomenal self wearing the foolish pelt of one's vices, ultimately leads to the gaze inward through the mirror to insight. Through mimicry instinct reflects itself into awareness. Imitation is a primitive way of learning. Imitation is also a way of therapy: by miming just that behavior which is before me, echoing and mirroring with my physical reality, it may become conscious of itself without losing original ambivalence. When I become mute and foolish as the ape, joining the other's shadow, we become a polarity in identity. Together we form a unity, but are twins, and awareness can break through at the most simple level of reflection.

Jung points to the identity of upper and lower ape in "Dream Symbols of the Individuation Process," which was presented first at Eranos and later expanded in *Psychology and Alchemy*. In the first appearance of a square mandala in that series of dreams, a "gibbon is to be reconstructed."[33] At the instinctual level which is beyond ego-consciousness and therefore both below and above us, we are connected backwards to the "bestially archaic and infantile" and at the same time forwards to the "mystical *homo maximus*" and his archetypal intuitions, perhaps prophecies. The dreamer, the ego, is not in the center; the gibbon was to be reconstructed in the center. Robert Fludd, another man of science, in the early seventeenth century also placed an ape in the center of his cosmic mandala showing the relationship of Man, Nature, and Heaven.[34] The egocentricity of the High Renaissance and of the high scientific rationalism of our period call up the ape as compensation. Strive as we may to overcome this, there is yet that monkey in the middle who, with his long tail that stretches back into the archaic layers of the psyche, indeed puts in question the heights of our achievements. As the ego progressed so did its shadow. This psycho-historical fact Morus notes (and the work of Janson confirms): "Since the 16th century monkeys had been pushing their way into the foreground both in scientific and poetical literature."[35]

The monkey at the center — what is this grotesque vision? To live centered then would mean to live with a central axis to all that is at the threshold, represented by the ape of folly, anarchy, and vice, to be always hearing his music. To remain human would require remaining in psychic connection with the sub-human at the center, remaining true to one's shadow-angel, true to one's own central madness, which is as well the wisdom of nature that is unconscious of itself and cannot speak in words. It would mean a wholly new feeling of respect towards our own "craziness,'" centering oneself around it and thereby centering it and giving it free space within to live. Irrationality would not have to be banned to the crazy fringe and treated as peripheral; irrationality belongs to the nature of the old wise man. Before we can gain consciousness of the wisdom of nature, which is how Jung in the passage above describes the old wise man, we would first have to be in touch with the unconscious aspect of the wisdom that is the ape. Our trust lets it become more familiar — our ape as *familiaris*, guide and companion. Consciousness then emerges from the threshold beyond the reach of the ego's senex order and puer dynamus. This consciousness of nature has the borderline quality of the *homo naturalis*.

Here we may re-integrate by means of mythological thinking some of the remnants of the nineteenth century that have hitherto been unaccepted by our ideals of a religious view of man. Nietzsche also demanded a new centering of man, where yea and nay, light and darkness, good and evil were to be superseded. But his superman was above, beyond good and evil, driven to that extreme by a puer reaction to a senex civilization. In the monkey, superman returns to the all-too-human, to below and within good and evil. The opposites are not transcended but rejoined from below, as a wound heals, through remaining within the tension of ambivalence in the neighborhood of the ape from where the problem of good/evil originates. So, too, Darwin's vision of the descent of man can be taken in another way. It is a mythical statement as well as a biological statement. It says that man is indeed lower than the ape who is superior in the wisdom of nature and who is man's "angel" as nearest intermediary with the natural aspect of the divine represented by that tail. Freud's development from Darwin remained confined by the nineteenth century. Our simian self became only the biological id of infantile sexuality, polymorphous perversity and the principle of pleasure. Freud never lost sight of the material facts of the ape below. Thus he did not see enough that the ape is also above. This upper aspect gives his statements a mythical counterpart, which now tells us that the id and infantile sexuality is a vital repository of "angelic messages" expressing the creative fantasies of the wisdom of nature. These fantasy-messages are *logoi spermatikoi*. That is, they are the seminal basis of consciousness produced by the ape.

We turn to the baboon, Thoth, for our final message. And each message is an angel that precedes the word it carries, the meaning that precedes the language in which it is encased, as natural light precedes our light. Thoth, scribe and teacher, who leads the soul to higher stages of knowledge, is perhaps the figure behind that ape of Picasso and the "gibbon at the center." From the dumbness of Thoth comes the Word. The language of nature is ineffable; it has only signs. That mute monkey, forming his glyphic signs, his phallic token always on display, is the reformer, re-orderer, and regenerator. In him gibberish and instruction, sexuality and logos, aged wisdom and Hermes are one. He is the scribe who through his records creates history, yet is himself without before or after.[36]

When Seth and Horus struggled, causing brightness and blackness to be separated, Thoth re-created the eye, having found it where

it had been flung by Seth into the outer darkness over the edge of
the world. (But light the candle and the edges of the room become
impenetrable blackness . . .) And the eye that the monkey re-creates is
the moon-eye, the left eye of the dreamer and feeler,[37] the inward eye
turned towards the primordial images of the milky way, restoring sight
and remembrance of a mute pre-verbal world of archetypal signs and
gestures. So the first month of the year in Egypt belonged to Thoth,
for he heralds in half-light new beginnings. So the "baboons of dawn"
as they were called, who adore the morning star and are that star, the
old ape our divine likeness with uplifted arms hailing dawn.

Our conclusion ends in the ambivalence of mythical images. Our tension is unresolved. In the soft light of the dusty world we cannot see
clearly. It may be day's end and a darkening of the light. The morning
star — is it Lucifer? The ape — is he man's fallen angel? The revelation
that is at hand, that Second Coming, may be the rough beast of Yeats
and Picasso, slouching towards Bethlehem. The beast may be but a
beast, the blood-dimmed tide of anarchy, a gibbering ape at nightfall,
the princely power, *simia dei*, its hour come round at last, bringing a
new reign of atavistic darkness. Or the soft light may be *Aurora consurgens* of a new millennium, of sun and moon together, *sapientia* and *caritas* conjoined, where wisdom and madness felicitously embrace each
other: an altogether new kind of day that the baboon heralds, and
gives us the eye with which to see it.

Either/or — yet one thing is certain: we cannot go down to the
ape, "the unconscious man within us who is changing" (Jung) and
transform the "essentially primitive creature" (Hoyle) on which the future depends without a metamorphosis of our main God, our own individual enclosed consciousness, sustained in its ego-tension and ego-
brightness by the senex-puer polarity. The individual does become
"the makeweight that tips the scales," for the restoration of the whole
man, his dawning into a new day, implies a prolonged acceptance of a
twilight state, an *abaissement* and rededication of the ego-light, softening by sacrificing each day some of its brightness, giving back to the
Gods what it has stolen from them and swallowed.

We may leave our transition of generations in ambivalence, with neither a beginning nor an end in the historical sense of the puer-senex division. These images from myth and nature may indicate a new relationship that is the oldest: our dependence as humans upon the divine light of natural consciousness. This soft light is pre-conscious, at the threshold always dawning, fresh as milk, at dawn with each day's dream, still streaked with primordial anarchy — the light of nature rising within each individual out of the unconscious psyche.

Notes

1. [This chapter has been excerpted from the final sections of the original paper "Senex and Puer: An Aspect of the Historical and Psychological Present," the bulk of which forms Chapter 1 of this present work.] — Ed.

2. E. Harris, "A *Caritas Romana* by Murillo," J. Warburg Courtauld Institute 27 (1964), pp. 337ff.

3. Photographic reproduction, ARAS Archive, C.G. Jung-Institut. Cf. *Aurora Consurgens*, (attributed to Thomas Aquinas) edited with commentary by M.-L. von Franz, (New York: Pantheon, 1966). p. 59 (milk), pp. 28–29.

4. H.M. Barrett, *Boethius* (Cambridge: Cambridge University Press, 1940), introduction by W. Anderson.

5. Ibid., pp. 77ff.

6. M. Ruland (The Elder), *A Lexicon of Alchemy*, trans. A.E. Waite (London: Watkins, 1964), pp. 221-22.

7. Peter Bonus (of Ferrara), *The New Pearl of Great Price* (London: Stuart, 1963), pp. 278–79.

8. "Exercitationes in Turbam XV," see *Aurora consurgens*, p. 264.

9. *The Song of Solomon*, 7:13–14.

10. See *Aurora consurgens*, p. 381, 106 fn.

11. C.G. Jung, *Collected Works*, vol. 14: *Mysterium Coniunctionis*, par. 385; *Collected Works*, vol. 10: *Civilization in Transition*, par. 579, 190; *Collected Works*, vol. 16: *Practice of Psychotherapy*, par. 539.

12. Wing-tsit Chan, *The Way of Lao Tzu (Tao-te ching)* (Indianapolis: Bobbs-Merrill, 1963), pp. 10, 21, 28, 55; 36, 43, 76, 78.

13. See my "Oedipus Revisited," in *Oedipus Variations: Studies in Literature and Psychoanalysis*. With essays by K. Kerényi. (Dallas: Spring Publications, 1991).

14. *Zohar* 2:122b–123a. Quoted in G. Scholem, *The Mystical Shape of the Godhead*, trans. Joachim Neugroschel (New York: Schocken Books, 1991), p. 53.

15. H. Corbin, "Imagination créatrice et prière créatrice dans le soufisme d'Ibn Arabî," *Eranos-Yearbook* 25(1956), pp. 178–79 [*Creative Imagination in the Sufism of Ibn Arabî*, trans. Ralph Manheim (Princeton University Press, 1969).

16. William Shakespeare, *The Tempest*, IV, 1.

17. O. C. Gruner, *The Canon of Medicine of Avicenna* (London: Luzac, 1930), Sect. 855, pp. 432–33.

18. Joel 2:28.

19. Acts 2:17.

20. *Tao-te ching*, p. 20.

21. C. G. Jung, "Picasso," *Collected Works*, vol. 15: *Spirit in Man*, par. 213. See E. Neumann, "Der schöpferische Mensch und die 'grosse Erfahrung'," *Eranos-Yearbook* 25 (1956), p. 31.

22. *Midrash Rabbah*, Genesis XIV, 10 (Cf. H. W. Janson, *Apes and Ape Lore in the Middle Ages and the Renaissance* [London: Warburg Institute, 1952], p. 135); Jung, *Collected Works*, vol. 14, par. 589, 602.

23. H. Zimmer, "Zur Bedeutung des indischen Tantra-Yoga," *Eranos-Yearbook* 1 (1933), pp. 52–55.

24. Heraclitus, Frag. 98–99 (J. Burnet, *Early Greek Philosophy*, 4th ed. [London: Black, 1948]); Plato, *Hippias Major*, 289 A-B; Plotinus, *Enneads* VI, 3, 11.

25. C. G. Jung, Seminar Report on Nietzsche's *Zarathustra*, X, pp. 51ff. (privately mimeographed, quoted by permission). Original seminar notes available as Mary Foote. ed., *Psychological Analysis of Nietzsche's Zarathustra: Notes on the Seminar Given by Prof. Dr. C. G. Jung (Zurich, Winter 1935)* (Zurich: 1934–39). Reprinted as J. L. Jarrett, ed., *Nietzsche's Zarathustra: Notes of the Seminar Given in 1934–1939,*(Princeton University Press, 1988).

26. E. T. C. Werner, *Myths and Legends of China* (London: Harrap, 1922); J. Bredon and I. Mitrophanow, *Das Mondjahr* (Wien: P. Zsolnay, 1953); A. Waley (trans.), *Monkey by Wu Ch'eng-en* (London: Allen/Unwin, 1942, 1965).

27. J. Hastings, *Encyclopaedia of Religion and Ethics* 11 (Edinburgh: Clark, 1909, 1953), p. 486a.

28. J. Gonda, *Die Religionen Indiens* I (Stuttgart: Kohlhammer, 1960), p. 316.

29. W. C. McDermott, *The Ape in Antiquity* (Baltimore: Johns Hopkins University, 1938); Janson, op. cit. sup.; L. Hopf, *Thierorakel und Orakelthiere in alter und neuer Zeit* (Stuttgart: Kohlhammer, 1888).

30. V. Elwin, *Myths of Middle India* (Madras: O.U.P., 1949), p. 226.

31. L. Ginzberg, *The Legends of the Jews* I (Philadelphia: Jewish Publ. Soc., 1961), Vol. I, p. 168; see R. Riegler, *Das Tier im Spiegel der Sprache* (Dresden/Leipzig: C. A. Kochs, 1907), p. 8.

32. P. Ammann, "*Musik und Melancholie bei Marsilio Ficino*," diss., C. G. Jung Institut, 1965.

33. C.G. Jung, "Traumsymbole des Individuationsprozesses. Ein Beitrag zur Kenntnis der in den Träumen sich kundgebenden Vorgänge des Unbewussten," *Eranos-Yearbook* 3 (1935); *Collected Works*, vol. 12: *Psychology and Alchemy*, par. 164ff.

34. F. A. Yates, *Giordano Bruno and the Hermetic Tradition* (London: Routledge, 1964), pl. 10, "Nature and Art." From Robert Fludd, *Utriusque cosmihistoria*, I, p. 3.

35. Morus (R. Lewinsohn), *Animals, Men and Myths* (London: Gollancz, 1954), p. 199.

36. R. T. Rundle Clark, *Myth and Symbol in Ancient Egypt* (London: Thames & Hudson, 1959), p. 254; H. Bailey, *The Lost Language of Symbolism* I (London: Benn, 1912, 1957), p. 69; *The Hieroglyphics of Horapollo*, trans. G. Boas (New York: Pantheon, 1950), pp. 66–70.

37. A. R. Pope, "The Eros Aspect of the Eye (The Left Eye)," diss. (C. G. Jung Institut, 1960).

Appendix A

At some moment between the Eranos Conference of last summer and this meeting of 1967, we moved into the last third of this century. Moments of this sort belong rather to the fantasies of time than to the chronometry of clocks and calendars. So we cannot with accuracy point to the hour when this transition occurred, because the "hour" depends not on rational measurements but upon arbitrary fantasy factors such as what happens to time when calendars are changed, when this century began, when the first century began, when the historical Jesus was born and with him the "time" of our age.

Despite these obscurities, we are now metaphorically but one generation from the twenty-first century. We are nearer to it in measurable time of clock and calendar than we are to the nineteenth. More, we are nearer in measurable time to the man of the twenty-second century than we are to the man of the early nineteenth. Napoleon (d. 1821), Byron (d. 1824), Jefferson (d. 1826), Beethoven (d. 1827), Hegel (d. 1831), Goethe (d. 1832) are more distant than the unknown presences of the year 2100.

This concluding third of our century is also the concluding thirtieth of this millennium; and so we are in the fractional sixtieth of the calendar aeon of the Sign of the Fishes, the Sign of the Christian Age, the myth of time within which we take our historical orientation. Fifty-nine generations stand behind us in this aeon; one stands before us, the last and concluding one, and the transitional one that carries us into the next millennium, and the time of Aquarius. Transition of millennia in one generation echoes the metamorphosis of the Gods that took place at the beginning of this era by its founder, who lived but one generation. The senex-puer polarity is given by the historical situation in which we are.

[This passage was taken from the original opening of the 1967 Eranos lecture on Senex and Puer (see Chapter 1 above).] — Ed.

Appendix B

To make this point more clear let us turn to Leonardo da Vinci. The critical event in his early memory (as Freud and Neumann [1] have written) was indeed the bird that descended to him in the cradle. Leonardo lived with his grandmother and with two successive stepmothers; his natural mother married again and seems to have disappeared from Leonardo's life. Leonardo has a fantasy, which he recounts as if it were an actual memory from infancy, that a *nibio*, opened his mouth with its tail and struck him many times upon his lips. This bird was *not* a vulture, as Freud and then Neumann have declared. Neumann, despite noticing that a *nibio* is not a vulture and so correcting Freud's error, nonetheless sustains it by retaining the mistranslation as symbolically correct in order to analyze, along with Freud, Leonardo in terms of the mother-complex. [2]

No. The bird, which came to Leonardo in his vision, was a kite, a relative of the hawk and like it a variety of the genus *falconidae*. (Hawk is the wider term, kite one of its varieties.) We have here to do with a symbol that can best be amplified from Egypt where Freud turned for his symbolic equation vulture = mother. But it is now the equation: hawk, kite, falcon = Horus = puer. The solar hawk descended upon the Kings at their coronation and was a spirit-soul (*ka*), and the hawk in a series of other contexts is a puer emblem *par excellence*. [3]

Because of the specific puer significance of this bird, the dual mother theme in Leonardo, on which Freud and Neumann base their interpretative case of his genius, may rather, and more correctly, be understood in terms of a discontinuity in the mother relation owing to the early intervention of the puer archetype in its apparition as a kite and which Leonardo kept as a valued memory. (I have not examined the biographical material enough to tell whether the intervention of the *nibio* image occurred precisely at a time between two of his many mothers. But I do not think the literal aspect of discontinuity is as important as are the two factors: the intervention of the puer and the discontinuity in mothers.)

Leonardo's interest in flying, his love of birds, as well as his supposed vegetarianism and homosexuality, may thus have a "hawk" in the background rather than a "vulture" and may be grasped as part of puer phenomenology rather than as a mother-complex. The various usages of the word "kite" in English emphasize the puer implications. A kite is a flying, triangular, light framed toy, a favorite of small boys, and a kite is "one who preys upon others." The term refers also to the highest sails of a ship which are set only in a light wind.

Moreover, the "case" of Leonardo seems paradigmatic for both archetypal psychology in general and the psychology of genius in particular. By ignoring the true significance of an image (in this case the hawk-falcon-kite), one can attribute a crucial event of any life wrongly to an inappropriate archetypal constellation. Then genius is not viewed authentically in terms of the spirit and its early call but is rather attributed to peculiarities in the fate of the mother. Because the vulture-or-kite quarrel stands for the conflict in perspectives between mother and puer, we can see how important an investment early psychoanalysis had in the mother archetype and how there was a consequent misperception and repression of the puer which is only now beginning to be revalued . . . A lesson we may draw from the Dionysus and the Leonardo examples is that what we see is determined by how we look, which is in turn determined by where we stand.

Notes

1. S. Freud, "Leonardo da Vinci and a Memory of His Childhood," in *The Standard Edition of the Complete Psychological Works of Sigmund Freud*, ed. James Strachey, 24 vols. (London: Hogarth Press, 1953–74), vol. 11; E. Neumann, "Leonardo and the Mother Archetype" in *Art and the Creative Unconscious*, trans. R. Manheim, Bollingen Series (New York: Pantheon, 1959).

2. Neumann, "Leonardo," p. 14: "Against the background of archetypal relations, the bird of Leonardo's childhood fantasy, considered in its creative uroboric unity of breast-mother and phallus-father, is symbolically a 'vulture' even if Leonardo called it a 'nibio' . . . For this reason we are perfectly justified in retaining the term 'vulture', which Freud chose 'by mistake,' for it was through this very 'blunder' that his keen intuition penetrated to the core of the matter . . ." (i.e., "the symbolic equation vulture = mother" [p. 7]).

This vulture was "seen" by Oskar Pfister in Leonardo's painting of St. Anne with Virgin and Christ Child as a negative form in the blue cloth that drapes and links the figures. Jung too "saw" a vulture in that painting. In a letter to Freud of 17 June 1909, Jung writes that he has seen a vulture (*Geier* in German) in a different place from the one seen by Pfister. Jung's vulture has its "beak precisely in the pubic region."

Strachey, who edited Freud's works for the Standard Edition, said the hidden vulture idea must be abandoned in the light of the kite-hawk-falcon (nibio) which was Leonardo's actual bird. But Neumann responds to this by saying that, in Pfister, Freud, and in Leonardo too, "the symbolic image of the Great Mother proved stronger than the actual image of the 'kite'" ("Leonardo," pp. 64–66). The power of the archetypal image of the Great Mother certainly dominated the psychoanalytic interpretation in all these commentators, but this does not establish that it also dominated Leonardo in the same way.

For a succinct devastation of Freud's Leonardo thesis, based on the vulture-kite confusion, see D. E. Stannard, *Shrinking History: On Freud and the Failure of Psychohistory* (New York: Oxford University Press, 1980), pp. 5–21.

3. See Chapter 5 above, "Notes on Verticality," for an extended working of this theme.

[This passage appeared originally in the latter part of section VI of "The Great Mother, Her Son, Her Hero, and the Puer," Chapter 4, above.] — Ed.

Index

Adler, A. XXV, 216
Agamemnon 238
Albertus Magnus 260
Alexander of Pherae 170
Ali, Mohammed 85
Alkmaeon of Croton 271
Altschule, M.D. 247
Anderson, W. 341
Aphrodite-Pothos 183
Apollo Belvedere 245
Apollodorus 242
Apollo-Hermes 112
Apollonius of Rhodes 242
Apuleius 85, 95
Aristotle 185, 261, 271, 285, 292, 295, 299, 305, 316
Arnaud, G. 300
Arp, H. 103
Artemidorus 155
Asclepius 155
Assmann, J. 176
Auden, W.H 105, 112
Auerbach, E. 236, 246
Aurelia 274
Autolykos 112
Avicenna 191, 342

Bacchus 152
Bachofen, J.J. 156, 244
Bacon, F. 304
Bailey, H. 343
Baird, J. XIV
Bandmann, G. 306
Barfield, O. 68
Barrett, H.M. 341

Basquiat, J.-M. 311, 314
Baynes, H. 69
Beethoven, L. van 345
Bergin, T.G. 304
Berry, P. 149–150, 240, 247, 270, 304
Bertman, S. 246–247
Bespaloff, R. 156
Binswanger, H. 69
Blanton, Jimmy 311
Blavatsky, H.P. (Madame) 276
Blume, M. 242
Boer, C. 305
Bohrer , K.H. 111
Bonus, P. 341
Bowra, C.M. 155, 242
Bredon, J. 342
Breton, A. 102
Brody, D. 191
Brown, N.O. 111, 165, 177, 181, 186, 191, 244, 255–56,
        286–288, 303–304
Brun, J. 243–44
Bruno, G. 343
Burnet, J. 342
Burri, M. 111
Byron (Lord) 345

Cain 194
Cambray, J. 177
Campbell, J. v, 68, 94, 142, 154, 243
Caravaggio 327
Cassandra 112
Castiglione, B. 295
Castorp, H. 223
Circe 147
Chakra, V. 296
Chappel, C. 110
Chardin , T. de 264
Charybdis 147
Chastel, A. 305
Chatterton, T. 311
Clark, W.R. 94
Cline, P. 311

Cobain, K.   311, 314
Coburn   299
Coleridge, S. T.   280, 299–300
Conrad, J.   281
Cook, A. B.   110
Corbin, H.   53, 69–70, 180, 190–92, 295, 304–305, 342
Cowan, L.   XIV
Cratylus   182
Curtius, E. R.   35, 59, 67, 69

Dalai Lama   76
Daphne   92
Daumier, H.   279
Dean, J.   311
Delcourt, M.   157
Descartes, R.   71
Detienne, M.   244
Diana   92
Dimock, G. E.   246
Diogenes Laertius   304
Diomedes   238
Doty, W. G.   111
Dryer, M.   279, 311
Dumézil, G.   299–300
Dunn, I. J.   56, 69
Durand, G.   191
Dürer, A.   263, 300

Earhart, A.   311
Eckhart (Meister)   127
Ehrenberg, V.   191
Eilberg-Schwartz, H.   177
Eily, B.   177
Eliade, M.   33–34, 67, 70, 176, 243
Eliot, T. S.   264, 268, 306
Elliott, R. C.   279, 300
Eluard, P.   111
Elwin, V.   342
Empson, W.   285, 301
Erasmus   268
Euclid   285
Eumaeos   182

Eumenides 243
Eurydice 156
Evans-Pritchard, E. E. 178

Faust 104
Finley, J. H. 246–47
Fisch, M. H. 304
Fischer-Homberger, E. 303
Fontenrose, J. 142, 151, 153–55
Fitzgerald, F. S. 138
Foote, M. 95, 342
Ford, Henry 80
Fordham, M. 56, 69
Fowler, W. W. 299
Frabotta, B. 305
Frankfort, H. 94
Frazer, J. G. 244, 247, 313
Freud, S. IX, XVII, XXIV, 47, 79–80, 127, 132, 134, 138, 152–53, 166, 177, 185, 191–92, 241, 247, 285–86, 288–90, 294, 302–305, 339, 347, 349
Fuhse, F. 300

Galinsky, G. K. 153
Ganymede 61, 110, 126, 150, 160, 280, 311
Genet, J. 198, 213
Gide, A. 98
Ginzberg, L. 342
Goetz, B. 69
Gonda, J. 342
Goodenough, E. R. 153, 305
Goullart, P. 76
Goya 284
Graham, H. 177
Grant, M. 154
Graves, R. 112, 176, 178, 182, 242–243, 245–246, 301
Grinnell, R. 154
Grönbech, W. 111
Gruner, O. C. 342
Guggenbühl-Craig, A. 68–69, 149, 299

Hakkert, A. M. 245
Hallie, P. P. 246

Hamilton, J.R.   242, 311
Haring, K.   311
Harlow, J.   311
Harris , R.E.   176, 341
Harrison, J.   143, 155, 243
Hastings, J.   342
Hector   225
Hefele, C.J.   94
Hefner, H.   81
Henderson, J.   xxi, 116, 149
Hendrix, J.   314
Hephaestus (Hephaistos)   119, 154, 184, 214, 242
Hera of Argos   154
Herakles   153–154, 180
Hercules   84, 87, 104, 133, 140–143, 145–146, 150, 154–156, 175, 184,
        215–216, 226, 243, 288
Hermaphroditos   169
Hermes   XX–XXII, 69, 80–81, 99–102, 104–109, 111–112, 119, 136, 143,
        159, 165–168, 171, 177, 182–183, 186, 188, 192, 216,
        222, 238, 244, 273, 339
Hesse, Eva   127, 311
Heyer, G.F.   149
Hildegard of Bingen   257
Hinks   110
Hippolytos   183
Hobbes, T.   158
Homer   151, 185, 188, 240–41, 296
Hopf, L.   342
Høst, A.F.   303
Hottentots   243
Hoyle, F.   30–31, 65, 67, 70, 333, 340
Hull, R.F.C.   XXV
Hydra   141

Ibn Arabî, M.   342
Isaac   208

Janson, H.W.   338, 342
Janus   54
Jarrett , J.L.   342
Jaspers, K.   188
Jefferson, T.   345

Jeremiah 254
Jesus 57, 76, 140, 150, 165, 192, 194, 199, 201, 206, 208, 224–227,
311–312, 345
Joplin, J. 311, 314
Julius Caesar 223
Jung, C. G. IX, XII, XIV, XVII–XIX, XXII, XXV, XXVI–XXVII, 30, 37–38, 40, 46,
50, 59–61, 64, 67–69, 71–75, 79–80, 82, 85, 91, 94–95, 101, 109,
111–12, 115–17, 120, 127, 130, 135, 139–40, 143, 148–153,
155–57, 180, 182, 185–86, 190–92, 201, 204, 208, 210, 213,
236, 239, 243–44, 246, 272–73, 276, 299, 301, 306, 319, 328–29,
331–34, 336–38, 340–43

Kaegi, W. 306
Kazan, E. 214
Keats xxv, 76, 89, 158, 311, 320
Kelsey, M. T. 94
Kerényi, K. 69, 100, 111–12, 142, 151, 153–56, 184–86, 191–92,
242–43, 341
Keuls, E. 168, 171, 177–78, 245
Kierkegaard, S. 259
King Lear 280
King of Epirus 157
King Saul 328
Kirk, G. S. 304
Kluckhohn, C. 65, 70
Kristeller, P. O. 306
Kronos of Hesiod 281
Kronos 42, 59, 110, 155, 241, 253–54, 261–66, 271, 277–79, 281, 284,
290, 297. 300, 304, 307, 332
Kronos-Saturn 41, 43, 47, 49-50, 60, 254, 258, 266, 305
Chronos 281, 300
Kudlien, F. 303
Kugler, P. 245
Kuster, E. 155

Laing, R. D. 325
Lancelot 311
Lange, K. 300
Lawrence, D. H. 79, 177
Layard, J. 242
Leonardo 346–47
Lévi-Strauss, C. 65, 189, 243

Lewinsohn, R. M. 343
Lewis, C. S. 115, 305
Lindsay 177–178, 243
Lloyd 244
Lombard 311
Lopéz-Pedraza, R. 111–12
Lovejoy, A. O. 300–301
Lowinsky, E. E. 306
Lua Mater 299
Lua Saturni 299
Luce, J. V. 247
Lykourgos 215, 242
Lysippos 97

MacDermott, V. 78, 94
Maenads of Dionysus 156
Magna Mater 115, 146, 224
Mao 33
Mary Magdalene 177
McDermott, W. C. 342
McGuire, M. 192
McLean, M. 156
Medici 295, 300
Medusa 147
Meiklejohn, J. M. D. 302
Melville, H. 192
Menelaus 238
Menuhin, Y. 311
Mercurius-Hermes 50
Messias 65
Miles, C. A. 110
Miller , D. L. 94–95, 240, 247
Minerva 301
Mithras 180
Mitrophanow, I. 342
Monick, E. 177
Moore, T. XIV, 150, 305
Muller, C. O. 304
Mus, P. 295, 305

Napoleon 345
Needleman, J. 89, 94

Neoptolemo 157
Neumann, E. 63, 69–70, 95, 111, 142, 149, 152–54, 162, 242, 342, 347, 349
Nicholas of Cusa 285, 315
Nilsson, M. P. 152, 154, 171, 178
Nitzsche, J. C. 316
Nixon, R. 81
Nock, A. D. 142, 154, 304

Odysseus VII, XIX, 88, 95, 104, 106, 147, 156–57, 161, 176, 182–85, 188, 191, 214–16, 235–41, 246–47; cf. Ulysses
Oeri, H. 300
Ogden, C. K. 302
Otto, W. F. 69, 100, 111–12, 151, 177, 245
Ovid 156

Panofsky, E. 68, 70, 110, 270, 299–300
Parker, Charlie 311
Parmenides 285
Parsifal 226
Pausanias 110, 242
Pécholier, Dr. 303
Pegasus 216
Pelopidas 177
Pentheus 215
Persephone 91, 130, 147
Petrarch 238
Pfister, O. 349
Phaedra 147
Phaedrus 245
Picasso, Pablo 332–33, 339–40, 342
Pilate 200
Plotinus 307
Plutarch 177, 281
Pluto 132
Pope 343
Pothos VII, XXVI, 97, 110, 159, 174, 176, 179, 182–86, 188–91, 238–39
Pozzo, L. XXIII, 326
Priam of Troy 157
Prometheus-Hephaistos 185
Pyrrhos 156–57
Pyrrhus 157

Radin, P. 111
Ramakrishna 127
Raphael 158
Redgrove, P. 245
Riegler, R. 342
Ripley, G. 65, 70
Rivière, M. 243
Robb, N. A. 176
Rohde, E. 155
Roheim, G. 154
Rorschach, H. 90
Rose, H. J. 300
Rossi, P. 304
Rousseau, J. J. 192
Rousselle, E. 70
Rubens 327
Ruland, M. 341
Rundle Clark, R. T. 176, 343

Sabazius 155
Sagittarius 335
Saint-Exupéry, A. de XIX, 67, 192
Sandburg, C. 80
Sartre, J. P. 187, 198, 213
Saturn XI, 37, 41–44, 47–48, 54, 56, 60–61, 63–64, 68, 70, 92, 131–32,
    150, 171, 226, 238, 241, 244, 253–66, 268, 270, 273–79, 281–84,
    287–88, 290–97, 299–307, 313, 320, 324, 327–28, 330
Schär, H. 94
Scherrer, M. L. 157, 242
Schiller, F. 176
Schlesinger, A. 34, 67
Scholem, G. 69, 330, 342
Schopenhauer, A. 167
Schuster, J. 111
Schwartz, S. 243
Scorsese, M. 177
Sells, B. 94–95
Severson, R. XIV
Seznec, J. 68, 111
Silenus 141
Simon, M. 153
Skinner, B. F. IX, XXV

St. Anne   349
St. Augustine   167
St. George   117
St. Nicklaus   97
St. Sebastian   311
St. Thomas Aquinas   202
Stanford, W.B.   156, 246–47
Stannard, D.E.   349
Starobinski, J.   300, 303
Stein, M.   111, 154, 242, 304
Steinberg, L.   177
Stevens, Wallace   71
Stroud, J.   v

Tagore, R.   127
Tasso   268
Taylor, C.H.   246
Taylor, T.   299
Telemachus   240
Telesphoros   60
Tertullian   72
Thass-Thienemann, T.   110
Theophrastus   306
Thomas, Dylan   183
Tristan   184

Ulanov, A.   245
Ulysses (Ulixes)   235; cf. Odysseus
Usener, H.   304

Vaschide, N.   243
Vergil   156, 237, 246
Voltaire   268

Wake, C.S.   177
Walker, D.P.   306
Weishaupt, A.   299
Wender, D.   247
Wenzel, S.   270, 301, 306–307
Werner, E.T.C.   342
Westropp, H.M.   177
Whitmont, E.C.   154

Wiener, P. P.   306
Wilder, A. N.   94
Wilhelm, H.   178
Willetts, R. F.   112
Winckelmann, J. J.   244
Wind, E.   63, 70, 153, 176, 243, 307, 323
Wolff-Windegg, P.   68
Woolf, V.   304

Yates, F. A.   343
Yeats, W. B.   32, 67, 333, 340

Zagreus   152
Zeus Chthonios   119
Zeus of Olympia   98
Zimmer, H.   92, 333, 342
Zoja, L.   150

About the Uniform Edition

Spring Publications takes pride in publishing, in conjunction with The Dallas Institute of Humanities and Culture, the uniform edition of the writings of James Hillman — the lasting legacy of an original mind. The pioneering imaginative psychology of James Hillman that soon will span five decades has entered cultural history, affecting lives and minds in a wide range of fields. For the creativity of his thinking, the originator of Archetypal Psychology and author of *A Terrible Love of War*, *The Soul's Code*, and *The Force of Character* has received many honors, including the Medal of the Presidency of the Italian Republic. He has held distinguished lectureships at Yale, Princeton, Chicago, and Syracuse Universities, and his books have been translated into some twenty languages. The American public showed its appreciation of his approach to psychology by placing his book, *The Soul's Code*, at the top of the best-seller list of serious works of nonfiction.

The cloth-edition set of 10 volumes the UNIFORM EDITION of the Writings of James Hillman unites major lectures, occasional writings, scholarly essays, clinical papers and interviews — arranged thematically. Each book cover is embossed with a drawing by the American artist James Lee Byars.